T0367263

BLOOD ON THE RISERS

A novel of conflict and survival in special
forces during the Vietnam War

MICHAEL O'SHEA

authorHOUSE®

AuthorHouse™
1663 Liberty Drive
Bloomington, IN 47403
www.authorhouse.com
Phone: 1 (800) 839-8640

Published by AuthorHouse 02/25/2015

ISBN: 978-1-4918-1381-2 (sc)
ISBN: 978-1-4918-1380-5 (hc)
ISBN: 978-1-4918-1379-9 (e)

Library of Congress Control Number: 2013915503

Print information available on the last page.

PROLOGUE

A N ANXIOUS FIFTEEN-YEAR-OLD SERVICE BRAT returns home, eagerly, after a decade of living abroad, after a childhood spent growing up in serenity in the recently defeated Empire of Japan. His new home is an obscure sector of south Texas, a hot, mostly barren landscape, its barrenness relieved by scattered palm and mesquite trees accenting the broad expanses of impenetrable brush and cactus. He quickly adjusts to the immense culture shock, but it isn't long before his docile world crashes around him. The unexpected dread of nuclear war brought on by the Cuban missile crisis confronts him, confounding his carefree existence. Then, just a year later, while he stands leisurely outside his high school shop class, his cherished Catholic President, John F. Kennedy, is summarily assassinated. In horror, the teen listens on a car radio during recess to the incident taking place in his own state.

Stunned by the events unfolding in his young life, he struggles with the reality that even his new favorite TV shows, *Father Knows Best* and *Leave It to Beaver*, are rapidly being overshadowed by the evening news broadcasts. Night after night, black and white images of American boys dying in the steamy jungles of a distant land shock his fledgling, adolescent sensitivities.

With his peers confronted with the same grim circumstances, he makes the simple commitment to serve his country, internalizing the martyred President's exhortation. Many of his classmates make profoundly different choices: seeking either deferments of convenience or refuge in Canada. With his decision made, he sets out on a life-altering quest to fulfill his obligation to his beloved country and to himself.

Along the way, he faces severe challenges, none more intense than his endeavor to preserve his basic values, his morals, and his honor, but he is ultimately comforted that his integrity is still intact. His quest is supported by the cadre of brave and honorable men he encounters, who help to mold his character throughout the process.

Just as paratroopers with firm grip rely on the chute's risers, young men require a vital substance of stability to adhere to as well, so they can retain their intrinsic values, their lofty aspirations, their full canopy of hope. But inevitably, as they journey through life, there is blood on the risers.

DEFINITIONS

ris·er \'rī-zər\ *n*: One of four vertical wide nylon straps that attach to the cape wells of a paratrooper's harness. The other riser ends are attached to the numerous suspension lines sewn into the outer rim of the main canopy. The paratrooper holds on to the risers, using them to steer the canopy. By pulling down on a selected pair of risers, the paratrooper can either run with the wind or turn into the wind, thereby slowing the lateral drift.

DE OPPRESSO LIBER: Latin for "Liberate the oppressed," the motto of the Special Forces regiment.

CHAPTER ONE

THE TALL GOLDEN COASTAL GRASS below danced and swayed in an eerie cadence with the crisp winter wind. Warden Howard Nicholls quickly banked the gray Piper Cub to his left, diving through the billowing gusts toward the small herd of javelina that was frantically scurrying for cover. He flashed a mischievous grin and gunned the engine to quicken the scavengers' pace. The portly lead sow squealed sharply in terror, her thick, black, spiny bristles fully erect as she crashed headlong into the mustard green thicket of thorny mesquite and prickly pear. Coveys of nesting bobwhite quail scattered wildly into the brisk morning breeze. Nicholls eased back on the controls, laughing heartily as he left the surly band of marauders desperately burrowing for cover. He had been airborne since just before dawn, searching the vast expanses of the King Ranch for his favorite prey: outlaw hunters, human predators of the brush.

Nicholls turned south, staying close to the tall deer-proof fences, erected at great expense to keep the cattle and deer in, and the poachers out. Peering through faint spider cracks in the yellow Plexiglas, he strained keen eyes to get a good count of the mature bucks chasing the large herd of whitetail into the thickets below. The swollen necks of the suitors verified the emerging ritual, each dutifully intent on expanding the endless herds of whitetail on the King Ranch.

Local hunters had waited all summer, sweltering in the south Texas heat, cleaning and sighting-in their favorite rifles, longing for the spicy taste of venison sausage, flavored by the smoldering embers of roasting mesquite. Chill blue northers blowing down from Canada engendered the necessary testosterone, enticing both the hunter and his prey with the blustery elements of dominance. Adrenaline saturated the spare, frigid air.

Nicholls continued south, past the ponderous Big House, headquarters for the world-famous King Ranch. He skirted the sleepy town of Kingsville below, carefully scanning the skies ahead for the jet aircraft practicing touch-and-go maneuvers at the naval air station just south of town. Pulling up on the stick, he keyed his mike:

"Ahhhh, Sierra One-niner. This is Bird Dog Twooo-three… Aahhhh, I'm gonna ease over to the Brimmers' stretch and check out the *senderos* below the creek bed."

"Roger, Two-three," crackled the reply. "I'm about fifteen from the loop, and I'll head that way to cover."

The game wardens stationed near the Ranch worked in tandem, a necessary tactic derived from years of experience in detecting armed infiltrators. They thrived at performing their dangerous job, tracking and apprehending wetbacks and trophy hunters, both groups intent on not getting caught in the pursuit of their prey. The wardens were damn good at their job, and the outlaws knew it.

* * *

Miles away, two prone figures peered quietly over the caliche mound into the barren creek bed below. Their squinting eyes focused on the two does and the nimble yearling grazing cautiously on the salty grass clumps scattered throughout the arroyo. The trio took turns nudging the fallen mesquite limbs away from the meager but welcomed meal.

"It's colder than a witch's tit," Jim whispered. Shuddering, he turned his large head away from the gusting swirl of chalky dust, in time to see his friend mouth a silent reply.

"Pussy."

Jim nodded with a sardonic grin, then returned his attention to the deer meandering below. The boys held their vigil, as they had done since before dawn, shortly after they had slid under the fence just south of the Brimmer place. Clad in jeans and worn letterman jackets, they continued to scan the surrounding brush for any sign of movement. An occasional clumsy armadillo or jackrabbit was the only encroacher in their stoic watch, teasing them into sudden anticipation for the crescendo that would signal the end of the hunt.

"He's out there all right," Jim whispered. "I can smell him."

Mike drew a slow, deliberate breath in through his chilled, moist nostrils. *El muy grande.* He smiled, twitching his nose as the moisture trickled to his mouth. "Just don't miss, Jimbo."

Mike's veiled words had barely left his tight lips when the trio below set into a brace, their erect ears pointed directly at the boys on the dusty crest above. Mike's eyes widened as he sensed the compromise of their position. Breathing ceased, taut muscles strained, as wide eyes surveyed their perimeter. Then, as if on cue, the three deer rotated in unison and turned their attention to a scrub brush thicket behind them. With broad haunches poised to bolt, the deer stood motionless, glaring at the muscular intruder crowned with a magnificent rack of antlers. He stood silent, yet ominous, surrounded by the thick underbrush and scraggly mesquite trees, his horns glistening despite the early-morning haze.

Mike heard the faint click of Jim's safety releasing the trigger lock on his .308. It was his shot to take. The big ones always belonged to Jim, it was understood. Mike didn't even bother to touch his own safety. Jim wouldn't miss. He never did.

The size of the rack didn't matter to Mike. He was there for different reasons, to relish the beauty of the wild before him and, more importantly, to share the exhilaration his best friend was experiencing at this climactic moment.

Intent on shedding those lingering remnants of puberty, Mike struggled with his emotions, confused in the paradox of his emerging manhood. He didn't mind shooting javelina. They were horrid creatures, short, squatty, dirty, and reputed to be quite vicious. They even looked mean, their sharp, curved tusks a constant threat to man and beast alike. But deer—now, they were different. Every time he hunted with his friend, he drew from deep within to mask his compassion whenever a deer was in their sights. Today would offer no exception.

The elusive lord of the brush strode proudly down the rise and approached the trio. Proclaiming his arrival with a loud snort, he strutted confidently over to the larger of the two does, slowly circling behind her. Mike braced for Jim's shot. But as the buck continued to move alongside his prospective mate, Mike realized the time was not right. Jim was *very* deliberate: He would wait for the clear shot. He prided himself in not wounding animals and allowing them to run off and die a lingering death.

He knew exactly where the shot would be. Just below the head, in the middle of the neck. Clean. Painless. Final.

The buck continued to circle in front of the tense doe, then abruptly turned to face her. His towering rack remained erect, his mere presence demanded submission. He took two more steps and stopped. Neck to neck, *Muy grande*, finally in clear view for a broadside shot.

Booooom!!!!

The deafening report startled Mike. The result left them stunned. The doe dropped hard to the creek bed, quivering wildly as the warm blood spewed from the gaping wound above her eye. The startled buck sprang vertically into the air, leaped over the other frantic deer, and bounded up the embankment into the safety of the heavy brush.

"Ya missed!" Mike yelled. "Ya hit the wrong fuckin' one!"

As Jim had squeezed off the round, the massive buck had dipped his head to nudge the reluctant doe. The hollow-point projectile had shattered the far antler, exploding with fragments of metal and chunks of ear into the head of the anxious doe beside him.

Within seconds, silence settled over the arroyo. The distinct aroma of spent gunpowder lingered, unaffected by the gusting wind sweeping through the brush. Below the boys lay the product of their quest, a quivering doe, suffering and near death. Jim sprang to his feet and scampered down the jagged incline to the wounded deer below. Mike uncovered the bag containing their deer trolley and followed him down, kicking up clouds of white dust in disgust along the way.

Jim leaned down and picked up the shattered antler. "Fuck! I can't fuckin' believe it!" he grunted, slinging the remnant of his "trophy" deep into the bush.

"Been huntin' long?" Mike quipped. "You'll like it when ya learn how."

Jim drew his long Buck knife from its scabbard. "An' fuck you too!" he snorted. "The sombitch moved right when I shot. Fuckin' bastard!"

He knelt down beside the shuddering doe. With one powerful motion of his Buck knife, he cleanly severed her jugular. She responded briefly, tensing outright with a spastic contraction, emitting her final froth-filled gasp. Jim rolled her over on her back while Mike positioned a mesquite branch behind her neck. He picked up her front legs and slid them behind the branch, exposing the chest cavity for field stripping.

"Dad's gonna be pissed," Jim grumbled, spreading the doe's legs. Careful not to rupture her draining bladder, Jim made a stab incision between her teats. Mike noticed the milky secretions flowing uselessly from them, and for a moment, his thoughts fell back to the playful yearling that only moments before had entertained him with its carefree antics.

"Gimme a hand," Jim demanded, handing Mike the bloody knife.

Mike bent over and inserted the blade into the bloody hole. He pressed forward, ripping through cartilage and bone, gasping as the sharp odor fermented the crisp air. Jim pulled the intestines and other organs free and directed his friend to sever the last remaining tissues. They grabbed the bloody mess and shuffled over to the nearest thicket, where they lobbed the evidence as deeply as possible into the prickly pear. Jim scooped up a handful of caliche and rubbed the dirt over his forearms and through his hands, letting it absorb the globs of thick blood and membrane.

"Been here too damn long. Let's get her on the trolley!" Jim ordered.

Mike tore open the plastic trash bag and pulled out the parts of the makeshift frame. The boys had fabricated the strange-looking device from Jim's brother's bicycle tire and some scrap aluminum they had scrounged up in his dad's welding shop. Mike thought it looked more like a one-wheeled rickshaw, but since Jim didn't know what that was, they just called it a trolley.

The boys struggled to balance their load, starting and then stopping several times as the uncooperative corpse slid off the slick frame from one side to the other, mocking their attempt to escape the scene of their poaching. As youthful adrenaline interfered with their speedy departure, they simply cursed each other.

* * *

Less than a mile away, Warden Calvin Kruetter eased his gray Plymouth off the Old Loop Road and onto the narrow coarse asphalt of Farm Road 84. The long, straight blacktop stretched for miles, bordered on the right by the King Ranch fence line and on the left by the endless rows of milo farmed by Brewster Walton and his bastard sons.

Kruetter scanned the thick brush, looking for movement or any colors that did not blend in with the winter landscape surrounding the Ranch. His supercharged Plymouth idled slowly past the dry culverts, spooking only a few cottontails and horned frogs in its path. A dim morning sun glared through the light haze, as though intent on burning off any lingering low clouds before noon. The warden, mindful of the daily rendezvous for taquittos and coffee at Pearl's around nine, glanced at his watch. With an hour to spare, he returned his attention to the brush line and the critters within. *Nothing here*, he thought, pressing down on the accelerator.

Picking up speed, he reached down to roll up the window, and he caught a brief glimpse of a reflection deep in the brush. He eased his shiny boot from the accelerator. The Plymouth rolled to a stop. After a slight moment of tense contemplation, Kruetter backed up for another look.

A trail of broken, bent brush led back into the thicket beyond. Stepping out of the sedan, the warden unhooked the hammer loop from his sidearm and moved cautiously out into the weed line. The low-lying sage could not hide the intermittent tire tracks left in the patches of dirt between them.

Kruetter smiled as he scanned the thickets on either side of the trail, listening intently as he moved forward into the mesquite grove ahead. *Here comes Santa Claus, here comes Santa Claus,* he hummed slowly, peering cautiously over the rims of his silver aviator's sunglasses. "Gotch yo' asses this time," he said, smirking. "No way outa' this one, you dumb-ass sonsabitches."

He followed the trail through the brush until, finally, he spotted the source of the reflection, the windshield of a pea-green '59 Fairlane, backed into a thick clump of sage, obviously to avoid detection from the road.

"Bingo!"

He moved quickly to the car, which was empty except for a yellow and green box of .308 hollow points lying on the floorboard in the backseat. He felt the hood of the car for heat. As he ran back through the brush to his own car, he repeated the Fairlane's license plate number.

"Bird Dog Two-three, Bird Dog Two-three... This is Sierra One-niner. Over."

"Aaaahhh, roger, One-niner. This is Two-three. Over."

"Two-three... Aaahhh, we may have some fence traffic over here on Eighty-four, just south of Sarita Creek." Kruetter scanned the brush again before continuing. "If you pop the plug and come in from the east along the creek, you may be able to spook 'em. Don't have a body count, but they're not bow hunters, that's for sure. I'm gonna pull back down the road so they think they got a clear shot back to town."

"Aaaahhh… Roger, One-niner. I'm about, ohhh… one-zero out. This is Bird Dog Two-three… Out."

* * *

The boys made their way along the barren creek bed toward the fence, cursing the patches of soft mud disguised below the thin layer of dust and silt. Jim's huge arms began to ache as his heart pounded the cadence with every step. "¡Dalligas!" he shouted the Spanish slang for "Let's clear out!" Then: "We gotta hook 'im up, Shorty!" He frequently employed this invocation lifted from the TV series *Outlaws*. "What'sa matter? Your damn leg broke or what?"

Mike didn't answer. He tightened his grip on the slings as the trigger guards on the guns bounced on his back, etching painful red welts with every awkward step. He steadied the load with his other hand, crouching even lower to help push the trolley along.

Their pace quickened, aided by a long, flat section of the winding creek ahead, every turn concealing a potential hiding place for a Ranch fence rider or a game warden. Coveys of quail and dove scattered into the breezy sky, screeching a warning to the critters ahead as they circled away from the odd procession below. Moist patches of mud flew off the trolley's tire, splattering Mike as he struggled to keep up. He figured they still had a quarter mile to go and that it was time to make a change.

"Jimbo! Let me take the lead for a while. Here… Take the guns."

Breathing heavily, Jim gently lowered the struts to the ground. He walked back and took the guns from his exhausted friend.

"We need to stick another wheel on this sombitch," Mike remarked. "Who designed this piece-a' shit anyway… Alfalfa?" He was dismissively referring to the comic character in *Little Rascals*.

"Fuck you, and the horse you rode in on," Jim replied. "You're the one that came up with the damn 'rickety-shaw' idea, shit-for-brains."

"Rickshaws have two wheels, dumb-ass. It's too hard to keep *this* fuckin' thing balanced!"

"You sound just like an old fuckin' lady. Bitch, bitch, bitch."

"O-o-o-ohhh shit! Get down!" Mike grabbed Jim's shoulder and pulled him down hard as they both fell to the ground, feeling the sudden rush of air that followed the silent intruder as it disappeared over the ridge.

"Think he saw us?" Jim asked, flicking the chalky dirt off his unshaven face.

"Dunno, Jimbo. He had his throttle back. Didn't see him till he was right on us. He was comin' right down the creek bottom." After a pause he added: "Maybe he didn't, but I ain't gonna stick around ta find out."

"Well, *fuck!* Ain't this just a fuckin' bucket-a' shit?" Jim shook his head. "What the fuck else could go wrong? Must be on somebody's shit list today." He peered up into the empty sky. "We'll know for sure in a minute. If he comes back, we're dead meat. Gotta move, get the shit outa Dodge. I figure we got about ten minutes max to hit the fence line—fifteen if we're lucky. Pack it up. *¡Dalligas!*"

Leaving the deer lie was not an option either boy considered. They had killed it, and they would eat it. They knew the sky warden was on the radio calling for ground support. The challenge was to reach their car before his help could arrive.

* * *

"Sierra One-niner, this is Bird Dog Two-three. Over."

"Bird Dog… Sierra. Go."

"Aaahhhh, Sierra. We've got a coupla' bogies with at least one down moving east along Sarita Creek toward your location. Over."

"Roger copy, Two-three. I ran a check on those plates, and that junker belongs to Nathan Leary's boy, Jim." Before Nicholls could reply, Kruetter continued: "Been tryin' ta nail that smart-ass punk ever since he was in junior high. I'm gonna damn sure enjoy this one. Them acorns don't fall too far from the tree, do they?"

Nicholls broke the squelch on the mike, leaving a long pause before he answered. "Listen, Cal. I know what you're thinkin'. Just don't get over-anxious. Give him a lot of room to load up and head out onto the blacktop. We don't want to get him spooked and toss all the goodies before we get 'em out in the open."

"Don't you worry, Bird Dog. I'm gonna give him *aaallll* the rope he needs to hang himself. Can't wait to see the look on Nathan's face when he comes down to get his kid out of the lockup. Yessir, gonna really enjoy this one."

"Roger, Sierra. I'll see you at the courthouse. Bird Dog Two-three, out."

* * *

Mike strained as he lifted the lower stands of wire just high enough for Jim to slide the lifeless carcass under the fence. Jim passed the rifles through and then rolled under, cautiously surveying the clearing where they had left the car. While scanning the perimeter for any signs of detection, he held the wire high for his friend to scamper under. With his free hand, he sorted through the extra shells in his jacket, grabbing the key ring, and handing it to Mike.

"Check it out," Jim ordered, nodding his head in the direction of the car.

Mike moved into the brush line, skirting the large clumps of bristling cacti, careful not to brush against the menacing needles. He slowed his pace as the car came into view, pausing briefly to look inside before inspecting the trail for any signs of new tire tracks. Satisfied they had not been discovered, he turned back toward the fence, emitting a shrill whistle, a sound Jim had taught him, a sound that imitated a quail calling to regroup the covey. Within seconds, the trunk flew open, and the doe was tucked safely out of sight.

"If we get separated, I'll meet you at Foster's at sundown," Jim said. "I'm going down the brush line to the blacktop, to make sure nobody sees us getting back on. Pull the car outa' the brush, and when you see me signal, haul-ass down and pick me up."

He moved off into the thickets, slinging the guns over his broad shoulders. He moved quickly, collecting clumps of tiny jumping cacti as they painfully attacked through his worn Levis. Scratched and bleeding from the thorny mesquite branches, he finally knelt down and left the rifles. Then he low-crawled through the sage and coastal grass to a position where he could see the blacktop in both directions. The narrow farm road was clear.

But as he pushed back into the thicket, he heard a radio break squelch. Then: "Sierra One-niner, this is Bird Dog Two-three..."

Jim didn't wait for the response, he knew the consequences of that transmission. Moving back into the obscurity of the thickets, he backtracked about fifteen yards. He paused to cover the rifles with clumps of sage and branches. Looking to his right, he made out the dull gray paint of the warden's car, tucked closely against the brush line about fifty yards away, backed partway into a culvert ditch. He dropped to one knee and stared aimlessly at the small clump of sage near his dusty boot.

Options, options. What are the options? he thought, drawing a deep, calming breath. *They're just sittin' out there waitin' for us to make a move. Then they're gonna nail our happy asses. Can't make a run for it. There's only one way out! Damn! Dad's really gonna be pissed.*

He drew back and sat on the heel of his boot, recalling the lessons Nathan Leary had taught him over the years. *Never limit your avenues of escape. Always have more than one in and, especially, more than one way out.*

His dad's words seemed moot now. *I knew that,* he conceded. His head nodded up and down, collecting scenarios as he replayed his dad's exploits over and over in his young mind, discarding some immediately while expanding on others. *Can't bury the sucker. They'd just bring in the dogs and find it in no time.* His mind raced, head continued to nod up and down, up and down. Suddenly it stopped.

The old end-run sucker play! That'll work! I'll just get the deer and the guns, tote 'em back over the fence, skirt the line down to Foster's, and cross over there! Yeah. It's only 'bout four miles, n' we can always come back for the guns later.

His bright eyes widened as he finalized his plan. *Mike'll have ta drive the car out, n' when they pull 'im over, the only thing they can stick 'im with is trespassing. Hell, that's only a fifty-dollar fine. We can live with that! No guns, no deer—nada!*

The distinct grinding of the starter on the old Ford stifled his encouraging thoughts. Brittle mesquite thorns shrieked above the dull murmur of the engine, inscribing long, fine lines in the car's green paint job.

"Oohhh, fuck me!" Jim blurted. "He's gonna screw it all up!"

His heart sank as reality shattered his spirit. He turned once again to see if the gray Plymouth had responded to the sounds of the car moving through the brush. He sprang to his feet, pushing hard through the tangled thickness, finally emerging into the clearing near the road.

There's the signal, thought Mike, seeing Jim waving his hands over his head. Mike sped toward the road and slid to a stop beside his beleaguered friend. Jim's forlorn expression, coupled with the resigned droop in his shoulders, said it all: They were *not* alone. As the dust drifted past, Mike noticed the front end of a gray Plymouth perched awkwardly in the culvert. He turned back to Jim, but he knew the next decision would be his alone. His options were limited, his choice immediate.

With a sly grin on his face, Mike flashed the thumbs-up sign to his dejected friend. Then, slowly, he eased the Fairlane down through the culvert ditch opposite the Plymouth and out onto the blacktop. With the image in his mind of a warrior facing the enemy in the field of battle, he carefully positioned the aging car over the fading white center stripe.

Warden Kruetter stepped from his car and peered intently at the lone driver of the Fairlane. He looked back toward the brush line. *Is that Nathan's boy?* he pondered. *Didn't Nicholls say there were two of them?*

He turned his attention to the car and strode defiantly though the boot-high grass in the culvert, curious why its driver hadn't turned toward town or tried to run.

Mike's runway was in front of him, however. In a gesture reminiscent of a carrier pilot about to be catapulted off the deck, he turned briefly and saluted his hidden friend. Then he gunned the engine, holding the brakes steady as the car lurched upward against the strain of the revved-up motor. The tanned Polynesian hula dancer mounted on Jim's dashboard swayed invitingly with the vibration, smiling back at Mike while her grass skirt shimmied above her knees. The bald tires broke free, briefly spewing burnt rubber and white smoke. Mike accelerated past the startled warden.

Kruetter scampered back into his car, cursing the youngster while he fished out his keys. Jim heard the distinctive Chrysler starter crank, giving life to the supercharged 440 under the warden's hood.

"Yeahhh boy!" Jim exclaimed from the bushes. *Mike kin beat 'im top end,* he thought to himself. His old Ford had only a 292 engine with a Holley four-barrel, but the boys had replaced the drive train with a really high rear end for this very purpose. Jim ducked down as the warden's car spun through the culvert, showering the brush line with caliche rocks and clumps of sage as it spun back onto the blacktop. Jim shouted encouragement through the cloud of white smoke and dust as the warden fishtailed down the road. He knew his friend was creating a diversion, giving him time to get away. He quickly made his way back to where he had hidden the guns. His emotions soared while he strapped the guns together, then slid back under the fence and headed north toward Foster's for the hopeful rendezvous.

Mike watched the speedometer ease past ninety as he looked ahead for the intersection of the Old Loop Road. He glanced in the rearview mirror, mindful of the dark speck trailing behind. The boys had outrun the wardens before, but that was at night and Jim was driving. Jim knew all the back roads and ranch trails and made good use of the switch he had installed that would cut his brake lights when they ran without headlights. He dropped the gearshift into second, braking firmly as he slowed to make the turn. The fuel jets on the four-barrel swiftly kicked into action, vaulting the old Ford down the long, straight flattop.

Just don't turn your red lights on yet, you son of a bitch. I've got five miles before I have to slow for the first curve. Mike kept his foot pressed hard to the floor, one eye on the rearview, the other marveling at the speed of the telephone poles whizzing past.

What the fuck's he got in that thing? Kruetter wondered. He glanced down at his speedometer. *One-twenty-five, and I ain't gainin' an inch! He's gotta slow down for that West Loop curve.*

Mike knew that the curve ahead was long and gradual. *If I can just get past it before the bastard turns his red lights on, it'll be time enough.* Unlike Jim, he'd never run from the law before as the driver, and he decided that when he did see the warden's red lights, he would stop.

He eased off the gas pedal, slowing for the curve. Then he noticed the two red lights in the warden's grill. He put the gearshift into neutral and coasted around the gentle curve. Then he eased the old Fairlane off onto the shoulder, where he reluctantly turned the car off.

Kruetter gripped his wheel tightly. Nervously he accelerated into the turn. Hot rubber screamed, gripping the coarse asphalt as the car leaned precariously to the right. Tight knuckles held his track through the curve and past the young man leaning casually against the green car, arms folded, legs crossed.

Thick white smoke obscured the gray Plymouth, trailing it to a stop about three hundred yards past the lone motorist. The smoke had barely cleared when Kruetter reversed his course, backing rapidly and sliding to a stop in front of the green Fairlane. Stepping out of the car, he left the door open, legs spread wide, anticipating confrontation. He stood motionless for a moment, glaring intently, the heel of his right hand pressed down on his sidearm, the left slowly adjusting his gray Stetson. Moments passed before he stepped onto the edge of the blacktop, custom black boots shedding the last remnants of caliche as they slowly pounded their way toward the boy.

Mike stood upright as the warden approached. He put his hands in the pockets of his jacket, pretending a casualness yet still fighting his innate urge to apologize. He stepped to the front of the car, anxious to find out just how much trouble he was in. Kruetter's glare left little doubt.

The warden walked slowly past Mike and stuck his head into the open window. "Where's the driver?" he demanded.

"I'm the driver, sir," Mike replied with a sheepish smile.

Kruetter continued to survey the contents of the car. "You think this is a fuckin' game, don't you, sonny boy?" he asked calmly. He pulled his head from the window and stepped back over in front of Mike. His steel-blue eyes squinted as he studied the expression on the teenager in front of him. "I don't know you, do I, boy?" he asked.

"No sir."

"You play ball for King High?" The warden was looking down at the large *K* sewn on the front of Mike's jacket.

"I did," Mike admitted. "Baseball."

Kruetter smugly shook his head. "Didn't figure you played football." Then, sarcastically: "Otherwise, I'd-a' known who you were."

"Never learned to play it growing up, sir."

Kruetter grimaced. "Where the fuck you from, sonny? Mongolia?"

Mike shrugged. "You're close. Japan."

"All right, Tojo," Kruetter quipped. "Let's see some ID."

Mike reached into his pocket and pulled out his wallet. He slipped out his driver's license and handed it to the warden.

Kruetter studied the information on the license. "Shannahan... What's your dad do, boy?"

"He's the operations officer at the naval air station, sir." Mike's heart sank as his father's image came into view. *Oh shit! The Commander! He's not going to take this one too graciously.* The gravity of the situation became apparent.

Kruetter left no time for Mike to complete the lament. Raising his voice, he demanded some answers: "I'm only gonna ask this one more time. Where's the Leary boy?"

"I guess he's at home. That's where he was this morning when I borrowed his car. I was just followin' the creek bed, looking for Karankawa arrowheads and some artifacts—"

"Hey, *asshole!*" Kruetter yelled. "Look at me! Do I look like a dumb-ass to you? You still haven't got the big picture here, have ya? That car belongs to Jim Leary, and I want to know where the fuck he is! You're gonna show me where I can find him. *¿Comprende?*"

Mike's eyes tightened, defiantly staring back at Kruetter. He watched his own reflection in the warden's mirrored sunglasses. He didn't like anybody calling him an asshole, not even Jim. The word made the hair stand up on the back of his neck.

Kruetter had heard enough. He slapped his left hand hard behind Mike's neck, squeezing firmly as he pushed him back to the rear of the car. "Open the trunk, asshole," he ordered, releasing his grip as Mike straightened up.

Mike stared back at him, slowly reaching into his pocket for the keys. *I wish I'd-a' kept going.* His youthful veins expanded along with his disdain for Kruetter. In a moment the trunk was open, exposing the doe covered in dry blood and dirt.

The warden shoved Mike out of the way. As he leaned over the trunk, an expression of confirmation swept across his smug face. "Well, well, well. What have we here? One dead doe and one lyin' asshole. What a pathetic pair! And ya know what, asshole? I don't know which one is *more* pathetic. Guess we'll just have ta ask the judge about that one. I suppose you're gonna tell him you just found it in the creek when you was huntin' artifacts. Or maybe you—"

Kruetter's folly was cut short by a faint gunshot echoing in the distance. He peered over the trunk, neck erect like an old bird dog homing in on his prey. He listened with his head cocked to one side as two more faint reports followed in quick succession.

"Looks like you're gonna have some company at the courthouse after all. Lock it up, sonny boy."

Mike slammed the trunk shut, walked around, and turned the key into the door lock. Kruetter stepped from behind, took the ring of keys, slapped one of the silver handcuffs on Mike's outstretched wrist, and locked the other cuff securely to the door handle.

"Don't run off now, sonny boy," the warden shouted over his shoulder as he trotted back to his car. "We got a date with the judge, and it looks like you're gonna have some company!"

Mike ducked his head, shielding himself from the assault of gravel and dirt spewing from the spinning tires trenching their way back on to the blacktop. "You fuckin' bastard!" he yelled, shaking his head vigorously, trying to rid the debris from his jet black hair. While the Plymouth disappeared over the rolling stretches of the Old Loop Road, he pressed his pulsating forehead against Jim's car.

Probably some stupid wetbacks. Only rookies or wetbacks take more than one shot, he surmised. *Sounded like it was coming from Carl's. Shit, even I could figure that out.*

Carl, Jim's favorite uncle, enjoyed the coveted reputation as the Chief Resident Poacher. His small spread bordered the King Ranch fence line, with corn feeders strategically placed to lure the wildlife into his lair. Although the spread was infested with deer, turkey, and javelina, the boys found no sport in killing the grazing game. To them, it was just like shooting cattle in a field. Whenever Carl needed meat, he would just step out onto his porch, pick up his rifle, and drop whatever walked in front of his sights.

With time to reflect, and his adrenaline fading, Mike felt pretty stupid himself, shackled to an old Ford, on the side of the road, with a dead doe rotting in the trunk. He'd never been in any trouble before, at least not with the law. His thoughts kept drifting ahead to the Commander, who would be standing tall and menacing in front of the courthouse, hands on hips, censuring lips. "This is unacceptable" would be the opening volley. As he pondered the consequences of this escapade, Mike's spirit continued to sink.

As the eldest boy in the Shannahan family (though he did have a sister, Patricia, who was two years older), Mike shouldered a responsibility typical of all good Irish Catholic eldest sons: Set the example for his three younger brothers, a sacred task enforced with brutal zeal. He'd already let his demanding father down once, losing the appointment to the Naval Academy because of his grades. This transgression could prove more disastrous to their relationship. *He won't understand. I'll never be able to explain this one to him.*

Jim had always made their hunting trips so adventurous, so natural. Mike was fervently drawn to the excitement, the challenges, and especially the camaraderie the boys shared. Jim and Nathan had taught him to resent the fences and politics, which prevented them from openly pursuing their youthful, God-given passions.

The fences spanned from Kingsville to the Mexican border, set in place by Captain King and his predecessors on land stolen and hoarded, Mike had been told, in the years following the Civil War. The apparent victims of the theft were defenseless Mexicans and immigrant homesteaders. Jim's grandfather had tracked *Muy grande* in his time, and the folklore surrounding the King Ranch and its occupants made it easy for the boys to justify their transgression. It wasn't, however, a topic they brought up in confession.

The local tradition was totally inconsistent with the Commander's motto, a sacred creed Mike had been taught since his childhood days in occupied Japan. The words came easily to Mike: *Duty. Honor. Country.* The plaque bearing that West Point motto hung perpetually over his bed, ever since his father had presented it to him on his seventh birthday in Yokohama.

No. He'll never understand. And Mike knew why.

* * *

CHAPTER TWO

T HE DRAINED LONE STAR LONGNECK sailed out the speeding truck's window, spewing a wet, sudsy plume of foam on its trek toward the dented yellow sign.

"Yeeeeehawww!" the passenger shouted. As the amber glass shattered, fashioning yet another crease in the battered, rusting curve sign, he slapped the weary driver on the shoulder. "That's four in a row, Bubba!" he yelled, trying to drown out the country music blaring on the radio.

Bubba nodded passively, tugging instinctively on the brim of his frayed straw cowboy hat. His foot eased off the gas pedal, then quickly he geared down to get a better look at the familiar car parked on the shoulder.

"Check it out, Brian," he said urgently, turning down the radio and slowing to a stop.

"Hey, that's Mike! What the hell? Looks like he's handcuffed to the damn car!"

"That's Jimbo's car," Bubba remarked calmly. "But where the hell's Jimbo?"

Brian jumped out of the truck. As he walked toward the car, he unbuttoned his worn Levis. "Gotta take a piss so bad my balls are singin' 'Anchors Away.'" He stopped behind the parked car to relieve himself.

Bubba eased out of the truck and stretched his long, lanky legs. He walked cautiously toward the Fairlane, gazing around warily for clues to the curious scene.

"Hey, Bubba! What are you guys doin' way out here?" Mike's nonchalance barely tempered the obvious stress on his face.

Bubba reached into his shirt pocket, pulling out a red tin of snuff. He slowly deposited a pinch between his cheeks and adjusted the wad behind his lower lip before finally replying. "Been up to Schulenburg at Papaw's breakin' in my new two-seventy. Want a beer?"

Mike smirked. "You know I don't like that shit."

Bubba turned and leaned his back against the car as he slid next to Mike. He looked over his shoulder and yelled back to Brian. "Hey, dickwad! Get him a beer outa' the back!"

Brian quickly waddled back to the truck, buttoning his pants as he stumbled through the dirt and gravel.

"OK, I give up," Bubba confessed.

"Ahwww, we were on the Ranch doin' a little game conservation, and... we got spooked on the way out." Mike's head slumped in resigned chagrin.

"Where's Jimbo?" Brian handed Mike a frosted longneck.

"He's on his way to Foster's, I hope. He's got the guns, but the problem is that I've got a damn doe in the trunk."

"A *doe!*"

"It's a long story," Mike admitted, shaking his head.

"That's a double whammy," Bubba said, chuckling. "Where's the warden now?"

"There were some shots comin' from around Carl's place. He went over to take a look. He'll be back in any minute. You better not wait around. He was a real asshole."

"Well, *Shi-i-tt!* That's where we were headed. We really got into 'em up in Schulenburg, n' we're just bringin' a coupla' the smaller ones out ta Carl's for him ta make sausage outa'." Bubba spit a long stream of rusty snuff juice and wiped the dribble off his chin with the sleeve of his already stained khaki shirt.

"The Great White Hunter here got a little trigger happy." Brian shrugged, embarrassed by Bubba's confession. "They're not tagged... We're over our limit. That's all we need to do is get caught with 'em out here ourselves!"

"Well, hell, minor detail. I got some tags in my wallet." Mike struggled with his free hand to take his wallet out of his jacket. "Jimbo's wallet is under the seat, an' I know he's got a couple left."

"Well, let's get after it." Brian tugged at the locked door handle. "Where's the keys?"

"The Lone Ranger took 'em with him... But Jim's got a spare taped above the gas tank on the left side."

*   *   *

Jim carefully leaned the rifles against the knotty old tree. Then he slumped down beside it, pausing briefly to catch his breath. He reached down and gingerly extracted the clump of long, yellow cactus spines from his right calf. He knew the smaller ones would fester up and come out on their own in a couple of months. He was careful to leave the less painful ones for his girl, Birdie, to fuss over. He'd need some tender sympathy to soften Nathan Leary's fiery ire.

The silver top of Foster's silo gleamed in the distance, a welcome beacon at the end of his arduous jaunt. Jim covered the rifles once again and then made his way carefully to the edge of the road. A renewed sense of caution forced him back into the brush and down the fence line to a culvert with a wide drainage pipe leading under the road and into Foster's fields of milo. He crawled through the maze of spiderwebs, crushing the resident crickets and crawling insects as he made his way to the light at the other end of the tunnel.

Suddenly he froze. The slinky, rattling noise amplified as several more black-ringed tails joined their conductor. He watched in terror as the diamond-shaped heads sprang up in unison, blocking his path through the darkened cylinder. "Motherfucker!" he muttered, slowly backing away from the coiled nest of diamondbacks. His hands trembled and began to shake violently. He tried to calm himself, slowly backing the way he had come.

Road noise above halted his retreat. He listened anxiously as a car door slammed, followed by a bevy of muffled voices. He dared not take his eyes off the scaly serpents. While their symphony grew louder, their captive audience, perspiring with every beat, watched in mounting terror, afraid to move in either direction. *They musta' spotted me crossin' the fence,* Jim figured. *Motherfuckers.*

Anxiety turned to shallow panic, his adrenaline pumped furiously, feeding his emerging phobia. He was trapped: pursuing wardens above, deadly serpents below. His mind raced, the panic prevailed. Then he turned and scampered furiously back out of the culvert and up onto the blacktop above, right into a group of Mexican men unloading several rifles from the bed of a battered old pickup. Startled by Jim's sudden appearance, they quickly threw the guns back into the pickup, and as the driver sped away, the two remaining wetbacks scrambled after and launched themselves into the bed. Jim stood there trembling, then quickly gathered his thoughts and ran across the road into the lines of milo, zigzagging through the plowed rows to the safety of the farmhouse.

Foster's truck was gone. Jim sighed, cursing furiously while fending off the frenzied pack of yard dogs. He sat down on the long porch and tried to catch his breath. Beads of sweat mingled with the stubble of beard on his unshaven face. He listened to the clatter of pointed paws tap-dancing the length of the porch, flicking up scant remnants of flaked white paint as they pranced. It was some time before his thoughts finally settled on his friend.

He couldn't have gotten too far, he surmised. *Forgot to put some fuckin' gas in the car this morning. Oh well, just bin one-a' those days.*

* * *

Kruetter's gait accented his mood. "Get off your ass, Tojo!" he yelled across the road. Mike slowly pulled himself up, indifferent but responsive to the rude demand. "You know where the Kleberg County Courthouse is?" the warden inquired.

"Yessir."

Kruetter unlocked the shackles, then flipped Jim's keys up into the air. Mike watched them fall, offering a sarcastic smirk but making no effort to catch them. He rubbed the soreness in his wrist, staring back defiantly.

"Pick 'em up, punk."

Mike continued to rub his wrist, shaking his head slowly. He glanced down at the keys, then defiantly rolled his eyes back to the impatient glare of the warden.

"Don't even fuck with me, boy," Kruetter advised. "I'm just in the mood to open a whole can-a' whop-ass on your scrawny butt soon as look at ya. Pick 'em up, get yo' ass in that car, and head back to the bypass to Highway Seventy-seven." He pressed down hard on his sidearm. "You make one wrong turn before we hit the courthouse, n' I'll take that as a personal challenge. Feel froggy today, asshole?"

Reluctantly, Mike reached down and retrieved the keys. The short trip back to town would not afford him enough time to come up with a plausible excuse to ward off the inevitable barrage and tirade of the Commander. He ran several scenarios through his mind, but the only one that made sense was to just come clean and take responsibility for his actions. Jack Shannahan hated excuses, and his son knew that all too well. He could hear him now: "When you screw up—and you will—don't pass out any 'weak sister' apologies. Take your hickey like a man, learn from it, and move on."

I wonder if that applies when you really screw up? Mike pondered. *Guess we'll find out soon enough.*

He pulled in front of the old three-story courthouse, its brown-brick shell weathered from several decades of sustained coastal winds. Kruetter pulled in beside him and motioned Mike out of the car. The warden took the keys again, patted his prisoner down, and once more slapped the cuffs on him.

"Is this really necessary? I'm not going anywhere," Mike protested.

"Think you're somun' special, don't ya, sonny boy? Well, we don't discriminate here. All you criminals are accorded the same courtesies. It's da law." He grabbed Mike's arm, forcing him up the long walk to the courthouse, through the marble halls, and up the stairs to the second floor. The sign on the door read: *J. R. "Tiny" Vela, Kleberg County Judge.*

"They've called your father," Kruetter remarked, motioning Mike to sit in the chair in the corner. He turned his attention to the busty redhead shuffling through some papers on her desk. "Nellie May, will you prepare the standard complaint, hon? Delete the trespass portion, I didn't see him cross over. But include the illegal deer in possession."

Kruetter handed her Mike's license. She studied it briefly and followed up her perfunctory glance by asking, "Is this your first offense, Michael?"

"Didn't realize I'd offended anything, ma'am." His deep breaths drew in the sweet ambiance of her alluring perfume. "Heck, I was just out at the Walton's place combin' the creek bed for arrowheads when—"

"Just answer the damn question, punk!" Kruetter shouted. "You're about two words shy of an ass-whoppin', you smart-ass son of a bitch!"

The chamber door swung open, breaking the tension in the room. Mike watched a frail, elderly man shuffle through the door, followed closely by a tall, imposing figure of a man. Speaking in Spanish, the old *patrón* tipped his hat, nodding kindly to everyone as he continued his slow, painful odyssey to the exit. Mike turned his attention to the second man, whose mere presence, with hands on hips, forced the nervous boy to his feet.

"What the hell is going on out here, Nellie May?" the tall man asked, jet black eyes focused on the young outlaw in the corner.

Nellie May shrugged, appearing a little tense following Kruetter's outburst. "I don't rightly know, Your Honor," she meekly replied.

The judge turned to Kruetter. "Cal, do we have a problem here?"

"Nothing I can't handle, Tiny. Caught 'im with the Leary boy this mornin', just south of Sarita Creek. They'd been on the Ranch shootin' doe, and this one tried to run," Kruetter explained. "Had to shut 'im down around the West Loop. The Leary boy got away."

"Nathan's boy?" Tiny pulled a large red-checkered kerchief from his back pocket. He wiped the sweat from the folds of flesh disguising his neck. Then he addressed Mike. "How old are you, son?"

"I'll be eighteen in a coupla' weeks, Your Honor."

"What were you and the Leary boy doin' on the Ranch today?" the judge asked, a slight Tex-Mex accent apparent in his query.

"I wasn't on the Ranch, sir. Mr. Walton lets me prospect the creek bottoms on his spread for Karankawa artifacts and—"

"The twerp's lyin', Tiny," Kruetter insisted. "He's got a damn *doe* rottin' in the trunk."

The judge focused on Mike's hazel eyes. "Well, if that's the case, guess there ain't no sense debating the issue." He turned to his secretary. "Nellie May, has anyone called his parents?"

"Yes sir. His father is on his way down here now."

"Well, in that case, let's go take a look at the evidence." Tiny folded up his checkered bandana, stuffing it in his trouser pocket as he ushered Mike and the warden out the door.

The trio had just reached the bottom step to the courthouse when a dull gray Volkswagen bus pulled up in the parking lot. Mike cringed as the naval officer stepped out and adjusted his trouser leg over his brown flight boot. The gold braid on his visor gleamed in the morning sun, the black brim shading the fire in his eyes. As the naval officer approached, Tiny and the warden glanced at each other. They straightened their posture as the officer extended his hand, his sleeve revealing the stripes of his rank. "Jack Shannahan," he introduced himself. "This is my son."

"Tiny Vela. This is Cal Kruetter." The judge introduced himself and the warden. "I'm afraid we have a problem here with your son, Commander. Warden Kruetter apprehended him this morning with an illegal deer, and we have reason to believe that it was taken off the King Ranch. The Ranch is posted property, and as you can imagine, they don't take kindly to poachers killing their wildlife."

The Commander turned sharply to his son, the glare of disgust sufficiently conveying the message that the exorcism had begun. Mike knew that this was the end of his relationship with Jim, his adventures, possibly his life as he knew it. He felt the stinging pain of the chastising stare, searing an element of his soul, that part where he carefully nurtured his honor. "Was it worth it?" his father finally asked, his voice tempered with intense disappointment.

Mike did not reply. His lips tightened, frowning slightly, but he offered no contrition. Not yet.

"We're about to log the evidence, Commander," Kruetter advised. "If you would care to join us, it's over here."

Kruetter hurried toward the trunk of the green Fairlane, smugly glancing back over his shoulder to be sure everyone was following. He paused briefly, jingling the keys like a ceremonial bell. With his audience assembled, he slid the appropriate key into the lock, finally exposing the incriminating carcass for everyone to see.

The warden stepped back in amazement, a confused look captured his gaze. Tiny leaned slowly forward, silently counting the six points on the small buck's rack. He noticed the white tag, tied neatly around the base of the lifeless deer's antler.

"Gimme your knife, Cal," Tiny ordered.

Kruetter complied, haltingly unsnapping the small scabbard he wore attached to his pistol belt. As he handed Tiny the blade, his eyes skewed inquisitively, shifting attention to Mike, who was standing expressionless beside him. "You smart-ass punk," he whispered.

Tiny grunted as he leaned into the trunk and cut the tag from the deer. He stepped back and unfolded the small paper. He was breathing heavily while he inspected its contents: *Michael Shannahan. Taken in Schulenburg County. November 21, 1965.* Today's date.

Tiny held up the tag. "What's the meaning of this, Cal?"

Everything was in order. A legal buck, properly registered, with a tag from Mike's Texas hunting license. Kruetter calmly reached over and took the tag from the judge. He scanned the contents, then turned to Mike and grabbed him by the nape of his collar, forcing him back several steps from the car.

"You obviously haven't lived here in Texas too long, *asshole!*" Kruetter began. "We have a saying here I think you need to remember: 'You fuck with the bull, and you'll catch the horn!' I don't know how you did it, but this bull has got your number, punk. You *and* your smart-ass friend will regret ever getting up this morning! I'm going to—"

"Cal!" Tiny yelled, "that's enough!"

Mike broke the warden's grasp and stepped back, regaining his composure. "*Shinchōna hantā wa kashikoku emono o erabu... Nazenara tokidoki... Usagi ga jū o motte irunode!*"

"Don't hide behind that gibberish, punk. Say it to my face."

"Since you don't speak *proper* Japanese, I'd be glad to. We have an old saying in Japan, too: 'The prudent hunter selects his prey wisely, because sometimes... the *rabbit* has the gun.'"

"Cal!" Tiny shouted. "My office."

Kruetter gave Mike one last glare, tossed the tag to the ground, and stalked off toward the courthouse steps. Mike swiftly picked up the tag, walked back to the car, and closed the trunk.

Tiny wasted no time: "Looks like you and the Leary boy set ol' Cal up pretty good. Wouldn't surprise me if Nathan didn't have a hand in this, too." He pulled the bandana out one more time. "Cal's a pretty good man, Commander, but he and Nathan Leary go way back." He paused briefly to collect the beads of perspiration seeping along the folds of his neck. "I'd hate to see your boy here gettin' caught up in this feud. It really doesn't have anything to do with him."

Tiny reached into his breast pocket, pulled out Mike's driver's license, and handed it to the Commander. "We don't have any reason to hold your son any longer, sir. You're both free to go." Then he looked directly at Mike. "As for you, son, I caution you to remember this: While you're in *my* county, *I* am the rabbit."

Tiny turned and slowly walked back to the courthouse, leaving Mike alone with his dad. Although the Commander was still confused about exactly what had just transpired, he knew his son, and his instincts told him that the boy was surely guilty of something.

"So you've been hanging out with the Leary boy again. What were the instructions?"

Mike watched his father's chest swell, his gold aviator's wings perched above the massive forearms folded in tirade posture. He knew the boot tapping would be next, followed closely by the swelling of the blood vessels in the temple.

"He's my friend, Dad… my best friend. The judge was wrong. Jim didn't put me up to anything."

"What *were* the instructions?" the Commander repeated forcefully.

"You told me to find some other friends." Mike's voice dropped sheepishly.

"Just what was it in those instructions that you didn't understand?"

Mike's emotions swelled up in his throat as their eyes made contact for the first time. "The whole thing! I *knew* you wouldn't understand!"

"Understand what?" His father's arms slammed to his hips. "Understand that you're a disgrace to this family, a personal embarrassment to me? And what a *fine* example you're setting for your brothers! Maybe you'd like to have your mother come down here and visit you in jail!"

"Well, that about says it all, doesn't it? You're still pissed that I wasn't good enough to get into Academy, aren't you?" Mike stepped closer, folding his arms in rebuttal. "All you give a shit about is the goddamn navy. When's the last time you were even home for dinner? And how am I supposed to have any new friends anyway? They're all afraid of you!" Mike turned his back, afraid his emotions would compromise the point he was trying to make.

"I'm not through with you. Get back over here!" his father demanded.

Mike slowly turned to face his dad. "Well, *I'm* sure as hell through. Through with your incessant bullshit, through with always not being good enough, through with having to be big brother—go-for, patsy, yard man—you name it!"

The last word had barely tumbled from his mouth when the right cross whizzed past his ducking chin. He stumbled to his right, regained his balance, poised to ward off the next blow. In that split second, he realized that he had crossed the line, violated the sacred bond between father and son, altering their relationship forever.

Jack Shannahan turned and stalked away, leaving his son alone to contemplate the consequences of their encounter. Mike suppressed his urge to run after his father, apologize for his impudence, retrieve what was left of their bond. But nothing could be the same anymore. He realized that for the first time in his life, he had stood up to his father. He didn't feel good about it, but he was still alive.

The gray Volkswagen bus backed out of the parking lot, and as it turned the corner, Mike wondered where he would sleep that night.

*   *   *

CHAPTER THREE

IKE PULLED THE GREEN FAIRLANE out of the Esso station, turned onto the bypass, and headed south toward Foster's farm. He draped his arm over the long bench seat, his restless mind reflecting on the events of the last few weeks. He struggled with his emotions, confusion obscuring any direction while his young mind wandered through the vast abyss of unfulfilled dreams. His father's harsh words simmered above his heart, still scarring the moist fabric of his pride.

He called me a disgrace... *He never went that far before*, he lamented. *Maybe I am*, he concluded, feeling sorry for himself.

He recalled the judge's comment "*I* am the rabbit." *Yeah... a big rabbit with big horns!* He finally realized just how close he had come to destroying any chance he had to do something meaningful with his life. *That's all I need, a damn police record!* He wondered if they did background checks on the roughnecks in the oil fields.

Mike rolled the window down. Along with the brisk wind, the sweet, soothing scent of milo tempered the sudden gust of manure filling the car. He gazed across the highway at the large herd of Santa Gertrudis cattle, skirted by a smaller posse of quarter horses and thoroughbreds thundering across the grassy plain. He looked up and saw a squadron of orange and white training jets, banking sharply above the startled herd, flaps and landing gear down-poised for their final approach to the air base. He slowed down and pulled over to the shoulder, watching the dark plumes of smoke billowing from their afterburners. One by one, they broke formation, lining up their sporty chariots, practicing their approaches for the carrier landings they were training for.

"Lucky bastards," he murmured, envious of their skill and courage, resenting the ease they exhibited as they maneuvered the war birds into position. "Can't be *that* tough," he concluded. He waited until the last trainer disappeared over the horizon, pausing just long enough to satisfy himself that it didn't crash and burn. He was, after all, yearning to take someone's place in that formation.

The road to Foster's led Mike down a familiar lane. He'd taken this path many times before, under much different circumstances. The tall pecan trees still stood in front of the white two-story house, the perfect trellis to Barbara's bedroom, and her loving arms. A flair of Shalimar teased his senses as he drew a sweet vestige of her into his mind—her silky golden hair, her crystal-blue eyes, her long, firm legs. He smiled as he caressed her image and the young love they had shared over the last two years. His euphoria quickly transformed to youthful anguish, his heart still aching since their breakup several weeks earlier. She'd found someone new.

Mike peered out the window, trying to make out the car parked in the long driveway to her house. He saw a tint of red through the broad white fence surrounding the manicured lawn: a sports car, Corvette, with a blue officer's sticker prominently attached to the shiny bumper. "He might as well move in... *Fuck* her... and the horse she rode in on." He shook his head. "Goddamn *whore*."

He pressed hard on the accelerator, quietly cursing himself for even caring, cursing her for hurting him, cursing the aviator who had stolen her heart. "It's my own damn fault," he finally admitted. "What the hell do I have to offer her anyhow? Hell, I don't even *have* a car!"

He knew he couldn't compete with the men her sorority sisters were dating, but then they weren't around when he and Barbara had fallen in love. He had only himself to offer, and until now that had always been good enough. But *her* life was changing. It had become a different world, and with a little guidance from her new friends, she evidently felt the need to see other people. He struggled with feelings of being betrayed, vicious thoughts that struck at the very core of his being. His young heart ached, pleading desperately with his conscious mind to do something to stop the pain.

I need to take something positive away from this, he reckoned, recalling his mother's advice. She always put a positive spin on adversity. It was just her way. But now he had too much on his mind to deal with it objectively, so he tried instead to drown out his thoughts. He reached down and turned up the music, as loud as it would go.

"One hundred men will test today,/

But only three win the Green Beret,"

the radio blared. The words lingered in his mind. Finally: *Hell, if they won't let me fly 'em, guess I'll just have to jump outa' the damn things.*

He slowed to make the turn to the Old Loop Road, and with his turn signal blinking on, the wind dried the final tear from his eye.

Jim sprang to his feet and scampered off the porch, waving wildly as his old Fairlane turned off the blacktop and through the gate. Yard chickens and guineas scattered as Mike slid to a stop, relieved to see his brush buddy running toward him through the cloud of caliche dust.

"Yeahhh boy! I knew you could outrun 'im, you ol' sombitch!"

Mike slammed the door. "No thanks to you, rectum breath!" he chided. "What tha fuck were you thinkin', waving me down there with the Lone Ranger sittin' right there?"

"*Shi-i-tt!* I was just lucky to hear the damn squelch break on his radio! Sky King musta' tipped him off soon as he saw us... Sneaky bastards. Would'na been a pretty sight if we woulda' pulled out there with the guns and the deer. How'd ya outrun 'im?"

"I didn't... Well, I coulda', but he'd-a just had the highway patrol waitin' for me at the other end of the Loop. I figured you'd have enough time to get scarce if he took off after me. Anyway, we need to get out to Carl's. Bubba and Brian are waitin' for us... Where're the guns?"

"Hid 'em in the brush. We'll get 'em tonight. I ain't going back over there until the sun goes down, that's for damn sure."

The boys pulled out of the gate and back onto the blacktop. Mike surveyed the endless strands of wire and fenceposts to his right. "You might have to track ol' *Muy grande* on your own, Jimbo. Don't think this *gringo* is gonna give those bastards another shot at my sweet ass, especially not over there."

Jim turned with an inquisitive stare. "Candy ass."

Mike left the epithet unchallenged. Changing the subject, he began to relate the whole story to Jim, who especially enjoyed the last part, where Kruetter's threatening comments led the judge to believe that this was all just part of an elaborate conspiracy masterminded by his father.

"Dad's just gonna love this one. He hates that bastard. You know, they used to be best friends... long time ago." Jim paused, tweaking Mike's interest in what was to follow. "The ol' man snaked him—stole his best gal—but that's not the way Mom tells it."

Mike smirked. "Just think, Jimbo. The best part of you could have been runnin' down ol' Kruetter's leg."

"Fuck you, Chinaman!" Jim smashed Mike's shoulder with his powerful fist. He glanced back to the road and then looked over for an opportunity to land another lick on his laughing friend.

"No wonder he hates your ass," Mike replied, still grinning from the revelation. "Hell, I don't blame him."

"It's not my fault the son of a bitch couldn't keep a woman. Hell, if a man can't handle some competition, he oughta zip up his fly n' *dalligas*."

Jim's remark stung Mike, whose sensitivity was immediately aroused, sending morose thoughts straight to the red Corvette. A long hush followed, allowing the atmosphere to descend into a more somber mood.

Finally, Jim, acknowledging his part in the mood swing, broke the silence: "It's your *own* fault. You were up her ass too much, pal. She had the power, and that's something you *never* give a woman."

"How the fuck do you know?" Mike inquired defensively, his head turned toward the window, shielding his pain from his best friend.

"Hey! Who loves ya, Miguelito? Have I got *dumb-ass* tattooed across my forehead? I've seen ya! You had the sweet ass so bad that every time you went to take a shit, the damn tumble bugs had a taffy pull!"

Mike smiled. Jim's expressions were crude, but they always seemed to bear the point. "What makes you the fuckin' expert?" Mike asked.

"Experience, my man. And listenin' to good ol' Dad. He told me a long time ago that the way to keepin' a woman is to treat her like shit... and never, ever to give her the power. Once she gits the power, she'll just use it on you, fuck your life up for good. Or, she'll decide that since you gave her the power, you just ain't man enough for her. Next thing ya know: ¡Dalligas!"

"So that's why you treat Birdie like shit?"

"Got to. Ain't no other way. Gotta keep 'em in their place. They're comfortable in that there corral, and as long as you keep 'em in there, they won't be grazing on that greener grass down the road."

"Sounds pretty fucked up if you ask me. My ol' man never treated my mom like shit, and they've been together for over twenty years."

"It's 'cause he broke her in early, that's why."

"Bullshit! That's your ass talking 'cause your mouth knows better."

"Well, road-kill breath, who's gonna get laid tonight? Me… or you?" Jim smiled, confident he'd made his point.

Rebuffed once again, Mike turned his attention to the plowed fields and rolling hills beyond the Ranch fence line. The few miles to Carl's would take them by several old farmhouses and small rustic ranches, built decades ago by hardworking immigrants from places he had never seen. He enjoyed their jaunts along the country roads. They allowed his imagination to reconstruct Indian battles and Civil War skirmishes in the agrarian plains. Having lived overseas until he was fifteen, he now relished the chance to roam the land that he had been able only to dream about as a boy. He watched the sun begin its final salute to the milo and mesquite, adorning the horizon with a fantastic array of pinks and blues. At this moment, with his best friend by his side, there was no place on earth that he would rather be.

The billowing white cloud trailed the green Fairlane down the narrow road and past the rusty gate to Carl's tranquil domain. Jim swerved around the large potholes in the dusty road leading to the quaint white farmhouse, which was nestled atop a small rise festooned with shade trees and tall neat rows of oleander. He pulled to a stop next to Carl's brand-new fire-red Eldorado, just one of his many penchants for the finer things in life. They stepped from the Fairlane, chatting again about Kruetter and the close call they'd encountered on the Ranch.

"He's down at the slab out back, Jimmy," a sweet voice reported.

Mike glanced up at the house to see a tall, dark-haired woman, barefoot and clad in a slinky blue cotton housedress, one of her long, shapely legs dangled over the top step to the porch. Her sultry smile seemed inviting, alluring, even provocative. Mike stared at her intently, intrigued by her seductive manner, her full, enticing lips slowly sipping from the ice-filled tumbler. He tried to follow Jim, but while she teased him, slowly licking the moisture from her lavish red lips, he stumbled over a yelping yard dog.

Jim grabbed his friend by the collar, pulling him along. He offered a warning: "She's too fuckin' old for you, pencil dick. Hell, she's damn near *thirty!* You wouldn't know what to do with her anyway. She'd tear your skinny ass up."

"Well, I sure wish she'd get after it!" Mike replied, still looking back to get a final glimpse of the temptress leaning against the pillar. "Who the hell *is* she, anyway?"

"Just one of Carl's hussies. Women love that old son of a bitch."

The boys ambled down to the covered slab behind the house, obscured by the fading twilight and thick clouds of smoke spewing from several large adobe barbecue pits. Four deer carcasses hung from the rafters, attended by several figures methodically skinning and quartering the lifeless prey.

"I was just about to send a posse out ta round your dumb-asses up," a deep voice proclaimed. Carl reached into the cooler beside him, pulled out a wet longneck, and handed it to Jim. The wide cuffs on his outstretched arm were folded neatly, the crisp white shirt tucked flawlessly in starched blue jeans. His tall, slim frame towered over Jim. Carl was an imposing figure, heightened by the exotic snakeskin boots and gray flannel Stetson. Mike always admired his sterling silver buckle, accented with real gold-inlayed longhorns.

"Nathan finds out you let ol' Kruetter corner ya, there'll be hell to pay in the home front tonight, Pup," Carl advised his nephew.

Jim shrugged his shoulders, bit the top off the longneck, guzzled the chilled brew, and emitted a loud, animated burp. "Not after he hears the whole story, he won't. He never laid eyes on me. That son of a bitch is all hat and no cattle. It'll be a cold day in hell before—"

"Don't give me that crap," Carl retorted. "You'd be sittin' in the pokey if Bubba hadn't come along when he did. You might as well have stuck a sign in the damn ground with an arrow pointing to where you went in at! Who the hell taught you to leave a car anywhere near the damn fence line anyway? Davy Crockett?"

"Didn't think you could see it—"

"See? There you go again thinkin'. What'd your damn instincts tell you, boy?" Carl took a sip from his longneck, then calmed his anger with a second swish. "Got to feelin' you two were purdy good at getting in and getting out and not getting caught, didn't ya? Got careless... complacent for you college boys." His gray eyes were now bearing directly at Mike. "Let me tell both of you hotshots: Complacency kills."

Mike felt a little better. At least someone else was finally getting *his* ass chewed out for a change.

"End of lecture," Carl announced, suddenly cheerful. "Want a beer, Mike?"

"No... Thanks anyway... Don't really like the stuff. Got any Dr. Pepper in there?"

Carl looked at Jim with a puzzled expression. "You still ain't broke his ass in right yet, have ya? I know you got him cussin' like a sailor, but does he even like girls?"

"I prefer *women*," Mike replied. "Think I've had me about all I can stand of *girls* for a while. But thanks for askin' just the same."

Carl chuckled. "He's learning, Jimbo." Throwing his arm around Mike, he patted him heartily on the back.

"Don't forget this here ice chest full-a' sausage for your ol' man, Pup. I put a little extra *cajoles* in 'em just for him. Don't eat too much at one time," he advised, "or they'll be talkin' back to ya in the morning, Big'n. *¿Comprende?*"

"You bet," Jim replied.

The boys mingled with Carl's wetbacks, who were busy skinning and quartering the hanging deer. Jim spoke to them in Spanish while Mike tried to pick up the gist of the conversation. Whatever he was saying to them must have been funny, because they all broke out in laughter and turned their attention directly toward Mike. Embarrassed, he walked over to Bubba and Brian, who were busily stuffing the ground venison into sausage casings.

"You going to Dwayne's funeral tomorrow?" Bubba asked.

"Sure. Isn't everybody?" Mike replied.

"I still can't believe he's really dead," Brian somberly added. "Somebody said that he's not really in the casket. They couldn't find enough of him to fill a gunny sack."

"The marines from the base are gonna be there. Probably gonna give 'im a twenty-one gun salute," Bubba said. "His folks are takin' it pretty hard. Ma went over there today and brought 'em some food and stuff. Goddamn Commie bastards!" He spit a stream of snuff juice in disgust.

"Jason and Billy went and signed up yesterday!" Brian exclaimed. "They're goin' over there to whop up on those Chinese bastards!"

"Vietnamese, Brian," Mike replied. "The Viet Cong are Vietnamese, not Chinese."

"Whatever," he replied, annoyed at Mike's rebuttal. "They're all Commie bastards over there anyway."

"It's kinda ironic they're burying him tomorrow," Bubba remarked.

"Why's that?" inquired Brian.

"November twenty-second," Mike said.

"So?" Brian shrugged.

"Kennedy was assassinated two years ago tomorrow, Brian," Mike explained.

"He was one of the reasons Dwayne joined the marines," Bubba told them. "Ya know: 'Ask not what your country can do for you. Ask what you can do for your country.' Dwayne felt real strong about that. His dad was in World War Two, ya know."

"So was mine," Mike added proudly. *So was mine.*

Mike's mind began to wander, but soon his thoughts of Vietnam were cut short by Jim's loud voice calling for him to help with the ice chest full of venison sausages.

"See you boys tomorrow. And hey, thanks for all the help today."

He shook their hands and hurried off to help Jim with the ice chest, shaking Carl's hand along the way. They struggled with the heavy load, finally lifting it up and into the bloody trunk of the Fairlane. Mike peered intently through the open windows of the house, desperately trying to catch one last glimpse of the raven-haired maiden within. Feeling a little cheated, he reluctantly slid into the car, bidding a silent farewell to the woman who would star in his dreams that night.

* * *

CHAPTER FOUR

THE OLD FAIRLANE LOPED ALONG the long, deserted blacktop, scattering an array of nocturnal creatures in its path. A country and western ballad blared out the open windows while Jim rhythmically patted the metal dash, wailing his rendition of the old favorite.

"Far across deep blue water/

Lives an ol' German's daughter/

By the banks of the ol' River Rhi-i-inne!"

Jim clicked on the high beams, searching the dark culverts ahead. He exposed a mélange of tiny eyes, each transfixed by the fiery object hurtling toward them. Squadrons of bullbats traversed through the bright beams, each competing for a morsel of road kill for their evening meal. The fresh evening air, seasoned with the thick tang of wild game, enveloped the car. The unique aroma featured a melding of furry rotting flesh, tempered with a measure of ripe cactus and mesquite.

Mike gazed at the stars to his right, scanning the evening skies for his old friend Orion, his childhood companion. His father had told him that the constellation would always be there for him, no matter where he was. Then, just over the next rise in the road, a large herd of javelina appeared in the headlights.

"Hold on!" Jim yelled, swerving off the blacktop and into the grassy culvert ditch, chasing the terrified herd of pigs that were desperately looking for a break in the fence line.

Rocks and debris slammed into the undercarriage. Mike gripped the dash and armrest with all his might. He stared at Jim's hula dancer, her grass skirt flying over her head as his wild friend mounted his charge. "You crazy son of a bitch!" Mike screamed. "You're gonna kill us both!"

Jim focused on the task at hand, however, yelling like a cowboy riding a bull as the Fairlane slid ever closer to the fence line. The hairy pigs scattered for their lives, leaping into the barbed wire, squealing in terror as the green monster slammed into its first victim. Mike cringed as the loud thump echoed again and again. Jim swerved back to the left, barely missing the mailboxes on the side of the road.

"What the fuck was all that about?!" Mike yelled.

"I hate those nasty skunk pig bastards."

"If your old man saw you do that, he'd kick your ass!"

Jim was busy looking in the rearview mirror. "Check six," he advised. "There was someone sittin' down that road where the mailboxes were."

Mike turned and looked into the darkness behind them. "How do you know?"

"Saw the damn moon reflecting on a windshield. See anyone behind us?" Jim asked, concern mounting in his demeanor.

"Probably just some parkers." Mike strained his eyes for a glimpse of anything metallic. "I don't see any lights."

"He won't put 'em on till he gets as close as he can. He's trying to lull us to sleep over here."

Mike sighed. "Don't even *tell* me it was a game warden. The judge warned me today, Jimbo. If I get caught pissin' on the sidewalk, they're gonna lock me up and throw away the key!"

"Don't worry, little buddy. Ta get you, they're gonna hav'ta catch me… And that just ain't gonna happen, Miguelito. Two can play this game!"

He reached under the dash and flipped a small toggle switch, disabling the brake lights. The Fairlane kicked into passing gear just as Mike noticed the loop curve ahead. "Don't worry, I've taken it at ninety before," Jim bragged. "We have to get halfway around the curve before I cut the headlights. If he's behind us, he'll have to turn his lights on ta make it."

Mike braced himself, pressing his feet firmly on the floorboard. Jim eased over across the mid-stripe, lining up the Fairlane on the far shoulder. The curve approached quickly, and just as quickly, Jim accelerated, catapulting the old Ford through the curve and sending it speeding down the blacktop toward Highway 77, six miles away. Mike's heart pumped hard as he craned back to watch the curve disappearing into the darkness.

Suddenly, a beam of light illuminated the blacktop behind them. A chill ran through Mike's body as he watched the lights turn, then spin in the opposite direction, like lighthouse beacons traversing through the night. He followed the wayward headlights with his eyes, confused by the abrupt pirouettes they displayed before finally coming to rest, the smoking beacons beaming uselessly into the dark sky above. "He crashed and burned, Jimbo!" Mike yelled. "Maybe we oughta go back!"

"Did he roll it?"

"Don't think so. He just sort of spun out. Looks like he ended up backwards in a ditch."

"That'll teach that dumb ass to try n' sneak up on me. He didn't see no brake lights, so he figured he could follow me around."

"He might be hurt. We oughta go back."

"You know who that is, don't ya? It's fuckin' Kruetter! I'll let your happy ass out, and you can go back!" Jim angrily exclaimed. "He's got a damn radio, and you know he's callin' the world in on us now!"

Mike thought for a second. "You're probably right. He's probably not in a real good mood right about now."

Jim guided the Fairlane down the road, wasting no time in putting as much distance as possible between them and the Loop Road. He sped onto Highway 77, merging in with the full lane of traffic heading north from the Rio Grande Valley. Within minutes, Jim had positioned the Fairlane between two eighteen-wheelers hauling grapefruits from the Valley. A highway patrol car flew by in the opposite lane, lights flashing as it headed south toward the Old Loop Road.

"Don't worry." Jim patted Mike on the shoulder. "Dad'll say we were home all night."

"I just hope he's OK," Mike replied.

Jim pulled off the bypass, slipping through the neighborhood streets, and with the lights off, he quietly eased the old Fairlane down the alley behind his house. He pulled into the backyard, under the old chinaberry tree, and turned the engine off. "Wait here," he ordered. "I'll go in and check it out."

Jim walked through the backyard, around the clutter of old engine parts and go-carts, up the steps, and through the screen door to the kitchen. Within seconds he returned, with two cold longnecks in each hand.

Jim handed one of the beers to his friend. "Drink it, and I don't want to hear any shit, you lightweight," he ordered, sliding back into the driver's seat. Mike shook his head but offered no resistance.

"They're up at the Elks Club. Dwayne's folks are havin' a wake or somethin'." Jim lifted his longneck and guzzled half the contents.

"We goin' to the funeral?"

"Not me!" Jim was quick to reply. Then he belched loudly before taking another sip. "You seem to forget what happened at my cousin Don's funeral a coupla' months ago."

"Your cousin Suzie's brother over in Alice?"

"Didn't I tell you?" Jim asked, a little puzzled that Mike didn't remember. He finished off his beer, holding it above his mouth as the last drops trickled in. "My Uncle Wally jumped right into the damn grave with him! I couldn't fuckin' believe it! He just lost it, man... Jumped right in there, bawling his eyes out, callin' his name, cryin' for his boy." Jim shook his head. "Fuckin' tore me up."

He bit the top off another longneck, spitting the metal top out the window. "When he started tryin' to pry open the casket, the ol' man made me get in there to pull him out. Uncle Wally begged me to help him open it, so's he could climb in there with him. Fuckin' broke my heart."

Mike's senses reverberated as he imagined the scene. "I never met Don," he said reverently. "He was already in the service before I got here."

"We used to spend our summers at his dad's lake house up at Mathis. He was like a big brother to me—toughest son of a bitch I ever met." Jim paused, his mind focused on the lingering pain in his heart. "I still can't believe he's really dead. He was the first person I ever really cared about who got kilt."

Jim chugged the remainder of his second beer and tossed it out the window. Then he grabbed Mike's longneck. "Can't let it get hot. It'll taste like shit."

"What'a you think it's like over there?" Mike asked.

He waited for Jim to gather his thoughts. Moments passed. Finally: "I dunno. I hear it's pretty fuckin' hot, all year round. Don't think I'd like to sleep in those jungles with all those leeches and shit."

"I don't mean the weather. Haven't you ever thought about what it would be like if we were over there in the war?"

"Naw! Who'd want to go over there anyway? Those fuckin' Chinamen are just like fuckin' javelinas. They give me the creeps."

"Vietnamese."

"What?"

"Vietnamese, Jimbo," Mike repeated. "They're called Vietnamese, not Chinamen, you dumb-ass. You think everyone from Asia are Chinamen."

"Do not!"

"Bullshit! The first day I met you… Remember that? I told you I had just moved here with my folks from Japan. The first thing you asked me was if I spoke Chinese!" Mike laughed, grabbing the beer back from Jim. He took a swig, tried to burp but instead just wiped his mouth with his hand. "People from Japan speak Japanese, your Chinamen speak Chinese, and Vietnamese speak Vietnamese! Get it?"

"It's all *Gookanese* to me… And who gives a shit anyway? Give me that fuckin' beer back. You ain't old enough to drink it." He grabbed the longneck out of Mike's hand and quickly emptied it. In typical fashion, he belched, lifted up his leg, and released a loud, prolonged fart. "Shouldn't stink," he assured his friend, grinning widely as the stark odor filled the car.

Mike sat unamused. "I give a shit," he answered sternly. "And I would think that Dwayne and your cousin Don gave a shit."

Jim quickly replied. "That was a cheap shot. I know where you're goin' with this shit, and it ain't gonna happen. I ain't goin' nowhere. And that includes the army, and especially the fuckin' marines. I get seasick, and I'm afraid of heights. So I guess that about leaves me out all the way around."

Mike pondered his friend's response. "There's two of us sitting in this car," he finally replied. "Will the *real* pussy please stand up?"

Jim turned abruptly. "Look, you fuckin' hero, that's a real war goin' on over there, you know. Blood, guts, real live-ass bullets flyin' around. People are dyin' over there. What's the matter with you? Your fuckin' TV broke or *what?*"

"You think I don't know? Just who the hell do you think those guys are? They're guys like you and me. They're over there serving our country, getting their *asses* shot off, and we're over here drinkin' beer and chasin' skirts!"

"You're serious!" Jim exclaimed, incredulous at Mike's attitude.

Mike thought for a moment. "Yeah, I guess I am, Jimbo. Somebody's got to get serious about what the hell's goin' on over there. Doesn't it bother you at all? We're gettin'a little too old to be playin' cat n' mouse with the game wardens. I'm gettin' a little burnt out on venison anyway."

"Then get after it! Haul your scrawny butt over there to China-land and get your fuckin' ass shot off. I ain't goin' to *your* fuckin' funeral either!"

Jim grabbed the final beer lying on the seat. He tried to pry the top off with his teeth, but after several attempts, he finally reached into the ashtray for the church key. "Just gotta be the fuckin' hero, don'cha?" he chided, finally prying off the top. "Just gotta prove somethin' to your ol' man."

"I ain't no fuckin' hero," Mike protested. "You don't think I'm scared? You're goddamn right I'm scared. You're talkin' to the guy who couldn't believe that marines would get up from perfectly good rocks to charge those machine gun bunkers in *Sands of Iwo Jima*! I still don't know what the fuck they were thinkin'."

Mike grabbed the beer from Jim's hand, sloshed down as much as he could stand, and then belched loudly as he handed it back. "But ya know what? They *did*. And someday I'm going to find out if I have enough guts to wear their uniforms with the same pride. All I know is, ya gotta at least show up. Something made them get up from those rocks, and I'm not sure I know exactly what that was. Maybe it was fear itself."

He paused, tumbling the word over again in his mind. "*Fear...* God, what an ugly word!" he whispered. Lately he had been holding the word sheathed in slanted eyes, cloaked in black pajamas, encased in a surrealistic menagerie of rice paddies and hell. He refused to dwell in that awful abyss his mind insisted on resurrecting, allowing only brief interludes before he cast the demon out. "Hell, I don't know, Jimbo, but I do know this: I gotta find out for myself."

Jim stared at his young friend beside him. "You're outa' your fuckin' mind. You bin smokin' some loco weed or sumthin'?"

"Maybe I am. But I've grown up around fighting men all my life, and I've never seen one of them walkin' around with their shirt tails out, dirty shoes, bitchin' about what they were doing. They're all damn proud to wear the uniform... And it shows."

"It's 'cause they'd end up in the brig if they did," Jim countered.

"I thought your dad was in World War Two."

"He was. He was a Seabee, and he always told me not to volunteer for nothin'. He also told me that if God meant for me to be a damn soldier, I'd-a' been born with green, baggy, wrinkly skin!"

"Shit, Jim, he was only jokin'. They always say that about the service," Mike protested. "You remember when I had to stay overnight, when they found that problem with my kidneys during my flight physical at the naval base in Corpus?" he asked. "They stuck me in a smelly ward with some marines who'd been wounded over there. Some of them couldn't even get out of bed."

"So?"

"So… I was ashamed to even be in the same room with them. I just lay there for hours, just pretending to be asleep. Finally, this young Negro guy gets up, shuffles all the way down the ward to my bed, pushin' this metal stand holdin' a bag with some medicine shit in it. He wanted to know if I had any cigarettes. The poor son of a bitch had a damn tube stuck in him somewhere under his gown. I couldn't believe he was even walkin'!"

"Did he tell you what happened?" Jim was finally taking some interest.

"Said he and his platoon were near a beach at a place called 'Chew Lie' or somethin'. Said they were ambushed by a bunch of farmers in black pajamas who they thought were part of the village they were protecting. Kinda snuck up on them while they were havin' lunch." Mike paused, conjuring up the images the young marine had left him with. "Can you believe that? A bunch of fuckin' farmers in black pajamas shot up a platoon of United States Marines!"

"I told you they're just a bunch of Commie bastards."

"Doesn't that just piss you off, though?"

"They'd never sneak up on *our* asses," Jim replied confidently.

Mike sat there quietly. Convoluted images of dark, sweltering jungles swirled through his head. His mind's eye searched for the enemy concealed among the rotting leech-infested foliage. *Would I see them in time? In time to save myself? In time to save the men behind me? Would I survive?*

He looked at Jim, and with a firmness that verified his resolve, he simply said, "I'm outa' here."

* * *

CHAPTER FIVE

T HE SQUARE-JAWED MARINE ADJUSTED HIS cover and stepped from the guardhouse, awaiting the small white car approaching the base. He stood patiently at parade rest, watching the car pass through the shadows of the palm trees. He recognized the blue officer's sticker on the front bumper and snapped to, rendering a crisp hand salute. Mike waved back, noting the scowl on the corporal's face as he disgustedly dropped his salute.

"Goddamn dependents," the guard muttered, stepping back into the shack, retrieving his tattered copy of *Playboy* on the stool behind him.

Mike continued down the long boulevard, toward the circle where the A-4 Skyhawk was mounted on a concrete pedestal. The small fighter was reported to have the name of the first student shot down in Vietnam stenciled on the cockpit. He strained to read the name, but as usual, his eyesight would not cooperate. *I'm just gonna stop one day and find out who that guy was,* he thought.

He continued around the circle, past the large white administration building, shifting the Falcon into second gear as he headed for the flight line. The cool air vibrated with the steady roar of jet engines, afterburners accenting the constant thunderous pitch as trainers sprinted down the runway.

I belong here, he told himself, taking a deep breath of the burnt JP-4 jet fuel. He recalled the days when he could tag along to his dad's job at Naval Air Facility Atsugi, his office sequestered in the dark ground-control-approach (GCA) hut, surrounded by the radar men at their green screens vectoring the jets and other fixed-wing aircraft landing on the runways. His dad had let him eat his sack lunch in the shade of the hut, outside, some forty feet from the edge of one of the runways, where he could spend the whole afternoon so exhilaratingly close to the planes landing and taking off, where he could see the pilots as they waved at him. They were practicing their touch-and-go maneuvers for actual carrier landings. As he sat there waiting for the next jet to land, Mike would imagine what it must have been like catapulting off the deck and having a wingman at his side, the plane screaming through the sky, flying into battle. Just a sniff of JP-4 had ignited a special fire in his soul. He had desperately wanted to be a part of it, the cream of the crop, America's finest.

He would manage to handle the responsibilities of fringe benefits as well—the fancy cars, the fast women, the camaraderie at the O club. The dress whites were just an added bonus—clean, classy, and uncluttered. He had felt they were designed to accent the glittering gold aviator's wings he would wear over his heart. The fantasy would continue, but unfortunately, the grim reality that his hopes and dreams had crashed and burned with his failed flight physical now pitted his soul with anguish and remorse. There would be no white shoes for him.

Mike drove past the large hangars that housed the training squadrons on the base. He looked for his brother-in-law's Corvette, which was usually parked outside the VT-23 hangar. A marine lieutenant, Harry had flown an A-4 in Vietnam, just like the one mounted in the circle. Mike didn't know his brother-in-law that well, but he had questioned Harry's sanity for letting him pick up the Corvette to detail. Though the patch Harry wore on his flight jacket, *Back Alive in '65*, was intriguing, Mike had too much respect for his brother-in-law to inquire about his exploits. He wasn't qualified to ask.

Mike pulled the Falcon into the Operations parking lot. He picked an obscure area far away from the main entrance, and he paused for a moment to contemplate the task at hand, how to bridge the emotional chasm that had opened between his dad and him in the weeks since the altercation at the courthouse. He gripped the wheel tightly, collected his thoughts, and then made his way to the large building situated on the flight line. He stepped through the alcove, filling his lungs with that masculine aroma that defined the perimeter of any flight line. Consisting of a unique blend of jet fuel, tobacco, coffee, and leather, it was reputed to be tempered with fear and accented with that elusive element of honor. Again, his mind wandered back to Atsugi, to the carefree days of "Mikie, the shirt-tail boy." Mike felt he was really home—home among his boyhood images of manhood.

The ready room in front of him bustled with pilots in their baggy flight suits. He watched for a moment while student aviators mimicked their maneuvers, swooping and stalking, one hand after the other. Transient pilots watched passively, unimpressed by the rancor and enthusiasm of their subordinates while a lone sailor in dungarees with a black grease pencil updated the scheduling board.

Mike moved quietly along the wall and darted up the empty stairwell, away from the structured confusion below. On the third floor he turned and hurried down the long hallway past offices filled with busy sailors and marines, the long lines of aircraft parked below, visible through large, tinted windows.

"Hold on there, sonny!" a heavy voice demanded.

Mike turned to see a tall, khaki-clad figure striding toward him. Curious heads peered through doorways to see whom the chief petty officer was addressing. In no mood to alter his task, Mike quickly replied over his shoulder. "Just came by to see my dad."

"You're gonna have to do better than that. You're in a restricted area, sonny!"

Mike stopped. Embarrassed by the attention, he reached down and tucked his shirt in. He felt out of place—faded madras shirt, worn Levis, dirty white sneakers—an imposter in the midst of professionals. "I'm here to see my father, Commander Shannahan."

The petty officer scrutinized the young intruder. "*You're* Commander Shannahan's son?" he replied, an element of doubt lingering in his eyes. "Wait one minute, I'll be right back." He moved past Mike and hurried down the hallway.

Within moments, he reappeared in a doorway, motioning him to come. Mike stepped into the small office, a hint of his father's blend of pipe tobacco welcoming his arrival. "This is Ensign Lawton," the chief advised him. "She'll take care of you."

"Thanks," he replied, sensing the chief's annoyance as he brushed past him.

"Well, which one are you?" The ensign rose to shake Mike's hand.

Mike smiled, heartened by the friendly voice, even more surprised to see a woman in his father's office.

"I'm Lisa," she said. "Your father's personnel officer."

"I'm Michael… the number-one son," he added, a tag he had accumulated over the years.

"I thought I recognized you. But then you are a little older. Anyway, it's nice to finally meet one of Jack's sons."

Then, still firmly holding his hand, she added, "I've heard a lot about you."

Yeah, I'll bet, he thought, finding himself allured by the depth of her blue eyes. "Thank you, ma'am," he replied.

"Oh, you don't have to call me *ma'am*." She was blushing, still admiring the young man in front of her. She quickly measured his features, finding the Shannahan character in his face. His very broad shoulders quickly tapered to a firm, thin waist, giving his six-foot frame a very athletic shape. His thick black hair accented the bright hazel eyes, eyes that seemed nervous as they looked quickly around the room.

"Is my father here?" Mike inquired, breaking the trance.

"Oh, I'm sorry." Lisa straightened her skirt as she stepped out from behind the desk. "Yes. I mean he's here, but he went up to the tower to go over some procedures with the control officer. He'll be right back down, Michael. Would you like to wait in his office?"

"If you don't mind," he replied gratefully, nervous at the prospect of small talk with an older woman.

He pointed to the door behind her, and Lisa nodded. He closed it behind him, uttered a sigh of relief, and walked over to his father's desk. He stared at the clutter before him. Folders and papers filled the boxes on either side of the desk. It looked exactly like the Commander's desk at home. Mike sat down in the large swivel chair behind it, leaning back comfortably as he surveyed the room. The walls appeared as cluttered as the desk, full of certificates and awards the Commander had accumulated over the years.

If you don't really want to know, don't ask! read the caption on a framed cartoon among the certificates. *Typical,* he thought. His father always had the answer for everything. Mike could conjure up no reason to doubt it. It was all part of the intimidating prospect of one day having to measure his worth, his accomplishments, his exploits by the standards his father had set. Coral Sea, Midway, Savo Island, Tarawa—all destinations on the global map of experiences his father had endured. Names cloaked in honor, names revered by those who understood the magnitude of sacrifices made in that vast Pacific graveyard. It was a part of his father's life they had never discussed, exposed only by strangers' idle comments, nurtured in hushed conversations he had barely overheard through the years.

Mike browsed the vast array of memorabilia. Framed pictures of old airplanes, shipmates, and the carriers they had sailed on. Men standing on the folded wings of fighter planes, the ocean's winds buffeting their flight suits. Warriors of a past generation, each with his own story to tell. He studied their faces, looking for that common thread that he knew must be apparent. What he saw was a bond of friendship etched in the smiles that accented the obvious camaraderie they shared for one another. He wondered which of the men were still alive, and which of them had plummeted from the sky for their country in that terrible war. He was ever grateful that his father had not made that lonely, final dive. Now he was searching for a clue to the Commander's mystery, some telltale sign that would open the door to reveal that elusive realm of honor. His young, untutored mind left but mere scratches at that door.

Across the room a familiar face caught his eye. A young boy kneeling behind a monkeypod coffee table, holding two gold medals on either side of a small swimming trophy. He walked over to the small-framed picture, smiling when he realized that *he* was the boy in the picture. He studied the butch-waxed crew cut and freckles. *God! I did look like the Beaver!* To the right were various pictures of his baseball exploits, including one that depicted him tagging out the Okinawa runner at home in the Far East Championship in Tokyo, a shot in mid-swing at the plate. *Where did he get all these? He was never at any of my games.*

Continuing down the wall, he stopped to admire the picture of his mother beaming with pride as she pinned on his Eagle badge in Atsugi. It all seemed so long ago, a different world from where he was standing now.

"Your dad's very proud of you."

Mike turned, startled to see Lisa leaning against the doorway. "I'm sorry," he responded nervously. "I didn't hear you come in."

"I understand you're thinking about flight school." She offered him a bottle of Coke as she walked slowly toward him.

"Oh, thanks. You must have read my mind," he replied, taking the drink from her, his eyes wandering down her sculptured stockinged legs. "Well, that *was* the plan, but something came up, so I'm not so sure about it anymore."

Lisa sensed uneasiness in the young man, punctuated with the manner his eyes continued to avoid contact with hers. She smiled, turned, and started back out the door. "Well, if I can get you anything else…"

Mike's attention shifted to an uncommon yet distinct, utterly familiar laugh. And before Lisa could announce his visitor, the Commander strode through the door and over to his desk. Two officers in khakis followed closely behind. Mike backed closer to the wall, unsure of his father's response to his presence. All three men turned and faced him, his father's glare potent and menacing.

"Ron, Eddie, this is the number-one son, Mike," he stated, stepping back out from behind his desk.

Mike shook hands with the officers while his father casually explained that he was a freshman at the local college. Following a brief exchange about the football team and the ladies at the university, the two men excused themselves and left the Commander alone with his son. The door closed, and Jack quickly returned to his desk, shuffling through the papers as he stood ignoring his son.

"I didn't come here to argue with you," Mike began, "and I just want—"

"Does my wife know where you are?" his father demanded, cutting him short.

"What?"

"You heard me."

"Your wife? You mean Mom?"

"No, I mean my *wife*. Does she know where you are?" he repeated, staring up at his son as he leaned over his desk. "I don't give a good rat's ass how you choose to treat your mother, but I'll be goddamned if you're going to be disrespectful to my wife, not as long as you live under my roof!"

"Yesss," Mike replied meekly. "I just left there. She let me use her car."

"Fine. Then get out of here. I'm busy."

Mike stared back, mustering strength to finish the task he had been rehearsing in his mind. "Father, I came here today to discuss something important with you."

"Son, I don't have anything else to say to you," came the curt reply.

"So what do I have to do, *beg* your forgiveness? I'm sorry! You know me well enough to know that. I screwed up! You've always told me to own up to my mistakes, learn from them, and move on. I'm trying to move on. Why are you making it so hard for me to do?"

"It's always about you, isn't it?" his father replied calmly. Then he sat down in his chair, pushed the intercom button, and said, "Lisa, call the admiral's office and let his aide know that I've handled that problem in the tower."

"Right away, Commander," she replied.

"I'm not ungrateful for the things you've done for me in my life," Mike said quietly. "I'm just at a point where the life you've laid out for me seems in conflict with everything else that's going on in my head. I want some adventure, some challenges," he pleaded. "I need to find the answers to some stuff that I just can't find in college here."

"Want some adventure? Need a challenge? Join the Marine Corps. They'll put a challenge in your life!" Jack quipped sarcastically.

Mike took one last look at his father, shook his head, and started for the door. He grabbed the doorknob, turned, and said, "I thought you'd feel that way, Dad. And that's what I came here today to talk to you about." He opened the door. "As usual, I took your advice. I enlisted this morning." He turned and walked out the door.

"It was very nice meeting you, Lisa," he said, smiling. He walked down the long hallway, feeling right at home with the men in uniform passing by.

* * *

CHAPTER SIX

F IRST SERGEANT VIRGIL BOLTON HAD just sat down in his chair when he heard the loud rap at his door. He glanced up to see one of his student cadets standing in the doorway.

"What do you want, bolo?" he snapped. "Can't you see I'm busy?"

"Just wanted to say good-bye," the young man replied.

Bolton looked up inquisitively. "Say what? Get your scrawny ass in here, troop!" Bolton leaned back in his chair as the young man approached his desk. "Where you goin'? Knock some pretty young thing up and have to get outa' town?"

"Me? Whatever gave you that idea?" Mike smiled, brushing the comment off as just another dig from his mentor in the ROTC department.

Bolton was a career infantry grunt, and his face sported terrible scars from wounds received in a desperate bayonet charge in Korea. Reluctantly, he was spending his last year in the army as an instructor at the university. Mike had taken to him quickly, absorbing as much as he could while he struggled to decipher the old sergeant's jargon and the life messages they contained.

"I enlisted Airborne, Top," he addressed the master sergeant proudly.

Bolton's eyes narrowed. He stared intently at the young man before him, quietly pondering the decision his student had made. "So tell me, Shannahan, just how long have you had this death wish?" He rose to his feet, then sat awkwardly on the edge of his desk. "Didn't I teach you anything? Where do you get off *enlisting* in the army?"

"I thought that you'd be proud of me, Top. Can't wait four years. Hell, this whole thing'll be over by then. There's not gonna be another one like WW Two... or for that matter, even Korea. We gotta stop those Commie bastards now! They're killin' our guys, just like they did at Changjin Reservoir! You were there. What's the difference?"

"Where the hell did you learn to talk like that?" Bolton's mind suppressed the chilling screams of that icy battle. "A little melodramatic, don't you think?"

Then Bolton paused, refreshing his posture. "Son, there're well-trained men on their way over there right now. The best thing that you can do is stay in school and get your degree."

Mike stared at the old sergeant, not wanting to believe what he had just heard. "Is that what you did? Stay in school? I don't think so."

"Whoaaa there, pup," Bolton ordered. "We're talkin' a whole different ball of wax there. There were some pretty scary folks out there tryin' to reorganize the gene structure of the whole fuckin' human race. Or aren't you takin' world history this fall?"

"All I know is that some of my friends who served their country are dead, and that's a direct result of what the Communists are doing over there in Vietnam. Hell, they tried the same thing in Cuba in '62, and Kennedy put a stop to that, pronto. Krushchchev even said he was going to wipe us off the face of the earth at the UN. He said he wanted us dead! What more do you want?"

Bolton folded his arms, shifted his posture on the desk and looked Mike straight in the eyes. "Son, most of my closest friends *are* dead. And ya know what? They died with a nonchalance that most folks might call courage. Hell, some of them might even call it bravery, but the simple point is: They're still *dead!* Yeah, I still shed a tear or two now and then, but it don't matter. They're still alive to me and always will be until we forget 'em. But, to everyone else, they're just a name on a grave marker… those that were lucky enough to have one, that is. Some of the guys couldn't even pronounce the name of the goddamn place they died!"

"So, what are you saying, then?" Mike asked earnestly. "You don't think we should be over there?"

"I don't think *any* gook is worth the life of an American boy. But then I'm not a politician, am I? I'm just a first sergeant in the United States Army and, by God, a damn good one too! I'd be over there right now if I didn't have…" Bolton halted his comments, realizing what he was about to undermine his argument that Mike should stay in school.

"That's what I thought, Top. So don't act like you don't know what I'm talking about. Kennedy took his turn, and so did you. Now it's my turn, and I need to find out if I've got what it takes. My dad didn't *raise* me to believe in war. I haven't been *trained* to go to war. My dad raised me to respect men like you and to value your sacrifices. Believe me, I have, and it still scares the shit outa' me. Regardless, I've learned that I have a responsibility to fulfill… to a lot of people who mean something to me. And I guess you're one of them. If I've missed something along the way, just tell me!"

Mike paused, waiting for Bolton to respond. He offered nothing, though. Mike sensed a forlorn distance in his stare. "I came by today, hoping you could give me some advice. You know, offer a little guidance for when the shit hits the fan."

Bolton slowly shook his head. "You'll be all right, son," he said, with an affectionate calm in his tone. "It's not *about* war, it's just about the men who go to war." He reached behind him and picked up a large silver medallion off the corner of his desk. He cleared his throat and began to read the inscription to Mike: "Every man born of woman must die. Only those of us who are called to Glory choose when, and where, and why."

Mike allowed the somber words to float through his consciousness. His quiet stare prompted Bolton to explain: "You'll know what I'm talking about soon enough. Just keep your powder dry, son."

Bolton stood and shook Mike's hand. He embraced him firmly, patting him on the back while he tightened his grip. "I'm *damn* proud of you, Shannahan. Give 'em hell, trooper!"

"You know I will, Top." Mike saluted and walked out the door.

"Don't salute me, you bolo!" Bolton yelled after him. "I ain't no damn *ossifer!*"

Mike smiled at his deliberate provocation and proudly walked through the department, shaking hands with classmates, saying good-bye to the instructors, and in his good-natured manner, absorbing the routine ribbing from well-wishers and friends. His thoughts lingered on Bolton's words, and as usual, he really wasn't sure of the true meaning of his mentor's prophecy. *God, I hope I'm ready for this,* he thought, walking back to the car.

Within, he felt the trepidation of the unknown. He was not sure he could attribute it to the excitement of the moment, or simply that he was intimidated by the task ahead of him. Regardless, youthful exuberance prevailed. He broke into a run and hurdled the iron chain barrier around the parking lot.

The next few days ran together. His high school friends thought he was crazy, but each remark of theirs just bolstered his conclusion that he was entering a select fraternity, one that they were unwilling to join, whatever their reasons. Barbara's call was different, however. She accused him of trying to make her feel bad by running off and trying to get himself killed. Such a notion did have a certain appeal, but only after she'd made such a big deal about it. After all, he had been thinking that she didn't care anymore.

The time came for him to sort out his personal belongings and make sure that his responsibilities at home were taken care of. For example, he made sure that his role as the resident Big Brother was assumed by his next-in-line, Thomas. In a ceremonial rite of passage, he gathered his brothers together and presented the successor with his baseball glove and bat, the only possessions that he truly cherished. (The rest of his lifelong accouterments had already been passed down to his younger brothers, not always with his consent.)

The Commander had left on a cross-country flight the day of the last in a series of their recent confrontations. He would be back tomorrow, though, and Mike was not looking forward to another skirmish. With his father absent, Mike didn't have to fight him, or furtively sneak around him, to get together with his best friend. He called Jim, and the two made plans to celebrate Mike's departure with one last night on the town. His mother dropped him off at Jim's house, and it wasn't long before Nathan and the boys were out in the backyard, watching the sun settle under the long shadows of the old chinaberry tree.

Nathan got up from his lawn chair, reached into the cooler, and handed Mike a longneck. "Jim tells me you're gonna be a paratrooper," he said, sliding back into his favorite chair.

"That's 'cause he's a dumb-ass," Jim chided. Nathan's quick glare wiped the sheepish grin from his son's face.

"Yes sir," Mike replied. "I was hoping that we could enlist together, but Jimbo wasn't too keen on the idea. Seems as though he's got this thing about heights."

"Well, he'd better get over it. I think it would be a *fine* idea to have you both in the same unit," Nathan proudly concluded. "What do you think, son?"

Jim fumbled with the label on his longneck, staring aimlessly at the ground between his legs. Without looking up, he answered: "We already talked about this today, Dad." His words hinted at a resignation in his spirit.

"Well, you better give it some more thought. The paper says you've got until Wednesday to get your physical."

"What paper?" Mike demanded.

"He didn't tell you? The draft board delivered his notice today."

Jim sprang up from his chair. "Well, we gotta go, Dad. The girls are waiting for us at the dorm."

"You haven't even finished your beer," Nathan protested.

Jim chugged the remaining drops, threw the empty bottle in the gray trashcan, and headed for the Fairlane, parked under the tree. Mike shrugged, handed the full beer to Nathan, and followed his friend to the car.

"Don't you be out spotlightin' on no back roads tonight!" Nathan yelled after his son. "Word's out that Kruetter's got some spotters on your happy ass!"

"Don't wait up!" Jim yelled back, cranking up the vintage Fairlane for one last gallop with his friend in crime.

They backed out of the yard, spinning caliche and gravel as they headed down the alley and onto the boulevard toward town. Jim reached over and turned up the radio, flipping through the stations on the dial. Mike leaned over and turned down the volume, waiting for an explanation he felt was overdue.

"I ain't goin'," Jim finally blurted.

Mike sat there in stunned silence. Jim ran his hand through his long, wavy hair, nervously tapping his other hand on the steering wheel. The bright neon signs on the boulevard danced eerily on the dull hood, casting a surrealistic aurora through the dirty windshield. The Fairlane sped through several intersections, its mute passengers busy contemplating opposing destinations. Through the corner of his eye Jim studied Mike, registering the disappointment seeping through, despite the mundane expression on his friend's face.

Finally, he couldn't take it any longer. "Go ahead, goddammit! Spit it out!"

"Ain't got nothin' to say," Mike replied calmly.

Jim turned onto Santa Gertrudis Boulevard, the scenic approach to the large mission-shaped administration building at the university. He continued to glance over at Mike, nervously anticipating the worst.

"Pull over, Jimbo," Mike finally requested. Reluctantly, Jim turned into the next street and came to a stop under the streetlight across from the engineering department.

"I was hopin' you'd be gone before you found out," Jim stated with an apologetic fervor. "I knew you'd get all bent outa' shape over it."

"What are you going to do, fella?" With palms outstretched, Mike pleaded for a sane answer to his question. "If you don't report, they're gonna come lookin' for ya. You know that, don't you?"

"Yeah, I know. But if I ain't here, whata' they gonna do? Figured I'd head up to Alaska. They just started building this huge-ass pipeline up there, and welders are getting damn near twenty dollars an hour to start."

"They'll track your happy ass down in a heartbeat. Draft dodgin's a federal offense, dumb-ass!"

"Not up in Alaska it ain't. Shit, there's probably not a cop station within a thousand miles of where that baby's goin' in."

"Ain't gonna be the cops comin' after you. It'll be the feds."

"Well, then tell 'em to get after it. They ain't got no jurisdiction up in Alaska, anyhow," Jim claimed, a hint of defiance in his tone.

"Jimbo, Alaska is part of the Union. Or did you forget to color it in when you were in elementary school?"

"Well, fuck it then. I'll just head south to Mexico. I *know* they ain't got no feds down there, that's a fact."

"Look, all I'm askin' you to do is to think about the consequences of what you're doin'. What'll folks say? What about your dad?"

"I know, I know. Don't you think I've *been* thinkin' about it? Hell, it's all I've been thinkin' about!" He gripped the wheel tightly, pounding his forehead repeatedly against the rim. "God! I don't wanta die! Not over there in that stinkin' hellhole. Why can't we be fightin' the Cubans? Or the Russians? Anybody 'cept them spooky Chinamen. I seen 'em on TV, an' they don't fight fair."

"I still can't believe that you're really serious about this. You, of all people. Hell, you're already a hero around here. And oh, by the way... Just how does *that* feel?" Mike shook his head, a look of disgust prefaced his next somewhat sarcastic words about his friend's local fame: "Uh *huhh*, you're considered the best hunter in the county. *Shi-i-tt!* I've seen you take a buck down at five hundred yards, open sights! You've been captain of the football team, they call you 'Mister Fifty-five.' They'll probably *retire* that jersey number! And what about your reputation as 'stud honcho with the women'? Hell, those Commies in Vietnam wouldn't stand a chance against *the* Jimbo Leary!"

Jim leaned back, rubbing his forehead. "Yeah... Well, big fuckin' deal. And fuck you too! You know the best thing about huntin' deer, Mister Know-it-all?"

"What's that?"

"They don't fuckin' shoot back."

Mike shook his head, a slight grin parting his lips. Then, reverently: "That really fucked you up, didn't it?"

"What?"

"Seein' your cousin killed over there."

Jim took a deep breath. "Does it show that bad? I really loved that guy," he said quietly. "And I don't ever want to see my dad go through what Uncle Wally did." His head tilted slowly, recalling the scene at the gravesite. "No way, not ever."

A moist tear swelled in Jim's eye. His lips tightened, accenting his muscular jaw. Mike felt a sincere tinge of sympathy surge from his heart as he watched his friend, his mentor, his pal, slowly turn away and wipe the pain from his eyes.

Mike placed his hand gently on Jim's neck. "I'm with you, pal. Whatever you want to do is all right with me, fella. Hell, you know where I come from. Kinda' hard not to tote the flag after bein' around my old man all these years. It's just who I am."

Jim turned and smiled at his friend. A beer-stained hiccup triggered a round of chuckles, followed with the earnest laughter so common in the front seat of the old green Fairlane.

"One good thing about goin' over there, though," Jim added, cranking up the trusty engine in his old war wagon.

"What's that?"

"At least you're not gonna have to worry about taggin' them suckers over there!"

Familiar white smoke and cowboy whoops trailed the rusted Fairlane down the block, around the square, and as Jim's charmed hula dancer wildly swayed, across the quiet campus to the women's dorm.

*   *   *

CHAPTER SEVEN

T HE LONG BROOM HANDLE INCHED closer to the prone figure nestled snugly beneath the patchwork quilt. The probe found its mark, rousing Mike out of his realm of ecstasy and back to the reality of his bedroom. His unfocused glimpse of an imp in pajamas hurriedly scampering through the open door prompted an immediate threat of retribution for this most serious incursion. "You little shit!" he yelled. "You'd *better* run and hide! Your ass is grass, and I'm the damn lawnmower!"

Exhausted, he fell back into his dream world, desperately searching in vain to recapture the glorious image of the firm, perky breasts he had discovered the evening before. Veiled whispers mingled with the scent of Tabu his senses were tracking, callously interrupting his quest to rejoin Mandy in the backseat of Jim's love wagon. He slowly pried his eyes open, however, trying to focus on the image of his three brothers standing beside the bed, shabbily clad in a colorful array of mismatched pajamas. Seamus quickly slid behind Tom and peeked around the waist of his protector.

"Mom says that breakfast is ready," Tom reported firmly, his arms folded as though he had already assumed his new role in the household. "And she says we can't eat until you get up."

Mike's brow raised slightly. He was amused by the untainted earnestness of the committee before him, the ruffled hair, the abundant display of freckles, and the naïve looks on their shiny faces. "Circus in town, guys?"

"What circus?" Daniel asked, his eyes widening at the prospect.

"Never mind," Mike replied, shaking his head as he chuckled at the response.

"Mom says you're goin' to the army today," Seamus added. "Are they gonna give you a gun?"

"Yeah, a real big one. And I'm gonna come back here and shoot your little butt for wakin' me up like that!"

"*Maaaawwwwwww!*" he screamed, scampering out of the room and back down the hall. "He's gonna *shoot* me!" His high-pitched voice echoed throughout the house.

"That wasn't funny," Tom declared, chiding his older brother as he left to console the terrified tyke.

"Ahwww, you know I was only kidding," Mike called after him, chuckling, his revenge satisfied.

Daniel stood alone with his big brother. His serious look of consternation sobered the mood. "I don't want you to go," he said quietly. "Somebody might shoot you."

Mike looked into Daniel's bright eyes, which were glistening with the full tear that was slowly seeping over the lids. The dull pain was immediate, surging from his heart, leaving his respiration shallow and dull as he choked back his own emotions. "Come over here, pal." He reached out for his brother's hand. "Nobody's gonna shoot me. It's just not gonna happen, so get that outa' your mind right now."

"How do you know?" Daniel pleaded, wiping the tears away with his other hand.

Mike sat up, gently stroking his brother's warm, wet cheeks. "Because that whole thing going on over there's probably gonna be over long before I even get there!" he said confidently. "I gotta go through Basic Training and Airborne School, and there's at least six months right there!"

"I still don't want you to go!" Daniel slowly shook his head, his moist eyes imploring his brother to reconsider. "I won't ever get to see you again."

"Look, pal," Mike said firmly. "Sometimes us guys gotta do stuff that we don't really want to do. But that's 'cause we're guys and not girls. Now, there's some really bad guys out there doin' some really bad things, and us good guys gotta go find 'em and make 'em stop it. That's what big brothers are for: makin' sure the bad guys don't mess with the little brothers or sisters."

"Kinda' like cops and robbers?"

"Exactly! Only… just a little different." Mike paused, squinting his eyes as he tried to justify his message in his mind. "Now, your job is to take care of your mom and sisters while I'm gone. That's what little brothers are for. So you and Tom and Seamus have a big job to do until I get back. OK?"

Daniel shook his head in agreement while Mike's smile reinforced the notion that his departure would only be temporary, and was the right thing to do.

"Now, go tell Mom that I'll be there in a minute."

Daniel turned and hurried down the hall, leaving Mike to ponder yet another consequence of his decision. He hadn't anticipated the impact his leaving would have on his siblings, prompting yet another reassessment of his motivation. He lay back on his pillow, feeling selfish for just being concerned about his mother's reaction. He realized that he would miss them, too, and finally admitted to himself that he actually loved them. He made a vow to tell each of them that before he left that afternoon.

Tom peeked around the doorway. "Mom says your eggs are getting cold, and we're hungry. Dad called from the base, and he's on his way home, too, so you'd better get up."

The last statement was motivation enough. Mike sprang out of bed, slipped on his Levis, and headed down the hallway, savoring the full aroma of coffee and sausage. The Commander arrived during breakfast, but instead of taking his chair at the head of the table, he retreated to his bedroom—but only after Seamus finally let go of his leg.

Before long, the whole family had assembled. His elder sister, Patricia, arrived with Harry. The trio of Mike's younger brothers scampered to the driveway and fought over which of them would get to sit in the driver's seat of the bright red Corvette. The Commander finally emerged from the bedroom, clad in a brilliant Hawaiian shirt over a pair of baggy khaki pants. He immediately engaged Harry in aviator banter, exposing the gregarious personality that was so foreign to Mike, who sat, interested but uniformed, resenting the fact that his new status did not automatically entitle him to the enlightenment he pursued.

Mike patiently waited for a lull in the conversation, then quickly seized his opportunity. "I heard Johnson has requested Congress to approve sending over another fifty thousand troops," he proudly interjected.

Harry responded without hesitation. "They'd better hurry. Word is, the First Marine Division has just about got that thing all wrapped up."

Mike struggled to respond but found himself lacking spontaneity, challenged by his limited insight into the current political situation abroad. Embarrassed, he excused himself and retreated to his room to pack his bag.

The morning went by quickly, punctuated by the never-ending sibling rivalries, but the occasional stares from one or another of them left him restless and longing for the time to leave. Finally, his father assembled the family together. An uneasy hush settled over the boisterous household. *Say good-bye to your brother* was the simple instruction.

Laughing, keeping the moment light, Mike picked up Seamus, teasing him before setting him down. He was careful to shake Thomas's hand, passing the gauntlet with pride. He muffled Daniel's hair and struggled to keep his balance while little sister, Teresa, threw her arms around her favorite brother, kissing him firmly on the cheek. The high school junior blushed, clearing her throat while she straightened her skirt, fighting the tears as she stepped away. Pat was next, briefly embracing him, offering a peck on the cheek before saying good-bye.

He saved his heartfelt tribute for his mother, who was standing behind the fidgety group, nervously wiping her hands on her apron. He walked slowly to her and warmly embraced her, resting his head on her shoulder. "I love you, Momma," he said quietly.

"I love you too, baby," she replied, tears tickling his neck as she kissed him tenderly on the cheek. "Please be careful, honey," she pleaded. "I'll be worried about you."

"Don't worry, Momma. I can take care of myself."

He kissed her lovingly on the lips, picked up his bag, turned, and walked out to the Volkswagen bus waiting in the driveway. The Commander followed, and soon Shannahan father and son sped away, Mike waving to the family he was leaving behind for the first time in his life. As the bus turned off Santa Barbara Drive into the boulevard, he turned and looked back, wondering if he would ever see them again.

Almost immediately, the Commander put him on the defensive. "I thought you said you had enlisted in the Corps," he began, reaching down beside him for his leather flight gloves.

"I didn't think you were even listening to anything I had to say," his son replied. "I merely said that I had enlisted that morning... that's all."

The Commander turned and shot a piercing stare but let the curt remark go unchallenged. "Why the paratroopers?"

"Sergeant Bolton said they were the best infantry unit in the army. I want to fight with the best."

Mike felt the urge to say so many things to his father, but he chose to suppress his feelings instead. He sat quietly, reflecting on the circumstances that had led to this day, still wondering if he had made the right decision.

"You probably think that I've been pretty hard on you," his father began again. "But everything that I have done has been to prepare you for this day, son." Mike looked at his father with wide eyes but said nothing. After a short pause, the Commander went on: "I can still remember that day thirty years ago, when my father took me down to the Brooklyn Navy Yard. It was a cold, rainy morning when I reported in."

Again he paused, taking his pipe out of the ashtray, repeatedly stroking the silver Zippo before it lit. He drew in several times until a large plume of white smoke drifted above the front seat, tainting the air with the sweet scent of chicory and walnut.

"I remember how I felt," he continued at last, his teeth gritting on the stem as he spoke. "And, I would have given anything to have gotten back on that trolley and just gone back home."

"Why didn't you?" Mike asked, feeling he was being set up.

"Three words, son... Along with the fact that your grandfather would have disowned me."

"I know. Duty, honor, and country, right?" Mike replied quickly, prompting another glare for his impetuousness. "Well, to tell you the truth, I'm actually looking forward to this. But I also have to tell you: You could have made it a lot easier if you would have had enough respect for me to share some of your experiences."

The Commander digested his son's remarks. Then, to avoid another conflict, he selected his own words carefully. "I wish it were that easy, son," he replied at last, trying to appease Mike with his conciliatory tone. "What did you want me to tell you? That your dad was a hero? Brag about how many Japs I shot down, how many ships I sank?"

"Well, no... I mean, I don't know. I just wanted you to tell me something... Anything!"

The Commander paused briefly, drawing several deep hits from the distinctive pipe clinched tightly in his teeth, gathering his words carefully to convey the true essence of his message. "It's not that I've been trying to keep anything from you, son. There's no mystery to war. Men die. Warriors find no solace in celebrating their own exploits. More often than not, the men they wish to celebrate their victories with… are no longer with us. It would be sacrilegious to boast or even pretend to relate without telling the whole truth. Sometimes it is too painful to relive those moments."

Then: "This whole thing is actually kind of unexpected," he said, casting a stern look of displeasure, "if you know what I mean." He took the pipe from his mouth, discarding its hot ash and tobacco out the window before he dropped it into the ashtray. "I pray to God that this thing is over before you get there, if only for your mother's sake."

Mike cowered back into his seat while the guilt monster crept back into his conscience.

"I have prayed to the Almighty above that I would never see any of my sons having to fight another war. God willing, I won't," the Commander continued fervently. "War is the most dastardly weakness of man, son. But it seems we never learn. I don't speak of it, because I loathe everything about it. Good men have made the supreme sacrifice only because of the cowardly ambitions of other men. If that doesn't make sense to you… it's because it doesn't."

"Then, why are *you* still in?" Mike asked.

His father shook his head, while the corner of his mouth eased upward, puckering his cheek, casting an indignant sneer at his son's remark.

"Never mind," Mike quickly added. "I know, stupid question." He felt foolish. He knew better than to think that he had acquired license to dent his father's classic veneer.

Mike turned and looked out the window past familiar white houses with towering pecan trees shading wide porches, down the narrow street to the stop sign. He watched the gold Nova slowing down as it approached the intersection. It was *her*. Their eyes met briefly before she turned away, speeding off down the street toward the university. Again, she was more beautiful than his dreams had embellished her—her flowing blond hair held firmly back by a yellow and white scarf. He closed his eyes briefly, and the remembered scent of Shalimar simmered above the twinge in his heart. His chest expanded fully, then slowly he exhaled her image, quietly pleading for God to help him break the spell.

"Make sure you call your mother as soon as you get there," his father insisted.

"I know, I know," Mike replied, his mind still drifting back from the fading fantasy. He took a long last look down Main Street as his father pulled to a stop across from the crowded bus station. He looked over at the long line of people waiting to board, people whom he would not normally associate with. Migrant workers, their skin dark and wrinkled from the unrelenting Texas sun—scarred and leathery, a testament to their way of life.

Together father and son walked across the street, and Mike smiled as a young rodeo cowboy struggled to stuff his saddle into the underbelly of the silver Trailways bus. Nauseous diesel fumes spewed from the idling engine, forcing an elderly Mexican woman to cover her mouth with her tattered scarf. A renewed sense of pride swelled within him. These were the people he was leaving to defend, common people like the young mother and the son tugging at her skirt. He walked up to the agent and presented his voucher.

"How much money do you have?" his father inquired, pulling his sweat-stained wallet out.

"Well, I found a hundred dollars in my wallet this morning. I'm sure Mom put it there."

"Well, here's another fifty." His father handed the money to Mike.

"Thanks." Mike also took the ticket from the agent. "I guess this is it, then."

As they were walking out together, the Commander placed his hand on Mike's shoulder. They both stopped. As Mike turned to face his father, he focused on the gold Nova parked across the street.

"Just remember who you are, son," the Commander said firmly. "You're the third generation of American Shannahans—an Irishman—off to do his duty to this great country. Life is a journey, son, and you are at the first crossroad of that arduous trip." He embraced his son, holding him tightly as Mike gazed over his shoulder, across the street.

The Commander stepped back and took his son's hand. As he held it firmly, he simply said, "*Croiche onoraigh.* See ya." Then he turned and walked away.

Mike stood there for a moment, baffled by the abruptness of his father's departure. He wondered if that was what *his* father had told *him* when he left him standing on the docks. He watched him stride back over to the Volkswagen van, alternating his glances between his father and the young blonde sitting in the gold Nova.

That's it? he asked himself. *See ya?*

Mike stood there, longing for the absent admission of his father's love, aware of the beckoning stare from the blonde across the street. Finally, he reached down and picked up his bag. He took the first step onto the bus. Then, holding on to the handrail, he leaned back out and yelled, "See ya!"

*   *   *

CHAPTER EIGHT

T HE SEEMINGLY ENDLESS STRETCH OF two-lane highway scratched its way through the flatlands of southern Texas. He watched the familiar rows of milo and cotton accented with oil rigs and herds of beef cattle give way to rolling plains and dairy farms, milking herds and grazing sheep, and mile after mile of virtually nothing. The heat from the grimy floorboard surged up through his tattered Adidas sneakers, compounding the queasiness brought on by the relentless assault of diesel fumes. He quietly cursed the driver for not missing that last skunk carcass. Tiny pellets of sweat formed above his dry lips. He was ready to puke. His eyes quickly wandered over the low-lying brush, hoping to catch a glimpse of wild game, or anything unusual to refocus his attention. He studied the flat grassy terrain as it slowly merged with a series of gentle hills but then broke abruptly into a rock-strewn landscape of jagged arroyos and cactus-cluttered cliffs. *I'll bet this was an old cattle trail,* he thought.

He imagined the old trail herders moving cattle along the rough terrain on their way from the grassy valley to "old San Antone." He studied the contours of the terrain, looking for landmarks where they would have camped for the night. His thoughts swirled from armor-clad conquistadors to half-naked Indians, sombreros, *vaqueros,* and cowboys in chaps. He wondered how he would have reacted to the primitive environment they dealt with over a century ago.

The bus rattled loudly as it rolled over the trestle bridge high above the shallow river. He searched the banks in earnest, envisioning the Mexican army led by Santa Anna bivouacked on their way to the Alamo. *Now those were some dedicated troops,* he surmised. *I can't imagine walking all the way up here from Mexico. That musta' been a real bitch!*

Now the vintage Trailways bus didn't seem so bad after all. By his calculations, it would have taken him over a month to make the trip to San Antonio on foot. As the bus rambled on, his respect for the men and women who settled and fought for this harsh, barren land soared. He couldn't imagine what was so special about it. Surely they could have found a better place to stake their claim. Miles and miles of scrub and mesquite, accented by an endless array of useless rock and caliche. The more he studied it, however, the more it began to take on an allure of its own. Before long, he had answered his own question. *I wish it were all mine,* he concluded, understanding why it had been worth fighting for… and still was.

His young mind swiftly painted a large stone hacienda on the rise above the Frio River. He endowed it with several sprawling oak trees, transformed the rocky abyss into a soft green lawn, and decorated the long, winding caliche road with neat white fencing. He imagined easing back into his favorite chair, careful not to snag his spurs as he crossed his dusty boots on the porch railing.

Carmelita's calico skirt danced in the breeze, her full cleavage teasing him as she bent over to serve him a tall glass of iced tea. The mint leaf tickled his nose as the gentle breeze cooled the sweat on his tempered brow. This was the perfect spot to relax after a long day of branding cattle and herding the horses that were grazing in the back forty beyond.

For the next four hours, his mind wandered through the decades, assuming different roles and characters as the bus brought him through the hill country and into the modern reality of the expanding metropolis before him. He searched the boulevards and streets, hoping to catch a glimpse of the Alamo. He wondered what it would look like, surrounded by tall brick buildings, a lone outpost, consumed by history and the valiant sacrifices of her defenders.

Then suddenly, it was there, across the plaza, the symbol of independence and pride for so many Texans, a true source of inspiration for the men and women who forged their legacies with the blood of the brave men who died there. He envisioned the ghosts of those brave souls above the ancient parapets. In total awe of their valiant sacrifice, he vowed to emulate their courage. He was standing alone atop the smoking ramparts, bloody saber in hand, when the bus swayed violently into the depot.

He stepped off and was greeted by the unfamiliar smells of the city as well as the raucous noises of traffic and construction, each noise blatantly out of tune with the other, reminding him of a monstrous orchestra tuning up for a concert. The stenciled sign above the doorway quickly caught his attention: *Military Inductees Report to 397 Broadway*, with a large arrow pointing across the street. He wasted no time slipping in and out of traffic to make his way to his final destination, where he delivered his packet of papers to the man in uniform at the front desk. Nervous anticipation gripped him as he studied the soldier before him, noting the khaki uniform's firm creases, its two rows of ribbons under the light blue long-rifle badge, its collar brass gleaming brightly in the dull-lit room.

"You'll report back here at zero-seven hundred hours, sonny," the uniformed man said. "That's seven a.m. for you *civilians*." Then he handed Mike a voucher for the Bluebonnet Hotel, gave him directions, and sent him on his way.

Mike walked slowly down the busy sidewalk, looked in the store windows, and noticed that most people were, at the very least, indifferent to one another as they passed by. Every person he greeted avoided eye contact with him, ignoring his clumsy attempts to blend in with them. Each storefront he passed emitted a slightly unique and unfamiliar odor, a subtle advertisement for the goods being sold inside. Gone were the flavors of milo and mesquite, replaced with the hint of oiled wood floors, musty leather, and week-old trash. The smooth coastal breeze had been transformed into a concoction of diesel and monoxide, lingering beneath the tall brick and granite buildings that blocked out the setting sun. The chill air thickened the blend of vile vapors, and with each step, Mike developed a growing aversion for this big city so far from home.

He turned the corner and tripped over a disheveled man slumped up against the wall of the building. He quickly apologized, and as he instinctively placed his hand on the fellow's shoulder, the man grabbed him and held on tightly. "I haven't had anything to eat for three days, sonny," he stammered.

Mike looked past the scruffy beard into the bloodshot eyes of the indigent, stunned by what he saw. He looked down at the filthy hand grasping his arm, jagged fingernails packed with dirt and dinge. The man's tattered clothes, layered indiscriminately without regard to color or texture, reeked of latent sweat and crusty body odor.

"Can you spare a dollar?" the man asked, his yellow teeth blending with the jaundiced tinge of his wrinkled skin.

Mike felt desperation in the firmness of the man's grip. He pulled back, wondering how someone could have possibly arrived at this paltry destination in life. His compassion guided his hand into his pocket, and as he pulled out the loose money he had there, he knew the man would need more than a dollar to get a good meal. "Here, old man." Mike selected a crisp new five-dollar bill from the pocket's meager assortment of cash (he left the money his parents had given him neatly folded in his wallet).

The vagrant quickly snatched the money from his benefactor and hurriedly stuffed it into the confines of his rotting garb. "God bless you, sonny," he muttered, struggling to get to his feet.

Mike shook his head, turned, and continued down the street. He didn't want to look back. He'd seen enough. He remembered the shame-laden Japanese beggars who lived in the caves behind his house on the bluff overlooking Yokohama Harbor, most of them still attired in remnants of the uniforms they had worn in the war. He had brought them parcels of food, and they had taught him how to play Japanese checkers. He had cherished their muted friendship and the special way they had made him feel welcomed in their damp, candle-lit lairs. It had truly been an exciting time for him, filled with adventure and intrigue. That is, until the day the Commander discovered the destination of his after-school rendezvous.

The large, vertical Bluebonnet sign snapped his mind back to reality. He watched the hotel doorman approaching him, mouthing words that were quickly lost in the clamor of the passing traffic. "I said: Did you give that honky drunk some money?" the Negro doorman asked forcefully.

"Ahhh, yeah, I did," Mike answered, puzzled by the question. He was hungry."

"Hungry, my ass, fool! Didn't your momma teach you anything? I've been tryin ta get rid of that sombitch for the last month. He's bin glad-handin' the guests here and makin' a nuisance of himself. He's gonna stick around here as long as bleedin' heart suckers like you keep givin' him money ta get his rotgut with!"

"The man said he was *hungry*," Mike reasoned.

"Oh yeah? Does *that* look like a diner to you?" The doorman pointed across the street. Mike had to turn around to look. He watched the man stagger up the high curb and limp directly into the crowded liquor store.

"Well, at least he knows where *he's* goin'," Mike retorted with a grin, "and that's a lot more than I can say for the rest of us." He brushed by the doorman and into the lobby of the rustic old hotel.

This place smells like a coffin, he judged, noticing the long, worn banister leading up the spiral stairs. The heavy wood panels in the lobby had long since lost the luster of their prime. They were laden with heavy murals and paintings whose oils had cracked over the years of neglect and abuse. He waited for his key, admiring the symbols of the Texas legacy prominently portrayed within the opulent, decorative frames. "Wouldn't surprise me if Santa Ana had stayed here on his way to the Alamo," he jested.

The clerk handed him his key and directed him up the staircase to the second floor. His room complemented the dank décor of the establishment, complete with the resident musty odor and a dark space on the far wall where he imagined some western picture must have hung. He threw his bag on the floor, turned, and fell backward onto the sagging bed. *Guess I've got a lot to learn,* he figured, recalling his encounter with the vagrant drunk.

He thought of his mother, wondering how her afternoon had gone, confident that she would have given the man money for a meal as well. He lay there for several minutes, staring at the yellow stains on the ceiling, wondering what his day would bring tomorrow. He felt inadequate, focusing on the slim stem legs of the stable cockroach perched on the ceiling above. He stared, aware that there was no sustenance within grasp, wondering why the scavenger had exposed itself to that extent. He watched it for minutes, mesmerized with its patience, aware of the inevitable futility of its quest. He felt he shared with it that predicament: totally exposed.

He sat up, reached over, and turned on the television at the foot of his bed. The snowy image of a familiar newscaster emerged into view, followed by the daily images of war he was becoming so accustomed to.

"U.S. forces launched Operation Crimp today," the announcer was saying, "the largest operation of the war to date. With an estimated eight thousand troops involved with the operation, military spokesmen have indicated that the purpose of the campaign is to locate and destroy the Viet Cong headquarters suspected to be located in or around the area just south of Củ Chi in Bình Dương Province. Patrolling and razing of the area has yet to locate any sign of the elusive enemy."

Those bastards are probably on their way back to Hanoi, Mike reasoned. *That's why they can't find 'em.* "Chickenshits," he said aloud. He fluffed his smelly pillow, eased back down on the bed, and watched with interest as the reporter gave the latest casualty figures of the day. Within minutes, the mental tasks he'd endured blended with the soft audible lullaby of traffic below, easing him into a deep sleep.

Hours later, he awoke confused, stirred from his slumber by the constant tone of the test pattern from the television at the foot of his bed. He realized that he had neglected to call his mother, as he had promised his dad he would. It was too late now, however. He set the dented alarm for six a.m. and then switched off the set. He lay back on the bed, folded his arms, and with a deep cleansing sigh, began his search for Barbara in the lonely confines of the darkened room.

* * *

CHAPTER NINE

THE SMALL BLUE GUIDON REVERBERATED along with the slow, morbid cadence of the stout drill sergeant. Two hundred dusty black boots mimicked his tune, each troop focused on the helmet in front of him. Their chalky green uniforms were accented with chevrons of sweat, a testament to the grueling regiment of the training they endured. Mike stared in respectful awe as the column passed by, not a smile evident in the heavily laden formation of infantry. Bulging green backpacks harnessed to poised, proud shoulders did not hinder their repetitive gait. He watched the perforated muzzles of their M14s listing slowly above the formation, modern implements of battle so deadly in the hands of the trained warrior. He felt the unmistakable surge of pride flow through his veins, pounding with each precision step guided by the low, guttural pace set by the drill sergeant.

"They're from Tigerland," a hushed voice behind him reported, referring to the junglelike advanced training camp at North Fort, the northern part of the base.

"How do you know?"

"Just look at their faces. Next stop: Vietnam!"

The comment intensified Mike's building curiosity. He studied their web gear and made a mental note of how many magazines their ammo pouches held. He wondered how many of them were walking dead, destined to pay that ultimate sacrifice.

"*If* I *die* in-a *com*-bat *zone!*" the drill sergeant bellowed, triggering an immediate response from his troops: "*If* I *die* in-a *com*-bat *zone!*" Then: "*Box* me *up* and *ship* me *home!*"… "*Box* me *up* and *ship* me *home!*"

"*Sound* off!" was the sergeant's call in the famous Duckworth chant. "*One* two!" was the troopers' cadence response, shouted in perfect rhythm stressing each syllable where all their left feet met the ground.

"*Sound* off!" "*Three* four!"

"*Sound* off!" "*One* two *three* four! One two... *Three-four!*" the final pair of numbers shouted as a single syllable.

"*Hup* two your-'a *left* four!" "*Hup* two your-'a *left* four!"

Mike felt the goose bumps ease as the column moved down the street. He suppressed his urge to run after them, staring down at his shiny new boots below the dark-green bloused fatigues. *I'd never get away with it,* he lamented.

He turned and stared at the rest of the recruits behind him, blank faces, young minds, each immersed in individual, personal reaction to the ominous cavalcade of troops. Shaved heads with white sidewalls covered by bland green baseball caps, an unimposing lot of confused and apprehensive boys, unceremoniously clad in baggy, unstarched fatigues, anointed only with the courtesy of plain white nametags—all of the recruits recent acquisitions, now the property of the United States Army. Keenly familiar with the training regimen he had before him, Mike shook his head in resignation, longing to leave the group he was in and join the ranks of those seasoned troops from Tigerland. He looked back at them in envy, gritting his teeth while the last troop of the formation disappeared around the corner barracks.

"Hurry up and wait, hurry up and wait," Mike muttered in disgust. "That's all we've been doin' for the last three days! Hurry up and wait." He sat down on his green duffel bag, stuffed full of web gear and his steel pot. An inner layer of white boxer shorts and long green socks softened his perch as he stared at the endless forest of tall pine trees beyond the barracks. Their unique fragrance filled his lungs as he sighed again, impatient to begin his new life in earnest.

He stared at the large white sign across the street: *Welcome to Fort Polk, Louisiana, Birthplace of the Infantry Soldier.* He smirked as he read the following well-wishing underneath the welcome: *We wish you good work and happy training.* "What do they think this is?" he said under his breath. "Disneyland?"

"Fall in!!" a thundering voice demanded. The scattered band of recruits scrambled to their duffel bags, nervously looking at one another to make sure they were responding correctly to the unfamiliar command. Then they stood motionless, wide-eyed and submissive, tense and cringing in anticipation of a subsequent command.

Mike watched out of the corner of his eye as a tall Negro sergeant strode out in front of the formation, turned slowly, and faced the new recruits, his eyes cleverly hidden beneath the tilted brim of his hat. "My name is Drill Sergeant Otis Massey," he began loudly. "I will be your sister, your brother, and yes, even your mother for the next eight weeks!"

Mike smirked. *Here go,* he thought. *You're gonna have to do better than that. I've already seen this movie.*

Before he had time to relax his grin, Sergeant Massey had assumed a position within inches of his face. "Do I amuse you, Private?" he asked softly, staring deep into the focused eyes of the recruit before him.

"No, Sergeant," Mike replied. "I'm just glad to be here."

Massey held his stare, exposing the clear white surrounding his extremely dark eyes, eyes that took their time evaluating the truth in the recruit's quick response. He looked down at Mike's nametag and registered a mental note as he turned and addressed the formation.

"I have been assigned the formidable task of turning you people into an effective fighting force of soldiers. This man's army has given me eight weeks to make that transition, and it will be possible only with your commitment to hard work and your strict dedication to the task at hand."

He paused, looking directly at each individual in the front rank before continuing his remarks. "If you do not pay attention to detail, expend your greatest effort to make that transition from citizen to soldier, do everything asked of you by your drill sergeant... you *will die* in Vietnam!"

Well, that just about covers it all, Mike told himself, carefully easing his eyes around the formation, gauging the reaction of the stoic troops around him.

"You will pick up your personal belongings and proceed single file to the trucks waiting to transport you to your company area," Massey informed them.

The bumpy ride to the company area led them through the main areas of the base. Formations of men in white T-shirts engaged in calisthenics emerged in the dusty fields behind the endless rows of barracks that made up the core of the base. Long lines of infantry trailing blue guidons clogged the main thoroughfares en route to their final destination. Through the rails of the long cattle truck, he marveled at the faceless humanity, toy soldiers at the mercy of the drill sergeants harnessing their youth, their stamina, their collective destinies. There was no voice to their toil, rather a benign submission consistent with their status—GIs, grunts, dogfaces, foot soldiers—all demeaning terms held for the essence of the army, the Queen of Battle... the infantry.

He would be different. He held no desire to march into battle, as just another anonymous dogface to be hurled at the enemy. He felt *his* destiny was sure to fulfill his ambitions, and although his journey would begin here among the conscripts and young patriots, he would face the enemy designated by a single term that heralded his arrival into battle: *paratrooper*. As he imagined gathering his silky canopy in his arms, the cattle truck jolted to a halt between the mazes of white barracks just off the main road.

"Un-ass those damn vehicles, you gutless maggots!" a booming voice demanded.

The stampede that included a five-foot plunge from the open tailgates resulted in only minor injuries—bruised shins, scraped elbows, impacted pea gravel protruding from various extremities. The frenzied mob finally settled into a mass of confusion, like a corralled herd of sheep silently awaiting the next dreaded command.

"How many of you criminals haven't been slapped today?" the unnamed first sergeant yelled as he moved excitedly between the bruised and soiled recruits. "That looked like a goddamn jailbreak!" he continued, flailing his clipboard above his head for emphasis. He continued his tirade, grouping his expletives into an endless stream of insults that were occasionally accented with an odious spray of heated saliva. The rant subsided only when it was apparent to everyone that he had, in fact, run out of demeaning expletives.

"When I call off your name, you will collect your equipment and fall in behind your individual platoon sergeant. Understood?"

"Yes, Sergeant!" the repentant mob replied in unison.

"*This* movement, unlike the previous maneuver, will take place in a *military manner*! Is *that understood*?"

"Yes, Sergeant!"

Mike watched the gangly first sergeant wipe his mouth with his handkerchief and then, with a clearly strained and angry voice, begin the roll call. The lengthy recital gave the young Texan recruit time to study the men he would spend the next eight weeks with. He noticed the particular manner in which the recruits replied when their names were called, and the ease or the struggle they experienced in moving their equipment to their respective platoon areas. They formed the ranks with all forms of manhood—short, fat, tall, and slim. They moved with varying degrees of intent, some with attitude, and it was evident to him that most were just plain scared. When his name was called, he moved smartly, feeling Sergeant Massey's eyes follow him to a position in his platoon.

Without further incident, the company was formed. For the time being, the unruly mob had been converted into an actual company of basic trainees, each at the threshold of his career in the United States Army.

"If you have prior service, or if you have done any time in ROTC programs, drop your gear and step forward."

Mike hesitated briefly, then complied with the first sergeant's instructions and moved to the front of the formation. He joined the other twenty men who had left the ranks and was instructed to report to the armory in the building to the front of the formation and draw a weapon. They returned, each with an M14 rifle they were instructed to unsling. Then they were told to stand at ease.

Soon Sergeant Massey called the group to attention again and ordered them to dress right. Then began the manual of arms, the rigidly timed series of positions and maneuvers each soldier performs with his weapon. For fifteen minutes the sergeant drilled the group, gradually intensifying the regimen, exposing the awkwardness of the less proficient as well as the skills of the more talented. Mike felt confident, relying on his hours with the college's King's Rifles drill team, his precision evident with every snap and slap of the wooden stock.

Sergeant Massey pressed on, his cadence calls clearly focused on thwarting Private Shannahan's performance. Frustrated, he finally gave the command that brought the competition to an end. "Orrrderr aahhmms! At ease!"

Massey moved to where the company's eight other drill sergeants stood conferring with the first sergeant, making notes on their clipboards and occasionally glancing back to the group of privates standing at ease. Within minutes, they approached the small group, selecting men to act as squad leaders and platoon sergeants. Mike watched as they slipped black armbands on their favorites, some with two stripes denoting squad leader, others with three stripes indicating the wearer was one of the acting platoon sergeants for the company. Massey had already chosen four men by the time he stopped in front of the young trooper.

"Nobody gives a shit whether you can march or not, but you've got a lot of snap to your moves, troop. I like that. Shows me you work at being good. Pride's an important factor in this man's army, So's takin' orders." He slid the three stripes up Mike's arm, one eye squinting, still searching for something in Mike's eyes. "Don't make me regret this, Shannahan."

Sergeant Massey stepped back, came to attention, and issued his order. "Take your post!"

Mike quickly executed a half-right step and moved smartly to his position in front of his platoon. Coming to an abrupt halt, he did an about-face and came to parade rest. *Flawless,* he thought, fighting the urge to look down at the three stripes he'd just been presented. *Not bad. That was easy.* He felt very relaxed out in front of the formation of recruits behind him. After all, one thing he had learned in his years as a service brat was that rank has its privileges, and right now he was the ranking recruit in his platoon. The fact that an element of *responsibility* played a key role in that position never crossed his mind.

*   *   *

CHAPTER TEN

"I F YOU DO NOT PAY attention to this block of instruction, you will *die* in Vietnam!"

Mike stared up at the instructor with disdain. He slid back in his chair, folded his arms, and mentally challenged the sergeant to tell him something he didn't already know. For the past four weeks, every instructor, from the rifle range to the infiltration course, had uttered that ominous warning. Even those few troops who actually believed it initially now had their doubts.

"This apparatus before you is the M-eighteen-A-one antipersonnel mine, more commonly referred to as the Claymore. When the blasting cap is inserted into the receiver well, like so, Mr. Claymore is not our friend."

Mike shuffled his feet in the sawdust floor of the massive tent used as a classroom, seeking a comfort level to sustain him for the next three hours of boring dissertation on a mine he'd already trained with in ROTC. As he settled into a relaxing posture, the firm hand on his shoulder startled his senses.

"Outside, Shannahan."

Mike looked up to see Sergeant Massey standing over him. The sergeant nodded toward the rear of the makeshift schoolroom, beckoning him to follow. He stood and, with a bewildered look on his face, acknowledged his classmates' curious stares. *Maybe they found that* Playboy *under my bunk*, he wondered, apprehensive about this sudden interruption in his training.

Looking over Massey's shoulder, he recognized the company executive officer standing at the entrance of the tent waiting for him. He quickly surveyed the stern look on Lieutenant Mauney's face and determined that whatever it was, it wasn't good. *I'm in deep shit now.*

He stopped in front of the lieutenant, came to attention, and rendered a snappy salute. "Private Shannahan reports!"

Lieutenant Mauney returned his salute and ordered him to stand at ease. "Based on your battery tests taken at the processing center, your scores indicate that you have the aptitude to qualify for Officer Candidate School, Private."

Mike's eyes widened. He barely recalled the tests he had taken at three a.m. the night he arrived at Fort Polk.

"Don't look so surprised, Shannahan. Those tests, along with the recommendation of your platoon sergeant, qualify you for an opportunity to appear before the board to determine your future value to the army. Is that something that you are interested in, Private?"

He glanced at Massey, a little confused at his apparent nonchalance with regard to the proceedings. Without changing his expression, the sergeant seemed to offer a transparent nod of approval.

"Yes, sir."

"Good. You will accompany Corporal Jenkins here back to the company area, where you will change into khakis and report to the OCS Board at thirteen hundred hours. Any questions?"

"No sir!"

"Good luck, troop."

The pair saluted, and Mike followed Jenkins to the waiting jeep for the ride back to the company area. "This beats the shit outa' riding those damn cattle trucks," he remarked to his driver, putting his boot up on the edge of the open door as he relaxed in the thinly padded seat.

"You're a real dumb-ass if you let them send you to OCS," Jenkins claimed.

"Why's that?"

"When's the last time you took a look at the casualty reports in the *Army Times*?"

"Haven't."

"That figures. I suggest you stop at the PX and git yourself a copy… You'll see."

"See what?" Mike replied, somewhat annoyed.

"Charlie's no dumb-ass." the corporal said, referring to the Viet Cong enemy. "They're killin' more second louies than us grunts over there. It's a fact!"

"Bullshit!"

"Ain't no bullshit, troop. They look for that long whip-ass antenna the radioman's carryin', then they just shoot the guy standing next to him. That's the LT," Jenkins reported, a smirk accompanying his remarks. "It ain't too hard to pick out the damn officers over there… the guys reading the maps, the shiny brass, the ones getting saluted—"

"Everyone knows not to salute officers in combat," Mike replied sternly.

"Yeah, but what if your men don't like your ass? Then what?" Jenkins turned and watched his passenger pondering his comments. "See what I mean?"

The conversation had taken the edge off of Mike's enthusiasm. He turned and took a close look at Jenkins, recalling his noncombatant status as a clerk typist assigned to the orderly room. Jenkins was a rear-echelon type, never to be in harm's way. "Well, that's just the difference between you and me, Corporal."

"How's that?"

"If I make the *Times*, it ain't gonna be for overdue library books, and it sure as hell ain't gonna be in the obituary column."

He turned and watched the tall pine trees give way to the bland array of troop billets, his mind focusing on the questions he could be asked by the board of officers. He put Jenkins's comments out of his mind, attributing them to the prevalent attitude of army troops toward second lieutenants. Within minutes, he was standing in front of his wall locker, sliding an altered paper clip inside the seam of his collar, a trick he'd learned in ROTC back in Kingsville. He carefully positioned his shiny brass on the stiff collar, then quickly turned his attention to his low quarters protruding from beneath his bunk. He'd spent hours spit-shining them, applying layer upon layer of flame-melted polish to fill in the pores of the leather. He carefully dusted the tips with a cotton ball, then cautiously set them aside to continue dressing.

"Standin' tall… and lookin' good," he remarked, admiring his handiwork in the latrine mirror. He adjusted his overseas cap and then took one final look. "Gig line straight, brass in order, brim two inches above the eye. Do it!"

He walked stiffed-legged out of the barracks and headed to the battalion day room, where the board was convening. He was careful not to break the creases in his trousers, and he prayed that his deodorant would do its job today.

The battalion adjutant met him at the door and instructed him to report to the ranking officer seated in the next room. His anticipation soared as he entered the room, quickly surveying the five officers seated behind the long wooden table. He recognized the gold oak leaf on the ranking officer, the major who was seated at the center of the table. Mike stepped up in front of him and saluted.

"Private Shannahan reports!" he remarked forcefully.

"At ease, Private."

Mike relaxed as much as he could, immediately noting the rows of colorful combat ribbons worn by the committee of officers. His eyes quickly focused on the parachute wings displayed above the pocket of the major he had saluted. The officer didn't seem like a paratrooper. A thin gray line outlined the bald spot on the top of his head, and the pink puffiness in his cheeks and neck displayed more than a passing appetite for the culinary arts. *Probably couldn't cut the mustard,* Mike thought.

"Shannahan, you've been recommended to this board for consideration for Officer Candidate School," the major began. "This is an informal inquiry, so I encourage you to be candid with your remarks, son. First, tell us a little about yourself and what brought you to the service of your country."

Mike disclosed his brief history, obviously proud that he was the son of a naval officer. The board listened with interest, nodding with approval as he used the inherent jargon and terms known only to a service brat. With patriotic flare he positioned his statements to reflect his responsibility to his country, along with his willingness to lay down his life to preserve its principles.

"That's all very interesting, Private," the major commented. "But we're looking for leaders in this army, so what makes you think you have what it takes to command an infantry platoon in combat."

"I've obviously never been in combat, sir, but I know those who have. They've all been leaders of men, and I've done what I can to model my life after those things that they have told me are important."

"Such as...?" inquired the captain seated at the end of the table.

Mike thought a moment, then responded. "Lead by example. Never ask more of your men than you are willing to expend yourself. You can never command respect, you must earn it."

"If you were given a dangerous mission, what's more important, the mission or your men?"

This must be a trick question, Mike surmised. *I'd better take my time with this one.* "In ROTC we were taught that our primary responsibility is the welfare of our men. There are no degrees on the value of our men's lives... but there are degrees on the overall value of the mission." He paused, choosing his next words carefully.

"You're quibbling, Shannahan," accused the captain during Mike's pause.

"I guess you want me to say that the mission takes priority over the welfare of my men, but that's not the way I see it. I think the important thing here is to have the ability to complete the mission without unnecessarily risking the lives of my men. If that means adjusting the operational order, then so be it. I think what sets our army apart from the Soviets and the rest of the world is our men's ability to take charge of the situation without having to rely on getting everything approved by higher-ups before making a decision."

"It doesn't always work that way, Private," the major retorted.

"What are your political views on the war in Vietnam, Shannahan?"

Mike looked intently at the first lieutenant asking the question and watched him lean back in his chair, one arm cocked on the armrest while he leisurely patted his lips with the index finger of his other. Sensing a degree of arrogance in the officer's query, the nervous troop felt he was being set up to debate politics that he was just learning to appreciate.

"I don't have any political views on that, sir. I'm a soldier in the Army of the United States and report ultimately to the Commander in Chief, the President of the United States. It would be inconsistent with my enlistment oath to have any other views. I fully support the President and the people who elected him." Quietly he thanked Sergeant Bolton for that answer, but as he suspected would happen, the lieutenant followed up with a quick response.

"Does that mean you would obey an unlawful order given to you by a superior officer?"

"Well, sir, if it were an unlawful order, then I am compelled *not* to obey it."

"Wouldn't that be a court-martial offense if you refused to obey an order given by a superior officer?"

"Well, sir, I'm not a lawyer, but my senses tell me that if I felt that an order was indeed unlawful, it would be my responsibility *not* to carry it out."

"So, what *would* you do, and who's to say what is or is not lawful?"

"Well, sir, that depends on the situation."

"You're quibbling again, Shannahan," came the curt reply.

Mike felt the beads of perspiration build on his temples. It was becoming obvious to him that they were attempting to expose him for what he was: a naïve young man, a mere neophyte, untutored in the intricacies of the political world he'd stumbled into on his own. He'd studied the Military Code of Conduct in school but was in no way an expert on the topic. His interests had never involved politics, and he barely knew the philosophical divergence between Democrats and Republicans.

The questions continued, some with obvious answers while others challenged the young man to search deep within for a response. He found himself relying on his father more and more, imagining what the Commander would say, how he would react to the situations the board presented.

Finally, it was over.

"That will be all, Private Shannahan," the major informed him. "You can return to your company now."

Mike saluted, did an about face, and left the room. Shuffling down the steps, he shuddered as the chill air met the damp remnants of his interrogation, his back and armpits seeping through with sweat. He felt numb, uncertain how his answers and bearing held with the board. He slowly rehashed the questions over in his mind, reviewing the responses for any telltale sign of accord he may have missed. The inquisition left him feeling anonymous, unsure of his performance, wondering if he really *did* have what it took to be a leader of men.

He stepped through the door to the barracks. The long lines of empty bunks and footlockers guided him down to his room at the darkened end of the bay. His footsteps echoed through the deserted quarters, emphasizing the fact that he was alone. Tossing his hat on the footlocker, he fell exhausted on the relative comfort of his taut bunk. "This sucks," he complained aloud.

His mind quickly made the familiar trip back to the lazy days of his life in Kingsville—his mother, his brothers, his sisters, the evening jaunts with his best friend. He longed for the carefree existence he'd grown to repudiate, and however trite that life seemed to him at the time, he now missed it, *deeply*.

Of all the emotions he'd explored and endured over the past month, the facet of uncertainty now dominated his psyche. The loneliness was bitter but fully anticipated. He'd repressed the numerous urges to call Barbara, defining that tendency as an element of weakness. The long lines of homesick troops sequestering the lone pay phone offered another deterrent. He'd continually recommitted himself to persevere, to reject those selfish emotions that drove some in his company to desertion. The one thing that was certain was that he no longer had control over his own destiny. The anxiety that accompanied that stark realization pressed heavily on his mind.

Just do your job, and get the hell out of here. Can't worry about those things you don't have control over, he reminded himself. *Just get into jump school, and things will take care of themselves.*

He brushed the board out of his mind, reverting to the goal he had set for himself when he'd enlisted. He would deal with the challenges ahead in Basic, confident that he would emerge unscathed, ready to join the ranks of the elite, the cream of the crop: the paratroopers. "I ain't gonna be nobody's cannon fodder," he proclaimed proudly. ********

CHAPTER ELEVEN

TWO HUNDRED AND TWELVE WEARY men stood motionless beneath the clear blue Louisiana sky, their dark green fatigues faded to olive, revealing the toil of their months of intimate contact with mother earth. Long, faint shadows from their empty barracks cast a bleak chill over the formation of the nervous troops. Tense, focused eyes held firm on the tall captain before them, each of the troops dealing with the building anticipation of the captain's next command.

"Sergeant Delaney, dismiss the company!" the captain ordered.

The first sergeant saluted, turned, and ordered his platoon sergeants to take charge of their platoons.

"Fall out!" Mike yelled over his shoulder.

The last word had barely cleared his lips when a rush of humanity surged past him. Within seconds the bulletin board in front of the mess hall was surrounded by desperate men pushing and shoving to read the list of names the orderly had posted only moments before. Mike stood back, watching the frenzy unfold, fully aware of the consequences of the moment. Men were searching the rosters for their names, praying for an assignment to anywhere but Tigerland, the land of the living dead.

The ominous destination, hidden deep within the towering pines in North Fort, plagued the consciousness of every man in the company once they had learned of its eerie mission: to prepare American boys to fight the enemy in Vietnam. Tigerland hosted the final training cycle before troops shipped out as replacements in the escalating war in Southeast Asia. A few relished the thought, but most secretly prayed for a noncombat assignment—driving trucks, maintenance, cooks, rear-echelon administration—*anything* but Tigerland.

"Just look at 'em," a familiar voice behind him chortled. "Bunch-a' scared pansies lookin' for a ticket outa' this man's army."

Mike turned to rebuff Sergeant Massey's comment but held his tongue while his eyes admonished the drill sergeant.

"Well, most of 'em, anyway," Massey conceded with a smile.

"There're some damn fine troops in my platoon, Sergeant, and you know it," Mike said. "I'd be proud to serve with them anywhere, anytime."

"Sounds like you're lettin' your alligator mouth overload your tweety-bird ass, Shannahan. But the bottom line is: You just don't get it. The fun and games are over, troop. I admire you stickin' up for your men, but the fact is that I've been doin' this long enough to know who'll show an' who'll go. Hell, I might as well call the MPs right now on a bunch of those jokers. Save 'em the time from havin' ta go round 'em up."

"Not from my platoon, you won't," Mike replied confidently.

"Shannahan, part of being a leader is having the ability to evaluate your men—their strengths, their weaknesses, what motivates them. Then, and only then, will you be able to harness their abilities to function as an effective fighting force. What you need to realize is that *summa'* those guys over there got the 'I gotta git outa' here an' home to Momma' syndrome. It's written all over their faces!"

Massey adjusted the brim on his hat, fumbling with the leather strap that held the tilt in place. He put both hands on Mike's shoulders, cocked one eye, and delivered his message: "Know your men, troop. And when you take the time to *genuinely* get to know them, then, and only then, will you emerge as an effective leader. Rule number two: Learn how to take advice. It may sound foreign to you, but it's a fact: *Sergeants* run this man's army. The brass just translate our dogface doctrine into proper English for the politicians to make war with."

The young troop struggled with the sergeant's last comment but embraced the gist of his message. "My dad was a first-class bosun's mate when I was born," he said proudly. "He worked his way up through the ranks, but he never forgot where he came from."

"So he learned how to shit and defecate at the same time," Massey remarked.

"What?"

"Sorry, I just couldn't resist," he apologized, chuckling. "For your future reference, Shannahan, ossifers urinate, enlisted men piss. *They* retire to the latrine to defecate, while we dogfaces have to settle on just takin' a shit."

Somehow, Mike just couldn't visualize the Commander partaking in *any* bodily functions. He shook his head in disgust, prompting a response from Massey.

"You also need to learn how to lighten up, Shannahan. Seems to me that you're lettin' your military bearing get the best of you. Time to take a break. Anyway, troop, where you headed tomorrow after graduation?" he asked, changing the subject.

"Well, I was hoping to go home to Texas, but my dad got transferred to the naval base in Brunswick, Georgia, last week, so I guess I don't have anywhere to go. Not a lot of places you can go on seventy-eight dollars a month," he complained, patting his near-empty wallet for emphasis.

"Don't you have friends you could visit with back in Texas? You've got a week's leave before you have to report to your next assignment."

"Not really. Didn't live there very long." There was a forlorn tinge in his response. His mind quickly wandered back to the tense phone call with his father the previous week, and his cheek tweaked as he recalled the brief conversation.

"Your mother fainted when she answered the door." Mike remembered how his father had admonished him about the effect of the solemn visitors in uniform knocking at his parents' house. *"Bruised her right knee and elbow in the fall."*

"Is she okay?"

"Just couldn't stay away from him, could you?" the Commander had replied, ignoring his son's concern about his mother but giving him more hell about Jim. *"They wanted to know if you knew where he is."*

"What difference does it make? They'll never catch him anyway."

The immediate dial tone had chastised his impudence, widening the crevice that had recently begun to mend. He quickly brushed the incident aside and told Massey of his decision to go on ahead to his next assignment. "Guess I'll just report in early and get settled in before the rest of the guys get there. Can't dance anyway."

He watched the last of the troops move slowly toward the barracks, their moods varying from somber to virtually ecstatic. Finally, he slowly ambled toward the bulletin board, projecting a nonchalance inconsistent with the anticipation brooding deep within. He found his name on the fifth column. He traced the line with his finger until he matched the destination code to the right: *AIT, North Fort.* Advanced Individual Training in Tigerland. *Massey was right*, he concluded. *Party's over.*

That night he joined his platoon at the brigade canteen, young men drawn together to celebrate a lasting achievement: They'd all made it through Basic Training. The 3.2-percent near beer flowed throughout the night, bonding the brazen soldiers together in the way they had hoped it would, some of them destined to be lifelong friends and comrades, others just an ink blot in the *Army Times.*

Early the next morning, they passed in review as brothers, comrades— pressed khaki uniforms, shiny marksmanship badges accenting the lone National Defense ribbon projected on their swelling chests. All heads held high as they marched in front of the relatives and army brass, the colorful reviewing stand anointed with flowing flags and symbols of patriotism. Never again would they harbor such innocence as they did now, marching proudly behind their nation's flag, the ultimate symbol of their commitment to their nation, a nation soon to be torn and socially decimated by the very strength that had made it so great.

Mike was oblivious to the discord sweltering within the ranks of his brethren at home. He considered that the men he knew who had deserted their post were simply more concerned for their own personal welfare than they were champions of a greater noble cause. In his view, not one of them was a partisan of peace, a disciple of democracy, or even a man of character. They were nothing more than deserters, rebels *without* a cause. Or if they did have a cause, it was just a selfish, individual one.

Although the desertion rate was relatively small, the number of draft dodgers was growing at an alarming rate. Mike couldn't help but think of Jim, and what must have really compelled him to make such a drastic decision. Mike tried not to think of his friend as a coward, but the more he thought about it, that notion seemed to be the only logical conclusion. As much as he missed him, he was glad that he would never share his foxhole with him. He felt the same about anyone who so blatantly chose not to serve. *Don't want anybody on my flank who doesn't want to be there,* he often thought these days. *For whatever the reason.*

*   *   *

Spring finally found its way to the red clay and tall pines of central Louisiana, bringing with it an array of showers and a rebirth of nature that collided with the new training cycle for the men in Tigerland. The hard red clay soon turned to sloshy mud, its difficulty compounded by a burst of foliage and thorny vines that held the trainees captive, tearing unmercifully at their flesh and fatigues while they traversed the countryside. Night raids, circle ambushes, fire and maneuver—repetitive exercises, designed to hone their combat skills—left no time for reflection, remorse, or even regret.

The long road marches with full gear often led them back into South Fort, a deliberate excursion they all relished. They took great pleasure marching through the reception station, chanting aggressive *jodies* (sassy, even slightly subversive, cadence calls designed to release tension), which they used with their numb swagger and worn gear to taunt the new recruits. They often joked about replacing the guidon with a skull and crossbones, a suggestion quickly rejected by the veteran platoon sergeant.

Mike was beginning to enjoy the training, a regimen that enabled the troops to use their own ingenuity in planning missions, a regimen that gave them the flexibility to improvise as long as they continued to succeed. Gone was the constant shouting and demeaning, as if the platoon sergeants themselves had bestowed an unspoken respect for the young men who were just weeks away from the sting of actual battle. Desertions had diminished, and men who were clearly not cut out to be in combat had been reassigned to other training disciplines, out of harm's way yet still able to serve their country.

In just over three months, Mike found himself adjusting well to the discipline and structure of the army. Life in Tigerland was not at all what he had expected. The training was tough, but the men knew that the more they learned, the more would their chances for surviving the combat zone improve proportionally. Two of their most cherished commodities had become chow and sleep, with rack time emerging as the clear winner.

The men with families or girlfriends back home spent most of their available time writing letters or standing in the endless lines at the phone booths. Alienated from family and without a girlfriend, Mike spent more time spit-shining his boots and honing his newfound appreciation for country and western tunes on the radio. Buck Owens and George Jones taunted him daily, tweaking his fragile emotions with ballads and laments that constantly reminded him of Barbara and the painful memories he carried in his heart. He identified with the lyrics, extracting from them a deep solace of pseudo-contentment in the fact that however remorseful the tune, he was not alone in his pain. He just wondered why it wouldn't go away.

The young troop lay in his bunk early one Saturday evening, reading the latest edition of the *Army Times*. His room, situated just inside the company day room, shielded him from the boisterous cantankerisms prevalent in the other company bays. Mike had earned the position of trainee field first sergeant, due to his performance in Basic as well as his overall ranking among the troops assigned to his company. With his new title came the perk of a private room to bolster his authority, along with a private latrine, a privacy the rest of the troops made sure was consistently violated.

He'd just turned on the radio when Buck Sergeant Ray Tolliver stepped inside the door. "Get your shit together, Shannahan! We're outa' here!"

"Where we headed?" Mike asked, pulling his boots out from beneath the bunk.

"We're on a *need to know* basis tonight, troop, and right now you don't need to know. Just get your shirt on and meet me behind the supply room in the parking lot."

The men liked Tolliver, a young Louisiana boy just back from the conflict in Vietnam. His brash demeanor held firm during training, but he always found time to mingle with the troops in the bays at night. The vivid stories he told about the war intrigued the young troops, but he always gave a positive spin on the adversity that he had seen. Unlike the other sergeants in the company, Tolliver wore the CIB, Combat Infantry Badge, above his pocket. The large yellow patch with the horse head and black stripe that he wore on his right shoulder informed the uninitiated that he had fought in combat with the First Calvary Division. The men and the other sergeants respected the uncommon symbols of a true and tested soldier.

Mike laced up his boots and hurried out the back door and over to the parking lot. He saw Tolliver standing next to a blue Mustang, waving for him to get in. He opened the passenger door and squeezed into the front seat, suddenly aware that there were three other passengers packed in the rear. Tolliver started the car and slowly backed out of the gravel parking lot without turning on the lights. "You boys are in for a treat tonight," he claimed. "Just do what I tell you, and everything is gonna be just fine."

Mike turned and looked in the back, recognizing three of the four acting platoon sergeants uncomfortably packed like sardines in the rear of the Mustang. The dumbfounded looks on their faces told him that wherever they were headed, they didn't have a clue either.

"Take your armbands off and put 'em in the glove box," Tolliver ordered. "If we get stopped, just let me do the talkin'."

The Mustang turned onto the main road and headed toward the front gate of the post. Mike quickly surmised that whatever they were up to, it wasn't on the training schedule. "Sergeant, we don't have a pass to leave the post," he complained. "If we get caught, they're going to charge us all with being AWOL."

"Minor detail, Shannahan," Tolliver replied, a sheepish grin on his face. "Just let me handle the small shit."

Mike leaned back in his seat, quickly surveying the situation and looking for his options, given what he knew was becoming an untenable situation. A hint of alcohol entered his senses, and he slowly looked over at Tolliver to verify his suspicion. Within seconds, Tolliver reached under the seat, pulled out a pint of Jack Daniels, and took a long swig as they approached the guardhouse at the main gate. *We're all gonna end up in the stockade!* he thought, cringing as Tolliver slid the bottle back under the seat.

The dicey sergeant slowed briefly, waved two fingers at the MP, and drove past, down the main street into Leesville and then out into the dark Louisiana countryside, disappearing into the night. "Here, take a shot of this," Tolliver offered, tossing the half-empty bottle into the backseat.

"Where the hell we goin'?" demanded Syrett, the second platoon sergeant.

"Well, as I see it, you boys are entitled to a little poontang. Any objections?"

"Sergeant, if we get caught, it's gonna be 'Katy bar the door' for us, and you know it," Mike protested, using the expression well known in the South for the certainty of disaster striking. "We're not even supposed to be off the post in the first place, and in the second place, we're all in fatigues, and that's against regulations by itself!"

"I told you not to sweat the small shit. I'll take care of everything. Now just *shut the fuck up* and enjoy yourselves. We've got a long way to go before reveille in the morning."

Tolliver stepped on the gas, launching the Mustang into passing gear, loping along at breakneck speed between the towering pines of rural Louisiana. He turned up the radio, and before long, the boys accepted their fate and joined in, defiling every tune with an unharmonious interpretation of some of their favorite songs. Mike stared down the long, seemingly endless road, instinctively looking for the telltale reflection of untamed eyes in the headlights, finally content to gaze at the stars forming a sparkling trellis for their evening jaunt. Then, at its vast distance, he recognized his old friend Orion, perched brightly in his perpetual place in the heavens, ensuring Mike that everything would be all right.

Nearly two hours later, the crowded Mustang pulled off the main road and down a dusty gravel lane encased in majestic trees that darkened the evening sky. The road wound slowly through the countryside, finally exposing a lone, bright neon light at the end of the lane: *Welcome to Ville Platte.*

Tolliver pulled up next to several cars and turned off the engine. "Take off your fatigue shirts and unblouse your boots," he told them.

"You gotta be shittin'," Syrett complained.

"Just do what I tell you, and everything'll be hunky dory," the sergeant said, stepping out of the car.

Reluctantly, the boys complied, tucking their dog tags inside their undershirts as they followed Tolliver up the wooden stairs and into the dimly lit tavern. Mike immediately felt the scent of Shalimar rush to its sacred place in his heart. He searched the room, momentarily confused by the intoxicating concoction, quickly realizing that she wasn't here. Scantily clad women rose from the plush couches surrounding the room, greeting the strangers as they stepped up to the long split-rail bar.

"Hello, sweetie. I've been a-waitin' fow'a you all night, honey."

Mike drew back slowly, uneasy as the tall brunette pressed her incredibly soft breast against his bare arm. He felt the edge of the bar press deeply into his rib cage as he retreated, his pulse surging in the process. His mind quickly flashed back to the porch at Carl's, and the temptress's image emerged in all her glory. *My God, this could be her twin,* he mused.

"You're cute. What's your name, sweetie?" she asked, a provocative smile emanating from her full red lips.

"Mi… Mike," he answered, clearing the dryness in his throat. He quickly looked for reinforcements, and he was distraught when he saw the other boys being led away from the bar and over to the couches on the other side of the room. He was on his own.

"Didn't your mama tell you it's impolite not to offer a lady a drink?" she asked gently, stroking the back of his shaven neck with tender care.

"Well, yes, ma'am. What'll you have?" He fumbled to retrieve his sweat-stained wallet from his back pocket.

"Just a little bitty gin fizz will do just fine, honey. And please, just call me Rita."

He turned to the bartender and ordered her drink. "What'll *you* have, sonny?" asked the barkeep.

"I'll just have a Coke with some lime in it, if you don't mind. I'm driving," Mike lied, ignoring the dubious expression he received in return. He opened his wallet and stared at the assortment of fives and ones, careful to shield Rita from his life's worth, packed neatly behind his laundry tag.

"That'll be six bucks," the barkeep said, staring intently at Mike, who slid the exact amount across the bar. *God, this is an expensive place,* he thought, quickly counting the remaining twenty-three dollars left in his wallet.

He turned and handed Rita the drink, noticing that the slinky lavender lingerie she wore had conveniently exposed the essence of her right breast. His toes curled as his peripheral vision focused on her large, soft nipple, summoning a fitting response from his anxious loins. He was careful not to stare, trying to remind himself that no gentleman would take advantage of the situation. But he had to admit, these women were certainly the friendliest he had ever seen.

"Well, cutie, I guess you're here fow'a a date." She tickled his ear with the edge of the cold glass.

"Actually, ma'am, I don't have any idea why I'm here, but if you step any closer, I'm sure King and I would certainly come up with something," he said, referring to the expanding bulge in his trousers.

"Silly boy," she whispered, taking that final step. "Are you in the mood for a full date, or would you rather go with the half and half?" she asked coyly, batting her long lashes with sultry emphasis.

He hesitated, squinting his eyes while he tried to decipher her question. "Half a *what*?" he finally asked.

Rita withdrew her embrace, stepping back with a wicked grin on her face. "Now, don't tell me that you've never been to a joy house befow'a, sweetie."

Her smile sweetened, her soothing brown eyes ablaze with renewed desire. She moved closer again, taking his hand and placing it on her warm breast. "Now, don't you worry 'bout nothin', sweetie. I'll be *real* gentle, I promise you."

She squeezed his hand firmly, turned, and led him away from the bar and down a long hallway at the other end of the room. The red-faced trooper heard his friends laughing as he followed her into a perfumed room. A soft red radiance dimly illuminated the wide bed with satin-frilled pillowcases.

"You just make yourself comfortable, sweetie. I'll be with you in a minute." She pushed him gently toward the bed as she turned and stepped into the bathroom.

He sat there for a moment, stunned by the possibilities, intrigued with the opportunity, wondering if she was indeed going to *tear his ass up*, as Jim had put it. He still wondered what she meant by *half and half*, but at this point he decided that whichever half he got was going to be just fine with him.

His shirt was off in a second, the laces on his boots no match for his inspired fingers. His pants lay folded on the floor with his skivvies-clad manhood hidden snugly under the covers when the light went out in the bathroom. She emerged in silhouette, the shorty nightgown fully exposing her long, lovely legs as she drew near the bed. He longed for her body next to his, anxious to fill his lungs with the essence of her sweet ambiance, to absorb the soft, gentle texture of her skin.

"I see we're a little modest," she commented, sitting down at the edge of the bed. "That's nice."

She paused briefly, taking off her earrings and placing them on the table by the bed. Picking up a box of matches, she lit a scented candle. The flickering flame danced and swayed, then held firmly erect. Duly intrigued, Rita slid slowly under the cool satin covers.

* * *

CHAPTER TWELVE

T HREE LONG WEEKS HAD PASSED since the boys had completed their "mission," infiltrating morning traffic as they limped silently back to base. Mike often thought about Rita, but he kept his feelings sheltered, sequestering her deep within the confines of his pillow. It wasn't easy to accept that he had violated a pact that he had made to himself, but he realized the experience enlightened him to the true virtues of some "women of the evening." After all, it was only when he opened his wallet to pay for his laundry that he discovered she had left him with three dollars, the precise amount of his laundry bill. The balance she kept, a small bounty he was eager to pay for the lessons she revealed to him that steamy bayou night. Tolliver resumed his role as mentor to the men, never to even mention the impromptu escapade to the secluded Ville Platte. It was their secret, and the men understood why.

The vestiges of summer crept subtly into the green rolling hills surrounding the post, slowly toasting the fallen pine needles and hardening the moist clay like an unrelenting hearth. Seasoned men fell victim to the inexorable heat, succumbing to the soaring temperatures that plagued the mission at hand.

"You think this is bad? Just wait till you get 'across the pond.' You'll find out what hell on earth really means," Tolliver predicted.

With the final week of training upon them, the men began to focus more on the war. Mike took notice of the number of men reading newspapers and news magazines and talking about the units they hoped to join, and those they would rather not. The number of men gathering in the day room to watch the evening news grew steadily.

"The North Vietnamese Three hundred twenty-fourth Division crossed the DMZ today," the elderly anchorman reported, "encountering elements of a marine battalion around the village of Đông Hà. Initial reports indicated heavy casualties on both sides, and marine commanders have told us that the enemy is well equipped and that reinforcements will be needed to counter their advance. High-level sources in Saigon tell us that most of the Third Marine Division, some five thousand men, has headed north to engage the enemy."

"So much for Harry's prediction," Mike mumbled to himself, recalling his brother-in-law's boisterous claim the previous winter that the First Marine Division would have the war all wrapped up.

"In other news," the anchorman continued, "scores of college students in California burned their draft cards today, in protest of the government's effort to bolster the ranks of soldiers committed to the war effort in Vietnam."

"What the hell is their problem?" Mike inquired. "Don't they know that a lot of their fellow countrymen are getting their *asses* shot off for them? If *they* don't want to show up and do their duty, who gives a shit? I don't want them there anyway," he added, an element of passion accenting his voice. "Just shut up and get the hell outa' Dodge!"

"How do they get away with that?" another agitated trooper chimed in.

"'In the beginning of a change,'" intoned another voice, "'the patriot is a scarce man, and brave, and hated and scorned. When his cause succeeds, the timid join him, for then it costs nothing to be a patriot.'"

A sudden silence fell heavily over the room. The men stared at Private Jake Saunders, who was contentedly engaged in one of his countless novels, his legs loosely sprawled over the lone padded armchair. "Mark Twain," he casually remarked, apparently uninterested in joining the banter at hand.

"I read *Huck Finn* and *Tom Sawyer* in school," one of the men said, "and I don't remember him say'n *none* of that shit."

Several of the men chuckled, not noticing the orderly who stepped into the room and walked over to where Mike was sitting. "Here're your orders, Shannahan," the orderly said, tossing a large manila envelope into Mike's lap.

The men quickly looked at one another, and before Mike could open the large envelope, the room cleared, everyone heading for the bulletin board in front of the orderly room.

He took a deep breath and then focused on the lines following his name in bold print:

SPECIAL ORDERS NUMBER 152

Fol rsg dir. Asg to: 3151 Bn 4th Stu Bde Ft. Benning, Ga.

Sp Instr: EM for Airborne Training

Mike was assigned, in the "following reassignment directed," to Battalion 3151 in the Fourth Student Brigade, Fort Benning, Georgia, with special instructions as an enlisted man for Airborne training.

He felt the wind surging through his jump gear, eyes watering profusely as he peered out the aircraft's door, anxiously searching for the drop zone below. Brilliant turquoise tracers from the enemy guns streaked skyward in search of a target. He gritted his teeth, waiting for the jumpmaster's signal to enter the fight. Green light! He sprang out the door, into the fierce prop blast hurdling him back and down, his canopy deploying high above him when the familiar voice broke his fall.

"Hey, Shannahan! the excited trooper exclaimed. "I'm goin' to the First Cav!"

"That's great, Sam," Mike replied, stuffing the papers back into the envelope.

"Where's Tolliver? I've got to tell him the good news. He probably still knows some of the guys over there."

The men slowly returned to the day room, shaking hands, congratulating one another on their new assignments, assignments to actual combat units.

"Big Red One," McCarthy proudly reported.

"Fourth Division for me," his friend Collins said, smiling broadly with delight.

Mike noticed Saunders wander back to his favorite chair, picking up the worn novel as he slumped back down, sprawling his legs over the armrest as he continued his read. His blasé demeanor was intriguing, not a hint of emotion apparent in the news of his new assignment. Mike knew the draftee resented his call to arms, an untimely interruption of his premed studies at Texas A&M University, but he always performed well in training, never complaining or shirking his duties.

Mike respected Jake and was curious where the army was sending him next. "What'cha reading, Jake?" he inquired.

"Hemingway." Jake's eyes still focused on the novel.

"*The Sun Also Rises?*"

"*Farewell to Arms.*"

Mike stood there for a moment, hoping his silence would move Jake to engage him in conversation, but the tactic failed. "You don't pass out a hell of a lot of *free* information, do you, Jake?" he finally asked, a jovial tone accompanying his inquiry.

"Sorry, man." Jake closed the novel and sat up. "Just wanted to finish this chapter before I called my wife."

"Where they sending you?"

"Fort Benning."

"Hey, that's where I'm going! Maybe we could ride over together," Mike suggested.

"That'd be nice, but I've got to make a detour down to College Station to pick up Jenny."

Mike knew Jake was married, but he wondered why he would be taking his wife with him. Maybe he was going to be assigned as "permanent party" at the post—that is, permanently based at Fort Benning along with his family. Mike's curiosity was heightened. "What unit are you assigned to?"

"The orders say Fifth Student Brigade."

"Mine say Fourth Brigade... jump school."

"OCS," Jake reported his own assignment. "Guess we'll be neighbors."

The unexpected words stung Mike deeply. He now knew for sure he'd been passed over for the coveted assignment. "That's great, Jake," he replied. "You'll make a fine officer." He reached out and shook the draftee's hand with both of his, shielding his building disappointment as best he could.

He slowly walked toward his room and closed the door before he sat down on his bunk. His bruised ego consulted with his delicate mind, desperately searching for a positive outlook that he could deal with. He reached over and pulled the papers out of the envelope. As he read the orders again, his eyes frantically searched for *anything* that mentioned the Fifth Student Brigade. Nothing. Noticing that the following pages were not all copies of the original, he sorted through the rest of the paperwork, amused to read that he had been promoted to private first class and had been awarded the Expert Badge for the M60 machine gun. *Big deal,* he thought. *Who really gives a shit?*

After packing his gear in his duffel bag that evening, he made a reluctant call home to tell the family of his new assignment. He promised his mother that if he were able to get a weekend pass, he would be sure to catch a bus over to the coast for a visit. His father at first seemed indifferent, but when Mike said that another man in his company had received orders to Officer Candidate School, the Commander questioned him intently. Once again, Mike could sense that he had disappointed his father. But as that old familiar sensation emerged, he handled it with a new perspective.

"Here's the deal, Dad. I had a chance to get in. I gave it my best shot, and it didn't work out. I've dealt with it, so I guess if *you* need to deal with it, sir, then deal with it. Now, I *would* like to speak with your *wife* before I hang up."

With his new lone chevron sewn on his khaki sleeve, Mike boarded the ancient DC-3 for the flight to Atlanta. With the paper barf bag never out of arm's length during the tenuous flight, the bumpy ride reinforced his desire to learn how to parachute. As he strolled through the airport concourse, he witnessed the vast array of uniformed young men with overnight bags and manila envelopes, just another cornucopia of America's youth restlessly gathering at the various gates. He felt sympathy, not for their commitment but rather for the anxiety he knew they were experiencing.

The bus ride to Columbus led him through some of the most beautiful countryside he'd ever encountered. Bright red clay, captured by lush green grasslands, bordered with sprawling displays of the tallest trees he had ever seen. As usual, he painted his own perspective of the history of the region, watching in amazement as the legions of screaming Confederates surged over the distant hills, emerging through the white cannon haze. Large, tattered rebel battle flags flowed lazily in the warm Georgia breeze. Picket fences, plantation mansions, and rows of blooming white cotton perked his unrelenting zest for a nostalgic glimpse of the "Ol' South." *What a glorious land!* he thought. *God, I'm so glad I'm an American.*

Within hours, the bus finally left its shadowing of the winding Chattahoochee River and gave him his first view of the post he would call home for the next several months. *Welcome to Fort Benning, Home of the Infantry,* the large sign read.

"Finally…a *real* army post," he declared.

He retrieved his duffel bag from the luggage compartment and dragged it over to the cabstand across the street from the bus depot. "Fourth Student Brigade," he told the cab driver as he slid into the slick backseat of the old Checker cab.

He leaned forward, rolling the window down to draw in the fresh pine-scented air as it flowed through the musty cab. He noticed the manicured sidewalks full of men in uniform, most with the distinctive tall paratrooper boots, each moving with an obvious purpose, leaving him with the sensation of living in a present imbued with crested air. The cab slowed through the main area, pausing as men crossed the street in front of them.

These people are professionals, Mike thought, admiring the military manner the ranks greeted one another as they passed by. "Airborne, sir!" the enlisted seemed to say, rendering a crisp salute as they passed an officer. "All the way!" the officers replied, returning the salute. *This is more like it,* he felt, his pride growing with every salutation.

In the distance he saw what looked like a huge erector set, a massive menagerie of steel beams towering high above the barracks below. "What the heck are those things?" he asked the driver.

"Those, sonny, are the jump towers," the driver said. "They're two hundred and fifty feet tall, and you can see all the way to Alabama from the top."

"Are those new barracks the jump school?" Mike asked, referring to the tall, pink brick structures at the edge of the field.

"Nope. Those are new OCS barracks. They're killin' off those ninety-day wonders quicker than you can say 'Hồ Chí Minh.' Guess they gotta keep up with the demand."

"Sorry I asked," Mike said, staring longingly at the new barracks.

"You'll be staying up on the hill overlooking the airfield," the driver added. "It's only a coupla' miles from here."

"New barracks?"

"Nope. Well… they were when I was there. Let's see here, that musta' been back around the spring-a' '42. Ever heard of the 'Fight'n Five-oh-ninth Parachute Regiment,' sonny?"

"No sir, can't say as I have."

"Well, why should you? Hell, that was way back when JC was still just a corporal. But those were the days! Yessir! Met up with those *worthless*

French bastards at Youks-les-Bains. That's over in North Africa. Hell, you probably weren't even born yet," he added, looking at the boyish image in the mirror.

"Probably not."

"Didn't even use reserves in those days, sonny. No need to. They dropped us under five hundred feet, and if your main didn't deploy, you barely had time to stick your head between your legs to kiss your ass good-bye."

"How long were you in for?" Mike asked, staring at the driver's gruff wrinkled neck and the short white stubble of hair.

"Long enough to get my ass shot up. We jumped in twenty-five miles behind the Kraut lines at Avellino. That was in Italy," he said, looking over his shoulder. "Ended up reinforcing the beachhead at Anzio in '44. That's when I got it. Well, here we are, sonny. That'll be four bucks."

He gave the cabbie a five and stepped out in front of a small white orderly room. He stood there for a moment, briefly recalling everything he had gone through just to get here. Large replicas of Airborne patches and jump wings loomed everywhere, prominently displayed on the sides of the buildings and on colorful signs lining the streets. Looking down at his low quarters, he knew he still had some work to do. After all, he was still a *leg*, a derogatory term all paratroopers used to define anyone who was not a paratrooper. He picked up his duffel bag and struggled up the short flight of steps.

"Where the hell you think you're goin', leg?" the gruff voice demanded.

Mike turned around to see a short, squatty Negro first sergeant shuffling over to him. His severely bowed legs negated a normal gait, causing him to list from side to side as he maneuvered into shouting distance in front of him.

"Who the hell gave you permission to enter my orderly room, Private?" he demanded, the nub of a wet cigar molded in the corner of his mouth. Before Mike could respond, the sergeant issued his penance. "Get down and give me twenty-five. And when you're done, give me twenty-five more," he ordered, shuffling past Mike and up the stairs to the orderly room. "Goddamn legs," he muttered.

What crawled up his ass and died? Mike wondered, feeling the pain of the chalky white gravel embedding into his palms. *Was he talking about his legs or me?*

He quickly muscled his way through the first twenty-five, feeling the layers of polish crack and split on his shiny shoes as they strained under the pressure. He stood up, removing some small stones and rubbing his hands together hoping to get the blood flowing again.

"I said give me twenty-five more!" the sergeant yelled, stepping back out onto the porch with a clipboard in his hand.

Mike dropped, resuming his silent count as the sergeant thumbed through the papers he held.

"What's your name, trooper?"

"Shannahan, Michael B.," he gasped, working his way through the final five.

"Recover!"

Mike sprang to his feet, looking down at the new creases in the toes of his shoes, accented with the white chalky dust he wiped from his hands.

The sergeant sorted through the papers, in the process chomping down regularly on the cigar.

"What kind of name is that? German? Here it is... Shannahan, Fourth Platoon. I'm going to need a copy of your orders, Shannahan. Get your gear together and find a bunk in the Fourth Platoon barracks over there," he pointed across the street. "No one enters my orderly room without boots, troop. This is an *Airborne* orderly room. Now get outa' here before I do some squat jumps on your scrawny chest!"

"Yes, Sergeant!"

Mike grabbed his gear and jogged across the street, breaking a sweat as he struggled with his duffel bag. He stopped at the entrance, staring up at the large master parachutist jump wings hanging above the alcove. He dropped his bag, took off his scarred, crumpled shoes, and casually threw them in the trashcan before he scampered up the stairs.

* * *

CHAPTER THIRTEEN

"Attennn-shun!"

T HE OVERFLOWING BLEACHERS SPRANG TO life with scores of helmeted troopers setting into a firm brace. Mike felt the pressure of his chinstrap as he locked his heels, assuming his finest military posture. The sudden blare of military music filled the hangar, echoing off the suspended green cargo chutes, startling the throng of troopers amassed below. Just as swiftly, a Napoleonic figure with stark white hair made his way to the podium, his gleaming black paratrooper boots a tribute to the festive cadence of the march. Short, swift strides accented his tempo, like that of a maestro flaunting his sacred wand. His final step to the podium signaled an abrupt end to the pageantry and the beginning of his remarks.

"Airborne!!" he shouted.

"All the way, sir!!!" echoed the thunderous response.

"My name is Colonel Bill Weller, and I'm *damn* proud to be here with you *special* young men this morning."

"It's Wild Bill Weller," the sergeant next to Mike whispered.

"Who the hell is Wild Bill Weller?" he asked in response.

The sergeant's tepid glare left Mike feeling like a greenhorn. He could only shrug in ignorance.

"That's right," the colonel went on, "paratroopers are *special* people. Have been since we made that first drop in North Africa in World War Two. Since then, America's Airborne troopers have always answered the call to service. In Korea… and now in Vietnam. We are there to succeed when others do not. We are here to teach *you* the skills necessary to become a paratrooper. When you leave here, no one will ever *dare* call you a leg again."

He turned and spat, ceremoniously pulling his white handkerchief out of his pocket to wipe his mouth. His prepared bravado brought the men to their feet, laughing and applauding his patronizing parody.

"He's got three brass stars on his master wings," the sergeant snidely remarked above the laughter. "That about says it all."

"How the hell was I to know?" Mike replied, taking his seat. "I've been outa' town."

He sat intently watching the seasoned colonel inspire the troops by sharing a variety of historical distortions of comical proportion. With every anecdote, Mike relished the response of his fellow troopers—privates, corporals, sergeants, and captains, each being skillfully anointed into the brotherhood of the cloth. In this case, silk. It was a welcome baptism. He sighed deeply as a broad smile stretched across his cheeks, his heart warming each time the colonel paused and spat. He was finally where he longed to be, with the best, the bravest, bonding with his new brothers.

Festivities concluded, the inspired troops marched back up the hill from the airfield below, a new pride and *esprit* adding a snappy kick in their step. Mike's platoon formed up in front of the Forty-second Company billets, waiting for their "Black Hat" platoon sergeant to appear.

They didn't have long to wait. He emerged from behind the formation and strode defiantly to the front of the troops, where he paused to welcome them to his platoon.

"That son of a bitch looks like a coke machine with a head," a corporal muttered.

"I am *Blood* Brown," the huge sergeant began. "I *am* the meanest, most rompin', stompin' Airborne soldier there is. I hates my mama, I hates my papa, I hates my wife and children, but…I L o v e s the Airborne."

Mike stared at the long scar accenting his bulging biceps, flexed conspicuously with his massive hands poised on his thin waist. The bright morning sun reflected sharply off the shaved black head, reminding the trooper of the Khan's guard in *Ali Baba and the Forty Thieves*. The only things missing were the earring, curved saber, and plumed pants.

"And let me tell you maggots somethin' else," Blood Brown went on. "I use'ta-be a marine… and they are sissies compared to the Airborne. But most of all: I hate legs! Now all you leg scum get down and don't *ever* quit doing push-ups!"

The men dropped, pumping up and down, up and down, and within thirty minutes the final movement in the formation groaned painfully to a stop. They lay there totally exhausted, some too weak to even avoid the remnants of their breakfast deposited below them. If there was any question as to the rigors of jump training, Blood Brown had answered that with emphasis the first morning. *I'm glad we got that out of the way,* Mike thought. *That sausage didn't taste the same the second time around.*

Their toil in the next week strengthened their emerging bond: gut-wrenching runs, coupled with excruciating calisthenics and endless repetitive drills. Blood led the Black Hat instructors swarming among the weary, demanding that last painful push-up, that final distant mile. Reveille formations held with the last fading glimpse of the North Star. Working through the day in sweat-stained sawdust pits that clogged the evening shower drains. Swing land training, mock doors, parachute landing falls (PLFs), thirty-four-foot towers, push-ups, and runs. Pretenders fell by the wayside while the worthy steadily persevered. By the end of Ground Week, six men in his platoon had departed—one with heat stroke, one alleging torture, while the others just physically broke down.

That Friday evening, Mike sat on his bed dutifully counting the damp money in his wallet. He looked back down the bay, envying the men seated on their footlockers working on their boots, caressing their soiled spit-shine rags as though they were holy veils. "Thirty-three dollars and change," he concluded.

He reached for his garrison cap and scampered out the door. Within seconds he burst through the door of the Airborne PX and stopped abruptly in front of the stacks of boxes containing the coveted Corcoran Jump Boots. He grabbed the first pair of size 11 he found, tucked them under his arm, and headed to the checkout counter. Standing in line, he noticed a lieutenant thumbing through a magazine across the aisle. The officer appeared older than most of the first lieutenants he'd seen, but it was something else about the man that intrigued him. *That guy's strack,* he thought.

Mike continued his survey, noting the immaculate nature of the officer's jump boots, the crisp blouse in his tailored trousers, the rows and rows of colorful combat ribbons anointing his chest. Mike was careful not to attract his attention, looking away often yet still mesmerized by the warrior's presence. He quickly recognized the distinctive Purple Heart ribbon, nestled squarely in the midst of many others, too numerous and distant to be clearly discerned. Above the ribbons was the CIB, the shiny star in the middle indicating the lieutenant's second war. Mike sensed something unique about the man, and he stared more intently now, following the faint, scarred contours of his face, yet hesitating to dare look into his eyes.

"That'll be twenty-eight fifty," the clerk requested.

Mike reached into his wallet, and he dispensed all of his cash on the counter. Then he turned quickly, drawn back to the mysterious nature of the man. At that moment, the lieutenant's head turned sharply toward him, and clear, penetrating eyes focused hard on the young private. Transfixed by this expression, Mike stared through the challenge, then slipped deep into the man's soul. Torrid images of fear and despair were suddenly exposed, cloaked in lofty and pronounced feelings of confidence and compassion. This man had clearly been there, on the threshold of death itself. He'd faced the challenges, and he'd survived. Only the scars on his tempered soul retained the horror of his trials.

The rookie trooper had seen enough, and as the clerk tapped him on the shoulder, the lieutenant stepped toward him. "Did you get a *good* look at the elephant, troop?" he asked quietly.

Stunned, Mike slowly shook his head. "Yes, sir… I'm sorry, sir," he apologized for his impudence… and more.

The lieutenant stared back, gazing at the fresh young face holding those inquisitive and sensitive eyes. Then he smiled briefly and walked away. The dazed trooper reverently watched him depart. Then he noticed the man reaching behind his back to retrieve the rolled-up green beret he had neatly tucked under his belt.

"You're holding up the line, Private," the impatient clerk reminded him. Mike scooped up the change from the purchase, picked up the boots, tied the laces together, casually threw them over his shoulder, and wandered slowly out the door and back to the barracks. Walking down the aisle to his bunk, he seemed oblivious to the chatter and folly directed at his dull new boots. He tossed them casually under his bunk before he fell exhausted on his pillow. He quickly fixed his eyes on the maze of springs above him, his head swirling with concepts of terror. He rolled over on his side, drew his knees to his chest, and calmly drifted off to sleep.

By Monday, his encounter with the warrior had subsided into a deep new cavern in his soul, where it was carefully guarded by sentries solely devoted to his sanity. The assault on his physical being continued, allowing his mind to focus on the training while his alter ego carefully sealed the vault.

"Rig and run! Rig and run!" the Black Hats shouted, coaxing the students to speed up the rigging process. A dozen troopers scampered around the circular metal frame, attaching the silk canopy to the elevating apparatus. Mike stood anxiously by, adjusting the harness that would attach to the parachute the men were working on.

"You can see all the way 'cross the Chattahoochee ta Alabama," the next man in line said.

"Yeah, I heard," Mike coarsely replied.

The canopy rose above the plowed dirt field, taut steel cables and snap links clanked and clattered while he shuffled under the majestic umbrella. The Black Hat grabbed the dangling risers, snugly attaching them to the cape wells above Mike's shoulders. "Just remember to turn into the wind, Shannahan," he instructed.

"What wind?" Mike asked, watching the sergeant give the order to hoist.

The harness tightened around his groin, slowly lifting him up and into the air. Higher and higher he ascended, watching the men below turn into blurred shadows on the ground. Scanning the horizon, he watched the river winding lazily along its crooked path. *Must be Alabama over there. Big fuckin' deal. Guess now I've got somethin' to write home about.*

He looked over his shoulder toward the OCS compound, focusing on the company of powder blue helmets standing at attention in front of the barracks. He wondered if Saunders was down there, and if—

The sudden jolt startled him. The immediate descent directed sharp chills through his tense body. He gripped the risers tightly, desperately trying to remember what he was supposed to do next. *Watch the horizon. Knees together and slightly bent. Toes pointed down. What else? Oh yeah, where's the fuckin' wind?*

He only felt the air swirling around him, coming from every direction at the same time. Before he had time to turn in any direction, his boots plowed into the soft dirt, triggering his body to spin into a PLF just like he had practiced all week before.

"Recover!" the Black Hat yelled. "Rig and run! Get the next man up here!"

Mike pulled himself to his feet, unsnapped his risers, and jogged over to the next man waiting to slip on the harness. "Nothin' to it," he said with authority, popping his quick release. "Just remember to turn into the wind."

The men continued to practice their landing falls, suspended in agony in the swing land trainers next to the metal monsters. They ran continually, taking time out to work on their upper body strength with push-ups and pull-ups while waiting their turn to rehearse the mass exit techniques that would be put into use the following week. They were all ready for it to be over.

Blood made sure the days turned into drudgery, but the nights offered time for camaraderie. The canteen two blocks from the barracks provided just the respite the men needed.

"See those assholes over there, Shannahan?" a burly corporal asked.

"Yeah, those are those SEALs from Third Platoon," he replied, bobbing his head to the mellow soul music from the jukebox.

"They think they're all hot shit. Saw one of the Black Hats drop the short one yesterday for fifty, and the son of a bitch asked him, 'Which arm?'"

"Wise ass. Better not let Blood hear him say that."

"Heard they're gonna climb the towers tonight," he said, chugging the remnants of his beer. "Some of the Rangers bet 'em they couldn't do twenty-five pull-ups hangin' off the end of one of the spreaders."

"That's fuckin' stupid," Mike noted, shaking his head. "What's the damn point?"

"You know, my gun's bigger than yours. Anyway, a bunch of us are goin' down to watch. Wanna go?"

"Sure. Ain't seen a real messy suicide since back in Basic."

Before long, the animated navy SEALs concluded they were finally up to the task. Armed with a supplement of liquid courage, they led the entourage down off the Airborne Hill into the plowed fields below the towers. Meager sums of money changed hands rapidly, collected by those less ambitious spectators who were content to profit on the spectacle unfolding. Slowly, dark figures emerged below the structure, cautiously scaling the metal maintenance ladder to the top. Bright red aircraft beacons attached to the colossal structure flashed in the evening sky, sending an ominous warning to aircraft and intruders alike. The crowd below cringed as the first man pulled his way out to the end of the north arm, followed closely behind by the rest of his crew. They waited, occasionally shouting words of encouragement to the stationary figures above, who were clinging precariously to the slick metal frame.

"Those sombitches ain't got the sense God gave a pissant," the corporal said. "You couldn't get my happy ass up there in a million years."

The first figure swung below, generating a series of gasps from the astonished crowd. They watched him bob and weave, counting the pull-ups as he rapidly pumped them out. At twenty, they knew he was in trouble. He hung motionless, making no apparent effort to pull himself back up to the beam above him.

"He's gonna fuckin' fall," someone shouted.

"Help him! Somebody fuckin' help him!" the men yelled to the sailors on the tower.

"Use your belt! Wrap it around his wrist!" Mike shouted. "Hell, they probably can't even hear us."

He watched as the next man shimmied over to the dangling SEAL, grabbing his wrist while locking his legs around the metal strut. He pulled him up, reaching for his belt to secure a better grip.

"Don't let go now," Mike mumbled, emitting a long sigh of relief when the man finally swung his legs over the beam.

"Well, I've had just about all the excitement I can stand for one night," the corporal said, turning and heading back toward the hill.

Mike and the rest of the men followed, fully aware that they narrowly missed witnessing a senseless disaster. It was only the next morning when they realized that not everyone who went up had come down. The entire company watched in delight as the squad of Black Hats scaled out to retrieve the lone SEAL who apparently sobered up *after* he had reached the top.

"That'll teach them fuckin' squids," the corporal remarked. "Bet they don't talk their shit after this one."

In fitting tribute to his escapade, the humiliated but intact sailor was greeted by a chorus of army troopers, loudly defiling the navy hymn in deference to his aborted heroics. They cheered wildly and derisively as he took the final step down the ladder, trousers clearly soiled from the harrowing experience.

Mike felt a degree of sympathy for the young sailor, however, recalling his own public humiliation following a schoolyard fight. His buttocks still bore the memory of the brutal lashing he had suffered at the hands of Father Gerber. He watched the mortified sailor stumble through the plowed dirt, bare head tightly drawn down in shame. He had to pass in front of the formation of his tormentors, and as he neared the ranks of unsympathetic soldiers, a hush fell over the crowd. Mike saw his face, lips tightly clenched and drawn. He realized that despite his navy uniform, he was still one of *them*.

Instinctively, Mike began to clap, offering his lone approval in spite of the outcome. The corporal stared at him in amazement, then after seeing the expression on his face, shook his head in agreement and joined in the accolade. Within seconds, the clapping swept through the formation, followed by an escalating chant that pulled the sailor's shoulders back and drew his head erect.

"Airborne! Airborne! Airborne! AIRBORNE! AIRBORNE!!"

The sailor began waving his hand, then clasped them together in an acknowledgment of triumph. His fellow SEALs broke through the ranks, gathering him up on their shoulders, then in unison they responded to the shouts.

"All the way! All the way! ALL THE WAY!!!"

The corporal looked at Mike and patted him on the back. His broad, gleaming smile exemplified the solidarity they'd achieved. "Fuckin' A!" he shouted. "All the way!"

*　　*　　*

CHAPTER FOURTEEN

"Come to the edge."
"We can't, we are afraid."
"Come to the edge."
"We can't, we will fall."
"Come to the edge."
And they came. And he pushed them. And they flew.

MIKE READ THE VERSE, CLEVERLY posted above the door leaving the rigger's shed. He felt the impatient nudge from behind, prompting him out the door and into the marshaling area set up in front of the hangars. He took several steps out onto the tarmac and stopped, his eyes squinting as he pondered the parable. Turning around, he walked back toward the shed, through the hurried troops carrying their parachutes to the assembly area.

"Chicken out, Shannahan?" a troop from Second Platoon asked, laughing at his own snide comment.

"Naw, the rip cord on my reserve's stuck," he replied over his shoulder. "And I'm gonna get another one."

He took several steps before he heard that trooper scream in disgust. "Son of a *bitch!*"

He turned to see the sprawling white canopy dangling from the open reserve, loud shouts from the Black Hats accenting the malady. Laughing, he stepped back into the rigger's shed, turned, and read the lines again. He slowly nodded his head in approval. Smiling contentedly, he rejoined the rest of the troops, who were sitting on their parachutes with their reserves tucked securely in their laps.

"My name is Lieutenant Allen Kent," the tall bespectacled officer informed them. "You've got two choices this morning, men: Pay full attention to the following instructions, or leave the best part of your manhood on the drop zone across the Chattahoochee. The choice is yours."

The lanky lieutenant continued his briefing, recounting the jump commands, altitude, wind direction and velocity. He covered what to do in the event of a malfunction, a topic the troops had studied intently. Just when they thought they had already heard it all, the lieutenant calmly mentioned the procedure for a hung jumper. *Hung jumper? What the hell is a hung jumper?* Mike asked himself, totally unfamiliar with the term.

"Nobody said nothin' 'bout getting hung up outside that damn plane," a trooper next to him complained.

Soft murmurs quickly cascaded into a low rumble of protest, prompting the lieutenant to snap the easel with his wooden pointer. "At ease!" he shouted, restoring absolute silence to the fidgety group. "I say again: The procedure for a hung jumper will be that if you are conscious, check your reserve, place one or more hands over your helmet, and we will cut you loose from the aircraft. You will then deploy your reserve in the prescribed manner."

The men looked at one another, wondering why this hadn't been mentioned in their training. Before they could discuss it among themselves, the lieutenant added another step to the potential malfunction. "If you are unconscious, and we are unable to retrieve you back into the aircraft, every attempt will be made to secure you to the side of the aircraft. We will then foam the runway and land as soon as possible."

"Lieutenant," a brave voice bellowed. "Shouldn't we be taking notes?"

Mike turned to see Captain Lennox, his student platoon leader standing at the rear of the formation. Unlike the rest of the men, the captain already had his parachute on. He was standing with his arms folded, rocking back and forth on his boots, clearly annoyed. "You don't have to sugarcoat it, Lieutenant. Go ahead and give it to us straight. Why foam the runway? Afraid the sparks from the fillings in our teeth are going to catch the plane on fire?" The men burst out in laughter, grateful for the brief moment of levity before they faced that final step.

Within minutes, the order was given to saddle up, followed by the command to board the planes. The men struggled up the ladder to the ancient C-119s, still in service since the closing days of World War Two. Like waddling women on the verge of labor, they struggled with the cumbersome loads, awkwardly trying to sit down in the flimsy webbed seats. Their feet flailed out into the aisle, spread widely to distribute the weight.

It'll never get up in time, Mike thought, watching the white smoke billow from the engines of the old Flying Boxcar.

With the doors finally closed, the aircraft taxied away from the hangars and out onto the runway, where it stopped briefly to rev up the engines for takeoff. He stared up and down the aisle, watching the faces of the men he'd trained with, searching for that one expression that would tell him that he was not alone in his trepidation.

The man next to him poked him on the leg and asked, "Are we supposed to yell 'Geronimo' or somethin' when we go out the door?"

"Either that or something else," Mike quickly replied, feeling the accelerating vibration of the plane reach a high-pitched crescendo. The engines revved to their peak, then the plane quickly lurched forward and raced down the runway, vibrating, creaking, swaying from side to side as it gathered speed to lift off with its *special* cargo.

Get on up! Get on up! Get on up! Let's boogaloo, he hummed, pleading for the pilots to rotate and silence the clatter. The relic finally eased into the air and banked sharply to the right, gaining altitude for its brief trip to Alabama. The jumpmaster stood up and opened the side doors, exposing a breathtaking view of the Chattahoochee and the post below.

Mike drew in the wave of cool, fuel-scented air, etching a new and exciting pathway to the domain where he harbored his worth. *Prop blast. So that's what it smells like.*

He inhaled deeply, allowing the invigorating potion to swell within him, bolstering his courage and intensifying his resolve. *God, I love this,* he thought, smiling broadly as he watched the jumpmaster lean out the door.

The wind soared through the jumpmaster's spread legs, aviator goggles protecting his eyes as he searched the fields below. He turned and stepped to the center of the plane. "Get reaaddddyyy!" he yelled, stomping his right boot hard on the floorboard, pointing down the aisle like an umpire calling a strike.

The men responded in unison, stomping their boots, symbolically acknowledging his order.

"Stand uuuppp!" he ordered, using his arms to direct the action.

"Hook uuuuppp!"

"Check static lines!"

"Check equipment!"

"Sound off for equipment check!"

The rear man in the stick checked the static lines on the man in front of him, then slapped him on the butt and yelled, "OK"! The process continued until the first man pointed at the jumpmaster, relaying the fact that all of them were ready. They stood there, silently contemplating their fate, clutching their static lines, every eye held firm on the red light by the door.

"Stand in the door!" the jumpmaster demanded, placing the first jumper in the door, the wind wildly whipping through the open fuselage.

"Go-o-o-o!!!" He shoved the first man out, and the rest followed behind like a cascading stack of dominoes.

Mike hit the door hard, launching himself out and away from the aircraft. A solid block of hot air slammed him sideways, turning his tense body to the left as he watched the toes of his boots rotate skyward, puffy white clouds dancing above them.

"One thousand, two thousand, three—"

The opening shock drew his harness tight between his legs. The loud cracking sound of rubber snapping, nylon unwrapping, and silk canopy slapping the wind motivated his pegged pucker factor, his adrenaline response, to soar. Clutching his reserve with both hands, he kept his chin tucked tightly on his chest as the parachute deployed above him. He felt himself swinging from side to side, and as he lifted his head up and grabbed onto the risers, he saw the beautiful green canopy floating gracefully above.

Relieved, Mike finally exhaled, noting the eerie silence that surrounded him. He looked around at the sky full of parachutes floating leisurely about him. *What an awesome sight,* he thought.

"Geronimo-o-o-o!!"

Mike looked above to his left to see his friend Rat pumping his scrawny legs wildly as if he were riding an airborne bike. His outburst triggered an onslaught of cheers and hollers that filled the sanctum void with boyish screams of glee and sheer delight. The descending new paratroops yelled at one another as they slipped left, then right, turning in circles as they floated slowly downward to the drop zone below.

"Will the jumper with the malfunction please deploy his reserve?" the loudspeaker blared.

Mike quickly checked his canopy again, looking for a blown panel or torn shroud line. Turning to find the jumper with the malfunction, he watched the scores of fluffy white reserves blossoming in the bright Alabama sky. *Those guys are in deep shit now,* he thought, wondering how many push-ups *that* mortal sin equated to.

"Eyes on the horizon. Knees bent, toes down, and, oh yeah, turn into the wind." He spotted the wind arrow on the ground, grabbed his front and rear risers, and pulled down as hard as he could. The canopy began to rotate, slowing his lateral drift as he prepared to land. He waited for the shock, then realized that he was *standing* on the ground, the light-green canopy fluttering down on top of him. He quickly rolled through his PLF, a mandatory maneuver required to eliminate the showboaters. He certainly didn't want to suffer the consequence of 250 push-ups. Jumping to his feet, he popped his quick release and stepped out of his harness. He figure-eighted his suspension lines, rolled up the canopy, and stuffed it in his bag.

"Man, if they're all like this, I could really get into this shit in a hurry! It ain't sex, but damn near!"

He threw the heavy bag over his head, adrenaline still rushing through his tense body as he headed for the nearest truck, anxious to share his adventure with the rest of his platoon. The men loaded their chutes into one truck, then climbed into canvas-covered deuce-and-a-halfs, the two-and-a-half-ton trucks that were waiting to take them back to Lawson Army Airfield.

"Ya know, ah always wunted ta be wun-a dem-thair parry-a-troopers," the corporal said with a bad hillbilly accent, "an' now ah *arrr* wun!"

"Well, congratulations, Jethro. You've just won an all-expense-paid trip to beautiful and majestic Southeast Asia," another trooper joked. "Problem is, it's one way, and you have to bring your own coon dog and ammo."

The war, Mike reflected, sighing. It was still looming out there in the distant horizon like a phantom banshee, enveloped in so many indiscernible guises that the young trooper was struggling with the reality of it all. He quickly brushed it aside, asking the group who the jumper was that had the malfunction.

"Some guy in First Platoon had a Mae West," Rat told him, using the term that describes a canopy distortion resembling a gigantic brassiere. "I saw him spinnin' around tryin' to get his risers untwisted before he hit. The damn reserve didn't even slow him down. Got hung up in his main."

"That had'a hurt."

The jump had resulted in injuries to some of the men in Forty-second Company, but nothing more serious than twisted ankles and a couple of broken legs. The other men took that news in stride, unconcerned that they might fall victim to the same fate. With four more jumps to go, they pressed on with their training.

And their homework: Blood instructed them to memorize several Airborne drinking songs to prepare them for their initiation into the brotherhood. "A big part of bein' a paratrooper is rememberin' those who went before," he told them. "Always remember: Their honor is in our keepin'. An' don't you never forget that. Ya never know when ya might have ta whip ass or whip out a tune ta liven' up the place. Kinda' adds a little pizzazz to what otherwise might be a damn dull affair."

Mike jumped down off the tailgate of the truck, his tired body still tingling from the vibration from the 119. He noticed the crowd of men standing in front of the bulletin board outside the orderly room.

"The line assignments are posted," the corporal told him.

He quickened his pace, surprised that they would post the assignments before the final jump tomorrow. The men who were not already assigned to Airborne units searched for their names under the units that were listed. The 82nd Airborne Division, the 101st, the 173rd Airborne Brigade— those three topped the list. Mike waited his turn and then found his name at the top of the list for the 101st.

The Screamin' Eagles. He stared at the unit patch stapled above the list: black background with a white eagle's head featured within the shieldlike frame. He knew the history of the unit, most famous for their heroic stand in Bastogne, during the Battle of the Bulge. Their commander, when ordered by the Germans to surrender or die, simply responded with a single word: *Nuts!* One of the battle groups of the 101st combat division, the 327th Infantry, was also famous for protecting in 1957 the "Little Rock Nine," the black students who integrated Central High School in Little Rock, Arkansas, much to the dismay of Governor Orval Faubus.

"Hey, Mike! Where ya goin'?"

He turned to see his friend Rat walking toward him. "Hundred and first," he said proudly.

"You mean the one-oh-worst, don'cha? The ol' pukin' buzzards."

"Your ass! Where you headed?"

"Eighty-second, the All-American Division."

"Yeah, *Almost* airborne," Mike chided back. "You'll feel right at home there, ol' buddy."

"Well, I'm headed for the PX to get my patch sewn on before everybody else gets there. Wanna go?"

"My fatigues stink. But who gives a shit? Let's go."

The boys broke into a trot, over to the seamstress shop behind the PX. Within minutes, they had their new patches sewn on their left shoulders, making them the newest members of those proud units. Intent on celebrating, they stopped off at the canteen and, along with the rest of the company, commenced to break in their new patches and status as members of an actual Airborne combat division.

The revelry continued well into the night, the jukebox blasting a variety of songs while the men flaunted their testosterone in arm wrestling and drinking matches. The beer flowed freely, along with their sudden intense loyalty to their new units. Mike shook every hand he could find that bore the eagle's head on the left shoulder. Strangers were immediately transformed into brothers, new warriors of the cult, destined to lock and load together. And together, they would set out to encounter the notorious Mr. Charles, "party of the second part," the terms they used to denote their Communist enemy.

Mike slipped out the back door, out to the edge of the airfield beyond the hill overlooking Lawson Army Airfield. He stood gazing up into the stars for his old friend Orion when he heard the jukebox beckon his attention.

"If you want something to play with,/
Go and find yourself a toyyyy,/
'Cause, baby, my time is too expensive,/

And I'm not a little boy, no, no..."

The words nurtured by the smooth nectar of the voice, effortlessly coupled with the intrigue orchestrated beneath the starry night, captured his weary imagination. He listened, envisioning himself as that young man in the song, in total harmony with the message it conveyed.

"If you are serious, look, girl, look, girl, look girl,/
Then don't play with my heart./
It makes me furious, hmm./
...
Tell it like it is./
Don't be ashamed, let your conscience be your guide./
...
You know life is too short, lord,/
...here today/
...gone tomorrow."

Barbara slipped immediately back into his mind. He regretted that he lacked the artistic talent to serenade her with such a charismatic melody to draw her attention. He listened intently until the words finally faded, overtaken by the loud cajoling of the men inside. He stepped back into the fray, intent on finding out the artist and the name of the song he had just adopted as his own, intrigued by the fact that someone else shared the torment he endured.

"Ooohhh shit! It's Blood!" Rat yelled across the long table, nodding toward the door.

Mike turned to see the behemoth tormentor standing at the door with his hands on his hips. The smoky room fell silent. Only the jukebox dared to challenge his entrance. The men stared, wondering why he was attired in his khaki uniform and what he was doing at the canteen in the first place.

"We thought we'd stop by and have a drink with you cowboys," he loudly informed them, followed through the door by the other three Black Hat platoon sergeants. "Isn't anybody gonna buy us a drink?"

Men scrambled to the bar, pushing and shoving one another to accommodate his request. He took off his cap and tucked it in his belt, then stepped up to the bar, where he was quickly accorded adequate space and a cold beer. He held it out in tribute, then bellowed, "Airborne!!"

"All the way!!" the men shouted.

Blood raised the beer and quickly chugged the contents, then smashed the empty can into his forehead, smiling broadly as the men applauded his maudlin feat.

"I think the son of a bitch is shitfaced," Rat said quietly.

"Well, then, just don't do anything to piss him off," Mike replied.

"Piss *him* off? He was born pissed off! He probably gets up in the morning an' slams his head up against the wall just to make sure he stays pissed off all day!"

They watched him suck another beer down. This time he opted to just squash the container on the bar, his sledgehammer fist making short work of the metal can. "Where's the Fourth Platoon?" he demanded, looking around the crowded room.

Rat tried to hide his diminutive frame behind Mike, slinking down as Blood's keen eyes sifted the room. With a broad smile on his face, the massive sergeant made his way to the long picnic tables where his men were gathered, grabbing a full pitcher of beer off a table along the way.

"You boys bin practicin' your homework tonight?" he asked, taking a long swig of beer from the pitcher. He surveyed the unresponsive group, impatiently waiting for an answer. No one dared to reply, knowing full well what the consequence would be.

"Where's the 'short stick'?" Blood asked, looking intently down the tables for his favorite target.

The men slowly leaned back, exposing the cringing young trooper hiding at the end of the table. Rat peered sheepishly toward him, an apprehensive smile begging for pity emerging on his freckled face.

"Front and center, troop!" Blood commanded.

Rat quickly grabbed his beer, sloshing the remainder down as he struggled to get up from the table. Mike helped him up, a sudden surge of disdain flowing through him. He objected to Blood's common practice of picking on his stunted friend.

"Yes, Sergeant!" Rat yelled, his squeaky voice trembling.

"We would all like to hear my favorite song tonight, trooper. And you're going to lead it," Blood informed his prey. "Somebody DX that squawk box!" He reached out and swept the beer cans off the picnic table, leaned over and picked Rat up like a toy doll, and deposited him squarely in the middle. "Well, we're waitin'," he informed him, handing the empty pitcher to a troop to refill.

Rat scanned the crowd nervously, sheepishly staring back at Mike for encouragement. The room erupted in a prolonged series of catcalls and cheers. Mike could only shrug his shoulders and nod for his friend to proceed.

The scrawny paratrooper nervously cleared his throat. Then, staring up at the ceiling, he began his mournful lament.

"Beautiful streamer, open for me,/

Blue skies above me and no canopy..."

"No! Not that one, bozo!" Blood yelled, clearly agitated at Rat's choice. "I want to hear 'Blood on the Risers'!!!"

"But 'Beautiful Streamer' is the only one I know, Sergeant," Rat confessed.

"Un-ass my drop zone, you pansy!" he yelled, grabbing Rat by the front of his shirt and lifting him off the table.

With one long stride, Blood vaulted himself up onto the table, bringing with him the boisterous approval of the crowd of troopers, who were now standing and applauding wildly. The other Black Hats egged him on, clapping their hands and moving to the center of the room. "Show 'em how it's done, Blood!" one of them yelled.

Blood slammed his boot forcefully on the table, catapulting spewing cans of beer into the air. He leaned forward as he pointed both hands toward his frenzied audience. "Get reaaddddyyy!" he yelled.

Every man in the club slammed his boot to the floor, silencing their cheers as they awaited his next command. Blood pointed at the three Black Hats, cuing them to start the show.

"Zoom... Zoom... Zoom, Zoom, Zoom," the Black Hat chorus began, encouraging the rest to join in.

"Zoom... Zoom... Zoom, Zoom, Zoom."

Blood waved his hand, conducting the vibrant tempo for the background of *his* song. When he was content that the crowd was on cue, his hefty baritone voice filled the crowded room:

"He was just a rookie trooper, and he surely shook with fright/

As he checked all his equipment and made sure his pack was tight./
He had to sit and listen to those awful engines roar.../
He Ain't Gonna Jump No More!"
"'Is everybody happy?' cried the sergeant, looking up,/
Our hero feebly answered 'yes,' and then they stood him up./
He leaped right out into the blast, his static line unhooked.../
He Ain't Gonna Jump No More!"

The men followed the Black Hats' lead, providing the background and chorus to the lively ballad:

"Gory, Gory, What a Helluva Way to Die,/
Gory, Gory, What a Helluva Way to Die,/
Gory, Gory, What a Helluva Way to Die,/
And He Ain't Gonna Jump No More!"

Blood led the troopers through all the verses of the song, teasing them with his own version of several of the refrains. Then, in a slow, morbid tempo, the rest of the Black Hats joined him in the last stanza:

"There was blood upon the risers, there were brains upon the chute,/
Intestines were a-danglin' from his paratrooper boots./
They picked him up still in his chute and poured him from his boots,/
And He Ain't Gonna Jump No More!"

Foam gushed over the tops of the swaying beer cans, held aloft in tribute to the songmaster, his inspired rendition complete. Blood raised his fist in response, pumping it up and down as the men cheered him on. A shallow chant emerged, rapidly gaining volume as the men repeated the words:

"stand in the door...
Stand in the door...
Stand In the Door...
STAND IN THE DOOR!!!"

Blood granted their wish, slamming his boot on the edge of the table, slinging his long arms out to the side, huge palms grasping for the outside of the imaginary door.

In unison, the men shouted, "Go!!" Blood vaulted into the air, snapping into a tight body position, and when he hit the floor, the crowd began the count: "One thousand...
Two thousand...

Three thousand…

Four thousand!"

Mike laughed heartily, hugging Rat and rubbing the matted bristle of hair on his head. The camaraderie continued into the night, with toasts and boasts permeating the smoke-filled room, tempered only with the poignant tributes to those who had gone before.

* * *

CHAPTER FIFTEEN

"THEY PROBABLY DO THIS SHIT on purpose," Mike yelled at Rat. "Just to make sure we're ready to bail out of this motherfucker!"

"I think I need to go call Ralph," Rat replied, looking pale and queasy as the plane rambled down the runway.

"That's what you get for getting shitfaced last night, dumb-ass! I wonder if these old clunkers came from the factory with these square wheels!"

Mike hummed his regular tune, noting several holes in the fuselage where rivets once resided. *They probably used this old shitbird in Korea,* he imagined, staring at the worn metal floor, visualizing a row of brown jump boots from an era gone by.

Pinned to his seat, he felt the sensation of the plane lifting off, shooting up into the sky, and banking sharply to line up its run on Fryar Field Drop Zone, across the Chattahoochee.

The jumpmaster opened the doors, then reached down and pulled up the first man in the inboard and outboard sticks. Each of them in turn, pulled up the next man, straining to get them on their feet with the extra rucksack and equipment bag strapped to their rigging. With his jump commands complete, the jumpmaster pointed to both men, ordering them to stand in the door. They waddled forward, heavily burdened with the extra equipment they were required to carry on their final jump. The light turned green, the inboard jumper's legs barely cleared the door when the prop blast hurled him back into the fuselage, banging his helmet as he shot past. Mike awkwardly shuffled toward the door, struggling to stay upright as the men behind him pushed and shoved. As he went, he winced at the loud bash and bangs of men and equipment recoiling off the fuselage.

With visions of being dragged behind the plane, Mike dove forcefully through the door, out and away from the airborne magnet. The hot blast spun his feet over his head, leaving him in a headlong dive, his main deploying between his legs above him. The opening shock snapped his body back through the risers, and as the heavy nylon straps whizzed by his head, it tore off his helmet, chinstrap and all.

Stunned, he found himself sitting in the saddle, his bare head pinned firmly to his chest, unable to breathe with the risers twisted tightly behind his aching neck. He watched his helmet plummet downward, spinning and tumbling until it disappeared in a small wisp of dirt. He struggled frantically, kicking his legs trying to untangle the risers, realizing quickly he could breathe only through his nose. He pulled with all his might, desperately trying to separate the death grip the risers held on him. He pulled, straining with every ounce of muscle in his body, until finally, he started to rotate, with the fertile ground still rushing up to meet him.

In the corner of his eye he saw a large green canopy slipping beneath him. He tried to yell at the jumper, but his jaw held firmly pegged to his chest. He continued to rotate, praying the novice jumper below would see him in time to slip away. *He's gonna steal my fuckin' air,* he realized, still struggling with the risers.

The other jumper's firm silk canopy brushed gently on the soles of Mike's boots. He picked his legs up, hoping the jumper would slide by. His heart sank as he felt the risers go limp, the canopy above him fluttering and losing lift. He pulled the risers off his neck while the terrified trooper below him screamed for Mike to get off his chute.

O, my God, I am heartily sorry for having offended Thee—

With no time to finish his act of contrition, he watched his own canopy collapsing above him, fluttering like a fragile silk scarf cascading to the ground. Long suspension lines floated like swirling green spaghetti around him, tangling in his web gear, dangling from his head. He pulled the risers out in front of him, trying to regain his balance, trying to climb off the other canopy. His boots sank into the green marshmallow shell, sucking him down each time he tried to stand. Frustrated, he reached down and pulled the quick release on his equipment bag, then threw it to the edge of the canopy, the lowering strap uncoiling like an airborne anchor line. The weight of the equipment began to pull him to the canopy's edge, too, and he finally tumbled off, dragging his collapsed parachute behind him. He fell well below the terrified jumper, his expanding canopy gasping for air. When he realized there was no time, he reached for the rip cord on his reserve. The canopy suddenly filled, oscillating him wildly beneath the olive death shroud. He looked for the horizon but saw blue sky instead. He held his breath, then slammed hard into the ground, snapping his unprotected head unmercifully into the warm Alabama soil. The impact snatched the last remnants of air he held in his chest, and the pain rapidly gave way to total darkness.

Mike's inert body edged slowly along the ground, nudged ever so gently by the half-inflated chute, seemingly searching for a breeze to sustain it. The fickle wind quickly obliged, filling the invigorated canopy as his body bounced over the clumps of grass and brazen knolls. The movement stirred his senses. Cool, moist dirt surged down his collar, reviving the stunned trooper enough to reach up and grab onto the risers. Bright white stars clouded his vision while his bruised and confused mind desperately searched for a solution to his dilemma. Letting go of the risers, he crossed his arms, squeezing firmly on the cape wells attached to the canopy. They snapped loose, liberating him from the precarious joy ride across the sprawling drop zone.

He rolled over on his stomach, hands digging deep into the damp, bracing soil, every cell in his body searching for oxygen. He lay there in torment, his lungs deflated like the rustling silk beside him, his whole body aching, unable to move.

He saw boots close to him, warm hands removing the globs of dirt from the back of his neck, finally checking his pulse. They rolled him back over, pulled the safety pin off his quick release, and popped his harness. He felt them removing the lowering lines off his lift webbing, and as they pulled his limp arms out of the harness, he rolled back over and dug his hands back into the soil.

"You OK, troop?"

He couldn't answer. A low, guttural moan was all he could muster from the swelling pain in his chest. In defiance of his agony, though, he flipped his thumb up from beneath the dirt covering his embedded palms.

"I think he just got the wind knocked out of him, sir," a voice reported.

"Well, just don't try to move him until Major Simpson gets here."

Finally, a few shallow breaths of air slipped into his painful chest. He coughed several times, gasping as the foul mixture of dirt and air filled his lungs. He relaxed his grip on mother earth, spitting and coughing as he rolled back over.

"Take easy, troop," the medic said. "We're not in any hurry here."

Mike took a deep, cleansing breath, then another. "So this is what they mean by *crash and burn*," he tried to joke, his voice still raspy and coarse from the pain in his chest. "Did somebody put me out?"

The medic smiled. "You'll be OK. Don't see any messy bones stickin' out anywhere they're not supposed to be."

He heard a jeep pull up behind the small crowd of troopers, and as he was brushing the dirt out of the small divot of hair on his head, a familiar voice asked, "Are you all right, son?"

He looked up to see the white eagle on the officer's collar and immediately tried to get on his feet. He swayed, then fell, clumsily trying to salute before he hit the ground. "Airborne, sir!" he said, trying to get back up.

"Whoa there, troop," the colonel ordered, placing his hand on his shoulder, preventing him from standing.

He turned to the drop zone safety officer and issued his order. "Lieutenant Kent, I don't want this man moved until Major Simpson has checked him out."

"I'm fine, sir," Mike protested. "I guess I just had the wind knocked out of me for a while. I kinda' hit like a ton of bricks," he was embarrassed to say.

"I saw what happened, son, and you're damn lucky to be alive. Now, you just stay put until my medical officer has checked you out. You're not authorized to rearrange any body parts on my DZ here today, troop. Copy?"

"Roger that, sir."

"Just remember this, son. Pain is only temporary, pride is forever. Sergeant Major, hand me a set of those wings," he ordered.

Colonel Weller bent down and pinned the shiny silver wings above Mike's soiled pocket. "That was quick thinking up there, Private. I haven't seen that one before, but I guess there's no end to Yankee ingenuity."

"Thank you, sir," Mike replied proudly, his intermittent mind stressing to comprehend the colonel's remarks.

The medical officer determined that, at most, he had suffered a severe concussion along with bruised ribs and ego. He put him on light duty and ordered him back to the company area for rest. The comfortable ride in the medical jeep, as well as his shiny new status, ensured that the event wasn't a total disaster after all.

The warm shower eased the tension in his neck, and after stowing his wet tongs in his wall locker, he gingerly lay down on his bunk to reflect. He was somewhere between sliding off the intruding canopy and reaching for his rip cord when the orderly entered the bay.

"PFC Shannahan, report to the orderly room on the double. The first sergeant is waitin' for your ass" he reported with a broad grin. "And judging by the things he was sayin' 'bout your momma, you in deep shit, troop!"

News travels fast, Mike thought, opening his wall locker for a fresh set of fatigues.

As he bent over to tie his boots, a sudden nebula of faint white stars floated into view. He leaned back on his bunk, slowly shaking his head and blinking his eyes. He sat there for a moment, then got up and hurried over to the orderly room across the street.

First Sergeant Copeland stood impatiently atop the steps of the orderly room, braced for the encounter. Mike slowed to a walk, in no hurry to engage the wrath of the feisty bowlegged sergeant.

"Get your scrawny ass over here, troop!" he yelled, his short stogie planted firmly in his mouth. "You know what all this is about, Shannahan?"

"Yes, First Sergeant," he admitted.

"Get down and give me twenty!" he ordered, pulling the wet plug out of his mouth, spitting the remnants close to Mike's outstretched hands. "And count 'em out!"

"Just who you know in Washington, DC?" the sergeant demanded, leaning down and shouting in his ear.

"No one," Mike replied, breathing heavily between his count.

"On your feet!" The sergeant moved close to Mike's face, looking up into his eyes, the rancid odor of stale tobacco prefacing his every word. "What the hell do you mean, *no one*? I just got a call from the Department of the Army less than an hour ago about you, Shannahan. An' you just told me you knew what this was all about!"

Mike staggered back. His bruised mind tried in vain to make sense of the sergeant's ranting, the push-ups resurrecting the stars from the black hole in his brain. He felt nauseous, on the verge of collapse.

"Sergeant, I'm telling you I don't know *anybody* at the Department of the Army."

"Are you lyin' to me, troop? 'Cause if you are, I'm gonna kick your shiny white ass back to the fuckin' Neanderthal days if you fuck with me, troop! Get down and give me twenty-five more!"

Mike's head pounded with every stroke as he painfully pushed out the final five. He tried to stand but fell backward onto the sidewalk, his head spinning from the constant beat of his heart.

Copeland reached down and grabbed Mike by the collar, pulling him to his feet as the young trooper struggled to remain erect. The sergeant then grabbed Mike by both arms, ripped off his chevrons, and threw them on the ground. "You won't be needing these where you're going," he said. "Inside," he ordered. "I'm going to get to the bottom of this."

Mike painfully followed Copeland up the steps, pausing at the top to regain his balance and breath. He stood there for a moment, staring down at the series of threads where his hard-earned stripe used to be. Stepping inside, he watched the sergeant thumbing through some papers on his desk.

"You apply for OCS?"

"Yes, Sergeant."

"You want to be an officer, Shannahan?"

"I did, Sergeant," he said while clutching the desk with both hands.

"None of my friends are officers, Shannahan. And I don't like the DA callin' my orderly room fuckin' up my paperwork!"

"Sergeant," Mike replied slowly. "I *enlisted* Airborne. I didn't *apply* for OCS. I was selected to go before the board back in Basic six months ago. Yesterday, I got my orders for the Hundred-and-first just like everyone else," he explained. "I have no idea what this is all about. I thought I was in trouble for makin' a mess on the DZ today."

"*Troop,* DA doesn't just call up a training outfit looking for somebody who was *supposed* to be in OCS," he replied snidely. "Did you whine and cry to your congressman or somethin'?"

"I don't even know who my congressman is, First Sergeant. But if you are saying that you have orders for me for OCS, I feel it is only appropriate for you to cut the bullshit and just say so!"

Copeland bit down hard on the stogie, his right eye twitching erratically as it squinted closed. He stared long and hard at the young trooper leaning over his desk.

"Get your grimy paws off my desk, troop! Lock those heels when you are addressing me! I was jumpin' outa' airplanes while you were still jumpin' outa' high chairs! I got *boots* older than you are, troop!"

"Well then, you probably oughta throw them away, First Sergeant."

Copeland slammed his fist violently on the desk. Mike snapped back up, drawing his arms in as he stood at attention.

Copeland watched the fire swell in the young trooper's eyes. Those eyes seemed distant, possibly on the verge of confrontation, the veteran sergeant thought. He rolled the wet stogie around in his mouth, gauging the young man's demeanor and the candor of his response.

Finally, he relented. "Report to Building Three, Main Post," he told Mike, standing as he handed him the papers. "Ask for Mrs. Kelly in the Officer Procurement Section."

As Mike reached out to take the orders, the small stars in his mind formed a bright nebula of light. Sergeant Copeland watched in amazement as the young paratrooper's eyes rolled back in his head. He swayed left, then right, then fell hard in front of his desk, lying unconscious on the floor below.

Copeland walked slowly out from behind his desk. Placing his hands on his hips, he simply shook his head. "Pussy."

*   *   *

CHAPTER SIXTEEN

A Year Later, Somewhere in Central Europe

T HE SNOW-CRESTED TIPS OF THE mountain range emerged in the midnight darkness, their majestic splendor accented by the dim glow of the starlit night. Captain Pollifrone checked the altimeter, looked over to his copilot, and nodded his head. He carefully verified his vector, reached down, and slowly began to reduce their airspeed, listening intently in his headset as his copilot alerted the loadmaster. "Ten minutes out. Let's get this bird ready for the chicks to fly the coop."

"That's a *big* roger. Tailgate commiin' down." The delighted air force loadmaster activated the controls, and whirring hydraulics slowly lowered the massive tailgate on the C-130 Hercules.

With his thumb pointing up, he smiled at the twelve dark faces insipidly staring back. He walked over to the first man, who was seated alertly beneath a pile of olive green equipment, reached down, and helped pull him to his feet. "Ten minutes out, Sergeant!" he said loudly, his flight suit rippling as the rush of frigid air swirled through the open tailgate.

The tall, heavily laden team sergeant turned to his men. Signaling with his hands, he ordered them to stand up. He cautiously shuffled over to the large bundle in front of the tailgate, checking the taut rigging before he and the loadmaster pushed it to the edge of the wide, open platform. The lanky loadmaster hooked up the static line while the sergeant reached over and turned on the small amber light attached atop the canvas bundle.

He turned abruptly to inspect his men, the dim, amber cabin light shadowing his distinctive Native American features. He attentively checked the tie-downs on their weapons, the lowering lines on their rucksacks, and most importantly, the static lines on their backpacks. Satisfied they were ready to proceed, he stood back and silently ordered his men to hook up. The jump commands flowed flawlessly, a silent sequence they had all mastered in their vast repertoire of skills.

"Three minutes!" the loadmaster informed him.

The sergeant turned to the first man in the stick, whose firm features were awkwardly distorted by the streaky mélange of war paint, only his blue eyes evident in his blackened face. The sergeant grabbed the man's brawny arm, then drew him close and offered him some advice. "There's a little bitty creek down there, Captain. Try to land on either side of it this time, sir," he requested.

"Very funny, Val."

The team sergeant patted him on the helmet, then turned to help the loadmaster push the bundle closer to the edge. Through the open ramp, the men gazed attentively at the jagged white peaks looming menacingly above the massive gray tail, providing a stark contrast to the dark, hidden valley below. Within seconds, the green light flashed on, and the bundle was launched off the ramp, the small drogue chute deploying above the dim, blinking light. The men followed closely behind, trailing the airborne marker into the blue-dark starlit night.

Val checked his canopy, and as he pulled down on his risers, he slipped quickly to the right, dumping some air to catch up with the vague, blinking light. He counted eleven full canopies floating below him, each maneuvering to line up on the bundle drifting into the dark meadow below. Reaching below his reserve, he pulled his quick release, dropping his rucksack fifteen feet below him. As he watched the horizon disappear behind the towering pines, he hit the ground, rolled through his landing, and quickly recovered to collapse the canopy. Dark shadows hurried along the drop zone, each one headed for the blinking light at the edge of the open field.

Every man mastered his unique function, setting up a perimeter while Val turned off the telltale strobe. He quickly broke down the bundle, with the team retrieving their own equipment before he signaled them into the tree line. Setting up another perimeter, he checked to ensure the drop zone was secure.

"Jacques, where's the lieutenant?" Val whispered to the blond sergeant.

"He's over there with Sarconowitz, strappin' the generator seat to his ruck," the team medic replied. "Don't worry, I got my eye on him."

"Let's get this gear under cover and get movin' before the locals get wise to us."

They consolidated their equipment, pulling a large camouflage net over their parachutes and jump gear. With armfuls of fallen pine needles, they covered the pile, blending the cache to match the terrain beneath the trees.

"We've got fourteen clicks to go before sunrise, Top," the captain whispered. "Get them together, and let's move out to the first rally point."

The men moved quickly inside the tree line, out of the valley, and into the foothills above. They slipped into the darkness of the mountain forest, the starlight smothered by the impenetrable pine awning. For hours they traversed upward, through the towering trees and along the treacherous ridgelines that marked the upslope edge of the forest. With ancient logging trails as their guide, they skirted the sleeping villages below, ever mindful of the objective they must reach before sunrise.

"Have Ryker string up an antenna on that ridge over there," Captain Clay instructed the team sergeant. "We need to get our sitrep back to the SFOB. Send the XO up here to shack up the message."

"Roger that, sir."

Within minutes, the long wire antenna hung between two trees, adjacent to the direction of the send. Specialist-five Nelson, the junior commo man on the team, helped lift the thirty-pound generator off the top of the XO's rucksack, gingerly lowering the cylindrical power source to the ground. He quickly attached the leads, grimacing while he cranked the device up to speed. He smiled, thankful that the duty of jumping and carrying the monstrosity was left to the most junior man of all on the team, the lowly XO.

"Copy this message to the C-Team, and shack it up for Ryker to send," Clay told his young executive officer.

The XO pulled the codebook out of the large pocket in his trousers and began to copy. "Insertion complete... Negative contact... Mission continues... One-zero sends." He worked through the maze of letters in his codebook, printing a series of block letters for the senior commo man to send back to base.

With his work complete, the young lieutenant handed the paper to Sergeant Ryker, who quickly tapped out a series of *V*'s in the Morse code sender he'd attached to his thigh. Spec-five Nelson cranked furiously, loading the wire with enough energy to send the message in the blind. Within ten minutes, the team had sent their report, recovered their equipment, and were back on the trail to their objective. They moved with rehearsed precision, silently negotiating any obstacle they found in their way. Hours passed before their target finally came into view.

Captain Clay peered over the large, moss-encrusted boulder, scanning the quaint lakeside village nestled tightly between the sloping meadow and the frigid mountain lake. Smooth billows of lazy smoke filtered into the early-morning haze, partially obscuring the view of the massive dam below. Val tapped the captain on the shoulder, pointing out several weather-beaten gun emplacements and bunkers protecting the obvious approaches to the sprawling structure by air. He continued to survey his target and then, with his assessment complete, deployed the team to set up their surveillance.

Rucksacks slowly disappeared into the misty twilight, blending in with the smoky haze and gruff terrain, each cleverly assimilating with the landscape well above the target area. With the advent of dawn upon them, the men lay concealed, in position to strike at a moment's notice. The command element observed the traffic and movement in the village, as well as the activity on and around the dam. The men assigned to execute the strike prepared their demolition charges and time fuses, rechecking their loads and detonators.

The hours passed as planned, with no alterations to the op order necessary to fulfill their mission. Finally, the sun steadily edged down over the still and tranquil lake, drawing with it a veil of chill, crisp air. With its last rays caressing the silver peaks above, the men anxiously reassembled at the final rally point.

"Show time, gentlemen," the captain told them. "If we're compromised, this is rally point Zulu. You're all familiar with the others back down the trail." He looked at his two demolition specialists and smiled. "Do your thing, fellas."

Sarkie and Dodson stripped off their fatigues, exposing black wetsuits they'd donned for the occasion. The lieutenant followed suit, stowing his boots and fatigues in his rucksack, slinging the long, coiled strands of det cord and time fuses around his neck. He followed them down the steep incline, moving cautiously toward the tree line below.

"Hey, Lieutenant," Jacques called after him in a strong, hushed voice. "Don't drink the water. Fish fuck in it."

The XO looked back, shaking his head as he caught up with the other men. They carefully worked their way to the edge of the lake, thankful for the dark, rummaging clouds dipping low to meet the steamy mist floating up from the mysterious lake. Like monstrous salamanders, the trio slithered into the chilly water, silently towing their tenuous cargo toward the distant, silhouetted dam. Their planned route took them out into the depths of the lake, where they would then turn toward the most distant placement and from there work their way back along the dam toward the shoreline. The icy water seeped through the folds in their hoods, the constant trickle just enough to cause them to shiver. As they reached the end of the first leg of their journey, the inevitable finally occurred.

Sarkie grabbed Dodson by the fin, pulling hard. "I'm crampun' up, Fred," he whispered. "Can't zeem to get any zirculation goin' in my legs. I'm no gonna make it."

"You've got to," Dodson told him. "We're only about four hundred meters from the dam. Suck it up."

Sarkie stopped, reached down, and began aggressively massaging his leg. "Grab my load, Dodson!" Sarkie's head submerged as he continued to struggle with his leg.

The lieutenant watched the commotion, swimming up next to the pair to investigate. "What's going on?" he whispered.

"He's cramping up bad, sir. Don't think he can go any further."

"Can you make it back, Sarkie?" the lieutenant inquired.

"Vass the alternative, sir?" he groaned through his heavy Slavic accent.

"Well, remember what God asked Noah: 'How long can you tread water?'"

Sarkie dipped his head back into the icy water, wrestling with the muscles in his left leg. He struggled harder to loosen up the cramp, circles of small waves churning around him. He came up, gasped for air, and then coughed loudly as the cold water splashed in his open mouth.

A light on the dam lit up the darkness, searching the water around them for the unusual noise. The trio quickly submerged, holding their breath as the searchlights traversed the lake. They surfaced slowly, realizing that they were still too far out for anyone on the dam to see them.

"Sound really carries out here," the lieutenant whispered. "Dodson, you swim back with him. I'll go ahead and place the charges."

"You don't know *just* where to place them, Lieutenant," he protested.

"Center span. I helped you measure out the length of the det cord, so I guess that's about as far apart as I'm gonna be able to place them. We calculated fourteen feet below the waterline, and I'm carrying the cork line for that."

"It's my responsibility to place them, sir."

"Give me the loads, Sergeant. I can swim circles around you old farts anyway."

"You got it, Lieutenant," Dodson replied, reluctantly passing the lead lines to the breaching charges. "We'll leave the key under the doormat." He grabbed Sarkie by the nap of his wetsuit and headed back to shore, leaving the young lieutenant to complete the mission.

As soon as the two swimmers faded in the distance, Mike resumed his slow and deliberate swim toward the mammoth structure, trailing the semi-buoyant charges behind him. He felt the murmur of the busy turbines vibrating in the water, growing louder and more intense with every stroke. He watched the guards atop the huge span of rock and concrete, who were concentrating their attention to either side of the abutments. The rib supports of the center span came into view, their protruding beams angling down toward the water, shielding the view of the guards at either end of the colossal structure.

As long as they stay where they are, this will be a piece of cake, he thought, only his sharp eyes and the top of his head protruding above the still water.

He took several large breaths and then slipped silently below. The long fins accelerated him through the dark, wet void, his outstretched hand warding off any unseen obstacle in his murky path. The high-pitched volume of the generator stators amplified with his approach, guiding him closer and closer to his target. The sudden light change in the hue of darkness told him he had finally reached his goal. He slowed his stroke, then felt the slimy, moss-infested wall of the dam.

Surfacing slowly, he quickly gathered the satchel charges. His numbing fingers ached as he released the cork depth finder, quietly taking several deep breaths before sinking down into the icy depths along the wall. He attached the first charge, anchored with a suction device, then traversed along the wall trailing the linking span of det cord.

Mike repeated the process three more times before he finally surfaced, gasping for air amid the masking rumble of the noisy turbines. He waited for a few minutes, mustering his strength, allowing his pounding lungs to resaturate with precious air. With the charges in place, he pulled out a green plastic bag containing three small M80 devices, pulled the rings on the split-tailed time fuses, checked his watch, and submerged. With his calling card afloat, the lieutenant sprinted away from the wall, kicking steadily through the dark, sullen sea, angling his retreat to the distant shore beyond.

Val watched two figures emerge tentatively from the water. He quickly lifted his binoculars, scanning the shoreline and beyond for the third. "We could have a problem here, Captain," he told the team leader. "Only count two swimmers."

"Get the team ready to move," Captain Clay advised him. "We may have been compromised."

Val followed his orders, consolidating the team for a rapid exfiltration. He watched carefully as the two dark figures emerged from the tree line, moving deliberately up the steep slope. Exhausted, they slumped down against the incline, breathing heavily as the captain questioned them.

"Where's the XO?" he asked.

"He's still out there," Dodson replied, still trying to catch his breath.

"Did you see those lights on the dam?" Val inquired.

"Yeah, Sarkie got a damn charley horse, and I guess they heard him gaggin'.'"

"Well, what happened to the lieutenant?"

"He took the charges and swam on to the dam."

"And you let him?" Val asked incredulously.

"I didn't *let* him do anything, Top. I wasn't going to argue with him in two hundred feet of water in the middle of the night! Anyway, he gave me an order, and I carried it out. Who's the officer here, anyway?"

"He'll be all right," Jacques added.

"He don't know shit," Sergeant Allen remarked with authority. The burly intel sergeant sat down on his rucksack and folded his huge arms in disgust. "I didn't hump all this way for that shavetail to fuck everything up," he objected. "You should have told him to go back with Sarkie. He don't know jack 'bout blowin' a dam," he said, scolding Dodson as he pulled out his Randall and began honing the razor-sharp blade on his leather scabbard. "He couldn't blow out a candle on his birthday cake. Probably can't even blow his nose—"

"That's enough of that, Joe," Val insisted.

"Get your gear ready to move," the captain ordered. "We'll give him five more minutes."

Jacques stared down at the lieutenant's overloaded rucksack, The ominous generator and stand lay unattended beside it. "Who's gonna hump the generator?" he inquired apprehensively.

"Nelson's the next junior man," Allen informed him. "Guess you're the lucky man, Jimmy," he said, still brooding as he stood and slung his weapon over his shoulder.

"There's some movement in the tree line, Top," Sergeant Ryker whispered.

The tense team turned their attention to the trees below, watching intently as the shadowy figure scampered up to their position. He bent over, numb hands planted firmly on his knees while he panted, gradually catching his breath.

Captain Clay went over to him, taking a knee as he questioned his exec. "How'd you do, Mike?"

He gave a thumbs-up sign, then stood up, walked over to his ruck, and sat down.

"I'm sure glad to see *you*," Nelson informed him.

"Thanks," he replied, looking down at the luminous hands on his watch. "Anytime now," he told them all, looking back down the mountain toward the dam.

The captain smiled. "Ryker, get that antenna strung. Harper, you help him. Nelson, set up the generator."

An abrupt flash lit up the mirrored lake, followed closely by three distinct booming reports that echoed through the silent foothills and beyond. Long, straight rays of light searched the empty lake around the dam as men scurried along the top edge, searching in vain for the phantom perpetrators.

"Copy this message, Shannahan," the captain told him.

Mike pulled the codebook out of his rucksack, his hands still trembling as he searched for his pen in his rolled-up fatigue jacket.

"Mission accomplished... Target destroyed... One-zero sends."

The men laughed and teased Nelson as he cranked the heavy generator. They were lighting up cigarettes and joking with each other while they waited for the message to be sent.

"There's supposed to be a real kick-ass *Gasthaus* down there," Jacques told them. "Bet there's some real big-titted *Fräuleins* down there, too," he said, smiling from ear to ear, his blue eyes hidden in the slits below his blond brow.

"We're two hours ahead of schedule," the captain told them. "Let's saddle up and get off this damn mountain. We'll huddle up on the main road into town."

Their "Operational Readiness Test" war-game mission complete, the team casually stumbled down the mountainside, laughing and cutting up as they assembled on the road below. Since the trucks to take them back to their base in Bad Tölz would not be arriving for another two hours, Captain Clay relented to their pleas and allowed them to reconnoiter at the local *Gasthaus*. The men leisurely strolled down the road, with their rucksacks and weapons, wetsuits and mountain boots, topped off with their coveted headgear: the Green Beret.

Captain Clay and his XO hung back, allowing the men their privacy as they hurried ahead.

"You should have come back with Sarkie, Mike," the captain chastised. "It doesn't sit well with the men when you try to show them up."

"Show them up? Hell, Denny, I was confronted with a *situation* out there, and based on the assets I had available, I made a decision. I swam competitively for over ten years. Workouts were two miles a day, by the way. If anybody was going to make that swim alone, tuggin' that gear, it was me."

"You still should have considered—"

"I'm not done," Mike interrupted. "At that point, when Sarkie coughed, the mission was already compromised. As the XO of the team, I felt that *I* was the most disposable asset. If I were exposed and captured, your two demo men could rejoin the team and continue the mission."

"I just want you to be *sensitive* to your role on my team," the captain explained, replacing his patrol cap with his beret.

"Well, I *am* sensitive! So far, my *role* has been to learn how to say 'nooky' and 'Can you spring for a pack of Luckies?' without an accent in Czech, jump and hump that goddamn generator, lose *all* my money in the knife-throwing contests, and have that overgrown ape medic of yours continually grab my ass and kiss me in the ear!"

"That's just his way of letting you know he's glad to see you," Denny added, chuckling at his young exec's candor.

"Well, the feeling's *not* mutual."

Denny laughed again, putting his arm around his new friend and offering his congratulations. "Good job," he said, patting him on the back.

"Thanks. I needed that. I think I'm getting that warm, fuzzy feeling already."

"Just remember, a lot of these guys started their careers in those god-awful mountains of Korea, and the rest of them, like Sarkie, were fighting Hitler in their own backyards. You can learn a lot from them if you watch and listen."

"I intend to. Humpin' the generator is one thing, but all this other shit they make up about being 'the XO's job' is gonna stop."

"It'll only stop when you make it stop," the captain informed him. "It's all up to you. They'll fuck with you till you howl at the moon if you let them. Respecting the rank is one thing, but respecting the man wearing that rank is the *only* thing."

"Guess that's why you're the captain, and I'm just the XO," Mike reasoned.

"These are some pretty special men. Proud to be the army's *very* best. They're not just going to respect you because you're a lieutenant and a graduate of the Special Forces officers course. You're gonna have to do a lot better than that, Mike. You're gonna have to earn it the hard way."

"So they think I fucked up tonight?" he asked, a slight resignation in his voice.

"That's not what I said. We accomplished the mission tonight, but if you *had* fucked it up, they'd run you off in a Minnesota minute. Just show them that you want to learn and are capable of making sound decisions, and they will go to the wall with you in a heartbeat. Don't ever hide behind your rank."

"What rank? The only thing lower on the chain of command on an A-Team is the goddamn road guard! I've been crammin' *years* of experience into the last six months, and it's really hard to catch up with those guys."

"They know that," Denny confided to him. "You've only been on the team for little over a month. You're not gonna out-hump them, out-jump them, outsmart them, or outdrink them. And you will *never* out-experience them. But don't *ever* get caught up in just following them. Trails are easy to follow. Get out there and blaze your own path. Take what you learn from them, and couple it with your own special talents you bring to the team. Move beyond intimidation. They expect you to *lead*. Do it."

Mike nodded his head, assimilating the guidance his new mentor had provided him, and quickly turned it into a challenge he would gladly accept. He adjusted the heavy load on his back, and as the young lieutenant marched down the narrow road with his captain, he knew the generator would be the lightest load he would carry tonight. And forevermore.

* * *

CHAPTER SEVENTEEN

THE BRIGHT MORNING STARS FLICKERED high above the Brauneck, the last in the chain of mountains comprising the regal Bavarian Alps. Well below the range's snow-crested peaks, a heavy morning mist sprinkled a faint vapor of dew on the fragrant edelweiss. The gentle mountain breeze wandered aimlessly throughout the highland meadow, garnering the fresh bouquet from the elusive plant blooming below the rugged fall line. A lone downdraft nudged it lazily down the slope, finally bestowing the sweet perfume upon the young man seated next to the tall, open window. Gratified, he peered pensively out into the benevolent darkness, watching the shadowy figures walking slowly toward the quadrangle for morning formation.

"That vill be aul fur today, klass," the portly matron informed them. "Tomorrow ve vill learn how to ask fur und receive information."

Mike looked at his watch. Six-twenty, he had time to get a cup of coffee before formation. He hurried out the door, across the gravel parade ground, and down into the cellar of the old three-story building. He walked into the team room, where Master Sergeant Valencia immediately greeted him in Czech, smiling broadly when he finished his salutation. Mike reached into his breast pocket and pulled out a spiral pad.

"What are you doing, Lieutenant?" he inquired.

"Writin' that shit down, Top," he said as he scribbled on the notepad. "I got part of it, but I'm going to make it a point to figure out just what you guys have been sayin' to me, talking all that gibberish. Better not have anything to do with my mother."

Val flashed his ever-present smile and took another sip of the steaming coffee before he set it down on the large round table. "Three minutes to roll call," he said, looking at the large Rolex on his wrist. "Wouldn't be late if I were you. Jack D eats second lieutenants for breakfast."

The image of the Group sergeant major floated through his mind. He looked at the coffee cauldron, then at his watch. Without hesitation, he turned and followed Val back up the stairs and onto the parade ground, where the mass of troopers were assembling by company. He took his place next to Captain Clay, and as the murmur of private conversations died down, the short, diminutive sergeant major called the men of the Tenth Special Forces Group to attention.

"Preeessseeennntttt aahhmms!"

The three line companies of Green Berets snapped their salute to the Stars and Stripes as it slowly edged its way to the top of the flagpole, spurred on by the echoing call of the lone bugler. The sergeant major called for a report, which informed the Group commander that all were present and accounted for. A series of announcements were made, and then the men were instructed to remove their shirts and prepare for the morning run.

Five miles and a series of shin splints later, the men gathered in the team room for the day's training activities. "We're going to start off this morning with Jacques's block of instruction on how to properly administer an IV," Val informed them. "At ten hundred hours, Sarkie will take over and give us a two-hour block on the proper placement of shape charges and the physics behind it."

Mike felt the weight of intruding eyes, and he looked across the table to meet Jacques's smiling glare. The imposing medic grinned, his eyes expanded in accented glee as he pointed to his forearm, with his finger mimicking a needle. The XO smirked, shaking his head as Val continued the schedule.

"After chow, Sergeant First Class Ryker will spend the next two hours instructing us on the implementation and use of the new 'Burst Device' for sending rapid encoded messages using CW." The team members all nodded their heads, anxious for any new innovation that would simplify the never-ending tasks they were asked to perform.

"When I'm satisfied that we all have benefited sufficiently from Sergeant Ryker's expertise, I'm going to split the team for this afternoon's PT."

The groans and moans prefaced Val's directive that half the team would participate in a ten-mile road run down to the village of Fleck along the Isar River. The other half would have the privilege of hiking the barren ski trails up to the "Crow's Nest" atop the Brauneck and back.

"I'm gonna check your rucks to make sure you're carryin' at least a hundred pounds. No exceptions, *Sergeant Lamont*," he informed them, staring directly at Jacques.

"Ahwww, come on, Top. My air mattress weighs at *least* a hundred pounds!"

The men laughed at Jacques's most recent antic, discovered only when Sergeant First Class Allen casually inserted his trusty, razor-sharp Randall into the medic's overstuffed rucksack. With the men in a good mood, Val helped Jacques set up the IV pole, hanging a bag of saline solution with various tubing and spreading out hypodermic needles on the table in front of them. The tall medic's demeanor changed abruptly as he began eloquently instructing the team on the various solutions available for intravenous delivery, insertion sites, sterile technique, and common pitfalls in locating a suitable vein for transfer. The obvious passion for his profession held the men's attention, along with the expectation that they would have to implement the techniques sometime in the near future.

"The next block of instruction requires that I demonstrate the proper technique for administering the blood supplement albumin," he told them. "Lieutenant, would you mind helping me out by rolling up your sleeve?"

As Jacques pushed the IV pole over to where he was sitting, Mike looked over at Denny. The captain ignored him, however, turning his head to whisper to Val as the rest of the men made room for the instructor. Gritting his teeth, the XO rolled up his sleeve and put his forearm out on the table. Jacques sat down next to him, snapping a long, wide rubber band he would use as a tourniquet.

"The first step is to secure the extremity, restricting the return flow of blood and creating a reservoir that discloses the location of the blood vessel," he began, wrapping the rubber strip around Mike's arm and cutting off the circulation immediately. "You can use a bootlace, reed, cravat, strip of palm—anything that will cut off the blood supply," he added, grabbing a long, thick needle from the table. "The larger the gauge of needle, the more rapid the supply transfer will occur. In a battlefield situation, time will be of the essence."

Mike cringed, watching Jacques screw the needle onto the glass plunger. The medic grabbed his arm, extending it outright and tapping for a vein in the crook of his elbow. "As you can see," the medic went on, "the needle has a beveled point. You want to insert the needle with the edge of the bevel against the skin. Like so."

Jacques *slowly* inserted the needle under Mike's skin, stopping to ask if everybody could see.

"Weren't you supposed to prep the site with alcohol before you did that?" Mike asked, perturbed at the deliberate slow pace.

"Oh yeah, I forgot," Jacques admitted, withdrawing the needle and laying it on the table. "This is not practical in a combat situation, but since the LT apparently has a phobia against little, tiny, germy thingies, we'll go ahead and make him feel better and apply a little alcohol."

Their eyes met while Jacques anointed his skin with the alcohol. The medic winked, his broad smile beaming as he continued his class.

"I say again: Insert the beveled edge close to the skin like so... Hmmm... Can't seem to find the vein. Let me try another spot."

"Lamont!"

"Sometimes you might have to try several different donor sites, depending on the size of the veins. No... That's not gonna work. Ahhh, here we go."

Mike's fist turned white as the medic continually stuck him with the large, imposing needle. Beads of sweat gathered on his temples as he endured the repetitive abuse. Mike stared at Denny, whose expansive smile indicated that he was enjoying this as much as the rest of the team.

With Jacques lining up for another excursion into his arm, Mike had finally had enough. He grabbed the syringe out of the medic's hand and stood up. "Jacques, if we were in a combat situation, I'd already be dead! How'd you pass dog lab anyway? Workin' on stuffed animals?"

The men laughed, amused at the lieutenant's outburst and Jacques's surprised expression.

"This ain't brain surgery here," Mike complained, sitting back down and looking at the red drops of blood seeping up from his bruised arm.

He took off the band, wrapped it around his other arm, and tightened the rubber cord with his teeth.

"After you've secured the tourniquet, the first step is to *prep* the site," he began, swabbing the cotton ball in a circular motion. Your patient may be unconscious, so if need be, grab his wrist and further constrict the veins between the tourniquet and the donor site."

The men sat up, watching the lieutenant tapping his own arm for a suitable vein.

"Once you've located a substantial vein, insert the needle at an angle that will engage the vein and travel along the same axis."

He slid the needle into his arm, lifting it up were everyone could see.

"Once you feel that you have achieved insertion, draw back on the syringe to verify this. You should see some blood appear in the vial. If not, you are not properly engaged, and you need to reinsert the needle."

He pulled back on the syringe, drawing a quantity of his blood into the clear vial. He quickly unscrewed the needle from the syringe, reached over, and attached the IV tube from the saline solution.

"At this point you will engage the proper solution for transfer, enabling a slight flow so that there are no air bubbles in the tubing. Then tape the delivery needle down to the patient's arm to ensure that the needle stays engaged."

He reached over for the tape, applied a figure-eight fold around the needle, and then released the flow valve, enabling the solution to drip into his veins.

"Any questions?"

Denny smiled.

The men of Operational Detachment A-1 completed their daily cross-training schedule, returned to their quarters, and changed into their field gear, complete with hundred-pound rucksacks and web harness. The split-team headed in opposite directions, with the captain taking half of the team down the winding road from the *Kaserne* to the river while the lieutenant marched up toward the imposing mountain trail beyond the steep meadow.

He set the pace, hiking vigorously up the nearly vertical path and into the shaded tree line above. The team pressed onward and upward, through the fragrant forest and into the boulder-strewn heights beyond. An hour passed, then two, before a voice from below halted the agonizing climb. "Hey, Lieutenant! How 'bout a break!" McQuerry complained. "Got to see a man about a dog!"

The rest of the team moved off the trail, anticipating the lieutenant to grant the junior weapons man's request.

"What's her name?" Jacques inquired, slumping down against a tree, pulling his arms out of the harness.

"Fuck you, Lamont!"

"All right, let's take ten," the lieutenant relented, slinging his ruck to the ground.

Mike walked off the trail and over to the edge of the cliff, gazing down at Prinz Heinrich *Kaserne*, Hitler's old SS officers' quarters, marveling at the vast beauty unfolding before him. Lush green meadows trimmed by the winding cascade of water flowing swiftly through the rugged and rocky Isar. Looking for the other half of the team below, he followed the river with his eyes as it disappeared into the fold of mountain ridges and distant trees. He sensed the conflict of nature emerge, and he wondered why men preparing for war could not find solace enough to prevent it when blessed with this vision of God's majesty.

"Where'd you learn how to do that, Lieutenant?"

Mike turned to see Jacques standing behind him. "Do what?"

"Were you premed in school?"

"Yeah," he replied, realizing what Jacques was asking. "Pre-*medevac*. They taught us that in OCS. Seems as though the life expectancy of a second lieutenant in combat had been calculated by some think tank, and they thought it was a good idea for us to learn how to take care of ourselves. Some things just *stick* with you, no pun intended."

"Well, the men wanted to know if you wanted in on the contest."

"Naw, I think I'll sit this one out. You guys tore me up last time, and I didn't even have enough left to get a Coke at the club."

Jacques flashed his patented grin and then rejoined the small group honing their knives, tossing sums of currency into the beret sitting atop the large moss-rimmed trunk. The lieutenant leaned against the crusted tree, admiring the skill and competitive nature of the men. Polished silver blades flashed through the fresh green backdrop, splintering pieces of bark as they slammed home into their target. He watched intuitively, inspired to continue his daily practice routine in the basement of "the Q," the term short for "BOQ," or bachelor officer quarters.

He noticed Sergeant Allen sitting alone against his ruck, patiently shaping a block of wood with his Randall, oblivious to the good-natured fun going on around him. The older sergeant intrigued the young officer, and he remained keenly aware of his antagonistic attitude toward him, a manner bordering on outright hostility. Mike was also aware that Allen had arrived a month before him, returning from the Fifth Group in Vietnam. Mike wondered about the circumstances leading up to his terrible wounds, purple scars that grotesquely accented the obvious void in his side. He wouldn't ask, feeling his idle curiosity only tainted the magnitude and honor of the solemn event. He slowly wandered over to him, sitting down and resting his forearms on his knees.

"I never asked you where you were over there," he inquired.

"It's better that way," Allen replied, without missing a stroke. "Couldn't tell you anyway."

"Classified?"

"That's right."

Mike nodded his head, understanding the constraints some of the men had on them. "Pretty bad?"

"Bad enough. No disrespect, but why don't you go over and get your war stories from some of the other guys, Lieutenant? I'm fresh out."

"I've heard enough war stories in the last year to start my own war, Sergeant Allen. They all start with 'And this ain't no shit.' It's a pretty big place over there, and I was just curious what part of the country you were operating in."

"Lieutenant, you should know that I don't want to be here," Allen told him, laying the scrap of wood on the ground. "I had my ten-forty-nine on Jack D's desk the minute I reported in to Group," he said referring to the 1049, the request form to transfer to a different unit. "As soon as it's approved, I'm outa' here and back to the Fifth. There's a real war goin' on over there, and it don't have anything to do with humpin' a ruck full of sandbags up a mountain, or pretendin' to blow some fuckin' dam in the middle of nowhere."

"You think they'll send you back after getting hit like you did?"

Allen turned and looked into the young man's eyes. "It's just a *flesh* wound, Lieutenant. It don't stop me from doin' my job in the least bit. And for your information, if they *don't* approve it, all I have to do is put a phone call into Mrs. A, and I'll be sittin' in the club in Nha Trang before you get off this fuckin' mountain anyway!"

Mike believed him. He'd heard of the legendary Mrs. A, a beloved figure sequestered deep within the confines of the Pentagon. A lady who could make dream assignments come true with the flick of a pen, rescue a warrior from the clutches of an incompetent commander with a few strokes on her typewriter, save the career of an errant solider with a mere phone call. The men revered her and, most importantly, trusted her with their lives.

"It's too bad officers don't have someone like her handling our assignments."

"Actually, sir, I'm glad you don't," Allen replied candidly.

"You don't have a lot of use for officers, do you, Sergeant Allen?"

"Let's just say that in my last assignment, I hadn't been blessed with the bravest and brightest, and let it go at that, sir."

"Well, I was an E-five before I was an O-one, so it's not like I just *fell* off the slop wagon. But there're some pretty squared-away officers in this Group, and I'm not naïve enough to count myself among them."

"Well, Lieutenant, before you start getting all full of yourself and thinkin' you're a person of some influence, try orderin' someone else's dog around for a while. See how far that gets you."

"I know who *runs* this team, Allen. But I also know who *commands* it, and I *do* know the difference. If you have a problem with your chain of command, I suggest you take it up with your team sergeant."

Mike stood up, brushing the debris from his butt, and as he turned to retrieve his rucksack, Sergeant Allen stopped him. "What *I* see, Lieutenant, is a young officer full of piss and vinegar out lookin' to become some sort of hero. I bin watchin' you. There ain't no place for *wannabe* heroes in Special Forces. It's just a dirty job with no thanks, and no need for it. You're just as dangerous as those damn cowards who break and run. You're gonna get somebody killed, and it ain't gonna be just you."

Mike turned and faced Allen, his tight lips and shaded eyes prefaced his remarks to the veteran soldier. "Ya know, Sergeant Allen, it's not just about me. It's about all these young buck sergeants and spec-fives who look up to guys like you and Top. And if you can't do better than carryin' that chip on your shoulder up and down this mountain, maybe you oughta go call Mrs. A. I'm sure she'll be more than happy to take your call."

Mike bent over and slung the heavy ruck up onto his back, leaning over to set the load while he snugged up the cinch straps. "You've got a wealth of knowledge that's called experience, Allen. And that's a damn valuable asset to any combat unit. But if you think that you're the only one who needs to suckle on that teat, well, this outfit and all the young troopers in it are really missing out on something special. I put my boots on the same way you do. And when they zip up that body bag, they ain't gonna be pinnin' any bars *or* stripes on the outside."

"Saddle up!" Mike ordered the men. "I bet the captain we'd be back before eighteen hundred, so don't make a liar outa' me."

"That *dog*, Lieutenant…" Allen told him. "He's got some sharp, *m e a n* teeth. Just make sure he doesn't bite you on the ass."

"I'll keep that in mind, Sergeant," Mike assured him. "And we have an old saying back where I come from in Texas: 'Don't ever squat with your spurs on.'"

He smiled, his tense eyes challenging Allen in earnest before he turned and headed up the trail.

* * *

CHAPTER EIGHTEEN

"**H**OW'S THE LANGUAGE TRAINING COMING?" Denny asked, pulling down on the edge of his beret as he and his XO emerged from the building.

"The hardest part is getting up at oh-dark-thirty every morning."

"Just be glad you don't have to learn Mandarin. Those guys swear their eyes start to slant about four weeks into it."

"My eyes are starting to slant just looking at that fat *Frau* they've got teaching that stuff. God, how'd you like to wake up every morning and have to watch that water buffalo roll out of bed?"

"Yeah," Denny, said, chuckling, "I think I've seen her grazing in that meadow just below the tree line before. Matter-a' fact, the guys refer to her as 'How Now, *Frau* Cow.'"

"Clay!"

The pair turned to see Major Reese, the B-Team commander, walking up behind them. They smartly saluted and followed alongside him as he continued to walk.

"Piper's headed to the Fifth tomorrow, so a bunch of us are going to help rearrange some of his brain cells with a few flamin' Mamies at the club tonight," he informed them. "I need twenty from each of you for the kitty."

The two officers contributed to the common practice of bidding farewell to one of their own. First Lieutenant Piper was just the latest of a continual exodus of men from the Tenth to their sister Group, the Fifth, in Vietnam. With each transfer, another slot opened on the small, twelve-man teams. The captains were the first to go, followed by the first lieutenants, leaving the second lieutenants to assume positions they were neither qualified for nor experienced in.

"He's headed for Mack-V SOG," Denny told him as they walked toward the BOQ, the bachelor officer quarters. MACV SOG stood for Military Assistance Command, Vietnam—Studies and Observations Group.

"I've heard of that," Mike replied. "Isn't that where Allen came from?"

"Yeah. They run some top-secret cross-border operations outa' Đà Nẵng. Real hush-hush."

The pair continued down the cobblestone street, past the snack bar and small PX, when a loud clanking sound caught Mike's attention. He peered through the open window of the gym, which was full of men lifting weights and heaving large leather medicine balls to one another.

"Who's that guy bench-pressing the Volkswagen?" Mike asked.

"That's Super Jew," Denny replied, smiling as he drew closer to the window. "He's the demonstration team leader. Great guy. Speaks Russian, German, Norwegian, and French—quite the linguist. Hangs out with the dynamic duo, Piper and Pressley."

They watched him lift the massive weights, every fiber of muscle clearly defined in his amazing physique, his skin-tight T-shirt soaked with sweat and on the verge of rupture. "That's a crime waiting to happen," Mike remarked, noting how much the guy resembled a Greek god, with his short, dark curly hair and protruding, slanted nose. "Remind me never to piss him off."

"Lieutenant David Rabin," Denny told him. "He's a sixth-degree black belt, too. Seen him stand flat-footed and kick out the ceiling lights in Piper's room. He just brought his team back in-country from submarine training down in Italy."

"Where do they keep the hay to feed him?"

The pair turned and made their way over to the BOQ, and Denny told Mike he would meet him later at the club. After checking his empty mailbox, Mike climbed the stairs to his room, threw his beret on the dresser, and fell exhausted on the bed. He lay there for a moment, breathing in the ambiance of fresh strawberries.

Strawberries?

He sat up, surveying his room for the source of the aroma. He could tell the *Putzfrau* had been there, because his change and loose brass insignias lay neatly sorted on the dresser. His curiosity helped him up, and he quickly walked over and threw open the window, gazing down on the empty courtyard below. As he turned and walked toward the bathroom, the scent grew more powerful. He went in.

"Son of a bitch!"

Red powder covered the tile floor. The sink, toilet, and tub were filled to the brim with a viscous, gelatinous substance. He leaned over the sink and cautiously dipped his finger into the blobby goop.

"Fucking Jell-O!" he yelled. "Motherfuckers! These guys apparently have too much free time on their hands. They're worse than the guys in OCS!"

Mike quickly decided that he would not let *them* get the best of him. He calmly reached down into the glutinous mess and pulled the drain on the sink, stirring the thick concoction with his hand. Within the hour, the last of the disgusting dessert slithered slowly down the drain. After changing his fatigues, he slid in behind the wheel of his "new" 1956 Mercedes and headed for the officers' club in Bad Tölz.

The ten-minute ride from the line company quarters at the Prinz Heinrich *Kaserne* in Lenggries brought him alongside the scenic Isar River. He watched the rapid, clear flow sliding over the shallow, rock-strewn riverbed, traversing through the farmlands in the valley, nourishing crops and livestock, and providing a vivid border for the artist's easel. He rolled down the window, allowing the fresh Bavarian breeze to dance freely in his hair.

Skirting the festive town of Bad Tölz, he turned up the hill to the main *Kaserne* on the road to Munich. He tapped the rim of the wooden steering wheel, competing with the Box Tops' beat blaring from the Blaupunkt mounted in the dash. His young spirits soaring, he smiled contentedly, slowing down as he drove under the Flint *Kaserne* archway, past the Tenth Group headquarters building in the sprawling quadrangle, and out toward the airfield and the colonel's quarters.

Within minutes, he had parked his new prized possession in the gravel lot next to the cottage-shaped club, and with the first hints of dusk flirting with the peaks of the adjacent mountains, he made his way through the noisy happy-hour crowd to the bar. He quickly found Denny seated between two strangers, actively engaged in a game of liar's dice.

"Whata' you having?" Denny yelled over his shoulder.

"I'll just have what you're drinking."

"Give him a red-eye, Gisela," he told the bartender.

"Mike, this is Hollis Stevenson. He's the team leader for ODA-26, a Russian team."

Mike shook his hand firmly, noting the olive-green woolen ascot tucked neatly under his collar, accenting the white first-lieutenant bar.

"And this is George Stanton. He runs the three shop for Bravo Company," Denny said, referring to Bravo's S3 Operations shop.

"Yeah, seen you around," the tall captain said, standing and offering his hand.

After that handshake, Mike turned back to Hollis, curious about his assignment.

"I know: What's a black lieutenant doing runnin' a Russian team? Save your breath, honky," he told Mike.

"Well, it did cross my mind," he replied.

"Look at my features," Hollis protested, turning his head sideways. "Notice the distinct aristocratic flair to the jaw line, the heavy Cossack brow accenting these dazzling steel-gray eyes? I'm not black. Just my skin."

"Yeah, right," Denny added. "Boris'll buy that one in a second."

"Who left the gate open and let you in?" Hollis asked, sipping a fresh Glenlivet, a sparkling diamond ring glittering as he extended his pinky finger. He gave the young lieutenant the once-over. "How'd *you* get into Group anyway?"

Mike looked at Denny, seeing him smile and roll his eyes. "Drank a lot of milk," Mike rejoined. "Isn't that how we all got here?"

"You must still be sucklin'. Bring your momma with ya? You don't look old enough to be weaned, much less wined."

"Gave it up last year for Lent. My girlfriend was getting jealous."

"You don't even look old enough to *have* a girlfriend. Musta' been the babysitter."

"Well, you have to take into consideration that I was born at a very early age. So I guess that makes me that much younger than you."

Hollis looked over at Denny and shook his head. "That's *all* we need around here, another smart-ass second lieutenant."

"He ought to fit right in, then," Captain Stanton added, looking past Mike and toward the door. "I see our guest of honor has arrived with his usual entourage."

Mike turned. His eyes widened, and his heart pumped with each slinky step of two beautiful blond creatures, their thigh-high skirts yielding the longest display of legs he'd ever seen. Lieutenant Piper smiled in triumph, obviously content with his escorts languishing snugly on either side of his tall, handsome frame. He walked slowly toward the bar, nodding casually at the well-wishers, his smug expression accenting the deep dimples in his chiseled face. Mike watched him carefully. The air of confident arrogance beamed throughout the room. Calculated strides of his German-made jump boots paraded him through the gauntlet of gawking ladies situated in the room.

"Where does he get those?" Denny asked.

"They pick *him* up," Stanton explained, getting up to make room at the bar for the guest of honor. "He's like the damn Pied Piper. They just follow him around, patiently waiting for a chance to play his flute!"

Mike stepped back, nodding at the former West Point football hero, snatching a whiff of fragrance from his stunning escorts as he backed against the wall. *Some guys have all the luck,* he thought to himself, noticing that everyone in the club had some interest in the trio.

His eyes continued to wander, admiring the local talent situated at various tables throughout the spacious room. Blond women, purporting varying degrees of appearance, desperate to meet an American officer who would immediately improve her station in life. Denny warned him of their intentions, but they all seemed so much older, diminishing his interest in any of them. Adorned in makeup, their features accented with dark liners. Pleasant dispositions obscuring devious motives. They probably weren't interested in him either, he reasoned.

Then he saw her across the room. Their eyes met for a second before he shied away. She challenged him, smiling as she stalked him with her sapphire-blue eyes, her coy demeanor flirting impatiently with his indifference. He gathered his thoughts, collecting his wits as he impulsively expanded his chest, turning slightly to present his profile for her review. He feigned confidence, adjusting his posture, flexing his large forearm as he lifted the tall stein of tomato-laced beer to his perspiring lips. He felt her eyes pandering to his ego, inspecting his taut physique while he carefully contemplated his next move. *Don't be obvious,* he told himself, buying more time before he knew he would have to reciprocate.

He hesitated, watching Piper ignore the pampering caresses of his lady friends as he joked and laughed with the men at the bar. Then he drew closer to the fray, intruding on the tempered camaraderie of the rowdy officers, relinquishing the opportunity for a potential rendezvous with the mysterious maiden.

"And there I was," he heard Captain Stanton telling them, "knee deep in hot brass and hand grenade pins, with nothin' between me and certain death but the '65 Swedish Bikini Team," he said, alluding to a Special Forces in-joke. "It kinda' reminded me of the time I was roundin' the Barbary Coast." He went on with his bizarre tale, nursing an Irish seafaring brogue: "Ayyy, there was a big blowup that night, I tell you. Kiwis and coconuts were flyin' across the deck. A lot of boys became men that night!"

Gisela set up the long row of shot glasses in front of the blustering men. With one smooth, traversing motion, she filled each to the brim with a rusty-colored liqueur, then she struck a long wooden match to set them all ablaze. Stanton grabbed one, holding it aloft while the blue flame flickered, announcing his toast to the attentive throng: "Here's to Teddy the Tuna:

We lift our glass, and say with pride…/

We'll be joining you soon, side by side./

So let your aim be steady, let your aim be true./

And till we see you again… *Fuck you!*"

The bar erupted with laughter. Majors and captains, leading the initiate lieutenants, grabbed the flaming shot glasses and drank the fiery brew. And with a final salute, all slammed the empty glasses upside down on the bar and concluded their tribute.

"As a matter of fact, I think the Tuna's exemplary service to the Group qualifies him for at least a *hymn!*" Stanton yelled.

"HIMMM!… HIMMM!… FUCK HIM!!"

Mike turned to Hollis and asked, "Why do they call him Teddy the Tuna?"

"The women all want to cuddle with him like a big teddy bear, and he always smells like day-old pussy," he replied, adjusting the folds in his makeshift ascot. "Don't worry, somebody will come up with one for you too, rookie."

Hollis stepped behind Piper and grabbed his head, leaned over, and kissed him wetly in the ear. "Don't you *ever* die, you sweet motherfucker," he told him. "I'll be right behind you."

Mike smiled, still getting used to the outlandish behavior of the men and officers in the Group. In the short time that he'd been assigned to the unit, he quickly realized that they parlayed and partied just as hard as they trained. Nothing would surprise him now, not after his consistent indoctrination under Jacques to the unique social traditions of the Special Forces.

Piper held his hands up, calling for quiet in the noisy, raucous bar. "I've only got one thing to say!" he shouted.

The crowd fell silent, waiting anxiously for his next remarks.

"Anybody that can't tap-dance is *queer!*"

Chairs screeched back from the tables as men vaulted from the tall bar stools. A loud frenzy of jump boots noisily rambled, shaking the dust from the raftered ceilings, the glasses off the bar. Mike quickly mimicked their lead, his beer sloshing wildly over the tall brim. *Thank God he didn't say polka,* he mused to himself, righting the remnants of his red beer on the edge of the wet bar.

He settled in at the end of the long horseshoe bar, nestled inconspicuously with his shoulder up against the wall. He watched the veteran officers spar with one another, buying one another shot after shot of strange-looking concoctions. Bottles of ouzo and Jägermeister littered the bar top, while the rowdy officers eagerly stuffed Gisela's revealing dirndl with green testaments of gratitude.

Through the maze of men and ladies, Mike's eyes made contact once again with the striking blonde, seated behind the flickering candle at her table. He smiled, mustering his courage as he sorted his way through the multitude of boisterous patrons blocking his way. He finally emerged, only to see that three other officers had joined her, each vying for her attention. She peered up at him, her alluring blue eyes offering regret while the three men turned to reject his advance. Somewhat befuddled, he turned and made his way back to the wet, crowded bar.

Hollis grabbed him as he slid past, pulling him over to the bar. "I've got some ladies stopping by later," he told him. "You interested in a little international relations?"

"Just what do you have in mind?"

"Use your imagination, cowboy. These are *French* chicks. Anything goes." Hollis turned to get Gisela's cluttered attention. "Hey, *Schatzi!*" he called to her, drawing a stern glare from the pretty barkeep. "What say you and me head back to the Q and do a little roll-around in the *Zimmer?*"

She slowly walked over to him, bent over, and placed her lovely chin above her clasped hands. Smiling sweetly, she softly provided him with her response. "Vell, that sounds zo-o-o nice, *Loit-nant*. But to tell you za truth, I'd rather masstingbate mit un pitchfork."

"Oooooou, that sounds interesting. Can I watch?"

"*Nein! Und* if you call to me *Schatzi* again, I cut off your *Wienerschnitzel* mit un ax."

"Ouch! That hurts just thinkin' 'bout it," he replied, grinning as she turned to pour another drink.

"You always talk to women like that?" Mike inquired.

"Women? What women? That's just a piece of ass, Shannahan. Get your shit straight." He snootily sipped from his icy tumbler, the jeweled pinky finger demanding attention from the young lieutenant. "She's Super Jew's main squeeze, and he's got this kosher thing about sharin' anyway."

Mike shook his head, amused at the dank candor of the lieutenant. "I bet you get your face slapped a lot, don't you?"

"Just a little foreplay before the main act, my man. I like a woman with spirit anyway. Makes my dick hard." He adjusted his ascot, pushed the bar stool back, and stomped his feet, adjusting the crisp blouse above his shiny boots. "See you around, Shannahan. I've got a special rendezvous that requires my immediate attention," he told him, smiling broadly as he winked and left the bar.

Mike watched Hollis as he strutted through the melee, casually slapping the outstretched hands that acknowledged his departure, pausing only briefly to carefully caress several dainty fingers in the process. The young lieutenant shook his head and smiled, wondering if he would ever be able to project the same confident nonchalance in the midst of so many strangers.

Envy quickly gave way to the task at hand, though. He lifted his heavy stein and rejoined Denny and Captain Stanton, who were dutifully mired in another tall tale of mystery and intrigue. He listened intently, studying the men's reactions to the endless banter, how they recalled humorous incidents in battle, accented occasionally by brief solemn sermons of true bravery.

Mike's attentive mind captured every word. He was grateful for the opportunity to eavesdrop on the exploits of true warriors, unabashed in hearing their detailed recollections of the battlefield and the essence of war. Their unbridled frankness surprised him until he realized that they were actually comfortable sharing their stories, as though there were an unspoken obligation each held to glorify and perpetuate the exploits of those they had witnessed fall beside them on the battlefield.

Their captivating words swept the young lieutenant away from the bar and into the highland jungles of that world he only imagined. They anointed him with sweat and dirt, his tight eyes stinging as he watched the lead element of the NVA creep down the narrow trail, his blackened hand clutching tightly on the firing device of the Claymore. He felt his heart pound as the endless line of silent intruders continued to pass through the killing zone, too many to fell with the fan-shaped blast of the device. The foreboding words caused his respiration to cease as he counted the enemy, clad in khaki, their black, butch hair hidden beneath the flimsy pith helmets they wore. Long, curved banana clips protruded menacingly beneath the deadly AK-47s. Sandals fashioned from old tires left faint tread marks in the dusty trail only a few feet in front of where he was carefully concealed beneath a thin layer of palm and elephant grass. He felt the symptoms of fear seeping through his veins, but *not* the terror of imminent death.

"And then what happened?" an excited voice asked, extricating the lieutenant back to reality.

"Well, it got pretty *western* awful damn quick," Stanton recalled, tightening his shoulders with a twinge. "This NVA stepped off the trail right next to one of the little people, dropped trou, and proceeded to take a piss right on his head." He paused briefly, taking a long swig from the tall beer, allowing the image of the North Vietnamese soldier pissing on the Montagnard to sink in before he continued.

"Yards don't take kindly to some NVA pissin' on 'em," Stanton resumed the story. "Especially not ol' Kapa Su. He sort-a' rolled over, pluggin' that damn piss hole with a quick burst-a' six from his Swedish K. The whole team opened up cuttin' those bastards in the kill zone in half. That really pissed 'em off, so they put the dogs on us, and we ran for two days before Covey finally got us out of there. Found out later it was a reinforced battalion from the Three-twenty-fifth NVA Regiment that'd just crossed the Fence up north of Mang Buk."

"You guys were lucky to get outa' that one," Denny commented.

"Can you imagine humpin' ol' Ho's trail all the way down from Hanoi, only to get zapped with your dick in your hand?" Major Reese joked, throwing another twenty on the bar, motioning Gisela to pour another round.

Mike lingered for another hour or so, nursing the remnants of the warm beer while he listened to the risqué jokes and soulful laments of the men around him. He wondered if he, too, would someday be able to pay tribute to those he served with, or them to him.

He forced the last snippets of tepid red foam from the bottom of the stein, and as he looked up, he saw a wooden plaque on the wall bearing a dark green shamrock. The two words contained in the decorative scroll immediately caught his eye. *Croiche Onoraigh.* He patted Denny on the shoulder, pointing to the placard on the wall. "What's *that* doin' here. I've heard those words before."

Denny looked up, then back at his young XO. "Surprised you don't know, *Irish,*" a chastising glare accompanying his quick answer. "Colonel Kelly put it up there a coupla' years ago. There're a lot of you shanty Irish in Group, and he thought it was a good idea to hang it in the bar. It's an old Irish saying: 'May you die with honor.' Denny smiled. "I kinda' like it!"

Mike's thoughts swirled back to the bus depot in Kingsville, and to the parting words of his father. *I bet that's what Granddad told him, too.* He motioned for Gisela to bring him his bill, digging deep into his pocket for the lone twenty he knew he had.

"You should stay away mit him," she advised, wiping the wet bar in front of him.

"Who?"

"*Loit-nant* Stefensen. He catch you mit trouble."

"Oh, he's all right. He was just kiddin' around. He already had a date with a coupla' *mademoiselles* anyway."

"You see! I tell you!" she exclaimed. "You should stay away mit them too! De French are good fur only *vun* ting," she reported, her index finger pointing up in the air, "und das is fur running avay from de Germans!"

Mike grinned and shook his head, handing her back the change from the twenty. Patting Denny on the back, he told him he would see him in the morning. Then he made his way through the dwindling party toward the door. As he passed the end of the bar, he noticed the striking blonde getting up from her table, talking anxiously to the officers as she stood, nervously fumbling with the small black purse in her hands. As he drew closer, she turned and smiled, walked toward him, and offered her outstretched hand.

"There you are, dah'ling." She squeezed his hand tightly as she glanced back at the stern-faced officers at the table. "I told these gentlemen that you had graciously consented to escort me home this evening. I'm ready to go if you are," she told him, the coy British accent and her vibrant eyes beseeching him to comply.

Before he could respond, she quickly bid good night to the men at the table, took his arm, and walked briskly toward the door. "You are truly my Sir Galahad," she whispered, "rescuing me in my time of need."

He felt confused, but instinctively he accompanied her to the door, feeling a slight perspiration seeping from her manicured hand. He held the door open, holding her arm firmly as they stepped down into the gravel parking lot. "Am I missing something here?" he asked, stopping her abruptly.

"Oh, don't be a bully. Can't you see I'm in a terrible predicament?"

He followed her anxious glance back toward the door, the dark silhouettes of the officers stood motionless in the threshold. "My car's over there," he said, pointing, as they stepped briskly through the parking lot.

He opened the passenger door and held her hand as she slid into the black Mercedes. Within minutes, the couple passed under the archway to the *Kaserne* and down the cobblestone street toward the bridge crossing the Isar into Bad Tölz.

"My name is Michael," he told her, reaching over to turn down the radio.

"I know. You're Captain Clay's executive officer. I saw you in the club with him last week when I was having dinner with some friends. Gisela told me who you were."

She reached into her purse and pulled out a shiny gold cigarette case. He watched her tap the end of the long cigarette on the cover before she lit it and leaned slowly back into the comfortable seat. "She likes you," she continued casually. "She said you're the only *true* gentleman in the place."

"Guess you can thank my mother for that. You *still* haven't told me your name."

"My name is Ewa. My friends call me Eve."

"Well, Ewa, am I still going the right way?"

"Just take a left after you cross the bridge. I want to take the high road back down to Fleck," she told him. "I just love looking down at the river in the moonlight." She took a long draw from the slender cigarette.

"Ewa... That's pretty. What kind of name is that?"

"It's Swedish. I was born in Gothenburg, but I went to school in England," she informed him, tossing the cigarette out the window.

The classy Mercedes vibrated over the thick cobblestone bridge, through the sleepy town, and out into the countryside, below the snow-capped peaks towering above them. The dark, narrow road wound just above the rushing waters, sparkling brightly in the moonlit night. He felt her nudge closer to him, nestling snugly as she rested her soft hair on his shoulder. Sharp scents of Chanel drifted swiftly into his realm of fragrances, a sophisticated blend of elegance and style, a bouquet he associated with distinction and class. And age.

Her hands gently squeezed his biceps, caressing his arms as she gazed past him toward the river. "Isn't this just grand?" she whispered. "It makes my toes tingle every time I see heaven dancing in the water like that. I find this the most romantic drive in all of Bavaria."

He felt her sigh as she snuggled closer. *What the hell did I get myself into?* he quandered, peering down at the long, slender legs as they drew up closer to his thigh, the dark, knee-high skirt climbing slowly above the gartered silk stockings. He heard her heels drop to the floorboard while her warm breath tickled his earlobe, the wet caress of soft, full lips slowly slid down his neck, sending a surge of empowering endorphins throughout the essence of his tense body.

"Please... Let's go closer. There's a little road up ahead that will take us down to the riverbank."

He slowed down and pulled off the paved road onto a dirt farm trail leading to the river's edge. As he turned off the engine, the tranquil sounds of rushing water enveloped the evening air. He felt her hand unbuttoning his shirt, reaching in to squeeze his breast, sharp nails biting into his firm flesh. "I knew you would feel like this," she softly told him, whimpering quietly as she kissed his open mouth.

Her aggressiveness stunned him, alerting his instincts to reject her advances, reassess his options, just make sense of what had transpired over the last thirty minutes of his life. Then, discarding any notion of caution or decorum, he impetuously embraced her, gently clasping her face and chin, kissing her softly as his strong arms gathered her closer. She responded with her hot tongue, forcing her passion on him with a frenzy of excited and spontaneous tremors, shuddering uncontrollably as his large hand enveloped her breast. They explored each other's damp bodies, frantically searching for the elusive signet that would captivate the moment, totally quench their quest for raw pleasure. He drew his mouth from her wanton lips, returning his caresses to her long, alluring neck, the bitter taste of Chanel persisting as he felt her shudder again, falling limp and submissive in the midst of his embrace. His hand quickly slid between her open legs, damp silk greeting his advance, the warm wetness accented with the sultry aroma of womanhood. Her legs spread wider, inviting his protrusion, moaning in full pleasure as his fingers gently encountered her succulence.

"Yes... yes... oh God, yes, Michael. Take me... take me" she moaned. "Take me now!"

"Here?"

"I don't care... I want you!"

He paused a moment, gazing into the sparkling eyes that captivated him more with every burst of starlight from the heavens above. He wanted it to be more than this. She deserved more than the front seat of a car, he reasoned. "Let's go back to my room in Lenggries," he suggested. "I have a nice bottle of wine. And some soft music as well."

"*Ladies* don't accompany gentlemen back to their rooms, especially to the BOQ," she scolded. "It's a haven for sluts and whores. I'm shocked you dare to even ask me!" She abruptly sat up and pulled her skirt down.

"I'm sorry, Eve," he apologized. "I've never taken a woman to my room. I didn't know."

"You must have seen the women come and go," she insisted. "I'm surprised they don't have a revolving door at the entrance. Take me home!"

Mike straightened his shirt, securing the last button as he started the car. As he turned back onto the paved road, Eve leaned over and turned up the radio. The soft vibrato of "Love Is Blue" eased the building tension, soothing the frayed sensitivities recently exposed. Yet he struggled with his thoughts, convinced he had meant no disrespect, wondering how he should have handled the situation differently. As the song lingered softly in the last stanza, Eve slid back over to him "I'm sorry, dah'ling. I just didn't want you to think I was a whore, that's all."

"I've always been taught that there's a time and place for everything," he replied. "And this *seemed* like the time, but certainly *not* the place."

"Of course, you're right," she conceded. "I have a better idea."

She eagerly directed the young officer down the road, past Prinz Heinrich *Kaserne* and over the bridge leading to Fleck. Within minutes the black Mercedes pulled to a stop in the small driveway beside Eve's secluded cottage. He stepped out beneath the towering pines, hurried around, and opened the door for her, his jump boots grinding loudly in the coarse gravel in his haste. He took her keys and opened the door, then slowly followed the trail of silk blouse and lingerie to her bedroom. He stood quietly in the doorway, sinfully admiring the cabaret unfolding before him. The dim light revealed an amazing creature, slithering on the bed as she struggled with her red panties, rolling down her stockings—one, and then the other. Full, flowing blond hair lay spread in contrast to the dark satin sheets displaying her attributes, her arms finally outstretched, beckoning him to join her.

"God, you're beautiful," he told her, unlacing his jump boots, then quickly discarding his clothes at the foot of the bed.

He felt her wetness engrave a line of lust from his chest to his loins as he slid up between her legs to meet her sweet, alluring lips. He kissed her deeply, succumbing fully to her captivating trance, craving to suckle amid her enticing breasts. He took her left breast in his hand, and as he leaned down to caress it, he noticed a framed picture on her nightstand.

A bride, and her apparent husband standing proudly beside her, a major's leaf pinned on the green flash on his beret. He froze.

"Who's that?" he asked, his eyes squinting in the dim light.

She reached over and slammed the picture down, pulling him back down to her.

"Wait a minute," he protested. "Who's that with you in the picture?"

"Michael, you're acting like a bully again."

"No, Eve, I want to know," he demanded, sitting up and pulling the pillow over his lap.

She reached over the edge of the bed, taking the gold cigarette case out of her handbag. Fluffing the pillow behind her, she slid up and lit the cigarette, sorting and flipping her hair before she answered him. "He's my husband," she relented, turning away as she blew a disgusted stream of smoke in the air.

"You're *married*?" he asked incredulously.

"Now you're *really* starting to bore me," she complained, folding her arms over her bare breast.

He stared directly at her, seeing the deceit spread quickly across her lovely face. His desire swiftly changed to resentment, then disgust. He shook his head, slowly got up, and went to the foot of the bed, sorting through the starched clump of clothes for his boxers.

"And you were worried that I'd think you were *just* a whore," he said softly. "Where *is* the poor bastard? Nam?"

"That's all you men think of, isn't it? Your goddamn war! You never think about the women you leave behind, do you?" she yelled. "What are we supposed to do while you're off killing people for no damn reason at all? Knit and crochet? Or maybe we should all get together for crumpets and tea?"

"Try being a wife. Strange concept, isn't it? But then, I imagine you do probably get a lot of in-coming and sapper probes during your tea parties, don't you?"

He tucked his shirt in his pants and sat down to pull on his boots.

"You self-righteous, warrior bastard! Don't preach to me, you hypocrite!" she yelled, kneeling up in the bed.

"Woman, it looks to me like he was a Special Forces major when you married him, so please, don't play the sanctimonious victim with me. My mother was the wife of a warrior, and I never saw *her* out picking up men in the officers' club when he was overseas, so don't even *go* there!" he said, his voice rising in contempt.

"I'm not your bloody mother, *bastard*!"

"Thank God!" he replied, shuffling his unlaced boots toward the front door. "There's a bright side to this charade after all."

He heard the patter of bare feet behind him, and as he turned, he felt the full vigor of her stinging rage as she slapped him forcefully in the face. He endured the assault, glaring back at her nakedness as he slowly shook his head in spite.

"And *that's* for *ignoring* me all night in the club," she said, flipping her hair as she turned and stalked back into the dim light of her empty room.

* * *

CHAPTER NINETEEN

MIKE WATCHED THE DARK SPECK closing in rapidly from his right while he steadily held his brace high above the rough sea of clouds below. Snow-capped peaks protruding above the soft cumulus skyscape provided perspective to his descent, frigid winds whipping loudly through his black jumpsuit as he plummeted toward the distant earth. He glanced at the altimeter strapped to his wrist: seventeen thousand feet and falling. The speck grew larger, swiftly tracking toward him through the dark blue sky, bearing down on him like a heat-seeking missile.

That son of a bitch is gonna hit me! Mike realized, flaring his body position, trying desperately to delay his descent. In a split moment, the streaking intruder passed within twenty feet of him, Jacques's beady eyes staring up through misted goggles as he shot through the icy sky below.

"You son of a bitch!" he yelled, his muffled protest captured by the tight oxygen mask. As the turbulence careened him from side to side, he cursed vehemently, and he desperately struggled to regain his stable brace. He quickly turned to the left, bringing his arms to his side, increasing his rate of descent as he tracked after the airborne prankster. Like a crooked arrow wobbling toward the target, he struggled to tighten his brace, straining fiercely to stabilize after his abrupt maneuver. His mind raced back to Kingsville, when he watched the smoking tires of Jim's Fairlane skid around another corner as he chased him through the city streets in his mother's white Falcon. Desperate to cut down any drag in his quest for terminal velocity, he felt his instincts force him to point his toes.

He watched the body below him start to flair. *I've got you now, you son of a bitch!* he thought, while gritting his teeth and focusing on the heavenly body floating casually below him. *This shit is gonna end right here, right now!*

Easing slowly into a spread position, Mike continued to rock and sway as he tracked the brazen medic from a position above and behind his unsuspecting prey. He struggled with his stability, ignoring the serenity of the ice blue sky, dutifully adjusting his attitude while maneuvering ever closer to his airborne target. Glancing again at his altimeter, he decided it was time to make his move.

At twelve thousand feet, he slipped swiftly next to the startled medic, grabbing onto his harness as he quickly pulled Jacques's silver rip cord. The small drogue chute immediately deployed above Jacques's muffled screams, loud snapping sounds of risers and canopy echoing in the brilliant sky. Mike swiftly fell away from the inflating Para-Commander, its green oval-shaped image oscillating wildly in the dark-blue sky above him.

Mike turned to focus on his altimeter, Jacques's rip cord still thrashing like a bullwhip in his gloved hand. He rubbed the frosted crystal, watching the gauge drop below the ten-thousand mark. The milky haze of thick, billowing clouds quickly shrouded his vision, leaving him in an eerie limbo as he hurdled through the chalky mist. His heart surged as if it were ready to burst through the nylon chest straps, his goggled eyes opened wide when he broke through the final layer of distorted haze. Forested lush mountains loomed in the distance off to his right, with several turquoise green lakes lazily reflecting the midday sun to his left. He picked up his landmarks, straining through blurred goggles to pinpoint the target: the open dirt pasture just to the left of the winding river below. The altimeter read four thousand, and as he rotated to the right, he prepared to pull the rip cord, bracing nervously for the ominous opening shock.

Hope they didn't fuck with my main, he worried, hesitating briefly before he slipped his thumb through the stainless steel loop. He felt the drogue flutter momentarily, just enough time to send a warning alarm though his frigid body. Rubber bunch bands snapped loudly in precision as the main exploded with a rumble above him, his harness straining fiercely under the abrupt deceleration. He looked up, rendering the usual sigh of relief as the majesty of the open canopy loomed prominently above him.

"God, I hope I never get tired of this," he pleaded aloud.

Gazing down at the shiny lakes, he gauged the wind as it painted faint, cascading wrinkles near the eastern shoreline. Snapping both rip cords onto his harness, he let the lofty breeze take him, pulling firmly on the toggle line as he began to spiral down toward his target. He glanced up to see several other canopies trailing above and behind him, orbiting downward on the same apparent trek.

This sure beats the shit outa' jumpin' with those damn T-10s, he told himself, soaring like an eagle, slipping left, then right, full circle—the whole world traversing below the nap in his new German jump boots.

Bright orange panels marked the target, and as he picked up the drift of purple smoke floating across the landing area, he stared intently at the scores of men standing next to the caravan of trucks and jeeps. *Somethin's up,* he thought as he watched the animated Major Reese flailing his arms, barking silent orders to the MPs, who were lined up with their shiny helmet liners sparkling in the bright afternoon sun.

Turning into the wind, he swayed slowly as the canopy flared, pulling down tightly on both toggle lines until his boots touched the ground. Gathering his canopy, he felt a sense of apprehension as several MPs scrambled through the dirt toward him. He instinctively tucked Jacques's rip cord into his shirt and slid it around to his back.

"Grab your gear, Lieutenant, and come with me," the lanky MP sergeant ordered.

"What's going on?"

"I don't know, sir," he replied, helping the lieutenant out of his harness. "We've been ordered to escort you and your team back to Lenggries immediately."

Mike gazed back up over the drop zone, watching the rest of the team maneuvering their canopies into the landing area. Staring up through the high clouds, he searched the bright sky for any sign of Jacques in the heavens above.

Shit, he's probably halfway to Austria by now, he figured. *Just hope nobody else saw what happened up there.*

He slung his gear over his shoulder and followed the bevy of MPs toward the waiting trucks idling on the edge of the freshly plowed pasture.

"We're a jumper short, sir," he heard the HALO (high-altitude–low-opening) committee sergeant tell the major. "Twelve exited the aircraft, but

I've only been able to eyeball eleven, sir," he reported, lifting the binoculars back to his eyes.

Mike stopped. "Looked like Sergeant Lamont had a malfunction at about ten thousand," he told the sergeant. "His main started to deploy as I went by him and—"

"I've got him over there at nine o'clock," an excited voice informed them. "Looks like he's at about seven or eight thousand, drifting south, southeast."

"Goddammit!" Major Reese shouted. "Get a tracker on him ASAP!" The red splotch of anger flowed instantly from his pug, rosy cheeks, indelibly anointing his wrinkled forehead like steaks of red war paint. "I want somebody there when that bozo hits the ground. Goddamn Hollywood jumpers! Goddamn 'malfunction,' my ass! I've got *his* main malfunction hanging!"

Mike cringed as he slowly walked toward the covered trucks, his mind evaluating the repercussions of his impetuous retaliation for Jacques's prank. He slung his gear up into the truck, climbed up, and slid in next to Sergeant Allen.

"Hope you've got your dog tags on, Lieutenant. You're gonna need them."

Mike's eyes narrowed. "What's that supposed to mean?"

Allen slowly reached into his pocket and pulled out his shiny Zippo. "They don't send an armed escort for any training exercises I've ever been on, Lieutenant," he replied calmly, then lit the Camel and took a deep drag off the short cigarette.

Mike looked around, finally noticing that all of the MPs *were* armed, and not just with their standard sidearm. Each of them was carrying a Thompson submachine gun or an M14 rifle. Beneath the black M60 machine gun mounted on the lead jeep dangled the telltale links of live ammo, bronze-tipped projectiles in their shiny brass casings.

"Could I have one of those, Sergeant?" Mike requested, nodding toward the cigarette between Allen's nicotine-stained fingers.

"Thought you didn't smoke, LT," Allen chided, reaching into his breast pocket and flipping a fresh butt over to him.

"I don't, but there's a lot of things I didn't do before I hooked up with you crazy bastards."

Allen feigned a smile, the deep dimple in his cheek revealing a lost temperament, once ordinary for him. "It comes with the territory, Lieutenant," he said before taking a deep drag off the smoldering butt. "Just makes it easier to look that elephant in the eye sometimes. You'll see."

"I have. We've already met."

Evidently puzzled, Allen paused, then reached over and lit the lieutenant's cigarette, his terse eyes delving with caution into the young man's confident gaze.

"Give me a hand, Lieutenant!" Val requested, beckoning Mike to help him up into the truck. He reached down and complied, then slid over as the team sergeant pulled the tailgate up and latched the rusty pin though the lock. Then Val slumped down next to Mike, stretching his legs out on top of the maze of parachute bags stacked in the middle of the truck.

Val turned and stared at the lieutenant, his focus widening as a smirk spread across his face. He glanced at the cigarette in Mike's hand and shook his head. "Didn't anybody tell you that'll stunt your growth?"

"Figured I'm tall enough already. Besides, I may as well smoke. I inhale at least half of the smoke you human chimneys pump out every day."

"So… what happened up there, LT?" Val asked quietly.

"Nothin', Top," he replied, folding his arms and settling back as the truck began to shudder. "Just a little overdue payback, that's all."

The team sergeant slowly shook his head. "You sure picked one fine helluva time to get even, Lieutenant."

"Roger that. But you know what they say back home in Texas, Top: *Caca pasa*."

The bumpy ride back to the company area in Lenggries allowed the men time to speculate on the purpose of their armed escort. Captain Clay reminded the men about the A-Team that had gone into isolation several months previously, when the Arabs and Israelis got together for another one of their two-day wars. That team's mission had been to jump in and provide security for the trapped American citizens in the U.S. Embassy in Cairo. Mike learned that the mission had been scrubbed only when a British SAS unit beat them there while rescuing their own embassy personnel. Each member of the team had their own scenario they shared, but one thing was certain: Whatever it was, they were going in together.

The convoy of jeeps and trucks rattled noisily over the cobblestone quadrangle, hastily pulling to a stop in front of A-Company headquarters. Mike stared briefly at the men piling sandbags around the entrance to the building, then he slung his gear on his back and followed the MP escort through the alcove. They made their way down the wide spiral staircase to the basement and passed more guards as they filed into their team room.

Within minutes, Major Reese strode through the door, clutching several large envelopes with the distinctive red *TOP SECRET* label on the outside of each. "This is a level-one alert, gentlemen," he began, leaning on the large circular table, his fists clenched and his expression drawn. "You will remain in isolation until the planning stage of this mission is completed. You will not have any contact with anyone outside this room unless authorized by me personally."

He paused briefly, tucking his shirt deeper into his trousers before he continued his remarks.

"Late last night, diplomatic Russian envoys, in the form of infantry and heavy armor, invaded the capital of Czechoslovakia in an attempt to reverse the democratic tendencies of the Dubček regime. There are reports of armed resistance, but the situation is still being evaluated. We, gentlemen, have been ordered to prepare to insert several teams to link up with the Czech partisans to support an organized resistance to the incursion and occupation. Your mission objectives are contained in these envelopes that the S3, S2, and area specialist will go over with your command structure during your O&I briefing. In the meantime, I suggest you inventory your gear and make ready for deployment."

Mike glanced over at Denny, gauging the reaction of his team leader. He felt an air of confidence and anticipation fill the room. Smiling faces exchanged nods of approval, competent warriors with a new mission to embrace, seasoned and tested professionals all—all, except one. *They're serious about this,* he realized, pondering the consequences of the event. He felt a degree of excitement, a moment of reflection, a series of diverse emotions, none that could hold the true essence of his spirit, or the imminent danger that loomed before him.

"Have that big ape medic of yours report to me as soon as they police his young ass up," Major Reese told the captain. "If he's not back by eighteen hundred hours, I'm going to enter him on the duty log as AWOL."

"Yes, sir," Denny replied.

Val's eyes followed the major out of the team room. He ran his hand through the sparse burr of black hair as his squinting stare quickly turned back to Mike. Before the team sergeant could consolidate his feelings with full expression, the lieutenant quickly got up and shuffled past the guards, calling down the hall to the major.

"Major Reese!" Mike slowed his pace as the major turned and stopped. "...Sir," he appended his rude interjection.

"What is it, Lieutenant? I'm rather busy right now. If you want to call home, forget it."

"About Sergeant Lamont, sir."

"No chance, Lieutenant. I'll deal with him myself," he told him, turning and starting up the staircase.

"It was my fault, Major. Sergeant Lamont didn't have anything to do with it."

Major Reese stopped, paused for a moment, slowly turned, and walked back down the stairs, staring intently at the young lieutenant. "This ought to be good," he said somberly, his hands wandering up to his hips while he surveyed the expression on the lieutenant's face.

"I got too close to him up there, and with the wind whipping through my goggles, well... I bumped into him."

"Go on," the major prompted.

"Well, as I was trying to slip away from him, I pushed off, and my hand must have slid through the loop on his rip cord handle."

Mike watched the small blood vessels in the major's hooded eyes swell in earnest, casting a rougelike tint that quickly engulfed and illuminated his pudgy cheeks. The wrinkles in his brow folded like an accordion as his pressing squint extinguished the flames in his eyes. Mike saw his own reflection in the major's rapidly dilating pupils.

Major Reese stared quietly, surveying the caliber of truth in the eyes of the young repentant before him. "That has got to be the *lamest* damn thing I have *ever* heard in my ten years in Special Forces, Lieutenant," he reported, shaking his head in disbelief. "Who the fuck do you think you are? Lieutenant Fuzz? Or is it Beetle Bailey? Bend over!"

"Pardon me?"

"Bend over, Lieutenant!"

Mike quickly obeyed the major's order.

"Now, spread your legs. Put your arms between your legs, and pull your fuckin' head out of your ass!"

Mike stared back at the major, hesitating as he pondered the absurdity of the order.

"Do it!"

The lieutenant quickly complied, awkwardly bending over as the humiliation quickly spread through his whole being.

"What the fuck were you thinking, Lieutenant?"

"I don't know, sir," Mike muttered. "I musta' had my head up my ass."

"There! Feel better? That's the oxygen flowing to your fuckin' brains now that you've got your fuckin' head out of your ass! You're damn lucky I don't have anyone to replace you on this mission, or I'd have your shavetail ass sortin' bunch bands in the rigger shed for the remainder of the millennium!"

"Roger that, sir."

The major stared at the young man, contemplating further consequences to amend the egregious infraction. The stare narrowed abruptly, a genuine hint of disappointment prefaced his next remarks. "I heard about you and Major Carlson's wife, Shannahan. I'm not impressed," he concluded, a distasteful scowl rendered as he departed up the stairs. "We have a moniker for charlatans like you over here," he added, leaning over the banister to make his point. "*Buddy fuckers*. And *we* don't forget."

"I didn't know she was *married*, Major," Mike protested, shaking his head as the vain words echoed in the hollow stairway.

"Jeeezus Christ! He must think I'm a total fuckup," he murmured to himself, squeezing his rolled-up beret in his clenched fists. *Nothin' like being the head turd on the shit list,* he lamented, making his way slowly back to the busy team room.

For the next twelve hours, the men of ODA-1 prepared for war. The top-secret briefings provided a format for planning their insertion, linkup, and order of battle for the pending mission. Strange men clad in civilian attire, some with heavy accents, and others deliberately bland in their demeanor, provided unique insight into the area of operation and the population therein. Dossiers complete with photographs of the underground elements they were to link up with were studied and discussed at length. Sarkie and several others bantered in fluent Czech with the clandestine emissaries, updating their intelligence while finding time to insert a levitating joke or two. Mike found himself laughing at the unintelligible wit, fully aware of the absurdity of his ignorance.

Sergeant Lamont's unceremonious reunion with the team drew only a few chastising smiles and indignant headshakes as the men pressed on with their own assignments. Mike's emotions drifted in cycles as he was taunted frequently by Jacques's intermittent stares. Major Reese's stinging comments had left a lingering degree of remorse in his mind. He seemed even more concerned about the other officers who might share the same conception of the events of that beguiling evening with Eve.

Struggling to put it out of his mind, he focused on the monumental task at hand. Piles of charts and maps littered the increasingly crowded team room while Master Sergeant Valencia completed numerous chits of requisition for the additional equipment the team would require. The lieutenant intermingled with the men as they worked on their specific assignments and responsibilities, his role in the mission not yet clearly defined by the detachment commander. One thing was certain, however: *He* would be jumping the generator.

As the hours drifted by, a detailed plan of action took shape along with the bundle being assembled in the wide corridor outside the team room. New uniforms were delivered. To ensure the anonymity of the infiltrators wearing them, they were divested of all markings. Crates of ammunition and explosives along with Soviet-made weapons and equipment lined the walls. Web harnesses and rucksacks were packed and unpacked, only essential equipment finding a home in the confines of their accumulating gear.

The young lieutenant made good use of his tattered Czech phrasebook. Constantly muttering, he relied on the book to interpret the seemingly indecipherable patter. He quietly recited the extent of his vocabulary over and over, as if cramming the night before a test. Frustration soon set in, and along with it, the realization that *"Frau* Cow" had deserved more attention than the lieutenant had been willing to give, a decision he now regretted profusely.

"Gentlemen, your briefback will be heard at oh-two-thirty hours in the wardroom," Major Reese informed them. "Finalize your operations order and prepare your maps for C-Team approval. The briefback will consist of operational planning, infiltration, linkup, contingency, and logistical requirements. Just make sure it jibes with the area assessment. You have two hours. Make good use of it."

Mike looked at his watch, the fantasy immediately transformed into sobering, stark reality. He felt he was finally at the threshold of his gravest quest. A faint chill encompassed his spirit as he urged his gatekeeper to bare open his sacred vault. *Whatever you do from here on out will constitute your worth in the eyes of others as well as in your own,* he told himself. *Move with purpose. Stay calm. Use sound judgment in your every endeavor. And for Christ's sake, don't let anyone see just how fuckin' nervous you really are!*

His thoughts clearly assembled, he strolled leisurely over to where Val and Denny were seated. He spun a folding chair around backward and sat down between them "What part of the briefback do you want me to handle, Captain?"

Denny looked over at Val. Then, with the team sergeant's nodding approval, he gave Mike his task. "I was going to handle this myself, but if you think you're up to it, you can take the security and codes portion of the ops order."

"Roger that, Captain."

He knew Denny was giving him a small task that he was familiar with, but he was still grateful for the captain's confidence in him. He gazed around the room, focusing on the faces of the men he would accompany to an uncertain war. They each assumed a new intimacy, which he would kindle and nurture within him. A diverse bond began to swell in his young heart: Brotherly admiration as well as a renewed sense of responsibility for their trust inspired him.

An hour later, he had made his final check on his equipment, drawn his basic load of ammo and explosives, and secured them neatly on his web harness and in his rucksack. The cardboard rolls of empty black tape spools littered the team room, and every piece of equipment was securely strapped onto web gear and rucksacks. The busy team of riggers secured the bundle in the hallway, and at precisely 0230 hours, ODA-1 followed their escort upstairs to the briefing room.

Mike stood attentively, keenly aware of the number of field-grade officers seated in the room. The unfamiliar uniforms of Allied NATO officers present at the briefing surprised him. He wondered what they were doing there, but then he realized that they were probably going to have some future role in this mission as well.

Denny's presentation flowed smoothly. He paused only for the occasional question from the theater staff representing the European Command Headquarters. He outlined the infiltration route, overflying the Czech border through northern Austria, where they would insert by air into the province of Jihočeský, 120 kilometers south of Prague, just south of the River Vltava.

The team opted for a quick insertion, with the Eleventh Air Commando Squadron from Sembach dropping the team at 650 feet over the forested area north of Dolni Mokropsy. They felt a HALO insertion left too many options for failure in that dense terrain. Key members of the team followed Denny's overview, providing insight into their portion of the operational plan with precise, unrehearsed professionalism. By 0330 hours, the plan was approved. The team collected their weapons and gear and made their way down to the waiting trucks. The armed convoy of MPs escorted the clandestine team immediately to the darkened airfield and the waiting C-130 Hercules.

Mike jumped down from the tailgate and leaned over to pick up his gear, when he saw the image of his old friend Orion bidding him adieu from his perch near the dark horizon. He sighed, his spirits refreshed as he boarded the darkened aircraft. He sat down next to Val, the constant noise and vibration from the four engines limiting their conversation to smiles and nods of anxiety and support. The large tailgate elevated and closed, muffling the high-pitched clamor to a constant dull humming, a sound that usually translated into an immediate lullaby for the troops within. Mike glanced at his watch: 0400 hours. He knew from the briefback that the flight would last only forty-eight minutes once they were airborne, the longest forty-eight minutes of his life, he reasoned.

His thoughts hurried back to his father, imagining his trepidation while he sat in his open, windswept cockpit, waiting anxiously to launch off the deck of the carrier. *I wonder if he felt the same way,* he pondered, squirming in his seat, fidgeting with his web gear and straps.

"Relax, Lieutenant," Val told him, smiling as the dull cabin lights flickered off the oily greasepaint on his hardened face. He handed the uneasy lieutenant a stick of gum, a time-tested device used to keep ears from stopping up on the rapid accent from airfields. "They've got some JATO-assist tanks strapped to this baby, so it could be a real quick ride."

The lieutenant focused on Val's compassionate stare. "Just don't let me fuck up, Top," he said sternly, unwrapping the stick of Spearmint.

"If you ain't got it figured out by now, LT, ain't no one in this stick is gonna be able to bail you out. Just keep on doin' what you've been doin' that got you this far, Lieutenant. Rely on yourself. In the end, that's all you got anyway. And by the way," he added, "the grab-ass and games end tonight."

Mike nodded his head in agreement, encouraged by the words of wisdom from the veteran team sergeant. He settled back in the nylon webbing, casting his eyes down the row of men seated on the opposite side of the aircraft while the war bird abruptly lurched forward along the taxiway. Most were still adjusting their gear, settling into their flimsy seats, waiting for the plane to make that last exhilarating sprint down the darkened runway.

Mike felt someone staring at him, then focused on Sergeant Allen, whose expression was fixed and poised. In the dim light, Mike couldn't tell if it was a smirk or a smile, but regardless, his delving eyes made his point.

The aircraft shifted to a stop. Several sweaty palms gripped the aluminum tubing, while others just continued to perform the tasks they were doing as the engines revved up to a deafening pitch. Mike waited for the brakes to release for what seemed like an eternity. He waited, and waited. Finally, with his peaking adrenaline nearly spent, the engines suddenly abated, slowing down to a frustrating idle. They sat on the end of the runway in the sullen darkness. For well over an hour, the men maintained their anxious vigil, praying for the dormant plane to launch them into that elusive realm of glory. They sat poised, ready for anything, anything except the inevitable.

The loadmaster quickly stood up, reaching up for the tailgate controls that slowly revealed the early morning sun beaming across the eastern mountain peaks and into the tension-filled cabin. He leaned over and cupped his hand as he relayed his message to Captain Clay. Denny slowly unbuckled his safety harness, stood up, and addressed his men.

"Stand down!" he yelled. "Our mission has been scrubbed."

* * *

CHAPTER TWENTY

C OLD, BLISTERING WINDS CAREENED FORCEFULLY through the sharp, towering peaks above the *Kaserne*, transforming the lush Bavarian meadows below into a bleak montage of brown and amber-yellow pastels. Flurries of soft white snow soon followed, and with the abrupt change in the weather and landscape, so came Denny's orders to the Fifth Group. Months had passed since their aborted mission, affording valuable time for the lieutenant to refocus his priorities and to rededicate himself to mastering the skills he knew would be necessary to fulfill his mission as a Special Forces officer.

The rigorous training routine affirmed to him that their unique mission was a valued component to global stability, with teams constantly deployed abroad for training in the disciplines they required. ODA-1 found itself consistently on the move, from Camp Darby in Italy, where they practiced submarine insertions, to the icy fjords of Denmark, where they refined their scout swimmer techniques. Mike especially valued the time the team spent training with the British SAS in the rugged highlands of Scotland, where he felt so close to the Emerald Isle of his ancestors.

The team had just returned from a grueling week of HALO training in the Pyrenees of northern Spain, when Denny found his orders waiting for him.

"I've recommended to the ol' man that you take over the team, Mike," Denny told him as he packed the last of his personal files into his tattered briefcase.

"I appreciate that, but I'm sure the men would rather just have Top run the team, if you know what I mean. That's a captain's slot anyway, Denny."

"Don't have any captains left to fill it, Lieutenant, so we're gonna have to improvise."

"Why doesn't that surprise me?" he replied, thumbing through the new *Army Times* on the team room table.

"Just keep your dick in your pants, and you'll be all right," Denny told him. "The men are comfortable with you, and Val gave you a strong vote of confidence as well."

Mike's temples squinged. He was pleasantly intrigued by this shocking revelation. He set the paper down, sat back in the folding chair, and promptly crossed his arms. "You know, Denny, ever since that night I ran into Major Carlson's wife, I've been paying a lot of attention to what is really going on around here. This place is nothing more than Peyton Place East." he said, alluding to the popular book, movie, and TV series about a sordid fictional New England town. "You wouldn't believe some of the midnight rendezvous and bullshit that goes on after dark."

"You think I don't know? They're just a coupla' renegades sewing their oats," he remarked casually. "Just don't get caught up in it. It's not a good career move on your part."

"Fuck that! The same hypocritical sons of bitches who gave me shit about her are standing in line at the end of the bar every night just waitin' for their chance to dip their wicks into somebody else's wife!"

"I know who you are talking about, and it's none of your business, Mike," Denny advised him. "Don't infringe on their leisure by letting them know that you even give a shit about what they think or do."

"I just don't understand why people even get married if they want to fuck around." Mike flipped through the newspaper. "It just doesn't make any sense."

"There's no such thing as a married man one hundred miles from home," Denny replied casually. "And on the flip side, you know the old saying: 'When the cat's away, the mice will play.'"

"Seems like everybody's got their own cute little saying to justify or trivialize the flaws in their character, don't they, Denny?"

"It's pretty convenient, don'cha think? But to be totally honest with you, Mike, it does take a special breed of woman to put up with an SF trooper. They have to put up with a lot more than the average army wife, and that's saying a lot."

"Whatever."

"I'm speaking from experience, my man," Denny replied, latching up the straps on the bulging briefcase and sitting down at the table. "When I got back from my last tour in Nam, I came home to an empty house, with a note attached to the fridge. She was *long* gone. So was everything else in the house... except for the hammock she'd strung across the living room for me to bivouac in. The woman even left a box of my favorite C-rations on the stove. The note said she thought I'd feel right at home there without her." He paused briefly, shrugged his shoulders, and finished his point. "And you know what? She was right."

"I didn't even know you were married."

Denny placed the briefcase on the floor, stood up, spun the chair around, sat back down, and rested his arms over the top "For about twenty minutes I was. But in all fairness, we can't tell them where we are going, or when we'll be back." He ran the tips of his fingers through his cropped blond hair. "And before long, the loneliness and frustration turns into resentment and insecurity, and that leads to emotional decisions they wouldn't normally make. Nothin's normal around here. We make our own rules. Society dictates decorum, politicians dictate policy, but warriors have a tendency to dictate their own terms as long as it doesn't interfere with their mission. You either understand that and accept it, or you move on."

"That still doesn't make it right," Mike replied, shaking his head in disagreement.

"Mike, don't read anything into the activities of these guys that you don't totally understand," Denny chastised. "To them, you are still a neophyte, an unproven entity, without any vital substance, existing in their midst only at their pleasure. It's not a question of *joining* the team as it is earning the right to participate at all. We've had this conversation before, Lieutenant," he concluded, a vague annoyance apparent in his tone. "You've either been there, or you haven't. There *is* no in-between. If they even tolerate you, *you* should feel honored. As far as their social lives are concerned, they can't turn the switch off and on that easily. And frankly, it's none of your goddamned business."

Denny stood and picked up his briefcase. He stomped his boots, drawing the crisp blouse down around the bottom of his trousers. "Get over it. There're more pressing issues you need to be focusing on anyway." He turned to leave the team room, but before he passed through the door, he paused to offer one last piece of advice. "Get yourself a nice little *Schatzi*, Shannahan. That'll keep you out of the club, so you won't have to put up with it."

"Yeah, right," Mike replied, returning his attention to the pages of the *Army Times.*

"Just remember the old adage, Lieutenant," Denny said. "'Discretion is the better part of valor.'"

Mike peered up from the wrinkled, lazy fold in the paper. "Ya know, Denny? Just when you were starting to make sense, there you go and fuck it all up with this tired old platitude justifying just what's fucked up with everything we've been talking about."

The captain stared back from the door, angry but silent.

"Here you go trying to equate discretion with valor," Mike went on, "and what the fuck *is* discretion anyway? A lame excuse for deceptiveness, infidelity, sordidness. What the fuck is it? I can guarantee you it does not equate in any fashion to valor, so why do you even use it in the same sentence?"

Denny remained silent, gathering his thoughts while the lieutenant straightened his posture for his next barrage.

"To me, discretion is just a synonym for deception," Mike continued, pontificating, "a vile attempt to veil the truth in a subtle pretext of a word that should be reserved for politicians. *Valor*, sir, is a virtue. Discretion is but a mere crutch convoluted by those who have never appreciated nor approached the realm of honor."

Mike paused, his respiration exceeding the volume of his straining pulse. Staring intently at Denny, he waited impatiently for a response. "What say you, sir?" he suddenly blurted, his intense eyes daring yet another encounter. "Tell me the difference. Tell me how valor evolves into honor with discretion. Better yet, tell me what the fuck I'm doing here in the first place if that's all there is to it?"

Denny continued staring, his eyes narrowing as he hesitated to respond. He was pondering how the young officer's words might have been those he'd uttered himself in times past. While he attempted again to recapture this memory, the junior officer tendered a final volley.

"And don't tell me it's a paradox or some other bullshit excuse. Men of honor have no need for flimsy discretion, or any other excuse to justify their deportment."

"Shannahan, shut the fuck up!!" Denny demanded, his tolerance depleted. "What nursery rhyme or fuckin' fairy tale are you quoting from? And furthermore, what the fuck do *you* know about honor in the first place? Who made you the official expert on valor and honor, Colonel Socrates? Something you read in a fuckin' book?"

He stalked back over toward the lieutenant, leaned over, and placed both clenched fists on the table before him. "*You* probably still believe in God, don'cha? From what I've seen in my life, I'm not sure He even remembers what planet we're on. Furthermore, you're letting your fuckin' age out of the playpen again, puberty breath!!!"

Mike stared at the captain's clear, focused eyes.

"I don't make excuses for anyone, Lieutenant," Denny went on. "But you apparently need to reassess your idealistic outlook on life and get with the real program here. It *is* what it fuckin' *is*! You need to alter your *self-righteous* global paradigm of life, or you're going to have to learn to deal with it any way you want. Either way. But if you're still having trouble accepting the facts the way they are, then maybe you need to make an appointment with the fuckin' Group chaplain. I don't have the time to reevaluate the meaning of life with you, so fuckin' grow up or ship out!"

Mike relented, slowly shaking his head in perplexed resignation. "I didn't mean to go off on *you*, Denny. I'm just a little frustrated with the whole thing. I guess I just expect things to be cut and dried, not all convoluted with *degrees* of truth and conscience. It just gets a little confusing to me," he admitted, running his hand through the emerging crop of dark hair.

"You haven't even *approached* the gates of hell yet, Lieutenant, so where the hell do you get off judging men who have spent more time in combat than you did in high school?"

"Don't you think everybody's made me *well* aware of that?"

"You get all tangled up in trying to figure shit out, Mike. You've got the rest of your life to sort it out. Give it a break. Just focus on what's important now. Sometimes, Lieutenant, you make me *really* wonder if you're mature enough to handle this shit!"

His captain's comments blistered Mike's pride, cutting deep into the cocoon nurturing his budding confidence.

"Didn't your dad teach you anything about life?" Denny continued. "You don't *have* all the facts. You haven't *been* there, so how the hell can you make a decision about anything? When *you* finally find yourself in front of a battalion of NVA trackin' your ass with dogs five clicks inside the Laotian border, you better be *focused* on getting your team back across the Fence. Chuck doesn't give a rat's ass about your fuckin' honor, he *pisses* on your quest for valor, an' he's gonna *zap* your virtuous ass in a heartbeat while you ponder the true meaning of life. If your camp's being overrun by a battalion of screamin', bugle-blowin' banshees, are you going to crest the berm and wave the flag, hopin' somebody is gonna see you all full of valor and honor? You're fuckin' not, I'll tell you that, Lieutenant!"

Mike's eyes downcast as he felt the critique take hold, soothing his impetuousness. The silence between them allowed him time to grasp the stark reality he tended to avoid. "I had very little one-on-one time with my dad," he added sheepishly. "He always stayed late at work. He never made much time to teach me about life."

"Sorry 'bout that, but just so you get it right, Lieutenant, I'll share a little parable that Colonel Kelly gave the men one night in the club. This so-called *charade* has the lineage and true-life sacrifices to support it." The captain sat down and leaned over the back of the chair, white-knuckled hands squeezing the back rest as he looked Mike squarely in the eyes. "'Men,' he told us, 'Special Forces is a mistress. Your wives will envy her, because she will have your hearts. Your wives will be jealous of her because of the power to pull you away. This mistress will show you things *never* before seen and allow you to experience things *never* before felt. She will love you but only a little, seducing you to want more, give more, die for her. She will take away from the ones you love, and you will hate her for it, but leave her you never will. But if you must, you will miss her, for she has a part of you that will never be returned intact. And in the end, she will leave you for a younger man.'"

"Never thought of *her* in that manner," Mike replied, smiling at the thought that he could one day share their passion for the mistress himself. "Colonel Kelly said that?" he inquired.

"James R. Ward, OSS Detachment One-oh-one, World War Two, Green Beret," the captain concluded. "They served together back in the day."

"You're absolutely right, Denny," Mike quietly responded, slowly getting up, pausing notably before he reached out and shook the captain's hand one last time. He placed both hands on his grip, nodding his head in agreement with his mentor's last statement. "You know, I value your advice. It's just hard for me to cultivate and accept lapses in character when it equates to something I've aspired to all of my life. After all, I'm the son of a *real* hard-core Irish naval officer," he explained. "You're totally right. I've got a lot to learn, and I just wish I had your perspective on how to get there from here. My dad wasn't too keen on sharing that sort of stuff with me."

Denny acknowledged the contrition in Mike's eyes and realized his role as mentor just might finally be taking hold upon the young lieutenant.

"I just hope you don't hold my lack of maturity against me, Denny," Mike continued. "I'll probably get a little older tomorrow. So in the meantime, just do us all a favor and don't forget to keep your happy ass in nametag defilade over there." Mike was using the common military slang for keeping one's head down, not exposing oneself to enemy fire.

Denny feigned a slight smile, unveiling a cloaked sigh of relief as he turned and left the team room. Mike watched him stride down the hall for the last time, still shaking his head as he headed up the stairs.

The lieutenant retreated back to the table, besieged with an element of inadequacy, and hesitantly picked up the paper again and sorted through the flimsy pages. He stared aimlessly over the unfocused print for several minutes, recounting the stinging remarks he knew he truly deserved. Finally, he found the casualty section, paying close attention to the rank and the names of those killed in action that month. A brisk chill expanded his senses, watering eyes focusing closely on the familiar name.

"Rat... Goddammit, fella," he whispered, recalling the days they'd spent in jump school together. He drew back in the chair, folding his fingers tightly together over his head. As he ushered Rat's jovial images through his mind, feelings of regret consumed him, feelings that he had betrayed his friend because he wasn't over there exposing himself to hostile fire. He sat silently, scarcely breathing while he offered a heartfelt tribute to his fallen friend.

Instinctively, he leaned back over the table, looking again at the small type that signified the end of a friendship. He continued to read, following the long columns of names that filled the page. Melnick, Mylinski, Peterson, and Sutter—all OCS classmates from his platoon at Benning. Brewer, Levine, Potter, and Wheatland—men he had known in Basic Training and AIT. All gone, all dead. He stared at the heading of the page again. *Killed in Action…*

An honorable fate, he reasoned, silently saluting their virtuous sacrifice in his mind. He continued to stare at the heading, taken deeply by the solemnity and honor it denoted. Nurturing regret, he warily wiped his nose with the inside of his palm, absorbing the moisture seeping in his eyes with the edge of his sleeve. *Nothing fuckin' discreet about that,* he told himself.

Loud shouts and clamor suddenly erupted outside the team room, scores of jump boots pounding up the stairs, men laughing, others joking as the noise echoed throughout the basement.

"Hey, what's up?" Mike yelled, looking down the hallway at the exodus of men clamoring up the stairwell.

"You're not going to believe it, Lieutenant," one sergeant shouted. "There's a convoy headed this way from Bad Tölz. Come see for yourself."

Mike scurried up the stairs, following the procession out into the quadrangle, where throngs of men lined the parade ground. Three ice-crusted deuce-and-a-halfs circled the frozen cobblestone quadrangle, the thick diesel exhaust polluting the fresh afternoon air. Mike watched the first truck pull off into the snow-capped parade ground, coming to a stop near the tall flagpole. He pushed his way through the melee, stopping next to Sergeant Allen, who stood stoically, arms folded, a disgusted look on his face.

"What's all this about?" Mike asked him, staring at the three large army trucks unloading a gangly group of officers in their dress greens.

"Well, you can bet it's not a fuckin' USO show," he replied, shaking his head. "There goes the fuckin' ghetto, Lieutenant. Time to make that phone call to Mrs. A."

Allen turned and walked briskly away from the spectacle, leaving the lieutenant to sort out what was transpiring. From each corner of the quadrangle, men swarmed out of the old Bavarian-deco buildings, quickly drawing the circle closer as the last truck pulled to a halt. Metal tailgates on the covered trucks slammed down in unison, and one by one, the shavetails stumbled off, dragging their overstuffed duffel bags behind them. Twenty-five brand new second lieutenants, their shiny gold bars sparkling in the afternoon sun. The men standing around him chuckled, most just highly amused at the spectacle of a long line of second lieutenants lining up with their duffel bags now in front of them. The new arrivals' faces portrayed a variety of expressions, ranging from bewilderment to embarrassment, accented by one striking and common element. Mike had to concede with that obvious factor: They all looked simply ridiculous.

*   *   *

Second Lieutenant Rich Mycoskie took a deep breath of the crisp mountain air, clearing his lungs of the musty canvas tinge lingering from the thirty-minute ride from Group headquarters. He dropped his heavy duffel bag in front of him and stared out at the large, casual crowd of laughing, flippant men staring back at him.

"Honey, I'm home," he finally said, intrigued by the diversity of the cajoling men lining the parade ground.

Mycoskie stared at the variety of uniforms. Some wore heavy, dark-green woolen tunics, accented by lighter, faded jungle-green fatigue pants. Others sported woolen mufflers or dark-green sweaters under the standard-issue fatigue blouse. He even noticed a few with freshly starched fatigues, but the one consistent factor that stood out to him was the distinctive, worn green berets on their heads, inscribing a monogram of professionalism to the entire gathering.

The gathered crowd seemed content on keeping their distance, arms folded passively, or at least one hand on their hips. The only movement Mycoskie detected was an occasional shifting of weight, and a lot of head scratching. He dusted off his class-A greens and then bent over to fix the blouse in his jump boots, one eye constantly fixed on the silent formation for any sign of hospitality.

"Well, here we are," he remarked to the other lieutenants around him. "But ya know what? Just lookin' around, I don't know half the guys here!"

*   *   *

"Look at zat one over zair at ze end of ze line," Sarkie told his XO. "He looks like ze Pillsbury Doughboy, all dressed up und novair to go!"

Mike stared at the tall, overfed young officer, who was nervously trying to mold the stiff beret on his melon-shaped head. Despite his best efforts, the edge of the beret would not lie down over his ear. It appeared more like a flat green mushroom than the stylish beret the men in the Group were expected to wear. Mike noticed some of the other second lieutenants with berets, each one of them struggling with the new headgear, pulling the edges down over the wrong ear, their efforts enhancing the delight of the assembled mass of veterans.

"Zair're a bunch uf fuckin' legs!" Sarkie exclaimed.

"I donno," Mike replied. "I think I see some jump wings on some of them. Just look at their boots. That'll tell ya."

"Look at that one in the middle, Lieutenant." Mike looked over his shoulder to see Val standing behind him. "He thinks he's a clown. He's not even wearin' boots."

"Yeah, Top, I noticed him too. He looks like an accountant in a baker's hat."

"I was thinkin' he looks more out of place than the Pope at a bikers' convention, myself."

"Zis oat to be goot," Sarkie said. "Here come ze major und Jack D."

The throng of men fell silent as the Group sergeant major and Major Reese strode authoritatively in front of the formation of new replacements. Without hesitation, they both executed a column left directly in front of the most conspicuous member of the entourage. The sergeant major's eyes focused sternly on the new lieutenant as Major Reese assumed a position squarely in front of the startled officer, whose beret floated squarely on the top of his pointed head, the black nylon tie strings dangling down to the top of his collar. Mike contended he looked more like a skinny British seaman than a Special Forces officer.

"And just what are *you* supposed to be?" Major Reese asked him, his hands drawn authoritatively up to his hips.

Lieutenant Olmstein swallowed hard. "What do you mean, sir?" he quietly responded.

"Give me that beret, Lieutenant," Reese demanded, impatiently waiting for the lieutenant to comply.

Olmstein hesitated, a nervous tremor twitched rapidly in his bony legs as he reluctantly handed his beret to Major Reese. The major promptly held it high in the air for all to see. His eyes staying focused on the trembling lieutenant, he ordered the sergeant major to his side. "Sergeant Major, will you kindly instruct these *bozos* on the proper etiquette of the wearing of the beret?"

"Roger that, sir!" Jack D stepped forward, taking Olmstein's beret from Major Reese and displaying it for all the new arrivals to see.

"This, gentlemen, is a Green Beret. It is not a hat!" he exclaimed, his froth-filled veins accenting his displeasure. "None of you have earned the right to even wear it. And by the looks of things, you may well *never* earn that right! But as long as you are assigned to this unit, it will be a part of your uniform, and by God, you will wear it correctly! Do I make myself clear?"

"Yes, Sergeant Major!"

"Men of honor have died wearing this beret, and many of them *I* have had the distinct honor of calling *friend*. Our late President John F. Kennedy once referred to this beret as—and I quote—'a badge of courage, and a mark of distinction in the fight for freedom.' If I ever catch any one of you wearing it like a Girl Scout, a pastry chef, a French pimp, or in any other unauthorized manner, I will make sure that you are transferred to the leg unit nearest to the Chinese border! *Any questions?*"

"No, Sergeant Major!"

His heartfelt tirade completed, Jack D tediously delineated the protocol of donning the beret in the correct manner. In spite of his in-depth block of instruction, many of the new recruits never mastered the simple art of wearing the beret, nor the implications such an honor entailed. The arrival of the neophytes quickly prompted an exodus of disgruntled veterans back to the steamy jungles and outback regions of that wretched land, Vietnam, that exodus being the ultimate paradox that characterized their trepidation, adrenaline, and honor. Mrs. A's phone line sizzled with desperate requests for transfers to the Fifth. The Tenth Special Forces Group was destined never be the same again after that chilly afternoon, not then, not ever again.

Within several weeks, twelve of the new recruits succeeded in promptly being ushered out of the Tenth Group, exiled to regular infantry units throughout Germany. The remaining young zealots acquired the demeaning tag of Spring Chicks and, as such, were naturally treated accordingly. Not allowed to wear the full green flash on their berets, they received a thin, half-inch green candy bar to wear below their rank. They answered reveille at 0400 every morning, and they struggled through a grueling crash course tailored after the Special Forces officers' course at Fort Bragg. Six weeks later, the survivors were assigned to A-Teams as executive officers, a move that instigated a second round of veterans requesting transfers and retirements.

Mike found himself actually enjoying the turmoil that ensued. *He* was no longer the focus of the trivial pranks and begrudging resentment. For him, the aggravating, petty harassment finally ceased, and the resumption of hazing fell squarely on the nerves and gumption of the selected new lot. His faded fatigues and newfound swagger provided him with the treasured anonymity he so longed for. His sudden promotion to first lieutenant and command of ODA-1 completed that treasured transition. Even Jacques finally acquiesced. It was a new ball game. The focus had changed and, along with it, Mike's attitude about his position in life.

The news from the States stung his zest for his fellow citizens. He was deeply disappointed by the revelation that his compatriots were carrying the NVA flag in the nation's capital—in support of his enemy! The Spring Chicks told of massive demonstrations, draft card burnings. "Happenings" had been staged over the past eighteen months—even outright defiance of the rule of law. Young men crowded the college campuses, seeking refuge from the call to arms they fervently sought to elude. Those unqualified to secure deferments simply left home and headed north to Canada. Mike wondered if they would run into his old friend, Jim.

*   *   *

CHAPTER TWENTY-ONE

THE RUSTY SNOW CHAINS ON the black Mercedes clanked loudly against the ice-capped cobblestone, spinning wildly as Mike coaxed it up the steep incline to the entrance to the vintage Prinz Heinrich *Kaserne*. He urged the car forward, patting the dash to the lively beat of the Box Tops blaring loudly through the pulsating Blaupunkt. Through the archway and around the corner, he felt his vocal cords twinge as he mimicked his *new* favorite tune, his mind wandering sporadically to find the right words. He turned into the gravel parking lot in front of the BOQ as the spirited organ solo trailed to a muffled end. Reaching over, he turned the radio off and slouched back into the worn leather seat while his mind recaptured the pressing issue of the evening.

He recalled gazing across the small dinner table, admiring the sparkle in Susan's light blue eyes. He watched her with veiled envy as she smiled adorably, gathering the last of the linen dinner napkins, meticulously folding them with dainty hands as she turned and disappeared into the crowded kitchen.

"You're a lucky guy to have such a lovely wife, John," he told his new XO, still wondering why he had married her on his way to war.

Over the past six months, Mike had been struggling with a nagging anguish, having witnessed wives and children being chaperoned into waiting staff cars to be ushered to the airport in Munich. Widows, orphans—each loved one now shackled with a new label, a somber and unwelcome destiny, all of them unwitting victims of the tragedy of war. He couldn't help but wonder if lovely Susan would suffer the same fate, and importantly, he wondered why his new executive officer would have even subjected her to that conceivable destiny.

"Met her at a sorority mixer at Rutgers," John had told him. "I was *smitten* so bad I had to go look the damn word up!"

A selfish notion, Mike reasoned in his mind. *Waiting at home for a distant lover is one thing, but to marry someone on the verge of going into battle is quite another,* he decided as he adjusted the heater in the car. *Heartthrobs can lead to dire consequences. I know,* he told himself. A twinge of self-pity tiptoed sheepishly into his consciousness.

Twwaaanngg!

He felt the car shudder as the left headlight went dark.

"What the fuck!!!?"

He looked up to see the distant muzzle flash just before the second bullet extinguished his other headlight. Throwing open the door, he dove into icy slush and slithered frantically away from the idling car. Struggling to scamper to his feet, he made a slippery run for the snowy embankment packed beside the gate to the officers' quarters.

Those were damn gunshots! he realized, peering cautiously over the frosty berm, the wet ice etching a chill pattern throughout his senses. Scanning the barracks where he saw the last muzzle flash, he focused on the open window with the dark crêpe drapes flowing outward in the crisp, light breeze. *That's shithead Hollis's room!* he noted, ducking back down as he gathered his thoughts.

He rolled over on his back and leaned on the embankment, the numbing slush swiftly seeping throughout his loins and down his outstretched legs. He pressed his wool beret hard against his ear, warming the lobe while he hurriedly collected his thoughts. *This is fuckin' bullshit,* he quickly concluded. *Those were live rounds!*

His anxiety rapidly dissolved to sheer anger as he sensed yet another macho display of pseudo-bravado from a "fearless" garet warrior, the rear-echelon type with staff job, the trooper who never sees combat. Sliding on all fours over to the car, Mike pulled the keys from the ignition and scampered around to the trunk. He carefully opened the lid just enough to retrieve his pistol belt and his .45 Colt automatic, then cautiously made his way around the compound to the side door of the barracks.

The hallway stood darkened and empty, and as he rejected the idea of chambering a round, he slid quietly through the door. He listened to the competing array of tunes echoing from behind closed doors as he slowly crept toward the center stairway leading up to Hollis's room.

"What's with the pea shooter?" the brazen voice inquired from behind. Mike turned sharply, confronting the figure leaning out of his room, a bottle of Löwenbräu firmly encased in his hand.

"Suppose you didn't hear those shots?" Mike inquired rather incredulously, recognizing Lieutenant Mycoskie, with his trademark deep, dark five o'clock shadow.

"And *that's* something new around here?" Mycoskie emptied his bottle as he stepped from the doorway.

"He shot my fuckin' headlights out!" Mike replied.

"Bummer. Got any beer in your room? I'm fresh out," Mycoskie confessed. "The *Putzfrau* cut me off." He held out the empty beer bottle.

"Fuck you." Mike continued up the stairs, holstering his sidearm as he made the turn up the second flight.

"Probably Hollis," Mycoskie surmised. "He stumbled in here about an hour ago with a coupla' *mademoiselles* he cornered in Munich. He was pretty fucked up, if you know what I mean."

"'Fucked up' is about to take on a whole new meaning," Mike replied, tracking a cold, wet trail up the remaining steps.

"This oughta be good," Mycoskie replied, scampering up the slippery stairs in his bare feet.

Mike positioned himself in front of Hollis's room, unzipping his wet fatigue jacket and slinging it to the floor. He reached down and rattled the locked door handle, then slammed his fist forcibly on the thick, solid door.

"Hollis, you motherfucker! Open the fuckin' door!"

"Get the fuck outa' here, honky," the muffled response floated through the door. "I'm busy entertaining Prince."

Mike stood back, and with a sharp thrust with his wet boot, he smashed the door open, shattering the threshold in the process. The sweet, pungent odor of sweat and sex quickly enveloped his nostrils, and visions of shimmering wet bodies entangled in awkward, enticing poses tempered his rage. A red silk scarf enveloped the table lamp, casting an alluring rose-tint glow to the menagerie of stark nudity on the bed before him.

"You sorry black-assed son of a bitch," Mike bellowed. "Who the fuck do you think you are anyway? Fuckin' Nat Love?"

"Hey, Hollis! Got any beer in here?" Mycoskie inquired, stepping through the remnants of the doorway and over to the side of the bed, smiling suggestively at the startled young women frantically pulling the damp sheets over their naked bodies.

"What do you honkies think this is? A fuckin' love-in? Get your own fuckin' bitches and leave the *brother* the fuck alone. I'm very capable of handlin' this myself. I've seen me and Prince dwell quite comfortably in this same scenario before," Hollis said, characteristically referring by name to his penis.

Mike noticed the 9mm Browning Hi-Power lying on the desk against the wall, two shell casings strewn on the floor below the open window. He walked over and picked one of them up, holding it up for Hollis to see. "Just what's your major malfunction, Stevenson?" Mike asked him. "You gone and let all this Green Beret shit fuck up your freakin' mind?"

Agitated, Hollis sat up in the bed, reaching over to retrieve the shamrock bottle of Glenlivet from the bedside table. He took a long swig and then handed it to the girl on his right. "I thought you were that wimp-dick Pressley. Figured he was shining those bright fuckin' lights in my room to fuck with me. Me an' Prince conducted a little E&E on his happy ass in Munich, you know," he bragged, recounting the "evasion and escape" adventure. "Bailed out with the babes while he was in the latrine at the Heavy Weapons Club."

"Wrong, rucksack breath. Pressley drives a fuckin' silver Jag. You shot out *my* fuckin' headlights, and as fucked up as you are, you could have hit me, you stupid motherfucker!"

"Not a chance, momma's boy. That piece has a certified match barrel, and I *always* hit what the fuck I'm aimin' at."

"Your fuckin' dick has always been bigger than your brain, Stevenson, and if you weren't in mixed company, this conversation wouldn't even be taking place. Just because these floozy-ass French bitches have an affinity for the brothers doesn't give you the right to fuckin' abuse everyone else, dickhead! And if I recall correctly, *you're* the one who thinks he's a fuckin' white man in a black man's body in the first fuckin' place. And another thing," he concluded. "You're paying for all that shit, fart-stain, and if it ain't fixed by the weekend, your sorry ass is going to find itself with your heels locked in front of the major!"

Hollis spewed out the last sip of scotch in a resounding spray, his mocking laughter quickly reverting to a coughing, wheezing, spastic attempt to regain his breath. "In front of *who*? Elmer Fudd? I got more shit on his honky ass than a ten-foot honey bucket in a fifty-foot shit well."

Mike stared intently at the unrepentant Casanova, cast a final look at the bewildered naked maidens, then threw the empty shell casing at the drunken lieutenant, and stalked briskly out of the room.

"Annnnnnn' what the fuck are *you* waitin' for, rookie?" Hollis demanded, noting Mycoskie's eyes surveying the distressed female creatures before him.

"Just wonderin' if you had any cold ones left," Mycoskie retorted. "But I'm not at all opposed to some sloppy seconds instead, you sweet Hamma knokka," he suggested, rubbing the long leg beneath the covers next to him.

Hollis climbed over the trembling girl, picked up the pistol from the desk, then turned to see Mycoskie scampering through the door and down the hallway to the stairs.

Mike locked the door behind him, threw his soggy jacket over the fetid, warm radiator, and slumped down languidly into the musty armchair in the corner. He stared at the makeshift bar he'd constructed, now totally unenamored by the three *Playboy* centerfolds he'd taped over the front. He focused casually on the fishnet hammock draped from the corner ceiling, along with the camouflaged poncho liner he used as a bedspread to complement the olive-drab bachelor décor. The chill room mimicked his mood, a fitting accent to the dreary thoughts surfacing in his bruised mind. He wondered just how long he would be able to maintain the charade before he admitted to himself that he was conveniently eluding the noble quest from which he would finally free himself or die trying.

I'm ready, he told himself. *God knows it's time.*

He walked over to the bar and retrieved the full bottle of Glenlivet from the bookcase behind. Grabbing one of the crystal tumblers he'd bought for his mother, he reached down and unbuckled his belt. Stumbling over to the window, he stepped on one leg of his trousers, then the other, dragging the wet garment along the cold, wooden floor. He reached down and slung it into the bathroom. Then he leaned over and scooped into the glass a handful of ice and snow from the window ledge. After carefully pouring in two fingers of the scotch, he turned on his stereo and retreated to the relative comfort of the armchair in the corner. *Thank God, I hate this shit,* he conceded. *Otherwise, I'd probably be one drunk motherfucker in the morning.*

He slung his legs over the padded armrest and cast his consciousness into the myriad of flagrant thoughts skipping through his tutored, yet mangled mind. He sipped on the concoction, trying desperately to find some solace in its mysterious bouquet. He sensed an ambiance familiar to his senses, yet he rejected the abruptness of the flavor, a sharp, distinct assault on his sensitivities. *Must be an acquired taste,* he surmised, rejecting his tendency to just put the drink down and go to bed.

My whole life has been a defiant parable, he concluded. *I've been in the army for three years, and I haven't even showed up,* he calmly admitted. *And... that's my fault.*

He swirled the sharp-tasting single malt, diluting it as much as he could with the icy slush in the glass. *The next thing you know, I'll be smokin' a bunch of Cuban cigars and hangin' out with Hollis. The Commander will really be proud of that.*

The music drew his mind closer to Barbara than he'd been in three years. It teased him with optimism, comforted him with compassion, then slammed him back to reality when his deepest thoughts finally seeped through the closely guarded vault and focused grimly on his old friend Rat.

A smoldering rage lethargically consolidated its strength but finally settled well within his soul, prompting a dire decision that he knew he either needed to make or live without honor for the rest of his life.

Then, as if on cue, the stereo added a subtle caveat to the evening: "Turn out the lights, the party's over."

*   *   *

Major Reese glanced up to see the young lieutenant standing in the doorway to his office. He noticed a manila folder tightly clutched in the visitor's left hand, and the faint smile on Mike's face seemed to set him at ease.

"What the hell do you want, bozo?" he bellowed.

Mike strode through the door, his confident gait halting abruptly in front of Major Reese's cluttered desk. "Just some paperwork that requires your endorsement and signature, sir," he replied.

The major leaned back in his chair, slowly clasping his hands in his lap as he crossed his bullfrog legs. He looked up into the young man's eyes, cautiously gauging the temperament of the lieutenant standing before him. He slowly reached out, palms up, took the folder from Mike, and began to read.

Within seconds, he closed the folder and spun it back across his desk. "Your ten-forty-nine requesting transfer to the Fifth Group is denied, Lieutenant," he responded casually.

Mike stood stunned. His eyes widened as he stared down at the portly major smiling up at him. "I don't understand, Major," he replied forcefully. "Why me?"

"Because, Lieutenant Fuzz, Group HQ has other plans for you. I just got your orders this morning, Lieutenant, and you'll be out of here within the week."

"Out of here to where?"

"Stateside, Lieutenant. Land of the hippies, Black Panthers, free love, acid rock, and draft dodgers. You oughta fit right in with your flattop, Shannahan."

The major reached across his desk to his "out" box and retrieved a stack of orders. He thumbed through the papers until he found the ones with Mike's name on them. He casually tossed them in his direction and continued as the lieutenant carefully picked them up.

"This goddamn 'balance-of-payments deficit' has finally caught up with us over here. The Group has been ordered stateside to some god-awful place called Fort Devens, Massachusetts. Colonel Kelly hand-picked the advance party, and your silly-ass name was at the top of the list, Irishman. Congratulations, Lieutenant, you're going home."

"But, sir, I don't want to go home. With all due respect, sir."

"Shannahan, the army could give a rat's ass what *you* want to do, Lieutenant. Now take your orders, and vacate the premises. You've got a lot of out-processing to take care of before your flight Friday."

Disheartened, the lieutenant came to attention, saluted the major, turned, and walked out the door.

"Where the hell *is* Fort Devens. Never even heard of it," he muttered to himself. "Massachusetts? What the fuck is in Massachusetts?"

His mind painted the scattered, foam-laden, rocky shoreline, the choppy bay dotted with the gaff-topped sails of the lobster fishermen's sloops, fishing nets shimmering above the wooden piers, *Old Ironsides* straining against her moorings. "I can just see myself now, slipping through the top of the maple trees onto the DZ. *Fuck!*" he quietly lamented.

* * *

CHAPTER TWENTY-TWO

WHERE WERE ALL THE PINE trees? There were a few here and there, but nothing like what he'd been used to. They had stood like silent sentries, welcoming him to every post he had been to before. He wouldn't miss them, he decided. They were certainly no match for the beautiful white birch and billowing orange broad leaves of New England that would be showing up later in autumn, months after the now-bare deciduous trees would bring forth their glory.

Mike had recently learned that Fort Devens had originally been purchased from local farmers and included about five thousand acres of prime land, some of which bordered the lazy creek flowing north into the Nashua River. Since the end of World War Two, the post had been home to the clandestine Army Security Agency, which was responsible for training officers and enlisted men in the fine arts of cryptology, linguistics, covert operations, and intelligence. There had not been any combat units there since the end of that war, a fact that generated a lot of local curiosity when it had been disclosed in the local news that a Special Forces Group would be calling their sleepy little post home.

The members of the advance party had echoed their apprehension as they were escorted through a series of old, dreary white World War Two barracks, greatly in need of a new coat of paint. Squares of loose white gravel outlined the assembly areas outside the barracks. The place had reminded Mike of the assortment of old wooden deathtraps he'd survived in Basic Training back at Fort Polk.

"Zis place fuckin' zucks," Sarkie exclaimed.

"Whad'a ya expect?" Sergeant Major Logan replied. "The fuckin' Taj Mahal?"

Mike shook his head. "Same old army bullshit. Guess we're gonna have to put on our coveralls and slap a layer of paint on the whole rotten place too."

"Vair ve supposed to set up ze team rooms?" Sarkie inquired.

"These *are* the team rooms," Logan replied. "These aren't our billets. Each team will have a floor for their gear and team areas. We'll have rooms at the NCO billets on main post."

Any excitement that accompanied the new transition quickly turned to despair. As the group was escorted through the post facilities, it was readily apparent that any form of proper military courtesy had subsided into the local civilian culture, wherein curious stares and nods replaced the customary crisp hand salute.

"Fuckin' legs," Sarkie protested. "Zat shit's gonna change ven ze Group gets here. Jack D iss gonna haf a field day wit zese bolos!"

For the next several weeks, the advance party coordinated the mundane tasks to prepare the ancient facilities for the arrival of the main body of the Tenth Special Forces Group. They toured the airstrip, armory, sleeping quarters, mess halls, and transportation facilities that would be required to support their training exercises.

One terrain feature was obviously absent: There were *no* mountains. *This ain't gonna work,* Mike had told himself. He'd been shocked to hear that the nearest mountainous terrain was at least two hours north, up into the White Mountains of New Hampshire. "That's a hell of a long hump," he concluded. "Any dams along the way?" he asked the escort officer.

The bachelor officers of the Group were quartered in Wainwright Hall, a dismal excuse for a BOQ, compared with the relative luxury of the Q back at Bad Tölz. Most of them decided to move off post and bribed or threatened the S1 admin folk to issue statements that on-post housing was unavailable. The problem, however, was that there weren't any apartments or houses for rent anywhere around the little local town of Ayer that they could afford, nor, for that matter, were there patriotic landlords who were willing to give the servicemen six-month leases. The men started looking around other nearby communities, and their luck greatly improved.

When the Group finally arrived later that month, Mike received his assignment as commanding officer of ODA-21, a Czech Team in B-Company of the Tenth. His old acquaintance, First Lieutenant David

Rabin, had earned the job as the company S3, in charge of operations and training. It was a major's slot, but the fact was there weren't any majors left in the company to fill it.

David was regarded as the best man for the job, despite the fact he was still wearing a hip-high cast from injuries he had received earlier, on an ill-fated demonstration parachute jump in Belgium. The herculean team leader had crashed and burned during an exhibition jump for the king and queen in Brussels. When Mike had gone to visit him in the hospital in Munich, he was still in pretty bad shape. He'd shattered his tibia just above his jump boots, and the thigh bone had snapped and protruded through his skin, which only added to the fracture disease that soon set in. He quickly developed pneumonia, and a subsequent infection just about wiped him out. The only thing that saved him was his intense spirit, coupled with the superb physical condition he'd been in at the time of the mishap. The word around Group was that the trio of nurses assigned to the orthopedic floor had provided routine, timely incentives to motivate his speedy recovery.

Together, the two bachelors found an old Victorian house in Lowell, an industrial town about thirty miles from the post. It was completely furnished with antiques and reflected the turn-of-the-century motif so common to the area. They moved in, and the only changes they made were to install their combination of stereo equipment in the living room, along with a coat rack to hold David's Bavarian walking cane. Like most young men of the era, they both loved music, and the superb quality of equipment reflected their elevated taste in fidelity.

The quaint two-story house had three bedrooms upstairs, so they decided to find another housemate to help share the rent. The officers in the Group routinely congregated at the O club for lunch, so Mike spread the word there that they had an available bedroom for rent. Lieutenant Rich Mycoskie had apparently lost out in the rush for apartmentmates, so he quickly took him up on the offer.

Rich enjoyed his reputation, which was, without question, as the most jovial character in the Group, the type of guy who could muscle his way into a crowded bar and, by the time he left, be on a first-name basis with everyone in the place (provided they didn't throw him out first). His persistent, bellowing laugh was highly infectious.

Rich moved in the next day. Mike heard the motorcycle pull into the driveway on the side of the aging house. He looked out the kitchen window and saw Rich straddling his 650cc Triumph, burdened precariously with an overstuffed duffel bag sitting upright behind him. His guitar was secured to the tall chrome backrest.

"What took you so long?" Mike asked. "You get lost?"

Rich deposited his aviator sunglasses in the top pocket of his leather flight jacket. "Green Berets never get lost!" he said proudly. "Get disoriented every once in a while, but we *never* get lost."

Mike smiled. "Where's the rest of your gear?"

"You're looking at it. Possessions preclude progress, and I'm a progressive kinda' guy. How you doing, Hamma knokka?" he asked, stepping up on the porch to shake Mike's hand.

The top-heavy bike abruptly toppled to the ground with a loud crash, followed by an extended, very dissonant phantom C half-diminished chord from the bruised guitar. Mike cringed as its hollow vibrations heralded his new housemate's arrival.

Rich didn't even bother to look back. He stood stout, but sturdy, and could easily cultivate a five-o'clock shadow by the first coffee break in the morning. His fair Celtic skin accented his dark beard, reminding Mike of the pastel of a hobo that his brother Thomas had hanging over his bed.

Mike was glad to have Rich join them. He'd at least have somebody to talk to after dinner, since David usually retired to the den and immersed himself in Russian technical manuals to improve his vernacular. (David had mastered five languages, four of them fluently.)

Mike showed his new housemate to his room, and they both stood in the small doorway looking at the small twin mattress against the wall. Rich asked if he could borrow some sheets, and Mike brought him some of the old white ones his mother had sent from home. He made the bed while Rich retrieved his duffel bag, and as Mike fluffed the pillows, Rich dumped the entire contents of the bag on the bed. "There!" he exclaimed with a heavy sigh. "I hate moving. It's such a pain in the ass. Let's go slam down a coupla' brewskies, you sweet Hamma knokka, you!"

"You want some help putting your stuff away?"

"Naaaaw! Minor detail. Wasted effort. It'll all end up in the same place anyway."

He was right. Over the next several weeks, Mike noticed the pile of clothes and underwear steadily growing. He finally stopped in Rich's doorway one night after work to survey the total magnitude of the phenomenon. *They haven't moved at all, just expanded,* he observed. He detected the subtle change in the tint in the white boxer shorts, though: slowly emerging to a dingy brown, gradually evolving into a greenish yellow. *Disgusting,* Mike thought, a slight tweak in his cheek as he imagined the mass expanding, like spongy mushrooms in the dark forest: upward and outward, nurtured by the stagnant variety of bodily fluids incubating within. He'd seen enough and promptly crafted a *Contaminated Area* sign, which he taped to Rich's door.

Mike told Rich that he thought he was a slob. David saw it a little differently. He told Rich that he lived in squalor, like a filthy pig in a sty. Rich agreed but did nothing to remedy the situation. The weekend following David's comments, Rich's floor in his room was covered in hay, with hardened ears of corn scattered across the surface. Undaunted, Rich cleared a path to his bed and ignored the brazen intrusion into his lifestyle.

It was an unlikely combination of personalities, but as the weeks turned into months, the three housemates actually became close friends. That fact did little to diminish the traditional SF spirit, though: They still found subtle ways to compete with one another, to mess with one another's minds. They manipulated uncanny responses by perpetrating the most egregious acts imaginable, all in the true spirit of the Brotherhood.

David bought a silver 428-hp Corvette, complete with slotted custom lake pipes down the sides. Mike countered with a classy white '64 T-Bird, outfitted with custom speakers and a new eight-track tape system. It took a couple of weeks, but Rich finally showed up with a '63 Chevy Biscayne. David told him he didn't mind the puke-green color, but the *Jesus loves me* mud flaps would have to go. Rich resisted for several weeks but finally relented to David's constant threats. Later the next day, the company sergeant major made a special trip to the S3 shop, curious as to when Lieutenant Rabin had given up Judaism and decided to become a Jesus freak. Rich had used epoxy to attach the mud flaps to the Corvette's fiberglass frame. The resulting bodywork to remove them cost him two hundred bucks, but he bragged that the shit David had caught from the rest of the company made it well worth every penny.

It seemed that Rich always found a way to get the last laugh, but he was no match for David's sheer strength, or his level wit. "Super Jew," the tag David had earned in Bad Tölz, proved invincible in the weekly arm-wrestling matches. He drew great pride from the fact that it took both of his housemates to pin him down. He still worked out at the local gym every evening, and his injury only served as an impetus for him to maintain his physical superiority over his younger peers. He hated his hand-carved walking cane, but he needed it to steady himself when walking upstairs or when getting into or out of tight places.

David had grown up in a tough neighborhood, a skinny pimple-faced Jewish kid in the suburbs of Washington, DC. At age twenty-six, he was one of the older lieutenants in the Group, and his maturity and poise established him as somewhat of a role model for the younger officers, such as Mike. It had been a bitter setback when the doctors told him that he had developed a nonunion in his tibia, that they would have to reoperate immediately and insert a metal rod in his leg. The healing process would begin all over again and would require at least another six months in a cast. There was no glory to his injury, and it began to take its toll.

The men of Tenth Group gradually adjusted to the new environment. They were not happy with the old World War Two barracks and team rooms, but they were glad to be back home for a change. But what a change it proved to be! Mike's America had been transformed into a nation in turmoil over the past several months: Black Panthers, Haight-Ashbury, flower children, public assassinations, riots in Chicago.

For the very first time, they *watched* what was going on over there, "across the pond" in Vietnam, and they kept a vigil for familiar faces every evening on the six o'clock news. Mike hoped he'd catch a glimpse of Denny, but most of the televised coverage concentrated on the conventional units, far from the perilous border camps manned by the men of Special Forces. Their concern for their comrades was overshadowed by their resentment of the seeping hatred they felt the public had for the men in uniform who were fighting the war, an affront they took very personally. They had to take it personally. It became a daily challenge, and the fighting men's honor was, after all, ultimately in *their* keeping.

The officers were shunned at local bars or accosted because of their obvious status. Short hair had become the Scarlet Letter, shared by all of the men in Group, a symbol so easily discernible amid the prevalence of long hair, mutton chops, and Fu Manchus. The older or married men wore their crew cuts with pride, but the bachelors considered their high-and-tights a stigma. The housemates tried to blend in with the locals: They wore wide, bell-bottom trousers and long, wide-collared flowery shirts. Rich even invested in a pair of elevated shoes and a wig, a fashion statement that quickly evolved into a social disaster. Still, they persisted, driven by innate desires, taunted and tempted by the sensual swaying motion of unshackled breasts, inspired and intrigued with the rumor of free love, the popular alternative to war.

They quickly discovered that if love *were* free, it was only free for those who conveniently espoused the psychedelic myths and hippie lifestyle of the era. The parameters had been drawn. Despite their youthful image, the housemates were a symbol of the establishment: inhibitors, collaborators, pawns perpetrating chauvinistic concepts, warmongers, truly unworthy of any semblance of intimacy.

The worn-out slogan *Make love, not war* did not apply to the jaded torchbearers of freedom and liberty, Mike reasoned. Thinking of the protagonist rascal in those sassy jodie cadence calls—whether male civilian Jody or his female counterpart Judy, the opportunistic civilians who do mischief stateside while soldiers were sacrificing overseas—he listened daily to both the current Jody and Judy screaming about the immorality of war while feasting on convenient copulation, totally neglecting the issue of the immorality of casual sex itself.

David held a very distinct opinion about the hypocrisy of the slogan, and of those who professed it. "If killing for peace is absurd and immoral," he proclaimed, "then fucking for peace is just as asinine. Unless, of course, you happen to be under the influence of PCP, LSD, or some other illegal substance. Then you can say the devil made you do it."

They regularly joked about the cunning and tenacity of their worthy nemesis, Jody, who had definitely developed the upper hand, burning his draft card in public, seeking refuge or asylum, hiding inside the college campus with deferments, encouraging the sexual liberation of women. All three men knew *they* were the patsies, the ones easily taken advantage of by Jody, especially when the liberal media regularly touted the "courage" of the draft dodgers who made it to Canada.

Their nightly forum usually convened in the den right after the video carnage known as the six-o'clock news. "Real courage is when you stand up and fight for what you believe in," Mike offered. "If these guys stood up and said, 'No, I'm not going to participate in an immoral war, despite the consequences,' then I'd have a lot of respect for them. I may not agree, but dammit, I can buy that type of conviction."

"That's bullshit!" Rich asserted. "Fighting in an 'immoral war' is not the issue here. It's the fear of getting killed, that's all. They could always serve in a noncombat arm. Most of them are just cowards hiding behind the few who really believe that crock of shit. Let them bail out to Canada! We're better off without them. Hope they freeze their chickenshit asses off!"

"Their agenda is better suited for an enclave of Buddhist monks," David added. "They're not all Hare Krishnas, but they want everyone to believe that their motivation stems from some sort of Pacifist Ideology. That since we are a country of diverse religions and ideological tolerance, no one will dare challenge their motivation—whether real, or adopted out of convenience."

"Yeah," Rich added, "I got their motivation hanging. Their fuckin' motivation is smokin' dope and gettin' laid by some braless flower child in the back of a microbus while groovin' to Iron Butterfly."

"What's wrong with that?" Mike asked.

"Fuck you, Shannahan!" Rich replied, trying to mask the smile that finally emerged. "*Wasza matka lubi osioł prącia!*" he spouted, drawing a confused stare from Mike. David chuckled, compounding Mike's frustration at his obvious lack of language skills.

"What'd he say?" he asked David, looking over to Rich in disdain.

"I didn't get the whole thing, but I think it had something to do with your mother and a donkey," he replied, still amused at Rich's broken Polish phrases, which he recited with vulgar regularity.

"*No seru na své matce a sestře,*" Mike blurted out, not sure if he had gotten his fragile Czech in the proper order.

"You guys are a piece of work," David observed. "Either one of you have any idea how ridiculous you sound?"

"And fuck you, too, you walking thesaurus," Rich remarked.

His superior status verified and intact, David brought the verbal duel to a conclusion. "Rich's right," he proclaimed. "This war is no different from any other war we've fought. *All* wars are immoral... Any killing is immoral if you want to get right down to it. The media has just done such a good job of bringing this war into America's living room that a lot of young men don't even have to hop a troop ship to find out what it's really like. Not like they used to. The mini-cam has taken all the romance and intrigue right out of the mysteries of war and turned it into a nightmare. What they've been able to see in their own living rooms has just plain scared the shit outa' them. And with all the talk about expanded consciousness and everybody doing their own thing, these guys have been able to draw sympathy from other Americans, who themselves are just as confused and shocked about what they see on the tube."

"What's so tough and courageous about bailing out to Canada?" Mike asked, smiling. "Now, if they were headed up to Peoria, I could see their point," he concluded.

"Fuck you, Shannahan!" Rich bellowed, shooting him the finger for the comment about his hometown.

Their conversations continued with growing regularity, but they all agreed that it was *their* commitment to their country that allowed Jody to hide behind deferments. They concluded that the televised slaughter of their brothers actually vindicated his protest and flight to avoid serving, while the "courageous" draft dodgers, deserters, and hippies thrived on the fruits of a free America, and of her liberated women.

The consensus that emerged among the three of them was that they were just red-blooded American men. The trilogy of sex, politics, and war had replaced religion as the topic taboo, one of the polarizing wedge topics that could be a hazard to friendships. They agreed that there was no clear-cut answer to the complex issues of the day.

David continued to support the notion that this war wasn't any different from the one their fathers had fought in Korea: Asian setting, DMZ, North and South, Communist insurgents supported by Red China, Russia, and other Marxist regimes. What did make it different, though, was the attitude of the American people, ignited and tempered initially by those who refused to fight. It was this public attitude, regardless of the motivation, which weighed heavily on the shoulders of the young men who carried Old Glory into battle, a solemn burden they had little room or stamina left to bear. Mike felt they were fighting the battle on two fronts: not only abroad but at home as well.

The housemates devoted hours debating the social and political atmosphere they were impacted by. Not one of them was opposed to differing points of view, as long as those views were heartfelt and not mere attitudes of convenience. The men were, after all, a small cross-section of America: a Catholic, a Protestant, and a Jew.

The one attribute they all shared in their collective gene pool was clear: their love of women, a fact that required no discussion. In pursuit of that noble quest, the three had ventured out for the evening in search of the elusive American breast, a phenomenon detected only recently beneath the tight-fitting sweaters of the coeds from nearby Lowell State. Intent on developing a "stable of talent," the trio had run reconnaissance patrols on the popular watering holes frequented by the mysterious coeds. They had selected primary and secondary targets and identified rendezvous points in the event their mission had to be aborted.

As they approached the Inferno, the primary target of the evening, they encountered two bouncers, who made it quite apparent that they were not the guests of honor for the evening. Following the brief "welcome" at the door, they found their way through the smoke and laughter and over to the long, crowded bar. As David stepped up to the rail, the trio promptly established a perimeter, then sent out a recon party to locate targets of opportunity.

Mike immersed himself into the raucous melody blaring from the costumed band's rendition of "Try a Little Tenderness." He noticed Rich stop beside a table of coeds and lean over. It wasn't long before he moved on, though, stopping at two more tables before he made his way back to the bar. "They're all on the rag," he said defensively.

"That never stopped you before," replied David.

"Maybe they just didn't like your face," added Mike.

"We'll see," Rich confidently replied, the wet ice trickling down his nose as he downed the tall glass of scotch and water and headed directly for the corner table on the other side of the room. Just before the song ended, Rich emerged on the dance floor, dwarfed by a tall, skinny creature with a dark, kinky balloon bouffant. He appeared to be having a great time on the dance floor, all six bars worth. Mike looked at David, shook his head, then turned, and leaned back on the padded armrest as Rich escorted his partner back to her table.

"Maybe he'll get lost on his way back," David commented.

Mike turned to take a sip of his drink when he felt Rich's hot hands slapping him on the back. "More scotch!" he ordered. "Nothin' to it. These women *love* me!"

"Rich!" David chided. "That broad is fuckin' ugly!"

"I know. I thought you were goin' to say something else," he replied.

"What? Something about her skin color?" David asked.

"Well, that too," Rich replied sheepishly. "No. That she's taller than me. I've never been with a woman who was taller than me."

"Hey, napalm breath, she's wearin' nine-inch fuckin' platform shoes, dickhead!" Mike informed him.

Rich remained unrepentant. He turned to the bar, raised his arm over his shoulder, and proceeded to start patting himself on the back. "Yooouuu sweeet-talkin' Hamma knokka, yooouuu," he loudly proclaimed. He gathered up his sloshing glass of scotch and took a long swig. "Got one rule I never violate," he told them, clinking the empty glass on the wet bar.

"And what's that?" Mike inquired. "Or maybe I shouldn't ask."

"Go ugly early, and avoid the rush at closing," he informed them.

"Well, she did have a *kind* face, I'll give you that," David remarked.

"Yeah? What kind was that?" Mike asked.

"The kind that could make a locomotive take a dirt road," David concluded.

Mike felt the gazes and stares from the other patrons around the bar. He shook his head in a veiled attempt to disavow his friends' repugnant remarks and retreated inauspiciously down the bar to order another drink. He stood there alone, enveloped in the misty haze of lingering smoke, gazing at the band through the fog created by the long, dingy mirror in front of him. He felt someone nudge his arm and turned to see a young brunette with a five-dollar bill in her hand, beckoning to the bartender. He took a chance.

"Band's pretty good, aren't they?" he asked her.

She turned briefly, their eyes never really making contact, then just turned back and walked to another spot in the crowded bar. Several other young ladies wandered up to his place at the bar, but none wanted to talk, dance, or even allow him to buy her a drink. *So much for the sexual revolution*, he told himself as he wandered slowly back over to where his friends were standing.

Mike grinned, pleasantly surprised to see David smiling as he carried on a conversation with a petite young lass with short, reddish hair. He introduced Mike to Sarah, and he explained that she had graciously offered him her bar stool when she noticed the full-leg cast beneath his bell-bottoms, which were held conspicuously together with the string of safety pins. Sarah quickly interjected that David had initially refused, but she had insisted. She was, after all, pursuing her ambitions in nursing school at Lowell State, down the street.

The trio continued immersed in casual conversation when a young man with a dark Prince Valiant haircut abruptly stepped in and asked Sarah to dance. He held out his hand for her to take, but she politely refused. He stood there for a moment, glancing back and forth at the two men, sneered, then turned and disappeared back into the bustling crowd.

Rich soon returned to the small gathering, finally having given up on his quest with the sepia queen, but only after she informed him of the monetary consequences of their further association. He wasn't having much luck with the ladies, and Mike even overheard him inviting them to barbecue some snake, or at least make a night jump with him.

Before long, Mike noticed Prince Valiant making his way through the crowd, flanked by three of his large friends. Very large. Two of them sported faded sweatshirts with the letters *BC* on the front, obviously the property of the football program at a local university. The other guy appeared taller and slim, his curly sideburns blending into his long brown Fu Manchu.

"You guys on leave or something?" Prince Valiant asked, pushing his empty glass between David and his new friend.

"Not exactly," David replied.

"Seems as though you guys are a little out of your element. Killed any babies today?"

David slowly pushed off the bar stool and stood up. He took one last sip of his drink and carefully placed it on the bar. He turned and took a step closer to the agitator, clearly bracing for a fight in front of him. "Ya know, fella, you've got it all wrong," he calmly told him. "But, to tell you the truth, I'm kinda' glad you brought that up. Ya know, I really get a little tired of all that crap about getting the blame for killin' babies and all. In fact, nothing could be further from the truth. And I just wish for once, you people would get that straight."

David then leaned over to his rival and, in a clear, distinct, yet hushed tone, offered his explanation: "See that beefy-looking guy over there?" he asked, pointing to Rich.

"Yeah? What about him?"

"*He's* the sorry bastard who *kills* 'em," David explained, shaking his head at Rich. "Me, I don't get involved in any part of that. The slimy little fuckers squeal too much. I just prefer to salt 'em down and throw 'em on the barbecue. They're real tender, and pretty damn good eatin'."

Prince Valiant abruptly stepped back. "You're fuckin' sick, man!"

"Just tell your entourage to move on, fella," David told him. "This is a private party, and we don't want any trouble."

Gathering his wits, the agitator promptly replied. "Well, if you guys haven't noticed, this is a *civilian* club. We don't take to *warmongers* comin' in here. So why don't you guys just go back to your base and sharpen your bayonets?"

"You're movin' in the wrong direction, pal," Mike told him, stepping up beside David to make his point.

"You guys think you're real tough, don't ya? Trying to impress the little lady here. Did ya tell her the only reason you're in the army is 'cause you couldn't make it on the outside? Seems to me you're even too ashamed to wear your fuckin' uniforms when you're not playing soldier boy or off busy murdering innocent women and children."

Prince Valiant glanced back at his friends for support, smirking confidently as he amped up his insults. "You don't wear it 'cause you know you'd get your ass kicked if you came in here wearin' your fuckin' monkey suit."

Rich stepped up to other side of David and stood in front of the biggest one in the group. "Damn, man," he said. "You look like you're big enough to stuff a whole barn *full* of hay all by yourself!"

The neckless hulk smiled, expanding his chest, and flexing his colossal arms.

"And fuckin' dumb enough to eat it all too," Rich concluded, staring the confused Goliath straight in the eyes.

Before anyone could respond, David turned back to the frightened girl behind him. "Excuse us," he told her, gently caressing her hand. Then he threw a ten on the bar and looked at Mike. "Let's go," he said calmly.

His words shocked Mike, for he clearly thought Prince Valiant had crossed the line. He'd never seen David back down from anyone or anything before. David grabbed Rich by the collar, and when he resisted, Mike took a firm grip of his arm and started moving him toward the door. They moved through the crowd with Rich protesting loudly, past the jeers and snickers and curious glances, out into the brightly lit parking lot, and into the dark, starless night.

The band played on, treating the crowd to a flurry of Creedence Clearwater, then tempered them softly with a somber ballad. Black lights reached out in the darkened room, illuminating colorful, psychedelic images in midair, while ladies' lingerie glowed brightly beneath their silky blouses and flimsy garb. Tall platform shoes slid silently along the dance floor, their movement guided by the union of flesh, and the soulful pleas of Procol Harum. An unsettled hush fell over the crowd, some straining to hear the words to the cosmic love ballad, others searching for some hidden meaning, but most for something to just hold onto.

This was the other side of America, the segment of his generation that Mike felt had passed him by, leaving him clinging to traditional values while *they* searched the universe for the true meaning of life. Ever since he had returned from Europe, he felt like a stepchild in his own country. He didn't condone their self-anointed right to use hallucinogens and other illegal drugs to expand their consciousness, thus enabling them to circumnavigate the heavens without ever leaving their apartments. He knew what they were about, but he just felt it was pretty stupid to fry your brain just to find yourself.

The evening wore on, the songs and scent of marijuana purging the smoke-filled room. The brass section of the band set the tempo for the next tune, stirring the crowd with the preamble to "Hold On, I'm Comin'." The show band set the crowd rocking, and hardly a soul noticed the men in khakis at the bar.

That is, until the song ended. Prince Valiant sashayed back to his table, glancing back over at the bar, seeing the uniformed soldiers standing there. He stared at their vague images: tan uniforms, black nametags, and black, shiny boots. "Take a look at the bar, George. Those chickenshit soldier boys are back!" he reported.

"I wonder what they're up to this time?" his burly companion inquired.

"Arnie, just leave them alone," the tall hippie requested. "They're not bothering anybody."

"Oh yeah? Well, Georgie, how'd you feel if one of those soldier boys was hittin' on your sister, Melinda?"

"I'd probably kick his ass. But she's not here. And they ain't. So what's your problem, Arnie? Why don't you just leave the poor fuckers alone?"

"Poor fuckers? Haven't you seen what those 'poor fuckers' have been doing every night on television? Haven't you heard about some of those massacres?"

"These guys don't look like some combat-crazed infantry dogfaces, Arnie. They're probably just some dumb truck drivers from Fort Devens. Hell, that big one has a damn cast on his leg. What'cha gonna do, pour a beer down it? Break the other one?"

"They don't fuckin' belong in here. I'm gonna tell them to get their candy asses out once and for all! Y'all comin'?"

Arnie got up and, along with the two ball players, skirted around the dance floor, through the crowd, over to where the soldiers were standing. George nurtured an uneasy feeling, watching his friend stop in front of the tall one with the cast.

"Nice uniform, boys, but I told you what would happen if you came in here looking like that."

"It's 'Lieutenant' to you, asshole, and that's precisely *why* we came back," David informed him. "You and I have some unfinished business."

"Oh touchy, touchy," Arnie mocked. "Did I say something to insult you?" he asked, looking over at his friends flanking him as he swayed from side to side.

"You *couldn't* insult me. Scumbags like you are nonentities. You have no meaning, no purpose in life. If you *could* have insulted me, I would have stomped your head back down through your scrawny ass in the first place. But you did manage to insult my uniform *and* the men who have died wearing it. They're not here to defend it, but we damn sure are."

Arnie confirmed his support as he looked back over his shoulder, making sure his friends were close behind him. "Yeah? Well, I'm glad at least some of you fuckers got what you deserved."

David's eyes narrowed. "We're through talking. Door's that way. Let's walk."

Arnie still felt pretty good about the odds. He felt certain he'd be able to take the cripple. All he had to do was to get one good kick in on the leg, and it would be over in a flash. He wasn't planning on getting close enough for the guy to hit him anyway. Arnie and his friends headed for the door, with David and his housemates close behind. A small crowd filed out behind them.

As the bright lights in the parking lot lit up the arena, Arnie turned to face his challengers. His eyes widened as he focused on the dark-green berets on the soldiers' heads. He sensed the sick feeling creeping into his stomach as he spotted the silver parachute wings over David's breast pocket. The silver bars on their berets and collars sparkled in defiance. He quickly realized he may have underestimated the trio. The bulging biceps on the cripple revealed a different story from what had been apparent when he was wearing the long-sleeved flowered shirt, and his companions' tailored uniforms exposed their taut physiques as well. "I suppose you want me to believe you are Green Berets?" he asked rather feebly.

"Oh, you saw the movie?" David replied. "You should read the book. It was much better. Wasn't it, Lieutenant Mycoskie?"

"Oh, much better," Rich replied.

"Wouldn't you agree, Lieutenant Shannahan?"

"Without a doubt, Lieutenant Rabin."

"But... you probably didn't have time to read it, now did you?" David went on. "That's a pity. You might have learned something about the American fighting man. But, then, I have a feeling that we can start that tax-free lesson right now."

"Thought you guys were from Fort Devens," one of the jocks said.

"We are," replied Mike firmly.

"They don't have any Green Berets stationed there," Arnie nervously observed.

"They do now," Rich reassured him. "You want to meet the rest of the guys? Who's playin' tomorrow night? Got any country and western bands? We'd love to show you how to do the two-step, but our real favorite is the *Circle ass-stomp.*"

Arnie took a step back, along with his friends. He quickly decided that the pending altercation may not be in his best interest.

"We decided that you needed a personal demonstration of what your taxpayer dollars are going for," David informed him. "Lieutenant Mycoskie, I think 'Tiny' over there is a prime candidate for your favorite *throat-crusher* move. Lieutenant Shannahan, the *BC* on the other one's shirt would make a good aiming point for your *boot print fandango.* I'll take the other two myself. I've got something special in store for them."

"Hey, guys… Ahhh, Lieutenants," George pleaded. "I'm really sorry about what was said back there. We hear you guys are trained killers. This shit ain't fair!"

"You musta' heard the old saying, chickenshit," David reminded him. "'Life's a bitch, and then you die.' But you can count on one thing," David added, noting that Arnie and his friends were nervously edging toward a retreat. "I'm *going* to kick your ass and teach you some manners. Here tonight, tomorrow, it really doesn't matter that much. You run, I'll find you. Shit leaves a pretty wide trail."

Arnie looked around, noting that his friends were shaking their heads, obviously not willing to pursue *his* vendetta. He was the first to break and start walking briskly through the crowded parking lot, and the burly jocks simply put their hands up and followed.

The three lieutenants took off their berets, rolled them up, and tucked them under their black belts behind them. The crowd parted in respect, allowing the trio to make their way back into the bar, the honor of their comrades fully intact. They had made their point, and while Arnie counted his blessings, they closed the bar in the warm company of some new friends.

* * *

CHAPTER TWENTY-THREE

"I WANT YOU TO COME ON, come on, come on, come on and *take it!/* Take another little piece of my heart now, babeee!..."

The shrill screams emanating from Janis reverberated into every corner of the house. David awkwardly stumbled down the stairs, frantically trying to get to the tuner to shut down the force-ten raspy voice tormenting his very consciousness.

"Oh! oh! have a,/

Have another little piece of my heart now, baby!/

Well, you know you got it if it—"

Skkkrrreeech!!

David leaned up against the antique bureau, gasping for air as the goose bumps settled over his naked body. Rich stepped through the long, beaded curtain from the dining room, casually holding a Löwenbräu in one hand and a silver razor in the other, his face laden with shaving cream. "Was gibt?" he asked in his typical cheerful manner.

David cocked his head toward him, lips tightened, blue eyes blazing. "I warned you, Mycoskie!" he said firmly. He snatched the LP off the turntable, held it up for Rich to see, and then, with relative ease, ceremoniously snapped it in two.

Rich's expression suddenly amplified, his favorite drinking companion brusquely defiled, violated, and destroyed before his very eyes. "Ohhh, you really know how to hurt a guy," he said, a hint of emotion tied to his resonant reply. His shoulders slumped as the full impact of his loss swiftly settled in.

David smiled. He'd delivered a telling blow, finally getting back at Rich for his constant annoying tactics. But, as usual, Rich would not let the transgression go unchallenged. "*En garde!*" he shouted, thrusting the double-edged Gillette forward, the spewing bottle of Löwenbräu cocked wildly over his head.

He advanced toward David in short bursts, his damp towel dropping indiscreetly to the floor while he sliced the air with his makeshift saber. David held up the broken record in defense, as the two squared off for battle in the crowded living room. Rich lunged forward, forcing his opponent back as he quickly parried. David's agility seemed severely hampered in close quarters. He banged his cast against the coffee table while he awkwardly maneuvered around the chairs and tattered ottoman.

Rich sensed his advantage. "*Przygotowanie do die możesz wieprzowych!*" he shouted in Polish, confident that David was too distracted to decipher the main words. "*Wasza matka ubiera rosyjski zwalczania buty!*" he spouted, pressing again for the advantage, driving David back into the coffee table. Lost momentarily in the heat of battle was the Slavic reference to David's mother's implied sexual orientation because of her preference for Russian combat boots.

David's new knee-high cast caught the edge of the table, tripping him into the Italian marble chess set he proudly displayed between games. He careened backward, crashing pawns and knights, kings and queens, reducing them to expensive rubble beneath the weight of his fall. Rich flopped on top of him in a flash, pinning him awkwardly between the overturned table and the couch. The combatants wrestled for position, with David's hand embedded in the thick shaving cream as they struggled.

Mike paused on the split landing of the stairway, staring down at the two naked men rolling around on the floor, shattered furniture and debris scattered around them. David turned Rich on his back and held his head in a decisive arm lock around his throat.

Mike leaned over the banister, astonished at the scene below. He listened to Rich gasping for air, prompting David to call for his immediate surrender. Rich stubbornly refused, lifting up his legs and then dropping his full weight down on David's stomach. David groaned in pain, tightening his grip as he struggled beneath Rich on the cold wooden floor. The vicelike grip cut the blood flowing to his adversary's brain. Then, in utter desperation, Rich reached below him and grabbed David's hairy balls, squeezing them with a firm grip. Super Jew immediately wailed in pain, the wail's pitch climbing an octave as Rich consolidated his demeaning grasp. Finally, David lurched into a rigid brace, eyes bulging, arms outstretched, submitting passively and totally to Rich's direction.

"Well, good morning, little buckaroos!" Mike yelled from the landing. "It's *such* a nice morning in the neighborhood, kiddos," he mocked. "Would you guys like some privacy, or what?" He walked down the stairs and into the forward edge of the battle area.

Rich relinquished his eunuch-molding grip and rolled over on the cold floor beside his gammy, groaning friend. Mike shook his head, walked through the beaded curtain, and tiptoed over the cold linoleum to the refrigerator. He pulled out a bottle of dark Löwenbräu, pried off the top with his teeth, then casually spit the cap into the overflowing trashcan on his way back into the living room. "Five o'clock in the fuckin' morning! What's the matter, Rich? Ain't got none lately, or what?"

"Super Jew trashed my goddamn album," he revealed, panting heavily.

"Good. He saved me the trouble. I used to like that bitch, but, Rich, there's more than one song on that fuckin' album."

"Don't like the others."

"That doesn't mean you have to play the same song a hundred fuckin' times to make up for it, dumb-ass!"

"Fuck you, guys! I put up with your *Madama Butterfly* and Mantovani shit!"

"Mycoskie, your ass is mine!" David moaned, struggling to his feet and over to the foyer. "You'd better sleep with one eye open, motherfucker," he advised, slowly hobbling up the stairs, gingerly dragging his bad leg behind.

"Clean this shit up, Rich. We got formation in an hour, and if you miss the run, it'll cost you a hundred bucks, fella," Mike warned him.

Within thirty minutes, the fracas behind them, the three lieutenants hit the door together. They jumped into their cars, each heading a different direction toward the post. The early morning ritual terrified the paperboys of the neighborhoods. They learned to just drop their bikes and run, seeking refuge on lawns, sidewalks, and on top of parked cars as the crazed trio rat-raced through the sleepy row houses and toward the on-ramp to Interstate 495.

It was just another mechanism they employed to fight the growing monotony of their jobs at Fort Devens. Ten-mile morning runs, repetitive training on such mundane subjects as riot control and community relations. The most intense assignments were the dreaded burial details. Escorting their fallen brothers back home for their families to bury always required weeks of mental rehabilitation for them, despite the honor associated with the event. However, the officers considered the mandatory guard mounts nothing more than trivial bullshit. Mike knew he didn't need a green beanie to perform these menial tasks, but the post commander, a leg, had taken it upon himself to reform the unruly troopers of the Tenth, drawing them slowly back into the fold.

The three lieutenants thought the army, like everything else in America, was going to hell in a handbag. Mike objected strongly when his team was selected to test a new prototype extraction ladder for helicopters, a gimmick recently developed by the nearby Natick Laboratories. He found himself dangling 250 feet above an old abandoned airfield, suspended precariously on a continuous-loop ladder, being slowly hoisted upward by a modified Volkswagen engine attached to the floor of the CH-47 helicopter. As he emerged through the small hatch in the bottom of the chopper, he had to immediately jump off before being pulled into the gearbox that was turning the retrieval sprocket. He had finally come down to this: a guinea pig for some crazy civilian scientists trying to make a buck off the war. He had his 1049 on Colonel Carter's desk later that afternoon.

The long drive home was filled with reflections. "The Age of Aquarius" blared on the radio, one of the few optimistic songs of the era. Mike was determined to fulfill his destiny, one way or the other. The Lowell exit sign brought him out of the jungle and back to reality just in time to miss it completely. Frustrated, he drove the T-Bird into the grassy median and back onto the westbound lanes to his exit.

As he turned onto their street, Mike noticed David's Corvette parked in the driveway. He was curious why his housemate wasn't at the gym working out. He walked up the back porch and through the kitchen door. He tossed his beret on the small table against the wall. "Honey, I'm home!" he yelled, sniffing a fusty odor in the air.

He turned to see David standing over the stove, still clad in his work fatigues, a white chef's apron draped around his neck. Mike stood there dumbfounded, watching him stir the steaming caldron with a broken broomstick, completely immersed in his task. At his feet lay a basket filled with white boxer shorts and undershirts.

"Hey, big guy, what'cha cookin'?"

"That motherfucker!"

"What motherfucker?"

"Mycoskie! Who the fuck else?"

"What the hell are you doing?"

"What does it look like I'm doing? I'm sterilizing my fuckin' underwear!"

"OK, I give up. I think I got the kosher thing down, but isn't this taking it a little too far?"

"The son of a bitch has the fuckin' *crabs!*" David shouted.

"I'm afraid to ask… but… how do *you* know?"

"I saw him last night from my window upstairs, syphoning some gas out of his Triumph."

"So?"

"He took it upstairs to the bathroom and scrubbed his crotch with it!"

"Oooouch! Are you shittin' me?"

"Do I look like I'm shittin' you?"

"Don't you think you're taking this a little too far? I mean, a big, tough guy like you worried about some little critters like that. They won't eat much. They're real itty-bitty, tiny thingies."

"Fuck you, *Gentile*," he replied.

"Is he out on his bike?" Mike inquired. "I didn't see it when I came in."

David laughed. "They stole it!"

"Who stole it?"

"The Hells Angels!"

"How do you know that?"

"What do I look like? The fuckin' yellow pages? What's with all the questions?" David complained. "The neighbors watched them do it. The fuckers just backed a truck up in the driveway, loaded it in the back, and took off."

"And nobody stopped them?"

"What were they going to do? Ask them not to steal poor Rich's bike because 'it's not nice'? Get serious. They did what any other neighbor would do: They took the license plate number, got a description of the truck, and asked me if there was a reward if we got it back."

"Rich's gonna be pissed," Mike concluded.

"Good," David replied as he continued stirring the pot.

Rich's reaction to the news was *very* intense, as if he had just experienced the loss of his best friend. He and Mike drove down to the police station to file theft charges against the local Hells Angels. After Rich filled out a pile of paperwork, the desk sergeant told him that he could forget about getting his bike back. That really didn't surprise him, but the detectives' response was not what either had anticipated: They were not even going to pursue the case, and they just laughed when Rich insisted that they could at least bring the owner of the truck in for questioning. They told him there was no evidence, asserting that the thieves probably had the Triumph in a hundred pieces already. The police weren't about to go on a wild goose chase just for some *soldier's* old motorcycle. Before leaving, Rich told them all in Polish that their mothers sucked donkey dicks.

On the way back to the house, Mike could tell that his friend seemed preoccupied. He barely uttered a word. Mike was astounded. It just had never seemed in Rich's nature to place such emphasis on anything of a material value.

Over the next several weeks Rich's typical jovial character had plunged into a somber, mysterious mood. He'd sit up alone late into the night, picking out some lonely blues tunes on his guitar and often sipping until dawn straight shots of Glenlivet. His daily movements became shrouded in secrecy. He disappeared for days at a time. Weeks went by where he left the post on Friday, not to be seen again until the 0600 run on Monday morning. Mike made it a point to bring him a clean set of fatigues, leaving them with his friend's team sergeant, Master Sergeant Sabolz. He had become the only one who seemed to get through to Rich.

It wasn't long though, before Rich's notoriety betrayed his lonely exile. Acting on reliable intelligence, several members of his Polish team mounted a reconnaissance mission deep into the Irish burroughs of Boston. They found their way to an old corner pub closely guarded by several of the neighborhood drunks, who were slumped irreverently against the red brick wall outside. It was about ten in the evening, and the tavern was packed with local patrons, mostly members of the over-forty persuasion.

The men waded through the smoke-filled room, setting up an observation point at the end of the long, wet, wooden bar. The rowdy clamor at the tavern was brisk, consistent with the rapid flow of alcohol. The deep, dark room extended well past the crowded bar, tables full of regular customers smoking and joking, totally oblivious to the strangers within. The men scanned the confines, along the stubby tables and crowded masses, toward the small, elevated stage at the end of the room. Staff Sergeant Klecki checked the latrine and the shaded corners, vetting the jovial clientele before reluctantly returning to the bar. Their beloved team leader was nowhere to be found. Dejected and concerned over the faulty intel, they ordered a round of Cuervo shooters and decided to partake in some of the local ambiance.

Just before 2300 hours, the loud jabber simmered to a halt. The men looked up from the bar to see a dark figure on the smoky stage adjusting the microphone in front of his guitar. He sat down on the tall stool, turned, and downed the remainder of the drink he'd placed on the amplifier behind him. The troubadour adjusted his strap and then welcomed the crowd. "Good evening, all you sweeeeet Hamma knokkas, you!"

A dim blue spotlight drew a bead from the rafters, casting a pale, chalky beam through the smoke and cheers from the crowd below. That audience knew him personally, and he responded kindly to their welcoming applause. Klecki turned to Sergeant Petrie, poking him hard on the shoulder. "I know, I know, I can see him," Petrie confirmed, gaping at their team leader, whose dark stubble beard had evidently been cultivated for occasions like this one.

Rich began with a flurry, setting the tone with a fandango longneck run on his guitar, then easing the crowd down with a splendid transition to his favorite blues melody:

"Trouble in mind, I'm blue,/

But I won't be blue always/

'Cause I know the sun's gonna shi-i-ine in my back door someday."

His men sat stunned. They had been totally unaware of the hidden talent possessed by their profane yet proficient leader. His deep, resonant voice filled the packed room with a simple, passionate outcry from his soul. He continued to massage their emotions until midnight, when a few more pieces of the puzzle slid awkwardly into place.

Rich strained to reach the last peaking notes of his favorite Orbison song, and the crowd rose to their feet, gleefully offering their profound gratitude for his mood-altering renditions. His last song complete, he stepped down from the stage and made his way to the table full of women seated in the front.

"They're all old enough to be his mother!" Sergeant Petrie remarked.

"Yeah, but look at all the attention he's getting," Klecki replied. "They all love his happy ass."

His men shook their heads in disbelief, a little embarrassed for their talented leader. They were just mere spectators as the old broads fussed over the elusive troubadour. He thrived in his new element, they concluded. The matrons obviously had something drawing him to them, but the men fully agreed that it wasn't the stuff dreams are made of.

Klecki finished his drink and reluctantly led the small group out the door. They had all ascertained that it was neither the time nor the place to rescue their leader from the clutches of despair. They had learned something about him that night. He'd shed his mask, exposed his soul, but far from the men who really cared about him, and only in the sanctity of strangers.

They would respect his intentions. There would be time.

* * *

CHAPTER TWENTY-FOUR

SPECIAL ORDERS NUMBER 118 EXTRACT

> *TC 230. Fol RSG dir. PRAP AR 55-28 Asg to: USAOS repl Sta Oakland Calif. For fur asg to USARV Trans Det (P5 TOA4XA) Long Binh APO SF 96384 (IDC-4); Aloc: 08-R-2120.*

MIKE'S EYES SPARKLED. HE FINISHED deciphering the orders, reached across the desk, and shook Captain Burton's hand. The portly S1 cocked a smile and shook his head. Mike had been bugging him every day for the past month, constantly inquiring about the status of his 1049. The young lieutenant was finally on his way.

Mike turned to leave when Burton yelled after him. "You're gonna have to extend, Shannahan. Your ETS is coming up in three weeks!"

"Minor detail. Type up the paperwork, and I'll sign it!" he yelled back, hurrying out the door.

He headed directly for the S3 shop, pausing several times to read the orders bearing his backward name. *Shannahan, Michael B.... First Lieutenant... Infantry... Long Binh... APO San Francisco.*

Long Binh, an exotic destination. Just the name was enough to conjure up preconceived images of what it might be like. The Highlands, he surmised, mountainous and rugged. He felt the strain of the ruck on his back as he shuffled through the gravel lot. Triple canopy, he'd need a magnum charge on his flare gun to signal the extraction choppers. *Don't forget that,* he thought. He sloshed up out of the marshy Delta reeds across the wooden threshold, tipping his beret to the S3 sergeant major as he walked past.

"Top of the morning to you, Sergeant Major!" Mike greeted him with a slight Gaelic brogue.

"Aiee, sir. And a fine one it is, at that," O'Leary replied, his smile following the Irish rogue prancing briskly down the hall.

David sat dutifully behind his desk, focused intently on blotting out the typos on the mimeograph paper with a small brush dipped in some sort of white solvent.

"Hey, big guy!"

"What are you in such a good mood for?" David replied, squinting eyes fixed on the task at hand.

"Movin' out." Mike sat down in the gray chair in front of the desk and propped his boots up on David's domain. The S3 ignored him, working hard at correcting the operations order in front of him. "Guess you'll have to get a new housemate, big guy. Unless you think you can handle the Polish Pervert by yourself."

David flicked him a disdainful glance and then returned to the task at hand.

"They say the *very* first thing you do when you get in-country," Mike continued, "is to call Nha Trang and let them know you're there."

"Get those filthy boots off my desk," David ordered. "And what the hell are you talking about? I've got to get this op order to the old man ASAP."

Ignoring the order, Mike spun the paper like a Frisbee across David's desk. It gathered a few loose papers, slid off the edge, and floated to the floor. David glared across the desk, slowly rolled his chair over, and carefully picked them up. His tense blue eyes shifted back and forth as he scanned rapidly through the garbled army jargon while Mike tapped the toes of his boots together, leaning back and forth in his chair, commenting on his new assignment.

Finally, David tossed the orders in his outbox, dipped the brush back in the small bottle, and continued to apply more solvent to his work.

"What's the matter with you?" Mike asked, a little puzzled at his friend's sullen demeanor.

David dabbed at the paper, reluctant to answer. "I'm getting out," he finally said.

"Outa' what? Your cast?"

David seemed irritated with the need to clarify his answer. He replaced the brush back in the small bottle, screwed the lid tight, then looked across to his friend Mike, and casually informed him. "Out of the army. I'm getting out."

"What! When did all this come down the tube?" Mike demanded to know, drawing his boots off the desk and leaning over.

"They told me my fracture resorbed, and now that leg's more than an inch shorter than the other one. I'm getting out on a *medical*," he calmly informed him, appearing indifferent to the circumstances.

"When?" Mike asked quietly, somewhat shocked by the disclosure.

"Next month. They gave me until the thirtieth."

Mike gazed across the desk at his friend. He watched compassionately as David's lips tightened, then followed the slight frown up to his china-blue eyes. David's blank stare contradicted his composure and did little to shield the despair in his heart. To Mike and his comrades, Lieutenant Rabin perpetually exemplified the epitome of the junior Special Forces officer. He judiciously honed every muscle in his body and, with equal precision, carefully calibrated every corner of his mind. Physically or mentally, he stood alone—his commitment to his men and his country absolute. The only inconsistency Mike had ever found in David's character may have been an overwhelming attraction he had for young maidens in cheerleading skirts, a compelling fetish Rich had exposed "quite innocently" through an unlocked door one evening.

Mike searched for something comforting to say. But all he could muster was the obvious. "What'cha gonna do?"

"Talked to the Israeli Embassy in DC today. There's a pretty good chance they'll offer me a commission as a major and let me finish my schooling over there. In between wars."

Mike smiled. *Good for you, Super Jew,* he thought to himself. *Ya gotta play the role right to the end.*

"I'd like to work with the Mossad," David added.

"What's that?" Mike inquired, not familiar with the term.

"Literally, it means 'The Institute,' a tag given to *HaMossad leModi 'in ule Tafkidim Meyuhadim.*"

"That's all Greek to me, but go for it," Mike replied.

"It's the national intelligence agency of Israel, kinda' like the CIA," David proudly reported.

"Well, why don't they just call it that?"

Mike was astonished with David's serious intent. And he knew that his friend would go out in style, off to war to protect oppressed people—and in this case, his own oppressed people. An *honorable* crusade to the Holy Land, not just a mercenary escapade of questionable morals. But despite his noble intentions, the burden of giving up his career with the Special Forces was still visible, and Mike knew exactly how his friend felt. He could only imagine the void in David's heart, but he equated it to being pregnant for almost three years, only to find that the growing embryo you'd been nurturing with care and compassion was nothing more than a hollow tumor, filled to the brim with false hope and shattered ambitions. For once, Mike knew he had something David wanted badly. For once, he *knew* he was right.

*　　*　　*

Mike waited for Rich to stop by the house over the weekend, anxious to share the news with him. The pride in his heart continued to swell, his honor finally at hand. As usual, however, the Group jester was nowhere to be found. The last time he had seen him was the preceding Thursday evening after work, when he was perched atop the steep incline on the roof of their Victorian dwelling.

David had vowed to kill Rich's newfound kitten, VC, that morning. The vicious threat followed another sleepless night spent fending off the feline's hit-and-run assaults on his person while he slept. Like those of his namesake, the attack cat's tactics were most effective when he operated at night. While he was on daytime patrol, or while planning a late-night ambush, he loved to lounge around the basement furnace and then leisurely track the black soot and grime over the furniture. White bath fixtures were adorned with greasy, daisylike paw prints, the same contrasting pattern found on the white sheets and pillowcases.

VC had crossed David's fabled "line" and was now doomed to a watery death or, at the very least, a high-speed rendezvous with a stationary object. David had taped a stick-figure reward poster of the cat on the kitchen door: *Wanted, Dead or Alive. "VC," a.k.a. "Kitty Kitty Kitty."* He offered a twenty-five-dollar reward for his capture, and he picked out a convenient seventy-mile-per-hour sign on Interstate 495 that he might throw the cat against as he sped past.

Rich had reasoned that David wouldn't dare harm a comrade of the Brotherhood, even if that comrade happened to be a cat, so he decided to put VC through jump school. He had taken the drogue chute off Mike's seven-gore T-U sport parachute and affixed the suspension line around VC's midsection.

Mike recalled pulling into the driveway and noticing a crowd of neighbors on the sidewalk staring up at the roof. He had looked up to see Rich struggling with VC, cursing loudly in Polish, carefully prying the sharp claws out of his forearm. Mike wasn't aware that he had arrived just in time to witness the fifth and qualifying jump. Rich held VC out by the back of the neck while he dropped the crêpe streamer to check the wind velocity and direction.

"What the hell are you doing up there, Mycoskie?" Mike had shouted.

"Hey, Hamma knokka!" Rich yelled from the parapets. "Mind moonlighting as the DZSO? We got an official qualifying jump here in progress!"

Rich began the jump commands, complete with the appropriate modifications. "Stand in the door!" he bellowed, the terrified feline dangling thirty feet above the makeshift drop zone.

Mike tried to reason with his housemate while the young boys in the crowd screamed "Go-o-o-o!" Rich smiled as he let go of the spirited kitten, only to have VC invert instantaneously and wildly, sinking all four sets of razor-sharp claws into the back of his outstretched arm. He roared in pain, then disappeared back behind the ledge of the roof, VC still hanging on for dear life. Polish epithets echoed loudly overhead, joined by the sounds of shingles tearing loose under the weight of the scuffle.

The baffled neighbors were waiting for the spectacle to continue when a screeching, furry figure flew into view, like a flying squirrel on its maiden flight, the cone-shaped drogue chute spinning uselessly above him. Mike conceded that Rich's ground-school training must have been effective: VC mimicked textbook terminal-velocity brace, stabilized head-up attitude, hair completely erect like a Halloween cat with his tail on fire.

The kitten hit hard, bounced again before rolling over, then darted out toward the street, only to get hung up in the picket fence by the wire-frame drogue chute still attached to his tiny body. Mike ran over to the frantic kitten and quickly tried to unsort the tangled lines holding him firmly against the fence. VC made it perfectly clear he was in no mood for any further attention, swatting and hissing as Mike tried to free him. The Special Forces first lieutenant moonlighting as DZSO quickly pulled out the demo knife strapped to his belt and, with several careful motions, cut the lines holding the terrified kitten captive. With a final shrieking howl, the animal darted out between the parked cars, down the narrow street, and up the hill toward Lindsey Street.

Rich ran from behind the house and down the driveway, panting and gasping when he arrived where the crowd had gathered. "Where is he?" he demanded, his bloody arms making poignant his query.

Mike shook his head. "*Pai ya,*" he told him and pointed up the street.

"Why didn't you stop him?"

"When's the last time *you* got in front of a B-forty rocket with claws?" Mike replied incredulously.

Rich remained pissed, David was elated, and Mike simply listed the cat as a deserter. He told his dejected friend it was probably just as well anyway. VC obviously didn't have the stamina or heart for this kind of thing, and from the northerly direction he'd headed, Mike assured Rich that he was probably well on his way to Canada to join the rest of the pussies.

*   *   *

Mike shielded his eyes from the rising sun as he stepped up to the entrance to Rich's team room early Monday morning. His friend's team sergeant sat calmly reading the casualty lists in the *Army Times*, sipping on a steaming cup of coffee in the empty room. Mike brought the paper sack full of clean fatigues over and set it down beside him. It was yet another disappointment when he didn't see Rich's smiling face at his desk.

"Seen my housemate, Sergeant Sabolz?"

"Affirmative, sir. But he forgot to wash behind his ears this morning. Sergeant Petrie's helping him get squared away for the oh-seven-hundred formation. Coffee?"

"No, thanks. Is he sober?"

"Don't know, sir. Sometimes ya can't really tell. Don't know if he's drunk or just looks that way. Could be hereditary, but I think it's 'cause he's just plain tired. I know one thing, though: I sure couldn't run with 'im.'"

"Got any idea what's floatin' around in his noggin, Top?" Mike asked sincerely, hoping he'd have at least part of the answer.

"Don't really know, sir. But somethin's got his gig line all out of kilter. The man must be down inside about somethin'. Sometimes when you're talking to him, he doesn't hear a word you say. Seems like his mind is a million miles away. Lately, it's just gotten worse. The last month or so he sort-a' went off the deep end."

"What do you mean?" Mike asked, pulling out a chair to sit.

"Well, ya know, he's been hanging out in Boston with a bunch of floozies," the sergeant began.

"*Floozies?*"

"Yeah. Older broads. You know: divorcée-seasoned barflies."

"No, I didn't know. I mean, I know he's been up to something, but he just comes and goes. Guess if he wanted me to know, he would've said something by now. He doesn't pass out a lot of *free* information, if you know what I mean."

"Well, we were all starting to get concerned," Sabolz continued. "He's been spending a lot of time over at the demolition committee shack. Sergeant Elder told me that he requisitioned a whole shitload of det cord and C-four last week."

"So?"

"So, we finished our demo training cycle two months ago, Lieutenant. We're not scheduled for anything requiring explosives until the ORT in July. If the C-Team gets wind of this, we're talking court-martial."

"What the hell is he doing with it?"

"Thought *you* might know, sir. Also, what the hell did he do with that old thirty-caliber Browning he put in his trunk last week?"

"*What?*" Mike stood stunned for a moment. Then: "Top, I gotta get back over to B-Company, but as soon as we take report, I'll be back to have a long talk with the man. Can you make sure he doesn't vacate the area before I get back?"

"Roger that, Lieutenant. But I can only try my best."

Mike hurried back through the old white barracks. The coarse gravel crunched with the rhythm of his pounding boots, past the empty coal bins, around the orderly room, and into the company area. He briskly took his place in formation just as Major MacLeod, the company XO, called the detachments to attention.

The detachment ranks had dwindled in strength with each day. Mike looked around the formation. A lot of familiar faces were missing. Playing palace guard just wasn't part of the SF creed. Like so many of the others, they'd gone home to their buddies in the bush, gone home to the Yards and Nungs, gone back to sleep in the jungle, to be serenaded once again with the menacing lullaby of the notorious "Fuck you" lizard.

Major McLeod detained the teams, conducting an impromptu Operational Readiness Test mandated by the post commander, just another impractical test to make sure every man had a functional gas mask in the event of a chemical attack. By the time the fiasco had concluded, and by the time Mike got back over to C-Company, just a circle of empty coffee cups and some papers were left on the team table. Rich and his men were nowhere to be found. "Gonna have to start calling the guy Spook," Mike proclaimed aloud.

He casually walked over to the team table to find something to write on. A copy the *Army Times* lay folded to the casualty section. He sat down, focusing immediately on the names underlined in pencil. *KIA... Dawson, Henry E., SSG... Edwards, James R., SFC... Clay, Dennis R., CPT, Infantry.*

He *knew* it. He had expected it would come to this. Now he couldn't disperse the images of Denny that were invading his mind. *Hope he didn't suffer.*

Mike picked up the paper and folded it closed, burying Denny's name deep within the crumpled pages of the tabloid. He got up to leave, the real purpose of his visit now obscured by more unanswered questions and the emerging emotions of remorse.

Suck it up, he told himself. He turned off the light and closed the door.

* * *

CHAPTER TWENTY-FIVE

IKE LAY NURTURING AN UNEASY sleep when he heard the dull thud. He stirred, straining to identify the muffled sound of something on the stairway outside his room. Weary eyes squinted toward the clock radio on the nightstand: 0120. Listening intently until the noise abated, he peered under the door to see if the hall lights were on. As though from a candle trembling in the wind, faint surges of light danced on the old oak floor, then disappeared completely.

He quietly slid out of bed, the cold floor adding a few bumps to the chill up his spine as he unsnapped the cover on his .45. He cupped his sweaty palm to muffle the slide of the pistol chambering a round, and he clicked off the safety. The rough plaster wall delineated thin white lines in his back as he slowly worked his way over to the door. Quietly, he turned the old glass knob, then spun through the doorway, out into the darkened hall, pistol leveled toward the empty stairs. He had barely taken the first step toward the landing when a cold blunt object parted the lower two ribs in his back.

"One sound, motherfokka, and I'm going to turn your dick into a sprinkler," the heavy voice whispered from behind.

Mike slowly raised his arms. A large gloved hand reached over his shoulder to grasp the muzzle of the cocked .45. He let go of the handle and, in the same motion, drove his elbow forcibly into the exposed rib cage of the startled intruder. The pistol bounced like an iron on the floor while he spun and delivered a snapping front kick deep into the stomach of the stunned assailant, sending him sprawling backward, crashing hard into the wall.

Mike picked up the .45 and turned on the hall light.

The heap at the end of the hall lay moaning and gasping for air, and as Mike watched in disgust, vomit erupted across the wooden floor, flowing freely under the door to David's room. He noticed dark-green camouflage paint on the man's face, the rest of his features concealed by a black ski mask, pulled low over his head. He looked like a commando—black sweater, dark Levis, low-cut army-issued Chippewa mountain boots.

Chippewas? Mike took a closer look as the dark figure rolled over into a fetal position, moaning, spitting long strings of saliva, and gasping for air. "Rich?"

He moved closer, careful not to step in the putrid mess seeping into the cracks in the wooden floor. He shook his head, gingerly releasing the hammer on the pistol. The sympathy he felt lasted momentarily, before he realized that only moments before he could have killed his friend. "You stupid son of a bitch!" he shouted.

Rich could only moan.

"This shit's gone far enough!" Mike bellowed. He turned and walked back down the hall, past sandbags stacked on the landing and into the bathroom, where he turned on the hot water. He leaned over the sink, his hands trembling as the adrenaline dissipated from his veins. Tired eyes tagged onto the rising vapor, rotated upward to the mirror, and suddenly focused on the reflection there. He jumped back out into the hallway, staring in disbelief at the green sacks of sand stacked up to the top of the railing. "This better be good, Mycoskie!" he shouted, his voice peaking as it echoed down the hall.

He went back into the bathroom and threw a towel in the sink. "You been listening to too many war stories, fella," he yelled over the rush of water. "I think that beret is starting to fry your brain. You better loosen the drawstrings a little bit. Before somebody does it for you!"

He wrung the excess water out of the towel, then headed back down the hall where Rich sat moaning, bent over in the corner, head between his knees. Mike held out the towel, drips of warm water splattering on the pitted wooden floor. Rich slowly reached up, grabbed it, and folded it over his face as the ends dangled between his legs. He sat quietly for a moment, then raised his head up and gathered in a breath of fresh air. Straining to reach over, Rich snagged the loop of the long silver flashlight with the ends of his fingers. He slithered over toward Mike and picked it up.

Click... click... click... click.

With a disgusted look, Rich flipped the flashlight up in the air and let it crash to the floor. "You fucked up my goddamn flashlight!" he complained, his voice resonating at a high pitch. "Son of a bitch!"

"Fuck your goddamn flashlight! What the hell were you doing sneakin' around at zero-dark-thirty in the goddamn morning, dressed like a fuckin' ninja? I coulda' blown your fuckin' ass away!"

"Aaagggahhh phewww," he slobbered into the damp towel. "I didn't want to wake the Ogre."

"He's not even here!" Mike replied, walking back down the hall to his room. "He's over at Sarah's. She's got a new outfit, red and white pleats, I think," he said, making a dig at David's fetish for maidens in cheerleading skirts. He turned the light on and put on an old pair of Levis hanging on his valet stand.

Moaning like an old man crippled with arthritis, Rich struggled to his feet and stumbled into the bathroom. He pulled a soiled towel out of the hamper and threw it over the mess on the floor.

"What's with the sandbags, Rich?" Mike asked, sliding the .45 back into its holster, his voice still tense and heavy. "Is this another one of your bullshit cosmic, mystic revelations? Should we be out building an ark? Or, better yet, out collecting animals and insects?"

Rich stuck his head through the door, his face still smudged with greasy green camouflage paint, beads of water clinging to the stubble on his chin. "Six *P*s, my man: Prior planning prevents piss-poor performance. Part of my contingency plan," he said proudly.

"Rich, we have to talk, fella. You don't live in fuckin' Cambodia. We let you do your own thing around here. We don't really mind when you're late with rent or the utilities. And the black lights and posters in the living room are really kinda' interesting. Juvenile, but interesting. But then, there's that nasty ol' rumor going around the latrine that you might be dealing in the black market with government property. Rich, I gotta tell you, it's just not funny anymore, fella."

Rich took off his wool cap and ran his hand through his thick black hair. "I didn't want to get you guys involved," he confessed.

"Involved in *what?* Rich, we're already involved! You're our housemate. More importantly, fella, you're one of us. I mean, we're not your typical Three Musketeers or anything, but for chrissakes, Rich!"

Rich turned and walked down the stairs, leaving Mike sitting on the bed, listening to the worn floor creak on Rich's way to the liquor cabinet. The ice clinked loudly as it hit the bottom of the glass, prompting Mike to put his shirt on and head downstairs to get some answers from his elusive friend. "Get another glass," he told him, trying the subtle approach for a change.

"Roger that." Rich pulled another tumbler out of the white wooden cabinet, splashed in a shot or so of Glenlivet, and handed it to his housemate. "Here's to shit in your eye," he proclaimed as he tapped the rim of Mike's glass.

"You want to talk about it?" Mike asked, his ears tightening from the strong bite of the brew.

Rich stirred the ice with his finger. He looked at Mike for a moment, raised his bushy eyebrows, and sighed. "Not really. But… it wasn't much… Only thing was, it belonged to my brother."

Mike waited for Rich to continue, but he just stared down at the floor. "Well, shit, Rich. *That* clears it all up."

"He gave it to me the day he left. Told me to take care of it. I… I guess I really fucked that one up, too." Rich stared up at the ceiling, eyes squinting and fixed. "But then, that's the kind of a sombitch I am." He coughed, clearing the building emotion in his voice. "I'll tell you something, though. The day they just came over here and just took it… That put a lot of things into perspective for me."

"Your bike?"

Rich downed the rest of his drink with one deliberate gulp and then reached for the bottle and poured another.

"I didn't even know you had a brother, Rich."

"I don't know either. He went MIA on my eighteenth birthday in the Nam. He loved that bike. And I went and let some worthless scumbags cut it up for spare parts. Now I have two scores to settle." He paused to take another long drink. Swelling tears pushed at his eyelids, then subsided.

Mike looked away. The intense pain spread quickly across the room, easily massaging the compassion in his heart. He thought of his own brothers. Thomas's white-blond hair tickled his nose. Though the bike ride to the O-club pool must have been uncomfortable for him, Thomas loved to ride up on the handlebars close to his big brother, his dusty bare legs pointing the way, his dirty small toes jiggling inward with every crack in the hot sidewalk. A brother's love, not often spoken, but measured by many subtle memories of tender moments. (Of course, Mike had a great deal of affection for his two sisters, too, but the bond he had with each of his three brothers had a special, masculine poignancy.) He offered a silent plea to the Almighty to protect the young tykes, his brothers, fighting off fleeting visions of cold bodies in obvious distress.

"What was his name?" Mike asked softly. Rich ignored him, staring down at his empty glass, his thoughts entangled somewhere between regret and utter despair.

Suddenly, he broke the morbid trance. He slammed the glass hard on the table, reached over, and patted Mike on the shoulder. "Got places to go, people to see, things to do. Thanks for the karate lesson, pal. Remind me to return the favor."

"Where the fuck are you going, Rich? It's two o'clock in the fuckin' morning!"

"Off to see the Wizard," Rich said, his jovial demeanor restored.

The worn Biscayne's rusty door hinges creaked, followed by its clattering valves nursed to life by the low-octane fuel in the nearly empty tank. Mike sipped on his scotch, his thoughts wandering from the brothers he longed to see to what was going on in Rich's unpredictable mind.

The rumbling engine suddenly stopped, and after the Biscayne's worn hinges groaned again, Mike heard the distinct sound of the trunk popping open. He smiled, shaking his head while listening to Rich mumbling to himself in Polish, his full voice rising and falling with a metallic clamor of what sounded like chains being pulled from the trunk. The Chippewas sounded heavier than usual as his frenzied housemate pounded back up the porch steps and through the screen door. The long, black, perforated muzzle of an old thirty-caliber machine gun appeared through the doorway. Then Mike noticed that Rich had an olive-drab ammunition box clutched tightly in his other hand. "Don't just stand there. Give me a fuckin' hand!" he pleaded.

Mike took the heavy ammo can and followed cautiously up the stairs. He could only watch in wonder as Rich positioned the old machine gun on top of the sand bags, pried open the can of linked ammo, fed the first round into the breech, and carefully sighted his fields of fire to cover the front door and foyer below.

Mike leaned up against the wall and folded his arms. "Ya settin' up for Halloween? Expect the kiddos to be fully armed this year?"

Rich ignored him as he firmed up the tripod on a stack of albums he'd taken from his room.

"Suppose ya already mined the front yard, lad," Mike said. "But did ya remember the Claymores for the porch? And how 'bout some good ol' toe poppers for under the doormat?"

"Good idea!" Rich replied facetiously, staring down the stairwell to the doormat on the floor.

"You're not going to tell me what the fuck's going on, are you?" Mike yelled after him. "Guess I'm just gonna have to call David and have him come home and straighten your silly ass out."

Rich rattled off a flurry of Polish as he bounded down the stairs. Stopping short of the beaded curtain, he turned and waved good-bye to his friend, who was standing at the split on the stairs.

Mike quickly vaulted down the last five steps and beat him to the back door. "I don't know just what the fuck you're up to," he spouted, "but this shit has just run out of funny!"

"It's not your fight," Rich concluded passively.

"So… you're going out to take on the whole band of bikers by yourself, right? Oh, that's *real* smart. That's not gonna bring your Triumph back, fella. You're probably gonna get your ass waxed in the process. What'cha gonna do? Steal one of *their* bikes?"

"Get out of my way."

Mike pressed his arm firmly against Rich's shoulder. I'm not gonna let you do it, shit-for-brains. You're out of your fuckin' *mind*!"

"What are they gonna do? Send me to Vietnam? Shi-i-tt," he moaned," I got my orders last Thursday. This kid is on his way. You know what the odds are for SF types coming back from over there, so you must have me confused with somebody who really gives a shit!"

Mike dropped his hand from his friend's shoulder. Rich had never talked to him about ever wanting to serve in Nam. He had less than four months left on his active-duty commitment. *He must have volunteered,* Mike immediately assumed, and a broad smile eased the tension in Mike's face. "Hell, guy, looks like we'll be going over there together. My orders came through on Friday."

Rich's demeanor abruptly shifted, and his eyes focused on the young man front of him. Mike had never felt the full attention of his friend's buttery brown eyes. Until now. They'd seemed patronizing, sometimes pretentious, but *now...* sincere and caring?

Mike gazed at the complex man before him, one who—he suddenly knew—had been shielding the depth of his fiber, suppressing the anguish that held him captive to a remorseful memory. A man with a mission.

Compelled by their joint commitment and encouraged by the abundance of scotch in their veins, the two Young Turks embraced tightly. Emotion and anxiety flowed reciprocally between the novice warriors. Each stepped back, strong hands still firmly gripping broad shoulders, focused eyes fixed to further verify their solidarity. Mike smiled first, promoting the mutual grins that slowly but easily evolved into an overture of warm laughter. Relieved, Mike seemed on the verge of tears. The two young men had finally consummated their bond. They knew that regardless of what the future might bring, in life or in death, from that moment on, they would always be true brothers.

Rich uncorked the bottle of scotch on the counter and poured another round. He handed Mike the warm, golden spirit and motioned him to follow. "Wait till you see this shit!" he bragged, opening the small door to the basement.

Mike followed him down the narrow steps, noting the fusty odor of fuel oil and decaying relics of tenants past. Rich stopped in front of the old workbench, clicked on the light bulb hanging by the rotting wire, and stepped back for Mike to see. The bench lay cluttered with old Christmas ornaments, pine cone wreaths, Styrofoam candy canes, and strings of old colored lights all tangled and broken.

"Are we back into the riddles game again?" Mike asked, not sure what Rich was presenting to him. "Christmas was four months ago, Scrooge."

Rich flashed a devious smile, reached over, and began tossing the frayed Yuletide remnants toward the darkened corners of the damp room. Below the maze of useless trinkets lay an old, fetid quilt, torn and tattered, lined with rusty water stains throughout. Mike took another sip of scotch as he watched Rich carefully undrape the molded structure he'd concealed. "Well? How do you like it?"

Mike moved closer into the light. The whole structure took up almost the entire workbench: houses, trees, tiny cars, even miniature mailboxes adorned the sidewalks his housemate had constructed with thin wafers of slate. "Rich, this is really nice."

Mike was obviously amazed at the detailed work Rich had put into the project. It looked like their neighborhood, houses close together, a few shade trees near the curbs, but the street sloped sharply up on one end, with a large two-story house set off by itself at the top of the hill. In front of this house were at least a dozen miniature mountain bicycles, the rear wheels backed up against the curb, front wheels turned in tandem, all pointing down toward the bottom of the street.

Mike had seen something similar in the window of a hobby store downtown. The only thing missing were the train tracks and locomotive. "Okay, I give up. What is it?"

"It's a mock-up!" Rich proclaimed excitedly, expecting Mike would grasp its significance.

"No shit. But what the fuck is it?"

"See this house?" Rich asked, pointing to the large one at the top of the hill.

"Yeah."

"That's where they live."

An uneasy feeling crept over Mike as he looked back at the bicycles. Motorcycles. *Hells Angels motorcycles.* Rich had put together an elaborate sand table of his intended target, just like they had been trained to do. He was determined to take them out. All of them.

Mike turned and looked at Rich. They smiled. Rich slowly nodded his head. "You're one crazy motherfucker," Mike told him, smiling and shaking his head.

"You with me, Hamma knokka? Could sure use a driver."

Mike looked back to the bikes on the hill. His thoughts carefully surveyed the mission at hand. Rich obviously had developed a detailed plan. *Besides*, he reasoned, *it would be a shame to let all those years of training go to waste.* He wouldn't even have to hump a ruck or worry about that damn generator on this one. He quickly balanced the task and consequences with the *character* barometer in his mind: *Duty, Honor, Country. No* real *conflict here*, he reasoned. Like the dreaded javelina, the image of the Hells Angels represented a torrid effigy at best. *Hell, the Commander might even condone this one*, Mike brashly mused.

"All the way!" Mike replied, finishing off the scotch. He flipped the empty glass over his shoulder and stared Rich directly in the eyes as the tumbler crashed on the floor. "Hell, I have a feeling we're going to need the practice anyway."

Rich released a broad, approving grin. "His name is Brad... Captain Brad Mycoskie."

*   *   *

CHAPTER TWENTY-SIX

Gang Violence Erupts in Local Neighborhood

LOCAL RESIDENTS AWOKE TO A *series of early-morning explosions, which were thought to have started several automobile fires and one two-alarm house fire at 1523 Lindsey St. Windows were shattered three blocks away from the site of the explosions, causing many residents to flee into the streets in the early morning darkness. The cause of the explosions was not immediately determined. However, a spokesman for the Lowell Police Department suspects foul play in the predawn incident.*

According to informed sources, a power struggle has emerged between the local chapter of the Hells Angels and the lesser-known Outlaws motorcycle gang. The two rival organizations are alleged to have secretly been vying for control of the illicit drug trade here in Lowell.

Irate members of the Hells Angels motorcycle gang have openly vowed for revenge in the incident. The explosions destroyed 16 of the member's motorcycles, while the ensuing fire completely destroyed their two-story house...

It had taken the night raiders exactly one minute and forty-five seconds to place the small slithers of C-4 joined with det cord on each cylinder block of the gang's motorcycles. A three-minute time fuse initiated the crescendo of destruction, just enough time for the car to quietly roll down the hill to the end of the street, providing a spectacular view for the fiery fusillade.

Despite his meticulous planning, Rich had never imagined that some of the gas tanks would be full of gasoline. Mike knew that was an honest mistake, given the source, but they both were relieved when they read that no one was seriously injured when the C-4 blew some of the flaming tanks onto the house and cars parked on the other side of the street.

They decided it would be prudent not to tell David about the successful raid. Consistent with most tactical operations, they agreed to adhere to the need-to-know philosophy. They figured the less he knew, the better off he would be. Rich had a difficult enough time explaining the Browning on the stairwell, but as usual, he bullshitted his way out of it, and after a couple of weeks of sleepless nights, they both wondered if it had been such a good idea after all.

*   *   *

The two outbound officers would have a thirty-day en-route leave before they needed to report to Travis Air Force Base in California for transport to Vietnam. Rich decided to take the northern approach to the base, through Peoria, in the northern homelands of America, while Mike would head south, first to Maryland, then back through the prickly pear and ragged mesquite of south Texas. The Commander had recently been transferred to the Naval Air Station Patuxent River in Maryland, on a flat peninsula jutting out into the rugged shoals of the Chesapeake Bay. Mike had never been there before, but as long as they had a marine guard at the gate, jets on the flight line, with Old Glory flying in front of the administration building, he knew he'd find the Commander on duty somewhere nearby.

The time had finally come for the alpine troopers of the Tenth to trade their worn Chippewas for the light, canvas-top jungle boots worn by the men of the Fifth. There would be no farewells to those who stayed behind, only firm handshakes exchanged until they would meet again. Mike knew the drill by heart. That's the way it was, and the way it would be.

Rich had just stuffed the last dirty pair of Levis into his overseas bag when Mike appeared in his doorway. "Sure you don't want to meet me in Vegas or somewhere a coupla' days before we report?" he asked.

"Wouldn't mind it, but I don't want to make any commitments just yet. Need to get back to Peoria and see what the folks got planned." He thought for a moment and then added, "Why don't we just plan on meeting a coupla' days early, but in Frisco. That'll give us plenty of time to engage in some serious brain damage."

Rich looked around the small room, under the bed and behind the dresser. He pulled out some lint-caked underwear from beneath the headboard and threw them into the trash. "Want yer sheets back?" he asked, pointing toward the bed.

Mike looked down and quickly shook his head. He peered disgustedly at one dingy off-white sheet, blatantly monogramed with a deep yellow elliptical stain, emblazoned in the center where Rich had slept. "Rich, I lent you those sheets months ago, fella. You never did wash them, did you?"

"Minor detail. Hell, I didn't want to lose the scent. It's a long crawl up those stairs, especially when you're half shitfaced at three in the morning."

"Goddamn, Rich!"

"Look!" he explained defensively, turning sideways and pointing his finger toward the bed. "There're a lot of serious memories embedded in those sheets, I'll have you know: Nancy, Lori… Shi-i-itt, I ought to frame the motherfuckers!"

"You ought to *burn* the motherfuckers!"

"Shannahan!" David yelled up the stairs. "Toth's here!"

Mike grabbed Rich's guitar and headed down the stairs. David sat neatly tucked behind the large cover of *Der Stern* magazine, sipping a hot cup of cinnamon tea, his leg resting comfortably on the ottoman in the den. Mike walked past him and into the kitchen and shook hands with the dark-haired Hungarian-born intelligence officer. Rich followed close behind, his duffel bag slung over his shoulder, spouting off his regular Slavic obscenities to their guest. Philip Toth laughed heartily, then blushed. Mike considered him about the only true gentleman in the Group, and despite the two years he had been there, Philip still had never really gotten used to the indignities and uncouth demeanor of his fellow officers.

His father had enjoyed his career as a Hungarian diplomat, but he had been an outspoken critic of the Soviet domination of his beloved country. Facing imminent arrest, he had taken his family in the middle of the night and fled to France, where he had promptly requested asylum. He had made that midnight move with nothing but his life and his family.

Lieutenant Toth maintained his cultured, aristocratic demeanor, despite his having ending up as a displaced person in the suburbs of Detroit in the early '60s. Mike had come to like and admire him and sought his company whenever he needed a break from the nonstop philandering of Rich and his cohorts.

"Rich, you'd better be very careful whom you say that stuff to," he informed him, smiling and shaking his head. "That's some pretty heavy Polish you're slinging around."

Rich strolled over to Philip, grabbed his head with both hands, and proceeded to kiss him wetly in his right ear. "Gonna miss ya, Tothie. Just guess I'm gonna have to learn this shit all over again in *Gookanese*."

Philip pulled away, calmly walked over to the kitchen counter, snapped off a paper towel, and methodically cleaned the saliva out of his ear. "It will certainly be a different experience without you around, I'll say that!" he proclaimed.

Rich expanded on one of his more hearty laughs, grabbed the guitar from Mike's hand, and walked over to the door. "Top of the Mark... Frisco... Thursday, the twenty-first... nineteen hundred hours... Be there, or be square!"

"Roger that," Mike replied.

"Oh, I almost forgot. I closed out my checking account, so write the Ogre a check for the phone bill. I'll square it with you when we get out to the coast."

Mike smiled.

"Good luck, Rich, and may God be with you," Philip added.

The sober remark caught Rich off guard. He stared back at Philip as if the blessing had cast a stigma of propriety he'd have to carry into battle. "If I make the *Times*, Tothie, just make it Glenlivet," he stated, referring to the customary toast so often performed as tribute to fallen comrades.

The screen door closed, and Mike listened to the loud creaking of the worn Biscayne's door as it rotated closed. The starter kicked in, and Mike heard the magazine hit the wall in the den, then flutter to the floor. "The shithead didn't even say good-bye!!" David yelled in utter amazement, hurriedly shuffling by like Chester chasing after Mr. Dillon.

Mike and Philip watched in comic admiration as David crashed through the screen door, screaming wildly at Rich as he pulled out of the driveway. Philip shook his head and laughed. "Never a dull moment around here, is there?"

They both stepped over to the window and laughed together as David ranted and raved through the car door window, arms flaying, chastising Rich for his rude departure. "The first time I ever encountered that guy," Philip recalled, "he was staggering across the old cobblestone bridge over the Isar River in Tölz."

Mike smiled, bringing up the lovely picture in his mind. "He and that moron Lauderson had been over to Takkies, that Greek place, doing some ouzo shooters," Philip added. "They were really hammered."

"I remember that night," Mike told him. "Wasn't that the night that they had to pump Lauderson's stomach because of all the shot glasses he ate?"

"Yes, that was the night. He was one of the Spring Chicks who got shipped out to some leg unit for 'conduct unbecoming.'" There were a lot of elderly German couples out for an evening stroll when they chanced upon them. I remember the fear in their faces when they encountered the two drunk Americans, arm in arm, singing some stupid song, kicking the ducks and pigeons off the bridge like beer cans into a gutter!"

"That's my boy, good ol' Rich. And we wonder why they call us 'ugly Americans.'"

A couple of hours later, David put his magazine down, hearing the jump boots step into the den. Mike stood silently before him, hand out, a regretful yet admiring expression on his face. David looked up, the sparkling star above Mike's jump wings caught his attention. He looked at the face staring at him, then back to the senior jump wings. They didn't equate, he theorized. But then, nothing in Group was commonplace anymore, and this was just another anomaly created by the war "across the pond," he reluctantly concluded.

David took Mike's outstretched hand and drew him close, firming the grip with both of his hands. "Don't try to be a fuckin' hero. Just use your head instead of your ass, and you'll be fine."

"Wish you were going with us, big guy."

"I'll be there with you. You know that."

Mike nodded. "Tell Sarah good-bye for me," he said as David followed him to the door. "I'll stop by DC on my way back. You better have some honeys lined up!"

"You don't have to worry about that!" David replied. "Keep an eye out for Shithead," he concluded as Mike slid behind the wheel. Philip leaned over from the passenger's seat and bid his farewell.

The white T-Bird backed out of the driveway for the last time, leaving David standing in front of the empty house. Mike gave his friend a crisp salute and yelled "See ya," smoking the tires as he sped down the street. The lone, imposing figure on the sidewalk sadly watched the wide red brake lights glow and then disappear swiftly around the corner.

The silver and white Navy P-3 Orion the Commander had sent was waiting on the tarmac when Mike and Philip arrived at the army airfield on post. Like an eagle in the midst of sparrows, it dwarfed the old green and brown army Otters parked alongside. Mike gave Philip an envelope with the title to the T-Bird, the last of his worldly possessions. He hadn't had time to sell it, and he knew Philip would appreciate traveling in style for a change.

A sense of finality followed Mike up the metal steps. He turned and waved to Philip, looked around briefly, and stepped inside. He was greeted warmly by that special aroma he'd missed so much, the traditional naval blend of masculinity, coffee, tobacco, and leather, with just a touch of jet fuel to sweeten it up. The aroma followed him to his seat. It had been more than three years since his senses had been anointed by that special concoction, and ever since then, he had had to settle for the army version of masculinity: leather, sweat, nylon, adrenaline, and a hint of fusty canvas.

Mike strapped in and gave a thumbs up to the pilots staring back at him. He was, in his mind, finally on his way to an ambiguous destiny, a providence he'd prepared for and knew was inevitable. He smiled broadly, and as the plane took to the air, he hummed the tune to one of his favorite melodies. *Get on up, get on up, get on up,/*

Let's boogaloo…

*   *   *

CHAPTER TWENTY-SEVEN

"**A**LL PERSONNEL WITH BOARDING PASSES for Flight Tango-two, Bravo-three-one-eighty-eight, report immediately to Gate Alpha-three for final boarding. This is a final boarding announcement for Flight T-two-B-three-one-eighty-eight."

"That son of a bitch!" Mike exclaimed aloud, scanning the hordes of khakis and dress greens, hoping to catch a glimpse of a beret.

He had spent the past three hours rehearsing what he would say to Rich, not that it would have any impact on his friend, he realized. At least they had a bar at the Top of the Mark, and anyway he hadn't really expected Rich to show up anyway. *If Barry Sadler had known Rich Mycoskie,* he thought, *he would have had to change a lot of the words to the song.*

"How much time do we have, Sergeant?"

"Most of the troops are already aboard, sir," the out-processing officer said. "But my guess is... about twenty-five minutes before they close the doors."

"Well, I'm going out front for one last look..." Then with authority: "Don't let them leave without me, Sergeant."

"You'd better hurry, sir. You've been assigned as troop commander for this flight," he said, handing Mike a thick manila envelope, the faded letters *COT* stenciled on the outside. "You must be the ranking line officer on this flight, sir. Matter of fact," he advised, "you should have already boarded."

Mike unzipped his small bag, stuck the envelope in, and slid it over to the edge of the counter. "Keep an eye on this for me, Sergeant. I'll be right back."

His frustrations turned to immediate concern. Rich was under orders to report to Travis Air Force Base no later than 1700 hours. Now it was 1900 hours, and technically, the motherfucker was AWOL.

He pushed past the lines of troops and airmen, through the crowded alcove and out to the entrance of the terminal. Standing quietly at the edge of the busy sidewalk, he marveled at the long lines of taxis and buses waiting to unload their somber cargo. So many farewells, so far from home—he wondered which of them would ever return.

He walked briskly away from the main entrance, stopping at the edge of the crescent-shaped terminal, looking in every taxi and car for a glimpse of his wayward friend. "Goddamn you, Rich Mycoskie," he muttered softly. "You're not gonna get away with this one. They'll have your ass this time for sure."

He felt a gentle tug on his leg, then another. "Mister… Mister," a quiet voice said. Mike looked down into the clearest, icy blue eyes he'd ever seen, peering up at him, wide and true.

"Mister… Are you a Green Beret?" the inquisitive voice asked.

Mike squatted down and rested his wide forearms over his knees. The boy appeared to be no more than five or six. Straight blond hair, the cut reminding him of the Dutch boy on the paint can. His black and white Keds looked worn at the toes, in sharp contrast to the new clip-on bow tie with his crisp, white shirt tucked neatly into his oversized khaki pants.

"What's your name, pal?" Mike inquired.

"Christopher… But sometimes people call me Chris."

"Well, Chris, my name is Mike. I'm pleased to meet you," he said, reaching out to shake the child's limp hand.

"Mommy said you are a Green Beret," Chris said with a serious look on his pious face. "I've never seen a real one before."

"Well your mommy's right, sonny. Have you ever met a soldier before?" Mike asked, glancing behind the young boy at the woman standing a few feet away. He noticed her folded arms, nervous fingers stroking the strap on her purse as though it were leather beads on a rosary. She seemed anxious, but a grateful expression nonetheless emerged through the rosy blush in her face.

"My daddy's a soldier," Chris proudly stated. "But he's not a Green Beret... Nope, he works with the infantry. They're the ones that get to wear the big round helmets."

"Well, you should be very proud of your daddy, Chris," Mike said, glancing over to the concerned mother.

"I know... He has some bright ribbons on his shirt just like yours." Then, after a little pause: "Can I feel your hat?"

"Sure you can," Mike replied, bending his head down for the boy to touch.

"It's real soft," Chris reported, rubbing his little hand over the smooth woolen fabric.

"Come on, Chris," the mother said, taking the young boy's hand and pulling him toward her. "The gentleman is busy, and we have to get back to Gramps. He's waiting in the car."

Then she looked Mike in the eye. "I'm sorry," she apologized. "We didn't mean to bother you... He just loves John Wayne," she explained. "That's his hero."

"Are you going to Vief-nam, too?" Chris inquired as his mother tugged at his hand. As the boy tried to turn and wave good-bye, he tripped over his little feet.

Mike watched as the young boy struggled for a departing glance back. When they stopped at their car, which was parked at the curb, he impetuously hurried down to stop them. "Chris!... Chris!"

Mike reached up and took his beret off, rolled it up, and handed it to the young boy. "This is just like the one that John Wayne wore in the movie, so I want you to take good care of it. You can tell your friends that. But you're the only one who gets to wear it... Promise?"

"Wowww!... Thanks, mister!"

"I gotta go now, so you take good care of your mother until your dad gets back... Deal?"

The young boy nodded his approval. As his small hands caressed and stroked the beret, Mike turned quickly and hurried back to the terminal entrance. He gazed down at his watch, then glanced back to take one last look down the crowded boulevard. Nursing a distinct feeling of being betrayed, he quietly cursed Rich one final time as he passed through the wide doors into the main terminal. He felt resigned to the disconcerting fact that he would be going over alone after all.

He regretted not having seen his siblings while home on leave, with Thomas and Daniel in North Carolina on a soccer tournament, and with Teresa out of state pursuing her business degree at St. Mary's. Seamus had succeeded in being exiled by the Commander to the Junior Naval Academy in nearby Leonardtown, Maryland, leaving Mike alone with his mother to absorb most of her Southern cooking secrets.

Comforting images of his mother were interrupted by a lone horn blaring in the distance, joined swiftly by a growing number of beeps and blasts from a variety of cars and buses. He looked back through the crowded alcove to see a worn-out-looking Chevy Biscayne zigzagging recklessly down the median, knocking over trash barrels, dodging pedestrians, and destroying scrub trees in its path. He hurried back out the door, bobbing and weaving through the crowd for a better view of the melee emerging. He watched the car jump the curb at the end of the median, speed around the jammed traffic circle in the inside lane, and abruptly screech to a halt in the base commander's reserved space at the end of the terminal.

The puke-green car belched dense clouds of white smoke, shuddered, then died. He watched the driver step out, slinging an old brown briefcase on the roof, fumbling with his beret, trying to get it centered with one hand as he forcefully kicked the door closed.

Mike ran his hand through his hair, shaking his head. *Some things just never change,* he thought as he pushed his way back through the doors, running briskly down the wide corridor, back over to the out-processing desk. "He's here!" he informed the sergeant. "Check his name off the roster... Mycoskie, Richard M."

"I still need a copy of his orders, sir," the sergeant replied calmly.

"Shi-i-i-tt!"

Mike turned and looked back toward the entrance, peering over around the men in uniform, anxious for his friend to appear. He glanced down at his watch again and then looked up to see Rich, striding swiftly toward the desk. The closer he got, the more evident was the full extent of his demise: his beret crudely torn above the green flash, the silver bar flickering, flopping up and down with every step. White teeth accented his unshaven face, and his stained, crinkled khakis were completely void of the required insignias of branch and rank. The empty belt loops remained overshadowed by the glaring black shiner he sported beneath his swollen right eye. His scruffy, unlaced boots appeared as though they had been shined with a Hershey bar.

"Hey, Hamma knokka!!" he exclaimed, obviously enamored to see a friendly face.

Mike stared down at the empty belt loops, then up to the telltale trauma to Rich's eye. "I'm not even going to ask," he told his friend, a resigned tone to his comment.

"Ooouuu…" Rich exclaimed, the obvious stellar grade of octane permeating his breath making Mike back up a step. "Excuse me, *Captain*. Where'dja get the railroad tracks?" he asked, referring to the rank insignia that indicated the promotion Mike had received while on leave.

"They came in the mail," he said, quickly shaking Rich's hand. "We're going to miss the goddamn plane, Rich! The sergeant here needs a copy of your orders!"

Rich smiled, slung the briefcase on the counter, unclipped the latches, and opened the lid, exposing a crumpled pair of seersucker pants, his black issue belt still threaded through its loops. He pulled them out and casually dropped them to the floor, shuffling through layers of papers and letters for his orders.

"You better hope the MPs don't see you, Rich. They might mistake you for a *real* army officer."

Rich paused suddenly, his pervasive grin gone, expression drawn down into a pathetic frown. He glanced over at Mike, then grabbed up the pants, frantically rummaging through the empty pockets. "Fu-u-u-cckk," he uttered as he pulled the belt out of the pants.

"Goddammit, Rich! Sergeant, can you call DA and get a verbal authorization for transport?" Mike inquired.

"Negative, sir. It's past twenty-two hundred hours on the East Coast, and everybody's gone home. If he had his allocation number, I might be able to do something, but without that… my orders are very explicit," he replied, watching Rich shuffle through the papers at the counter, mumbling to himself in Polish.

"You sure know how to fuck up a wet dream, Mycoskie!" Mike scolded. "I sure hope that whatever you were doing was fuckin' worth it."

"Captain, they've finalized the manifest," the sergeant said. "If you're going..."

The sergeant's voice faded as Mike's thoughts focused on the deep concern in his friend's face. He knew the consequences would be severe: *Failure to Report.*

"Come on, then... Walk me down to the gate," Mike said loud enough for the sergeant to hear. "You can straighten this out later." He picked up his own small overnight bag, grabbing Rich with his other hand and moving briskly through the crowded terminal.

"Man... I don't know what happened—"

"Just shut the fuck up, Rich! And take off that fuckin' beret. People are staring. Here, take my boarding pass. But don't use it unless somebody stops you. I'll do something to cause a distraction at the gate. You just make sure you get your feeble ass on board that goddamn plane. And, lace up your damn boots! Who the fuck dressed you this morning anyway?" He quickened his pace, moving ahead of his scruffy-looking friend, pulling the COT envelope out of his bag as he went.

Gate A3 remained crowded with family and friends, each quietly staring out the tall windows to the chartered 707 sitting on the tarmac, the red navigation lights dimly blinking in concert with the setting sun. Two air force airmen collected and counted the white boarding passes, oblivious to the tearful throngs, laughing and joking while emotion tore into the hearts of loved ones who were left standing only a few feet away. They both looked up to see the captain fumbling to retrieve the paperwork out of the envelope, hindered by the wide bag tucked under his arm. "Let me help you, sir," one lanky airman offered, reaching out to take his bag.

Mike raised his elbow, then dropped the pile of papers just as the airman pulled on the bag. The papers spilled on the floor, scattering on the slick linoleum tiles. "Jeeezus Christ!" he complained, standing until both airmen bent over to retrieve the scattered documents. "This just hasn't been my day," he said in a conciliatory tone.

"It was my fault, Captain," the first airman apologized.

"Naw... I just didn't have a good grip. My palms seem a little sweaty today for some reason."

"I can understand why," the airman replied.

Mike squatted down to help pick up the orders, catching a glimpse of Rich slipping out the door behind them. "How long's the flight, anyway," he asked, trying to hold the airmen's attention.

"Just about twenty-three hours, Captain. But, you'll have a layover in Hawaii for them to refuel. 'Bout an hour and a half... I'd get some sleep if I were you."

"That's not a bad idea," Mike agreed, standing as he took the orders from the airman and stuffed them back into the large envelope. "What do I do with these when we get in-country?" he asked, holding up the envelope.

"The Repo Depot NCO in charge will meet you when you arrive. Just make sure he gets these before anyone deplanes," the airman explained. "That's about it."

"Thanks." Mike turned and started out the door.

"Sir. You have your white boarding pass?"

Mike stopped cold, pretended to think for a moment, then turned to face them, his eyes shifting left and right, eyes squinting in supposed deep thought. "Damn!... Told you this hasn't been my day. I left it in the phone booth when I was talking to my mom... I'll go back and—"

"That's all right, Captain... We're already behind schedule. You're the last to board anyway. Good luck, Captain."

"Thanks..." Mike flipped a quick salute, turned, and stepped out into the warm evening air. There was no turning back now, he reckoned. He knew his destiny lay straight ahead, manifested in the form of a long, sleek 707, an unlikely aluminum chariot to carry him into battle. Somehow, it seemed so absurd to him. He'd always imagined it would be an olive-drab C-141. Certainly not a shiny Global Air Charter, complete with a light-gray-uniformed stewardess standing at the door.

Mike's heart pounded with every step, heavy jump boots pressing hard on the tarmac, deliberately bonding him to his homeland forever. Long-drawn breaths tasted the warm evening air, lightly seasoned with the sweet aroma of jet fuel, adding to the sense of finality in his every move. His last pace on the tarmac lingered a moment longer, then firm steps were replaced by the hollow clamor of jump boots on the aluminum stairs.

He lightened his stride, looking up into the sedate face of the veteran stewardess standing impatiently in the door. *She's probably a dubious agent of the Grim Reaper,* he teased in his mind, much like a similar proxy he had envisioned in an earlier dream... *Or at very least, Satan's mistress.*

Pausing briefly on the landing, he glanced over his shoulder at the sun-drenched peaks of the hills surrounding the base. The early evening twilight scaled the rolling slopes, creeping steadily upward, destined to extinguish the amber majesty painted by the setting sun. His searching eyes focused on Old Glory, flapping in the breeze, secure atop the tall mast centered in front of the terminal. He sighed, paying homage with pointed fingers, reassured in his ultimate quest in her honor.

Smiling, with his young heart at ease, Mike turned and stepped inside, encountering the stoic stares of hundreds of eyes. "Is this the flight to Tahiti?" he asked the impatient stewardess.

"Not for you," she replied curtly.

"That time of the month?" he inquired, not waiting for the response.

She grimaced as she watched him walk down the aisle. "You'll regret that remark," she sassed confidently, lifting up her clipboard, cracking her gum while she scanned the names for the COT.

The whine of the engines soon roared, and as the families and friends watched the big jet rotate out onto the taxiway, Mike watched Old Glory drift slowly down the flagpole. *She'll be folded and tucked... set aside for tomorrow,* he told himself. He knew she'd fly again, and again, waving good-bye to her sons, then beaming in the breeze when they returned, or dusted off to shield them from the grief of their families, draped lovingly over their remains when they returned to be interred forever, beneath the amber waves of grain.

* * *

CHAPTER TWENTY-EIGHT

HE WARM DROP OF SWEAT rolled from Mike's brow, lightly burning the corner of his eye as it rolled past his cheek and etched its way slowly onto his earlobe. He dared not move to whisk the irritation away. The ominous dark figure had paused at the foot of his bunk. Through the folds of the dense mosquito net, Mike's wide eyes searched desperately for a familiar feature. He lay quietly, stealing short, silent breaths of the hot evening air, cloaked heavily with the musky aroma of nervous, sweating men.

He'd spent hours fighting the heat, slipping in and out of a shallow slumber, listening to the faint drone of angry mosquito wings, constantly flipping his wet pillow for brief moments of cool relief. The evening distractions had run together: Distant thunderclaps, sounding more like deadly howitzers with every crescendo. An endless vibrato of cargo planes, hurriedly lifting off the nearby airstrip, their fiery JATO-assist speeding their departure. Illumination flares popped like vintage bottles of champagne, spewing oscillating shivers of light through the screen apertures of the wooden barracks. He couldn't remember whether he had slept or not. Nothing had changed. Except, that is, for the silent figure perched at the end of his bunk.

It moved—slowly, deliberately, silently lifting a dark object above the round metal bed frame. *I'm dreaming,* he assumed, *but it seems so real.*

Another flare burst high above the perimeter, fanning a million-candlelight glare over the flat checkerboard expanse between the base and Núi Cầu Hin and the other mountains surrounding Nha Trang, a mere mile away. Flickers of light danced through the lines of bunks, filtered by the flowing drapes of musty mosquito nets. He'd commented to someone earlier in the evening how the nets reminded him of flimsy cocoons, constructed specifically to incubate, languidly, the slabs of fresh meat flown in daily from the outside world.

The phantom froze, blending in with the awkward images flashing through the barracks, dissipating, then rising in concert with the distant light of the swaying torch. Mike's heart pounded a morbid cadence. He was gripped in fear by the ghoulish scene unfolding in front of him. He watched in silent distress as the barrel of the AK-47 slipped through the corner of the net, a silver-tipped bayonet parting the folds, unveiling a pair of catlike, ebony eyes. His jaw tightened, his breathing ceased, his whole being focused intently on the narrow black sapphires, glistening ominously in the last fading sparkle from the distant flare.

He glared up toward his own weapon, uselessly hanging from the head rail of the top bunk, out of reach, magazine empty. He anticipated the loud flash, the deafening report that would signal an end to his young life. His heart pounded fervently, demanding his limp body to react. His motor senses ignored the clear commands, however, apathetically refusing to respond. He lay paralyzed, captivated by fear, tormented by terror, his body mocking his innate instincts for survival. *O God, please don't let it end like this,* he pleaded. *Not my first week here. Not in a transient bunk. Not in my underwear.*

His arms felt as though they weighed a ton. They refused to reach up and grab the barrel of the gun that was pointed right at his head. He wondered if his bunkmates were dead already, their throats having been slashed by a silent team of sappers while he lay fretting about sleep in the stifling Indochina night. He strained to scream, to warn them. Nothing. Fear had silenced his voice. But not his heart. It continued to pound, louder and louder, faster and faster, until—

The terror shackles finally burst, catapulting him out of bed, through the maze of netting, and into the image of the apparition poised to strike. A deep, guttural howl followed, prompting several other nervous men to shout in alarm and scramble out of bed and through the bay doors to safety.

The bunk bed crashed around him, pulled to the floor as he wrestled to free himself from the labyrinth of torn netting.

"What the fuck's going on over there?" a loud voice demanded to know.

Mike struggled to stand but could only manage to reach a sitting position before the net held him back. His senses restored by his abrupt crash to the floor, he quickly realized that the whole episode had been conjured up in his sleep-deprived mind. "Jet lag is fuckin' brutal," he replied, feeling humiliated as he struggled to free himself from the tangled net.

One by one, the men returned to their bunks, shaken but relieved that the commotion was only imagined. Most were admin or support troops, destined for rear-echelon jobs that would keep them out of harm's way.

Mike ripped through the final strand of netting and quietly cursed himself as he righted the bed. He tossed the tangled net on the top bunk and headed to the latrine. Turning on the cold faucet in the shower, he stepped under the cool flow of soothing water, drenching his new olive-drab boxers and T-shirt. *Don't think I can put up with that kind of shit every night,* he surmised as he began to relax under the steady stream massaging his tense shoulders.

He finally regained his senses, turned off the water, and stepped out the rear door of the barracks to allow the hot evening air to absorb the remaining moisture clinging to his body. He stood there quietly, his dreary eyes scanning the moonlight reflecting in the rice paddies that formed a natural perimeter around the western edges of the base. The distant flares silhouetted the nearby mountain peaks, secure sanctuaries for Charlie to keep an eye on what was going on at the base, he concluded.

He started to walk down the dusty sidewalk along the perimeter fence, noting the lines of concertina wire and trip flares that crisscrossed out to the edge of the paddies. Ahead, he observed a figure, sitting atop a sandbagged bunker, a billow of chalky smoke lingering above him in the breathless night. He walked slowly, noting the dark image wore faded tiger fatigues, shirt open, trousers draped loosely over his unlaced jungle boots. Mike felt the man's eyes on him, although his head was facing out toward the paddies, the remnants of a small cheroot dangled loosely from his lips. The man seemed to be casually flipping a shiny object through his fingers. As Mike drew closer, he recognized the familiar profile, and as he stepped in front of him, the man stopped flipping the object and clutched it tightly. "Allen? Sergeant Allen?"

"Aaahhh, excuse me if I don't get up, Lieutenant," he said, obviously surprised when he realized who had interrupted him, and continuing to address Mike by his former rank. "A little late to be playing grab-ass in the barracks, don'cha think?"

A warm sense of security enveloped the young officer. "Somebody just had a bad dream," he replied, sheepishly staring down.

"Roger that, sir," Allen said, a soft resignation evident in his voice. "This whole country is a bad fuckin' dream."

"Don't know how anybody can sleep in this shit," Mike said, looking back toward the silent barracks.

"You just get in-country?"

"Yeah, three days ago. Haven't gotten a good night's sleep yet," Mike told him. "Just flew up from Biên Hòa today. Haven't had time to track down any of the guys from the Tenth. Who all's up here anyway?"

Sergeant Allen took a prolonged drag on the cheroot, leisurely inhaling the coarse smoke before spitting a sliver of tobacco into the air. "Well, sir, you just missed Sarkie."

"Yeah? How's that old fart doin' anyway?" Mike slapped the mosquito impaled in the back of his neck.

Sergeant Allen slid off the bunker, quietly gazing out over the perimeter wire and up into the dark Asian sky. After an extended silence, he looked down into his hand, his large, callused fingers tenderly caressing the thin metal necklace. He drew a deep breath, then grunting loudly, he launched the necklace high over the wire, far into the fields of rice before him.

"Donno, sir." A small, distant splash of a fallen comrade's dog tags prefaced his next remark. "You're gonna have to ask his next of kin."

Mike grimaced. The tall sergeant reached over and took his hand. "I'm a little surprised to see you here, Lieutenant. But you're just gonna have to get used to it."

Allen tightened his grip. Mike felt instantly that it was more than a greeting. "Right now, *Trung úy*, you're just like a babe in the woods," the sergeant said, addressing Mike as Lieutenant in Vietnamese. "Before too long, you'll be sleeping through the night without a pacifier," he assured him. "Ya just have to learn to give it up."

"Give what up?" Mike inquired.

"Good night, sir." Allen shook his hand, turned, and walked slowly away.

Mike noticed his old teammate's slight limp and, for a second, wondered what he had been doing here in-country. The thought passed quickly, though. This was Allen's life, he realized—his profession, his passion. *I envy his comfort zone*, Mike told himself, *and I just hope I don't have to go through everything he's had to deal with to get there.*

He considered Allen's sage advice. "Give it up," he repeated aloud. He *knew* what the sergeant was referring to. He'd heard other men in the Group allude to the very same concept. He just didn't know how to achieve that lofty state of mind. But he knew Allen was right.

His mind drifted back to a statement made by President Franklin Delano Roosevelt many years before. He recalled asking his father what the Commander in Chief during our frightening Depression and World War Two years had meant by it. "The only thing we have to fear... is fear itself." It hadn't made any sense to him then, and his father's interpretation had proved to be just as beguiling. But tonight those simple words finally fell into place for him. *If you can conquer the elements of fear, then you have nothing left to fear!* he realized.

He pondered the elements of fear: the enemy, being wounded, being captured, the uncertainty of his destiny. He concluded that he had no control over any of the outcomes, but they all had one common denominator: fear itself. *Fear serves no positive purpose,* he finally concluded. *It only exacerbates confusion in your mind, which inhibits rational thinking and promotes irrational behavior.*

He leaned up against the sandy bunker, gazing out across the tranquil expanse. A lull in the pyrotechnics had restored the serene mystique to the lovely countryside. *If Denny were here, he'd probably be telling me to shut the fuck up!* he mused, realizing his thought processes were cresting out of control. Yet, for the first time since he'd set boots on the tarmac in Biên Hòa, a sense of calm anointed his manner. He turned back toward the barracks, and with a renewed sense of purpose, he decided to leave his subconscious inhibitions on the berm to spar with the distant purveyors of the night.

Another flare lit up his path back to the barracks. He watched in amusement as the eerie images began their minuet, mocking him with every sway of their conductor's fiery wand. He stepped through the entrance to the bay area. Wide, terrified eyes followed his movement between the bunks. Rigid bodies, heels together, arms stiffly at their sides. *They're gonna have to get their own therapy*, he told himself as he imagined their anxiety contemplating their own encounters with the inevitable.

He searched for a fresh bunk. Then he slid off his damp boxers, pulled back the fresh white sheet, lay peacefully down, took a cleansing breath, and closed his weary eyes. Within minutes, the sound of sleep carried through the barracks, taunting the fragile souls of his weary comrades.

The predawn rain restored the tropical fragrance flowing through the malodorous barracks. The lone floor fan circulated the spicy sandalwood and bougainvillea, an ancient bouquet accented today with the hint of freshly issued jungle fatigues and stiff leather and nylon boots.

Mike flicked the beads of sweat accumulating above his shaven lip, blowing lightly to cool his tepid skin. Staring into the mirror, he held the left edge of his new beret while tugging down on the other end, a vain attempt to get it to fit properly.

"Cap'n Shannahan!" a voice echoed down the long bay area.

"Rrrroger!"

"The S-one requests your presence over at the C-Team HQ, ASAP... sir," the voice replied.

"On my way!" *Well, this is it*, he concluded, pulling the beret off and soaking the edges with a stream of cold water. He quickly wrung out the excess and then tried to shape it again. *That's gonna have to do*, he decided.

The mountains surrounding the Nha Trang base had drawn nearer with the morning light. Mike walked past the perimeter bunker and gazed out into a menagerie of tanglefoot and concertina. Subtle thoughts of Sarkie reflected off the placid film covering the stagnant paddies.

I'm really here, he confirmed, still a little hesitant about the profundity of his decision. Excitement mingled with boyish anticipation as he strode through the dusty compound, suddenly alive with an endless parade of dust-caked jeeps and raucous motorcycles. Their foggy red wakes anointed the hordes of pajama-clad mama-sans and young girls on their way to cook and clean for the American warriors, a domestic task they had perfected, a task passed from one generation to the next.

He felt the perspiration build on his temples and under his arms, large beads of sweat trickled down the middle of his back, irritating him as they began to soak the top of his trousers. The putrid scent of fuel oil permeated the growing aroma enveloping the base, an aroma suddenly enhanced by the blistering heat from the rising sun.

He looked closely at the variety of pedestrians. Some smiled as they passed, but most hid their faces below the wide brims of their pointed straw hats. He felt an inkling of their disdain, but he didn't blame them. He was used to feeling resented. It just came with the territory, he reasoned. He knew that to them he was just a foreign agent, certainly not a human being in their eyes, just a mercenary sent to further the goals and ambitions of the country whose uniform he wore. But he also knew that he was certainly no stranger to them, since other men like him had come before, the last horde bullying them in French.

The sweltering sun singed the shine on his stiff, uncomfortable jungle boots, while the temperature rose beneath his dark, woolen beret. He took it off, running his hand through his short, wet hair, noting that he hadn't seen many Americans on his way to the headquarters building. As he entered the inner compound, the grounds seemed deserted. He noticed an occasional trooper moving briskly from building to building, but he saw none lingering anywhere else.

He paused in front of a modest single-story building. *Headquarters, 5th Special Forces Group, (Abn), 1st Special Forces,* the light blue sign read. The forest-green flash of the Tenth was only one of nine Group flashes painted on the window awnings of the chalk-white building. Smiling, he adjusted his beret and strode proudly under the short portal into the Group adjutant's office.

Mike pressed down tightly with his toes, rubbing the soft, padded socks against the nylon-mesh inner soles of his jungle boots. The full blouse of his baggy jungle fatigues hung lazily over the tops, in stark contrast to the crisp, tailored ensemble he had normally, until recently, been wearing. He stood patiently, constantly annoyed by the enlarging trail of sweat his flowing armpits were spreading on his heavy new fatigue jacket.

"Sir, you're scheduled to depart Nha Trang Harbor at fifteen hundred hours," the S1 clerk advised him. "A navy barge will take you out to Hòn Tre Island for the combat orientation course."

"Do I *have* to go?" he scoffed, a slight grimace tugging at the edge of his mouth.

He refolded the uneven tucks in his sleeve while he contemplated the predawn runs up the mountain trail. He'd heard about the one-week course in the barracks, a course carefully designed to acclimate the men headed for combat assignments to the weather, a course including close-action combat drills in the jungles.

Same ol' shit. Hurry up and wait, he lamented, sorely gripped by the prospect that he'd have to spend at least another week before he received his combat assignment.

"Afraid so, sir," the young spec-four answered, smiling as he handed Mike back his in-processing paperwork. "Who knows, *Đại úy?*" the clerk said, using the Vietnamese for Captain, pronounced "die wee." "You might even get your CIB out there. Last class did. Made contact with the regional VC tax collectors."

Mike's eyes widened. "Really?" he asked, until that moment unaware that the island was inhabited. "They nail 'em?"

"Ruined their whole day," the clerk replied.

The rookie captain shook his head, wondering what had been going through their minds when they had them in their sights. "What the hell were they doing out there in the first place?" he asked. "That's kinda' like stowing away on a *kamikaze* flight! I thought everybody in-country knew we send our guys out there to throw some lead around."

The clerk just shrugged his shoulders and continued to type. "Just have a seat around the corner, Captain," he motioned. "The colonel likes to meet all the new officers coming into Group. I'll tell the sergeant major you're waiting."

Mike nodded, turned, and then returned to ask, "Oh, by the way... Do you happen to recall a Lieutenant Mycoskie reporting in the last day or two?"

The clerk blinked slowly, peering pensively over the top of his wire-framed glasses. "Friend of yours, Captain?"

Mike hesitated briefly, then conceded, yet contemplating the full consequence of his response. "We aahhh... We came over on the flight together. But aahhh... He sort of disappeared right after we landed in Biên Hòa."

"Wouldn't mention him to the Old Man if I were you, Captain," he advised. The MPs picked him up in Vũng Tàu two days ago. He was passed out in a jeep he had *requisitioned* from the Air Force in Saigon."

"Is he all right?"

"Suppose so, *Đại úy*. Might have some scars on his ass, though. The Old Man was ready to lock his heels and ship him off to some leg unit on the DMZ, but the word is: The XO saved his ass. Turns out Major Aldridge was with his brother when he was wounded in a bad firefight. Captain Mycoskie carried him out of the jungle and threw him on the last chopper out of a hot LZ somewhere along the Fence in Cambodia, then charged back into the tree line, singlehandedly firing up the bad guys trying shoot the chopper down."

"I heard he didn't make it back," Mike lamented.

"Never did recover the body."

Mike paused for a moment, recalling the bond he and Rich had established, along with the riderless Triumph parked in the driveway back in Lowell.

"You wouldn't know where I can find him, would you?" he inquired.

"No, sir. Top said the Old Man put him on a chopper and told the pilot to drop him off at some SOG radio relay site atop some steep mountain along the Laotian border. Told him that if he could find a jeep or a honky-tonk up there, he had his permission to get after it!"

Mike shook his head again. *Fuckin' idiot.*

Mike stepped back out into the hall and took a seat on the wooden bench in the hallway. The dark-paneled wall held the memories of critical engagements of the unit, portraits of their heroes, strange faces above familiar names: Donlon, Dix, Ashley, Zabitowski, and Howard. There were more, the powder-blue ribbon with stars conspicuously displayed in their honor. He stared at their faces, looking earnestly for some common denominator, some telltale expression he could recognize in the mirror.

His foray to glory ended suddenly, interrupted as the door to the colonel's office swung open. "Captain!"

Mike bolted up from the bench, stomped his boots to set the blouse, then strode briskly past the brawny sergeant major to stop in front of the desk situated in the center of the room. "Captain Shannahan reports!" he bellowed, his salute vibrating above fixed eyes.

"At ease, Captain!" Colonel Ryan barked back from behind the high-backed leather chair. "Have a seat. I'll be with you in a minute."

Mike chose the nearest chair, nervous perspiration building on his temples and upper lip. He sat quietly, staring intently at the shiny jungle boots propped up on the credenza behind the desk.

"OCS?" the colonel inquired, his back still facing Mike.

"Fifty-fifth Company," Mike was proud to say.

"Good… Excellent," the colonel commented, finally spinning around and standing up behind his cluttered desk. "Welcome to the Fifth Group, Captain," he said, his large hand outstretched.

Mike rushed over to accept the greeting, careful only to match the strength of the gesture. "Thank you, sir," he replied, smiling. He studied the colonel's face, gruff and laden with what appeared to be the remnants of adolescence acne. His hazel eyes conveyed confidence and concern, the latter of which was immediately verbalized to his new officer.

"How old are you, son?" a slight squint accenting the question.

"Twenty-one, sir."

The colonel nodded his head, delving deep into Mike's eyes. Then he sat back on the edge of his desk, resting his folded arms in his lap, pinched eyes still showing an element of doubt.

"I'd like to be assigned to CCN," Mike said, referring to Command and Control North, headquarters for the reconnaissance teams. "That is, with your approval, Colonel. I've had a lot of experience navigating hostile terrain, and I'm well at home in the bush."

A veiled smile eased across the Colonel's face. "And I know you'd do a fine job, son. But we've had some recent action down in Three Corps, and I've just decided to commit you to Colonel Anderson down in A-Company."

"Captain!! Captain!!!" a loud, angry voice echoed down the hallway.

Mike turned to see a dark figure moving deliberately toward the colonel's office, several men in quick pursuit. As they approached the open doorway, he noticed the layers of crusted, dried blood covering the ripped and jagged tiger fatigues.

"Stevenson?" Mike blurted. "Hollis?" The tall intruder wobbled past Mike, followed closely by Sergeant Major Bowen and several officers.

Standing in front of the desk, his bloodshot eyes riveted on the colonel, Hollis dug into his thigh pocket and pulled out his beret. Clutching it tightly, he shoved it directly in front of Colonel Ryan's face. It shook lazily in his hand, a lifeless symbol that drew everyone's attention.

"This belongs to you, sir," Hollis said, his dry, raspy voice quivering. "It don't mean *shit* out there in the woods, least not for you. You left my shit out there on the fuckin' tailgate one too many fuckin' times. I fuckin' quit!!"

He slammed the blood-soaked beret hard to the floor, turned, and pushed his way through the startled group of men crowded in the room. Mike cringed at the wide, open gash in his left cheek, his face contorted from thin, razorlike lacerations crisscrossing from his exposed, sweaty chest up to the tight, dirt-caked cravat tied around his head.

Mike stepped quickly to halt Hollis's retreat, his arm outstretched to draw his comrade near. A surge of compassion filled his heart as he looked into the shadowy, bloodshot eyes, the lurid stench of rotting skin filling his lungs. Hollis stopped short, glaring through Mike's sincere intent, looming ever awkwardly, more like a tormented biblical figure than his old comrade. His mangled left arm dangled loosely from his side, dark, moist skin concealing the full extent of his wounds.

Sergeant Major Bowen reached over and grabbed the arm, lifting up the fingerless palm for all to see. The dark boot string drawn deeply across the knuckles had mostly clotted the flow of blood from the crusty stub. Hollis sneered in disgust and pulled away from Bowen with a threatening glare. "Keep your fuckin' rear-echelon hands off me, *motherfucker*!!"

"At ease, Captain!" the colonel commanded.

Hollis turned slowly and stared at the colonel through his vision slits caked with stale sweat and dried blood. His cracked lips parted, revealing vivid, white teeth lined with thick, shady blood. He stood silently, as if in a trance, wavering above the small puddle of wet blood accumulating at his feet. Slowly, his parched tongue broke through the amber phlegm sealing his lips. "Who's gonna pay for this one, sir?" he asked softly, his distant stare defying a reasonable answer.

Colonel Ryan watched the trickle of blood curl around the jagged crease in the corner of his mouth.

"'Break contact...' 'Continue the mission,'" Hollis slurred, repeating the nonsensical replies he had received when pleading for rescue. He raised his bloody hand to wipe the oozing blood away from his lips. His body trembled, easing a swell of tears to his bloodshot eyes. He turned his head and spat a line of bloody saliva to the floor. "'Break contact...' 'Continue the mission,'" he murmured again.

Hollis paused. He lowered his head slowly, his raspy, cluttered breaths rising above the intense silence in the room. Mike hesitated, then moved closer, reaching out again to steady his tormented comrade. Hollis spun suddenly, pushing him away, another surge of adrenaline rekindling his abused spirit. "We're not goin' back out, Colonel. Not for nobody. No, sir, RT Saw's not goin' back across that fuckin' Fence! Not today. Not ever!"

He spat again, wiping the bloody drool from his chin. "Matter-a' fact, you *all* need to take a good look at my shiny black ass," he proclaimed, turning to ensure that all in the room would hear his message. "'Cause the next time you'll see it, you'll be following it through the fuckin' gates of hell!"

Hollis drew his good arm up, flipped a mock salute, then turned and pushed his way out of the office, his good arm steadying his paces as he staggered down the hall.

"Get that man some medical attention!" Colonel Ryan yelled. Several of the officers turned and scurried after Captain Stevenson, leaving the colonel and Mike alone with the sergeant major.

"I want some answers, Sergeant Major. And I want them now!"

Bowen stepped forward. "Walked into Buôn Ma Thuột early this morning, sir," Bowen explained, rubbing his hands together, hands stained with blood from trying to restrain Hollis. "He was the one-zero on the team we lost last week in Cambodia. They'd been on the ground two days when they walked smack into the NVA's Nine-five-Charlie Regiment's base camp."

"What?? Why wasn't I notified?" the colonel demanded.

"It was in the morning report, sir."

"Bullshit, Sergeant Major!! Don't hand me that crap!" He picked up the phone and pressed the button. "Aldridge! My office! Now!"

"They were able to break the initial contact, Colonel," Bowen went on. "But the team ended up on the run for three days, playing cat and mouse with Chuck's trackers. They hadn't taken any causalities, so the launch officer refused to extract them. That's when Chuck put the dogs on 'em. Their FAC lost contact after that."

"The one-zero called for extraction?" the colonel asked, stalking back and forth in front of his desk.

"Affirmative, sir. Declared a *tactical emergency* with the FAC and requested extraction… Seven times, sir."

"I want a full report from the rest of the team on my desk, ASAP!"

"Sir…" Bowen interrupted. "What's left of RT Saw just stumbled out the door."

Colonel Ryan turned his back, leaned over, and placed his palms on his desk.

"They just had medevac'd him in over at the Eighth Field Hospital, sir," Bowen added. "He musta' given them the slip."

"Get my chopper ready, Sergeant Major. I'm going to find out what kind of son of a bitch is running that FOB."

"That won't be necessary, sir. Major Dover's over at the Eighth Field, too. Captain Stevenson damn near killed him."

The colonel turned sharply, and then realized that Mike was standing against the wall. "We're through here, Captain. Report to your unit!"

Mike saluted, turned, and hurried out the door, maneuvering carefully through the smeared trail of blood and red boot prints etched in the tile floor. He stopped at the clerk's desk and with a stern tone issued his own directive.

"Specialist, Colonel Ryan has ordered me to report to my unit. Notify A-Company S-one that I'll be reporting in this afternoon. I'll be back in an hour to pick up my orders and travel voucher," he informed him. "And, by the way… How do I get over to the Eighth Field Hospital?"

The clerk leaned back in his chair. "Just follow the parade, sir."

* * *

CHAPTER TWENTY-NINE

IKE THREW HIS RUCKSACK INTO the back of the dust-caked jeep and climbed aboard. He cradled his new M16 in his lap, the muzzle resting awkwardly in the crook of his right arm.

"Where ya headed, *Đại úy?*" the driver asked, tugging his worn beret in place.

"Some place called Trà Cú. Ever heard of it?"

The young sergeant backed out of the small quadrangle in front of A-Company headquarters and quickly shifted gears as he sped past the wooden sentry hut guarding the compound. Mike waited for his answer, wondering why he was slow to respond.

"Colonel Anderson said it was pretty close to the Cambodian border, an old French outpost at the junction of some rivers," Mike yelled above the grinding gears.

"A-three-two-six. Captain McNutt's old team," the driver finally replied. "They tell you what happened there?"

Mike stared through the dingy windshield, recalling the S2's account of the fierce battle. "Yeah, I know," he conceded, wondering if a similar fate awaited him.

"A damn shame. Just a damn shame," the driver recalled. "It's a cold day in hell when we lose so many in one action, *Đại úy*."

Mike was relieved that he didn't know any of the men personally. Four of his team dead, two wounded. Over half the team wiped out on one sunny afternoon. Everyone said it just didn't happen in Special Forces, but it had at Trà Cú. He was on his way to replace those who had gone before. He vowed not to make the same mistakes that had led to their demise.

"They used to call it Hell on Earth. Now they're calling it the Slaughterhouse on the Nile."

"Sergeant, do you mind if we talk about something else?"

"Sorry, sir. I just—"

"How much further to the chopper pad?"

The sergeant glanced over at Mike and shook his head. "'Bout ten minutes, sir."

The episode at Group headquarters still stirred his soul. By the time he'd found the field hospital, Hollis's top-secret unit had extracted him, leaving behind some battered orderlies and eerie rumors of his exploits. Mike learned that he had been hit with small-arms fire four times and received puncture wounds from shrapnel too numerous to count. He'd seared off the bleeders with the hot barrel of his Swedish K, and according to the medics, that painful decision had saved his life. But the one exploit that confounded everyone was that he carried his dead one-one for two days through some of the most hostile terrain in Southeast Asia, only to lay him down gently in front of the launch-site commander in Buôn Ma Thuột. *The true nature of a man is confounding*, he admitted to himself, feeling remorse for the low regard he had held previously for the carefree Bad Tölz playboy.

Mike stared ahead through the muddy smear to what appeared to be a large group of school-aged children gathered along the side of the road. Waiting to cross the road, they yelled and waved at the small convoy of army trucks in front of the jeep. He smiled, adjusting his weapon so he would be able to wave back, although a little embarrassed by the whole thing. As they approached, he waved at the youngsters, then noticed the children's salutation was more explicit than he had imagined. Five-, six-, seven-year-olds, each gesturing wildly with the time-honored sign of American insult and contempt: Both hands, single, tiny middle digits extended in the absurd salute.

"Welcome to Vietnam, *Đại úy*," the driver told him, laughing heartily.

"They catch on pretty quick over here, don't they?"

"Don't worry about it, sir. You'll get used to it."

Mike stared back through the billowing dust. "I sure hope not," he muttered.

The work chopper strained, whirling blades cutting sharply into the thin, hot air, surging abruptly as it finally lifted off the hot metal pad. It continued to labor as it gained altitude, swirling higher into the hot, vaporlike winds stifling the thousands of American troops marshaled in the sprawling Long Binh Depot below. Mike leaned out the open door, straining against his seatbelt for a better view of the mammoth war machine. He watched convoys of trucks delivering their deadly cargo, crates of artillery shells and ammunition stacked on wooden pallets. Swarms of fork lifts scurried from truck to truck, resembling worker bees harvesting their honey.

A continuous maze of wood huts and shanties melded into an endless mass of human habitat, with small, white mini-clouds of smoke dwindling into the faint air, hovering aimlessly above the trifling cooking fires. *What a confined area for such a large depot,* he thought to himself. *How the hell does anybody know who's who around here anyway? Charlie could hide a whole damn division in those hooches,* he concluded. *Dumb fuckin' legs!*

The chopper continued to gain altitude, and with each revolution of the altimeter gauge, the temperature dropped five degrees. Mike reveled in the cool breeze flowing through his fatigue jacket, watching the dust-choked marshaling areas give way to a vast farmland accented with small, scattered villages. Tall, flowing palm trees lined the roads while tiny figurines toiled earnestly in the shallow rice squares, following close behind a farmer and his plow, fettered tightly between the wide haunches of a lethargic water buffalo.

He struggled to pick out the villagers and farmers as they went about their tasks. His eyes strained and scanned the playing field below, finally becoming adept at picking out moving objects. Recently alerted that he was, finally, in-country, he felt sure that at any moment, he'd catch the muzzle flash from some well-concealed sniper.

It all seemed surreal. A serene setting, with ordinary people, oblivious to the chopper carrying foreign warriors to fight *their* fight, to covet and defile *their* women—it just didn't make any sense to him at all.

He looked back over his shoulder at the door gunner behind him, lying slumped against the bulkhead, enveloped in blissful sleep, gloved hands tucked beneath the armpits of his Nomex flight suit, his large green helmet bobbing with every sway of the noisy chopper. Mike stared at him, wondering if he himself had looked that young when he was a private. He noticed the fuzzy growth above the gunner's lip, freckles and scattered pimples covering his Kansas face. *Does his mother know where he is?* he wondered.

Mike turned his attention to the wet, grassy terrain sliding beneath the length of the tattered skids. He noted that there wasn't any place for enemy troops to hide other than in these small villages. There were no lush rain forests, no perilous mountains, not even a ravine. Just an endless patchwork of fields and paddies, dotted occasionally with a small tree square sheltering scant dwellings with thatched roofs. This wasn't the ravished land in his dreams, the Central Highlands, the triple-canopy jungle hellhole they feared... and loved. This terrain was beginning to look more like the sprawling Florida Everglades to him: Long marshy stretches of elephant grass and clusters of reeds dominated the wetlands below.

Then, as if suddenly cast into a dimensional time zone, the ground below transitioned into a labyrinth of water-filled ponds. Hundreds of perfectly round pools dotted the wet plains below him, some small, some slightly larger, but all consistently round with dark dirt berms surrounding them.

The long, black perforated muzzle of the M60 swung sharply into view, drawing his attention away from the mysterious sight below. The chopper shuddered violently, flaring enough to cause Mike to grab hold of the aluminum rail on his seat. *Were we hit?* he wondered, looking back at the bleary-eyed door gunner chambering a round, then bracing his feet against the large ammo box below him.

Mike looked ahead at the pilots. Their casual manner quickly set him at ease. He turned back to the door gunner and lifted his palms up, shrugging his shoulders for an explanation. The gunner just shook his head, pulled his glove off, took a wad of chewing gum out of his mouth, and pressed it firmly on the up-strut beside him. Reaching up, he slid down the dark visor on his helmet, transforming the sleepy farm boy into a warrior of ominous proportion. Mike felt the gunner had seen action before, the black tint of the visor hiding the truth in his eyes, his masked fury tempered only slightly by the quick sign of the cross he made and the obvious act of contrition on his tight lips.

The pitch of the blades changed quickly, masturbating the cool air with a loud popping sound that rapidly transitioned to a more subtle *whop, whop, whop*. Mike didn't know what was happening, but he followed the gunner's lead and chambered a round in his M16. The first tracer round in his magazine slammed home just as the chopper tilted on its side, beginning a long, spiral rotation toward the ground below. His eyes broadened, he turned his head to the right, providing him an unobstructed view, the sheer force of the auto-rotation pinning him hard against the nylon seat. The ground rushed upward with distinct definition, exposing a winding, gray river below, its banks lined with the jagged remnants of palms and other trees. The gunner flashed him the thumbs-up sign, conveying to him that this was a controlled approach, designed to rapidly descend into hostile territory, minimizing the chance of their getting shot down.

Mike focused back on the small ponds, some empty as if they were freshly dug and intentionally lined with black soot. There were so many. They looked like craters on the moon, he imagined. *Craters?* he thought. *Shit! They're fuckin' bomb craters!*

His eyes quickly shifted to what looked like a small outpost, situated at the junction of a large river and a smaller canal leading south. The perimeter lay engulfed with piles of green sandbags, fortifying the numerous bunkers lining the outpost's perimeter. He noticed a smoke bomb spewing thick, red clouds of smoke on the other side of the canal. The camp and the bunkers were the first signs of war he'd seen since leaving the marshaling areas of Long Binh.

The chopper tilted back, the long, swirling blades grabbing a firm hold of the mass of air that halted their descent. The airship flared, tail boom swinging back and forth through a swirling cloud of red smoke, fuming hot air from the turbines assaulting the cabin from both directions. Suddenly, the misting cloud of smoke ceased, swept away by the whining blades, exposing a PSP pad, essentially a portable airfield made of interlocking steel strips, which was elevated above a sea of shallow, murky water.

Why are we stopping here? Mike wondered, looking out over a maze of rusting concertina and tanglefoot, the razor-sharp shards barely visible above the rippling shallows of stagnant water. He turned to ask the crew chief, only to see his rucksack fly through the door and the red-faced sergeant gesturing wildly for him to follow it. "Un-ass this motherfucker, Captain!!" he yelled. "Before you get us all killed!"

Mike popped the clasp on his seatbelt and sprang through the door, just in time to witness the first round impacting in the circuit of twisted wire and water. *Kaarruummmp!*

Mike rolled off the pad, showered by the hot shell casings of the M60 as "Junior," the young door gunner, opened up on the tree line across the wide river. He felt his new boots sink deep into the warm mud, and hot, turbid water filled his empty ammo pouches. The tall cascade of water and mud was still falling when the second round hit, hurtling globs of cordite-caked mud, laced with slivers of shrapnel, through the watery mist.

The chopper shuddered loudly as it lifted off the pad, the long tail boom swinging left, then right, dipping down only inches above Mike's head. A bright red line of tracers pecked at the distant shore, cutting and shredding palms before dancing off the water and tumbling into the tree line beyond.

The angry machine above him hovered for a moment, then eased its nose down, picking up speed as it zigzagged out of harm's way. Mike watched it skim above the ground, the heat from the turbine melting the air behind it. He felt abandoned, deserted, as he followed the Huey's desperate climb for altitude. He knew they were headed back to Long Binh, the invincible base camp, with yet another war story for their brethren at the club.

He sank lower into the steamy filth, hoping the distant gunner hadn't made the correct adjustment. His eyes scanned the shoreline, taut senses keyed for the next impact. He waited, his thumb searching for the selector switch on his M16, the soft mud sucking his boots deeper into the mire.

"Hey!! You over there!!" a voice shouted. "Did ya bring the mail with you?"

Mike peered over the top of the metal pad, eyes squinting at the tall figure standing atop a berm on the other side of the canal. He struggled to pull himself up from the clutches of the quagmire, reached over, and slung his waterlogged rucksack up onto the pad. "What mail?" he asked, startled by the man's indifference to the incoming rounds.

The stranger shook his head, stepped off the berm, and walked over to a small boat tied to a makeshift wooden dock. He started the engine and puttered across the canal, beaching the bow on the muddy bank. "Suppose they didn't send any flicks with you either, did they? Those chickenshit motherfuckers!"

Mike looked back across the wet fields to the distant shoreline and then turned to study the man in cutoff tiger fatigues and shower shoes. Tall and lanky, he had a confident, affable manner about him.

"Don't worry about that, Captain. 'Pierre' hasn't hit one yet. But I *will* say, that was the closest he's come in over three months," he explained, chuckling.

"*'Pierre'*? You *know* him?"

"Yeah, he's the local VC river watcher," he explained. "He worked for the French when they used this as an outpost. Keeps an eye on the PBRs and lobs a coupla' rounds of sixties at the mail choppers when they come in."

"Well, why don't you take him out if you know so much about him?"

"Well, sir, everything on the other bank of the river is the Twenty-fifth Infantry Division's AO. We have to get clearance before we return fire, and by that time, 'Pierre' is long gone. The indig say he grew up around here, and you'd never find him anyway. Hides out in the tunnels around here. Believe me, we've tried."

"Who are you?" Mike asked, curious why the man was not in uniform. "And what *is* this place?"

The stranger reached down and offered his hand, pulling Mike up onto the pad. "Braxton, Staff Sergeant Braxton, Robert E. Don't worry, sir. I'm on your side," he claimed smiling. "But everybody calls me *Bác sĩ* 'round here," he added. "Just means 'Doctor.'"

Braxton reached down, picked up the wet rucksack, and slung it over his bare shoulders. "Come on, *Đại úy*. I'll take you over to the camp, sir. I'm sure you'll want to get out of those wet clothes. And oh yeah, welcome to Trà Cú."

Mike followed him across the pad, drawing a degree of inner strength from Braxton's cavalier demeanor. He stepped up his pace to get a closer look at the thin black line of suture traversing the length of the puffy red incision on the sergeant's right calf. The guy walked without a limp, and Mike assumed the other small scabs were fragment wounds he'd received in the field.

They moved carefully over the slick, muddy berm, down into the small fiberglass boat nested in the reeds along the bank. Sergeant Braxton pulled the cord on the 40-hp Johnson outboard, and with the skill of a seasoned journeyman, he maneuvered the skiff across the canal to the makeshift slip on the other side.

They stepped up onto a dock supported by empty fifty-five-gallon drums that were flanked by a long line of wooden skids angling up out of the water. "What are those?" Mike asked, pointing to the strange inclined ramps.

"Those are the airboat ramps, Captain. They run 'em up out of the water so they won't bang into each other and tear up the fiberglass hulls," he explained. "The Filipino tech reps spend enough time patchin' up the bullet holes in 'em when they're in from runnin' operations down the Kinh Gẫy."

"Down the *what*?"

"The Kinh Gẫy. It's the canal we just crossed. It runs from the Vàm Cỏ Đông River there, all the way down to Four Corps. Straight as an arrow, cuts right through the Plain of Reeds. Kinda' like an expressway. We use it to move our troops deep into Chuck's backyard without havin' to hump through miles of waist-deep water spiked with exploding mackerel cans."

"Is that where—?"

"Yeah, they were just waitin' for us," he said softly.

Mike counted fifteen empty ramps and then noticed a large hull of a machine inside a tin barnlike structure above the empty skids. Several sweating men in cut-off tiger fatigues and welder caps were hard at work bolting down the wooden propeller on the large flat-bottom boat. The tall, green tail rudders caught his eye, a large white skull and crossbones painted on each, the words *Sat Cong* painted prominently below them. "What's the 'Sat Cong' for?" he asked.

"Oh, that. Well, *Đại úy*, the Cambodes like to scare the shit outa' Charlie. It means 'Kill Cong' or somethin' like that. Fucks with their mind before they blow 'em away."

"Cambodes?"

"Yeah. Didn't they tell you? We've got a company of KKK from the Third Mobile Strike Force runnin' our airboats," he explained, referring to the *Khmer Kampuchea Krom*, Cambodian nationalists. "Damn good troops, *Đại úy*. They're motivated. They kick ass. Not like the chickenshit VN we got here. They're down the Kinh Gẫy now, moppin' up some stragglers."

"Where do you keep the prisoners?" Mike inquired. "I'd like to see them."

Braxton smiled. "Bodes don't take no prisoners, *Đại úy*. They hate the Vietnamese. Won't even waste a bullet on 'em. They just run 'em down with the airboats," he told him. "Guess it's an ancient thing between 'em. Hell, we have enough trouble keepin' 'em from killing each other here in camp! They each have their own compound. We like it that way."

Sergeant Braxton led him up a muddy slope, through a worn chain-link gate and onto a rutted dirt lane that ran the length of the camp. Green, stagnant water filled the gullies on either side of the road, the entrances to makeshift shacks and bunkers only a footstep away from the thoroughfare.

"The strikers are gonna be pissed when they get back tonight, *Đại úy*. Since it's Saturday, we usually let them watch a movie outside the team house," he related. "We already showed 'em *Gidget Goes Hawaiian* 'bout six times already. But what the hell, maybe we can run it backward or somethin'."

They were walking together through the entrance to the inner perimeter when *Bác sĩ* was suddenly besieged by a gang of small, mostly toothless children. They tugged at his shorts, laughing and spouting a rampage of gibberish that needed no translation.

"We've got a bad problem with cholera and rats here, sir," Braxton began, picking up a small girl and hoisting her up around his neck. "Their parents send them out to catch them for dinner. And even if they don't get bit, they get sick when they eat them. The fuckin' things are infected from drinking the stagnant water. It's a never-ending cycle."

"What are you doing about it?" Mike inquired.

"Well, we put out rat poison in box traps, but the kids ate some of that, too. Wasn't a pretty sight, *Đại úy*."

Mike shook his head, noting that there was a lot of standing water and green mold wherever he looked. He stopped at a decaying bunker and poked his finger into the rotting sandbag. Red dirt and sand flowed freely to the ground. He looked at Braxton, then pulled on the angle-iron support holding the sandbags in place. The rusted iron snapped in half as several sandbags crumpled to the ground. "This whole place is a fuckin' disaster area, Sergeant," he told him.

"You got that right, Captain. The French built it, and it's been rotting here ever since W.W. Two."

Mike looked up to see another American walking toward them. His tiger fatigue trousers hung loosely over his unlaced jungle boots, his bare chest accented by the black shoulder holster holding his .45.

"That's the XO, *Đại úy,*" Braxton said. "He ain't right. He and the captain were pretty tight."

The young, dark-haired lieutenant walked deliberately toward Mike, his expression fully forlorn, a hint of repentance evident in his frown. "Captain Shannahan, I'm Lieutenant Dyson. We heard you were coming. I've requested to be relieved and transferred over to Mack-V SOG," he told him. "Nothing to do with you, sir. I just have to get out of here."

"I'll see what I can do to make that happen, Lieutenant."

"Thank you, sir," Dyson said, then turned and walked slowly back up the road.

"He blames himself," Braxton confided. "He and a coupla' the Bodes were out joyriding down the Kinh Gẫy in an airboat on the Fourth when they spooked an NVA squad setting up a fifty-one-cal on the bank. Chuck couldn't get the ammo out of the box in time to load it, so one of the Bodes cut loose with the thirty-cal on the bow. Cut 'em all down. They jumped out and hauled the fifty-one on board and *di-di*'d back to camp."

"*Di-di*'d?"

"Yeah. You know: Hotel Alpha, hauled ass. Gotta learn that one, *Đại úy.*"

"That's what started it?" Mike asked.

"Yeah. Out fuckin' around on the Fourth of July. The captain wasn't satisfied that they *only* had a squad down there. The fifty-one is crew-served and has a lot of fire power, so he and the Mekong mustered up some Cambodes and headed back down with a bunch of us to do a little recon in the area."

"That makes sense. Who's the Mekong?"

"He's the commander of the Cambodes. Real bad ass. Well, when we got back down there, we all got on line and moved inland. We crossed over the first paddy dike, and just before the lead element got to the second one, all hell broke loose. The bastards had them in a cross fire, cut 'em to shreds. The ones that were still alive… They let them lay there suffering, hoping someone would be stupid enough to try to crawl out over the berm and save them."

"That's it?"

"That, sir, was just the opening volley," Braxton went on. "Sergeant Clarkson radioed back during the ambush, and within thirty minutes, we had an eagle flight of a company of Twenty-fifth troopers airborne out of Củ Chi. Clarkson had both his legs cut off by a fifty-one. Took his boot laces and tied off the stumps while he called arty and air in on 'em. The Twenty-fifth company commander was dead before he even hit the ground. Our guys in the lead element bled out before we could get to 'em."

"What the hell did you run into?"

"Reinforced battalion of NVA regulars, sir. The two-hundred-seventy-first NVA Regiment had just crossed the Fence at Ba Thu and was headed for Saigon. We lost fifty-four U.S. KIA in that battle, *Đại úy*, fifty from the Twenty-fifth in addition to our team's four. The NVA lost their entire battalion, and most of their bloated bodies are still down there floatin' in that sea of death."

"That's a pretty heavy load to bear," Mike commented, acquiring a better understanding of the lieutenant's remorse.

"End of the line, Captain," Braxton said, carefully lifting the "China doll" off his shoulders.

Mike stared at the long, mud-block building. He grimaced as he surveyed the decaying structure, wide holes in the mud-caked walls exposing the rotten wooden frame supporting it. Rusting metal slats covered the roof, with moldy wooden shutters propped up over the windows to let the light in. He read the large sign over the door: *Condemned… But It's Home… Welcome to Sam's Place.* A chalk-white water buffalo skull adorned the threshold, held together by a rusty wire nailed above the tattered screen door.

"What's this?" he asked the *bác sĩ*.

"It's the team house, Captain. Welcome home."

* * *

CHAPTER THIRTY

IKE SURVEYED THE LARGE TOPOGRAPHICAL map on the wall with keen interest. He listened intently as Sergeant First Class Ed Daniels described the area of operations and outlined the recent enemy activity and tendencies of infiltration from the major staging area in Cambodia. The team intel sergeant identified the Cambodian village of Ba Thu, the unofficial end of the Hồ Chí Minh Trail, designating it with a red star placed on the vinyl map. "They've developed a large staging area here in Ba Thu, Captain," Daniels reported. "And it also serves as the headquarters for their SR-Three region." He described the enemy deployments in their Subregion III, inside Cambodia. "They have two major units: the Two-seventy-first and the Two-seventy-second Regiments of the Ninth NVA Division based there."

"That's a pretty hefty garrison, Sergeant. How many men are we talking about?" Mike inquired.

"Our best estimate is about fifteen hundred men in each regiment."

"How close have we been able to penetrate without crossing the border?"

"The air force has *seeded* the whole border with five-hundred- and thousand-pound bombs," the sergeant related. "We call the area 'AO Keep Out,' and we've instituted a three-thousand-meter buffer zone around the entire area. They're detonated by any metal object moving in their vicinity, so we just have to wait for them to make a run for it."

"How long does it take them to navigate the AO, generally?"

"Depends on their armament and the number of troops, *Đại úy.* They've been using motorized sampans for platoon-size units, and they can make it to the Vàm Cỏ Đông River before sunrise—if they're lucky."

There're hundreds of feeder streams out there around the Parrot's Beak. They only need less than two feet of water to navigate those sampans."

"What tactics are we currently using to stop them?" Mike inquired.

"The most effective is your basic night ambush at the junction of the feeder streams," Daniels pointed out. "They move men, ammo, and rice almost every night. Just a question of when and where."

"They're mostly two- to three-sampan convoys, Captain," Master Sergeant Walter Miller added. "We can usually take them out with a coupla' Claymores, and we can lay some det cord along the banks to mop up the survivors."

"How often do they try to move larger conventional units through?" Mike asked the burley team sergeant.

"That July move was a gutsy venture on their part, sir. They know that if we catch them in the open, we'll bring their world to an end," Miller confidently added.

"They like to make their big moves on holidays, sir," Sergeant Daniels remarked. "They know just when we will stand down and take a break. That's what happened on the Fourth. They almost made it to the river with that battalion... Until they ran into the XO."

"Well," Mike concluded. "Colonel Anderson made it very clear to me, gentlemen. My orders are to cut the lines of infiltration from the end of the trail through our AO, regardless of their strength. We need to make that happen."

"Did he tell you we have the highest kill ratio of any team in Three Corps, Captain?" the agitated team sergeant asked. "Up until a coupla' weeks ago, we were kickin' ass with the strikers. The damn LLDB and the Sidge would rather run than fight," Miller said, referring to the *Lực Lượng Đặc Biệt*, or official Army of Vietnam Special Forces (VN SF), and the CIDG, or Civilian Irregular Defense Group, which was drawn from minority populations. "But those Cambodes and our guys are getting the job done."

The briefings in the tactical operations center, the TOC, continued. Mike was briefed in detail for hours on the camp's Order of Battle and TO&E, a report that outlines the enemy threats, conditions, and limitations. It also included details on the camp's troop strength, heavy weapons, logistics, and current operations, including the 24-hour-a-day operations the team kept in the field at all times. He learned that the operations were always manned by two U.S. SF team members and two VN SF team members. The Americans acted as advisors, but, he was assured, they actually took charge when the situation warranted it.

The young captain was pleased that the TOC was one of only two areas in the camp that was air-conditioned, a luxury acquired by the team on a scavenger hunt into Saigon one weekend. The TOC also contained all the classified documents and encryption data used by the team. Sergeant Daniels informed him that the reinforced concrete walls and roof could withstand a direct hit from 122mm rockets and mortars. A backup radio network had been installed to ensure that if the camp was being overrun, they could still talk to the world to call in air strikes and artillery up to the very last moment.

Sergeant Miller informed Mike that the replacements for the men lost in the recent action were inbound, and the team would be back up to strength by the weekend. In the meantime, the sergeant wanted him to meet with the VN SF commander and the navy lieutenant who commanded the PBR boats attached to the south end of the camp. They had all had a good working relationship with Captain McNutt, and Mike wanted that to continue.

The VN SF captain was currently in the field with the 327th CIDG Company, so the team sergeant offered an alternative. "Let's take a walk, Captain," Sergeant Miller requested, closing the intel folder and returning it to the heavy file cabinet in the corner of the room.

Together, they walked down the long dusty lane, out of the fortified inner compound and toward the fighting bunkers occupied by the CIDG and their families. "There're some other things you should know about the camp, Captain," Miller began in earnest, a heavy Southern accent evident in his speech. "The camp's Sidge has been infiltrated by the local VC cadre for years," he told him. "Less than a month ago, Đại úy Tran, your counterpart, pulled the string on an intel op that he had been running for months. He rounded up over sixty VC infiltrators, including the commander of the Three-hundred-twenty-fifth Company."

"Here in the camp?" Mike asked, stunned by the revelation.

"Roger that, sir. He got word something big was just about to happen. He was probably right. Fact is, the B-Team thinks that the battalion we ran into on the Fourth was originally in position to overrun the camp with the help of those infiltrators in the camp strike force," he explained, wiping the beading sweat from his bald head with his handkerchief.

"Nothin' like havin' to fight the fifth column from within," Mike observed.

"Well, it seems that the LLDB higher-ups were a little hesitant in sending down some air assets to backload all the POWs back to Tây Ninh, so Đại úy Tran just shackled them all together, stuck them in assault boats, strung the boats together, and anchored 'em out in the middle of the river."

"From what I've seen," the captain replied, "that river has a pretty good current running through it."

"They were out there for three days, bobbin' and weavin'. They weren't a bunch of happy campers when the choppers finally got here to pick 'em up."

"So? What's the big deal?"

"Well, turns out that VC company commander's brother is a big wig in the Saigon government, and he wasn't too happy by the way the đại úy handled things. Word is: He's gonna have Đại úy Tran relieved and court martialed for mistreatment of the prisoners. Mainly his brother."

"What was he supposed to do with 'em?" Mike asked.

"Donno. There were too many of them to put into the Conex containers we normally use," Miller replied. "Thought it was pretty creative myself. Just another example of how high up the VC has infiltrated that fuckin' corrupt regime in Saigon. The đại úy is a pretty squared-away officer, sir. He's about the only LLDB here that's not corrupt. He's the *only* one we trust."

As they continued their walk through the camp, Sergeant Miller pointed out the three line-company compounds, cramped and crude shanties, each housing more than 275 CIDG troops and their families. They toured the 4.2-inch mortar pits and the American 155mm howitzer battery assigned to the camp from the Second Field Force. The sergeant showed Mike where the Kit Carson scouts resided and explained that they were all former VC who had taken advantage of the "Open Arms" Chiêu Hồi amnesty program to be repatriated.

Mike was most intrigued when they entered the Cambodian compound housing the strikers from the Mobile Strike Force Command, or MIKE Force, fierce indigenous troops trained and commanded by Green Berets. The distinction between the two ethnic groups in the camp seemed awkward and profound to him. He noticed that the Cambodes' skin appeared to be much darker and their features not as pronounced as their Vietnamese counterparts. They appeared intensely family-oriented, with their wives and children living with them in the decaying bunkers on the perimeter of the camp. The team sergeant explained that the living arrangements actually enhanced the security of the camp, since these men would be willing to fight to the death to protect their families.

Miller led him up to the berm overlooking the man-made canal while scores of small barefoot children followed closely behind, each hopeful for a morsel of food or a piece of candy, giggling and laughing as they looked up at the tall Americans.

"We've got fifty-five-gallon drums of foo gas on skids ready to light the whole canal on fire if they try to flank us from the other side," Miller told him, pointing out the barrels of napalm and the makeshift launching skids with C-4 propellants attached.

"What are all those boats down there at the end of the camp?" the captain inquired.

"That's the PBR compound, sir. Looks like they're maneuvering a fuel barge in place to refuel their holding tanks."

"Why are some of the men wearing black berets?"

Miller turned to him and gave him a snide, questioning glare. "Because they're in the fuckin' navy, Captain. Why did they build an eight-foot chain-link fence at the end of their compound thinkin' it would keep the bad guys out, and then place a Claymore halfway up on each support pole? 'Cause they're in the fuckin' navy!"

Mike chuckled, but before he could respond, Miller cut back in. "Why did they sandbag in a bunch of Claymores on the bows of their patrol boats?"

"I know," Mike replied. "'Cause they're in the fuckin' navy. My dad spent his whole career in the navy, Top. And he's still on active duty."

"That's why God gave me two eyes, Đại úy," Miller conceded. "So I might just have to keep one of them on you, just to be on the safe side. You might want to write him a letter and tell 'im he's got a whole bunch of his swabbies down here, and their oars aren't long enough to reach the water."

"Sure he'll be glad to hear that from me," Mike told him, smiling at Miller's opinions. "And ya really can't blame them, Top. Seems like everybody wants to be John Wayne."

"Never saw the Duke put a gun to his head and pull the trigger just to see if it was loaded," Miller concluded, handing out sticks of gum to the little ones tugging at his leg.

"Guess you got a point there."

"Anyway, that's why they have the fuckin' marines workin' for them. At least *they* know which side of the damn Claymore to point toward the enemy."

Sergeant Miller escorted the new team leader down to the navy compound and proudly pointed out the Claymores still attached to the aluminum poles holding up the long chain-link fence. Mike had hoped that he was kidding earlier, but that manner of mentality presented an even larger concern for him. The navy had constructed several buildings to house the crewmen for the PBR squadron operating under the protection of the Special Forces camp, and those buildings were outside the bunkers and defensive posture of the camp itself.

The compound sat strategically located at the very southern end of the camp, the most likely route, according to the briefings Mike had received, that the enemy would take to overrun the base. The obvious result of this configuration left the entire southern perimeter of the camp unprotected. Instead of calling in the Seabees to construct a viable defensive berm, with bunkers and fighting positions to defend their compound, they had erected what Mike considered mere Tinkertoys and a wire welcome mat for the enemy soldiers to clean their boots when they blew the Claymores during their ground assault. Once the navy compound had been breached, the team house and the inner compound would lie unprotected, just a casual stroll up the dusty lane.

"Where's our perimeter defense protecting this avenue of approach, Top?" Mike asked.

"They leveled it to put in the navy compound. The team wasn't happy about it, but the B-Team approved the annex with pressure from Group in Nha Trang. Didn't have anywhere else to put 'em."

"From what I've seen, the camp is protected by natural defenses on three sides. This is the only firm terrain to approach the camp, and we don't have any fighting bunkers to defend it."

"They were supposed to construct reinforced bunkers and wide trench lines with tanglefoot and concertina out twenty-five meters, Captain. But when they started digging, the water table just filled up the holes, so they gave up."

Mike shook his head in amazement. *We're more than twenty miles from the nearest element of friendly forces, and these jokers just left the back door wide open?* he thought to himself. "Did they send invitations out to SR-Three for the housewarming?" he asked Miller.

"Might as well have. I'm sure the devils within have gotten the word out to them by now. They're probably just rounding up some party favors."

The captain discussed the obvious defensive vulnerability with his team sergeant and was determined to rectify the security lapse once he met with the PBR squadron commander.

Sergeant Miller led Mike through the door in the navy compound's Quonset-hut-shaped building. The captain immediately felt the soothing stream of chilled air anoint his sweating skin with its comforting embrace. He hesitated, allowing the full flow to reinvigorate his body. Miller turned, noting the contented look on the captain's face. "Feels good, doesn't it, *Đại úy?*" he whispered, smiling. "Navy," he explained with a wink.

Mike watched Sergeant Miller walk through an open doorway and begin talking as he followed him in. "Lieutenant Bosworth, this is Captain Shannahan, our new team leader. He just got in-country from the Tenth Special Forces Group in Massachusetts."

The tall, heavyset naval officer stepped out from behind his desk and warmly greeted Mike, his firm handshake matched and then exceeded by the young captain's. The two men were immediately relaxed with each other, probably because a navy lieutenant is at the same rank level as an army captain. "Well," Bosworth said, "I'm from Nashua, just up the road from there."

"I know it well," Mike replied. "We used to jump into the White Mountains for our winter warfare and ski training."

"That's where I learned *how* to ski. Loved that area. Wish I were back there now," the lieutenant admitted. "This heat is about to kick my butt."

"Don't we all?" Miller put in, lifting up his arms to expose his drenched armpits.

"Feels great in here, though," Mike added.

"Yeah," Bosworth said. "Just one of the perks the navy provides us for being in the middle of a combat zone."

"I know," Mike replied. "I spent eighteen years in the navy. I know how they take care of their own. Especially when it comes to creature comforts and chow."

Obviously puzzled, Bosworth stared at the army captain in front of him, trying to deconstruct that last comment.

"The ol' man's a career naval aviator," Mike explained, smiling. "Ops officer at Pax River."

"*Outstanding!* I used to sail down the Choptank over to Pax River when I was at the Academy!" Bosworth happily stated. "Small world!"

"Well, that's interesting. I took you for an Academy man. Been around a lot of them in my days hanging around the flight line."

With the small talk positioning the two officers in proper perspective, the captain came straight to the main purpose of his visit. "Top was just giving me a tour of the camp, Lieutenant. And when I got to the end of the compound, I turned and looked back, and something really didn't look right to me."

The lieutenant leaned forward in his chair, an inquisitive look on his face.

"I looked down the main road from the airfield," Mike went on, "and I could see all the way to our SF inner compound, without any bunkers or fighting positions. The only impediments I could see to an enemy attack was some loose concertina and a chain-link fence."

"Yeah, we just had that erected a coupla' weeks ago," the lieutenant explained. "We put some Claymores and concertina wire out there to beef up the defenses a little."

"The Claymores I saw. They were strapped to the support poles."

"That's right. They're directional mines. They only blow in the direction they're pointed."

"Those mines, Lieutenant," Sergeant Miller broke in, "are a pound and half of C-4, with hundreds of ball bearings embedded in them. When you blow them, the mine has a back blast radius of at least five meters."

"When you blow them," Mike elaborated, "you're gonna take that chain-link down with them." Then: "I can send my senior demo man and engineer down here to help you reconfigure the placement of your Claymores," the captain offered, "so they can do the job you intended them to do."

The lieutenant sat quietly, slowly nodding his head as he pondered the consequences explained to him. "I'd appreciate that," he finally said. "By the way... We had a meeting with some folks from Natick Labs about some interesting new technology they brought to us," he said, changing the subject. "We need to discuss it with you, because it could affect your operations in the field."

Mike looked over at Sergeant Miller. They both shared the same puzzled look on their faces.

"They have developed some noise, motion, and magnetic sensors that can be concealed and planted throughout the area of operation," Bosworth continued.

"Sensors?" Miller inquired.

"Yeah. They're designed to activate when the enemy moves or makes a noise, or if a metallic object passes within a specific distance from them," he added. "Their locations are mapped on the grid square, and when activated, they send a radio signal back to our TOC, alerting our people that someone is in the area."

"Then what?" Mike inquired.

"We plot out the coordinates and send up a fire mission to the Second Field Force battery to take them out."

"Who-o-a-aa, Lieutenant," Miller protested. "Sorry, sir, but you are not authorized to direct fire missions *anywhere* in this AO. Regardless! We have troops out there in the AO twenty-four-seven."

"How are the sensors going to determine if the activations were created by the good guys or the bad guys?" Mike inquired.

"When we get an activation, we will call over to your TOC and ask if you have any troops in that grid square. If not, then it has to be the bad guys."

The captain looked over to his team sergeant. Miller continued to shake his head. "Don't like the smell of this, *Đại úy*," Miller complained.

"We're going to need more details on the program, Lieutenant, before we agree to any plan to seed the AO with sensors. Has this been tested at any other camp?"

"I don't know, Captain. They didn't say. I think this is their first try out of the box."

"Well, get back to me on that. I'll check with my highers and see what they think as well. In the meantime, put a hold on it."

The captain and his team sergeant shook hands with Lieutenant Bosworth and headed back out into the sweltering heat.

"What the fuck is wrong with these people?" Miller vented. "They can't even run up and down the fuckin' river without gettin' their boats shot out from under 'em. What makes them think they have any business playin' army out in the field?"

"Probably John Wayne's fault," Mike responded. "Stupid movie."

"Goddamn navy," Miller replied.

*   *   *

CHAPTER THIRTY-ONE

THE CAPTAIN STEPPED CAREFULLY INTO the loaded fiberglass assault boat, his web gear weighted down with magazines and grenades. The young Vietnamese commo man handed him the PRC-25 radio, then stepped aboard, taking his position at the bow of the boat.

"We go now, *Đại úy*," Thiệu, his college-educated interpreter said, giving the go-ahead to the driver, who was seated at the rear.

Mike watched the camp disappear in the distance, the thin radio tower steadily edging below the tall green reeds spouting above the canal's elevated banks. He leaned over the side to look ahead at the large squadron of assault boats laboring down the canal with their heavy cargo aboard. Lanky, white-feathered waterfowl scattered in all directions, their morning hunt foiled by the constant vibration of the churning propellers.

Mike sat up on the edge of the boat, peering over the grassy embankment into the wet fields beyond. He watched the series of abandoned rice paddies come and go, and he wondered what it must have been like here many years ago. He caught a glimpse of the tops of some trees, tightly clumped together, forming what he was told was a *tree square*, a mini-hamlet that sheltered the peasant families who toiled in the fields. Sorties of dusty gray dove streaked low above the formation, and Mike briefly reminisced about those carefree days he and Jim would pluck the tasty migrators before dusting them with flour and frying them in bacon grease. *Wonder if they have any shotguns back at the camp?* he pondered.

The overladen boats continued to traverse the narrow waterway for over half an hour, then slowed in unison as they navigated to a low break in the berm to discharge their cargo. Mike noticed that the men already onshore seemed to be milling around, joking and cutting up with one another as they waited for the boats to finish disgorging the troops—unloaded weapons slung over their shoulders, smoking and making a lot of noise, completely oblivious to the fact that they were in Charlie's backyard.

Mike stepped up on to the bank and called Sergeant Watson over to him. "Why haven't they set up a perimeter, Sergeant?" he asked the junior weapons man.

"This place is called the Hilton South, Captain," the sergeant replied. "Charlie knows we insert here. They won't mess with us here. It's sort of like an *understanding* between the LLDB and them."

"That's the stupidest thing I've heard since I got here."

"Well, Captain, we're out with *Trung sĩ* Nguyễn, sir," Watson said, referring to the Vietnamese Special Forces sergeant. "That shithead avoids contact at all costs. If you were hoping to mix it up with Sir Charles this week, the only way is if we get ambushed or spook some stragglers."

Mike turned to Thiệu and gave him an order. "Tell the *trung sĩ* that I would like to know what his objective for the day is." He walked over to where the *trung sĩ* was standing with the indig command element and listened as Thiệu relayed his message. He noticed that whatever Thiệu was saying to him obviously took longer than the question he had originally posed.

"He say we hunt for NVA and VC today," Thiệu explained. "We go to here… And then in afternoon, after *poc* time, we go here to RON." He pointed to several tree squares on his worn and tattered map. *Poc time* was the obligatory after-lunch nap, and *RON* was the remain-overnight position.

Mike took his own plastic-encased map out of his trouser pocket. "Show me," he told Thiệu, handing him a grease pencil to mark the route.

When Thiệu was finished, the captain took the map back and studied the route the interpreter had penciled in. He quickly noticed that the route to the tree-square objectives deviated from a more direct route, which would keep them parallel with the more prominent streams and tributaries that could be used to move equipment and men through the AO. "Ask him why we aren't going to monitor the larger streams that come across the Fence from Ba Thu," he ordered his interpreter.

Thiệu relayed his question and got a short answer from the *trung sĩ*. "He say *beaucoup* booby trap, *Đại úy*. We no go."

"Whatever," Mike replied, shaking his head in disgust. "Tell him to get this circus on the road."

Mike wiped the warm beads of sweat from his forehead and put his bush hat back on. He waited for the formation to head out into the knee-deep paddies that lay ahead of them. The terrain appeared flat as far as the eye could see. Modest clumps of chest-high vegetation dotted the vacant landscape, and the vast lake of stagnant water shimmered where the scores of dragonflies danced on the surface, intently devouring the rich larvae deposited by masses of nesting mosquitos.

"Đại úy," Thiệu said, putting the smiling boy in front of him. "This Cowboy. He carry you rucksack for you. He Đại úy McNutt numba' one."

Mike took notice of the young man's small black straw cowboy hat, the draw string pulled tight under his chin. Cowboy continued to smile, apparently pleased to assume the same role he had had with Mike's predecessor. His fatigue shirt lay open to the waist, and a plastic canteen and a lone ammo pouch hung loosely from his pistol belt, which also held up his drooping pants.

"Guess he's not expecting any action on this trip," Mike commented, staring at the empty space in the magazine well on his M16. "Just tell him to stay in front of me, so I can keep an eye on him," he told Thiệu, who then confirmed Cowboy's new position. Still smiling broadly, the boy opened the captain's rucksack, pulled out a tube of rice, and cut the plastic top open with a knife.

"What's he doing?" Mike asked Thiệu.

"He make dinner for you, Đại úy."

Mike watched the youngster pour some water into the tube, carefully measuring the amount before he set it on the ground, slits up. He then found the small packets of dried fish and peppers, tore them open with his teeth, and carefully poured them in the rice. He tied the two ends up tightly and then squeezed the mixture together, distributing the condiments evenly in the rice. Finally, he reached over, unbuttoned Mike's shirt, and slid the pouch of rice around to his back.

"What's up with that, Thiệu?" the captain inquired, a little perplexed at Cowboy's intimate maneuver.

"He make you dinner. Rice cook all day when you walk."

Mike looked over at Watson. The sergeant nodded his head, patting his side and indicating that he was currently incubating his dinner as well. "Thanks for the heads up," Mike snidely remarked.

He observed with renewed interest as the *trung sĩ* barked orders and pointed out the direction of march. The lead point man tentatively stepped off the littered assembly area and, with his weapon slung over his shoulder, began his slow, tedious trek through the knee-deep wetland. Each man sported a red and blue neckerchief, the identifying symbol of this particular CIDG company, a tactic Sergeant Watson had explained was employed by almost all the irregular fighting groups, each with its own color combination, to reduce the number of friendly-fire casualties. Their men had the tendency to wear the same garb as their nemesis, Sir Charles, the "party of the second part," Watson had told him, and the neckerchiefs helped a little to distinguish them.

Then the captain, taken aback, watched the limp rag-doll figure of the point man spin high into the air and the plume of pinkish red mist hang suspended above the body, which somersaulted back down and splashed awkwardly beside the line of men, who were now instinctively crouching in the marshy field. Mike felt the mild shock of the explosion as he dropped to his knee, the sharp report of the event reached his senses as the last wave of water and mud splashed down around them.

His eyes surveyed the scene before him, scanning the horizon for movement or muzzle flashes, his finger on the trigger, his thumb on the selector switch. A stunned silence lingered nervously over the formation while heads bobbed and weaved, searching for any sign of movement ahead.

"Watson!" the captain barked. The sergeant looked back and, in a crouched position, scurried back to the captain's side. "What was that?"

"Booby trap, sir. Too big to be the usual mackerel-can variety, sir. I'd say it was at least an eighty-two mortar shell with a trip wire or pressure plate," he reported. "They wanted to send a message with this one."

"Looks like Sir Charles just changed the rules," Mike replied.

"*Somebody* didn't get the memo," Watson agreed.

Mike stood up and walked up to the water's edge, Watson following him, while the men in the lead element were slowly making their way back to the assembly area. He noticed that the point man's body lay partially submerged, face up nearly fifty meters to their front.

"Is he dead?" Mike inquired, looking for any movement from the gravely wounded man.

"I would think so, Captain," Watson told him. "The impact alone probably rearranged his entire gene structure."

"Get a damn perimeter set up, Watson, and I want some flank security out at least a hundred meters in both directions," he demanded. "Thiệu, where's the *trung sĩ?*"

Mike pulled his map out of his trousers and studied the terrain features along the canal. Thiệu located the Vietnamese sergeant and pointed to his position in the mass of huddled men. Mike placed the sling on his M16 over his shoulder and grabbed hold of the pistol grip as he readied his weapon to the firing position. He walked briskly over to Sergeant Nguyễn and began speaking to him before Thiệu could catch up.

"*Trung sĩ*, we are in an exposed position, and the first thing we need to do is set up a perimeter, get some security out, and find out what the hell is going on here," he conveyed distinctly. "Tell him what I said, Thiệu!" he barked, an elevated tone accenting his displeasure.

Thiệu immediately complied, rattling off a series of indecipherable gibberish prompting a rebuttal of equally cryptic responses.

"What did he say?"

"He say men afraid to go. *Beaucoup* booby trap."

"Well, it's not like they didn't know where to put the damn things. This place looks like a trash dump for a fuckin' Boy Scout jamboree! Tell him to get a damn perimeter set up, and send somebody out to recover that body. And tell him I want to talk to him and his company commander to reassess the situation. It's obvious that this insertion has been compromised," he concluded.

Thiệu relayed his message while Mike set about locating Watson to determine what success he had had in getting some flank security out beyond their perimeter. "What's the status of the security elements, Sergeant?"

"Split up the Kit Carsons and sent them out a hundred meters up and down the embankments," Watson reported.

"Get my radio operator over here while I look for another insert point."

"Roger that, Captain."

Mike again pulled the map out of his pocket and studied the terrain farther down the canal to the south. There was no indication of any relief points because there was no elevation deviance in the map. Just perfectly flat terrain, much to his displeasure. He took the handset from the nervous radioman and called back to the camp.

"Red Bank Goose, Red Bank Goose… This is Goose One-zero, over."

"One-zero, this is Red Bank Goose… Go."

"We have one Victor November friendly down and need to have all the insert craft return to this location for extract to a new insert point, over."

"Aahhh, roger, One-zero… Understand one Victor November down. Do you require Dust Off, over?"

"Negative, not at this time. Inform the one-one that we will be providing new coordinates when we determine insert position, over."

"Roger… Wilco, over."

"One-zero out."

The captain made sure that the reluctant troops were consolidated, yet dispersed enough to cover all avenues of approach if they were hit by a ground force in the midst of the confusion and chaos created by the detonation of the booby trap.

He instructed Sergeant Watson to monitor the situation while he conferred with the Vietnamese Special Forces sergeant, *Trung sĩ* Nguyễn, and the indigenous commander of the 329th, a confident-looking man Thiệu called *Đại tá*, Vietnamese for Colonel. It became very obvious that they wanted no part in deviating from their planned excursion through the open plains, a route on which any movement could be monitored by the enemy from a great distance. Mike also concluded that the tactic was a deliberate attempt to avoid any contact with the enemy, who would be afforded enough time to elude the operation's slow, methodical pace through the Plain of Reeds. He decided that he would not tolerate this charade.

After listening intently, with all his efforts involving tact and reason exhausted, the captain told the *trung sĩ* that they would be moving south to a new insertion site, one less conspicuous than the Hilton South. He challenged himself, searching for the appropriate course of action, not relying solely on his own initiative but on keen instincts molded by mentors who had shaped his character and being. He drew from the wealth of knowledge that had inspired him, nourished him, allowed him to position himself among the legions of true warriors who had gone before. Valencia, Denny, Allen, Sarkie, even Jacques—men of character and distinction. They all had led him here, and it was finally *his* turn, with their honor in *his* keeping.

It's not always easy to do the right thing. Who knows what the right thing always is? But it's at least veracious to aspire to, especially when you don't know what the right thing really is. But then, when you attempt the profound thing, there is favor regardless of the outcome. Mike considered that, at least, was not a bad thing. *Guess there's really no right way to do the wrong thing.*

He knew what he had to do, in spite of any distracting rhetoric: *Take charge.* One man lay dead, and he considered that a shallow defeat, a senseless causality. He felt that *he* had allowed it to happen, so he vowed that it would not happen again.

He radioed back to the camp, requesting they contact any FAC in the area to assist him with a visual recon. They soon came back, informing him that a Bird Dog would be on station with fifteen minutes.

"We're moving south, *Trung sĩ.* Saddle up."

The captain urged the *dại tá* to order his men into the waiting boats. He watched several strikers load the point man's body, now wrapped in a poncho, into the boat headed back to camp. With the boats reloaded, he stepped down into the third boat and directed the lead boat to head south down the long, menacing canal.

Within minutes, he heard a firm voice echoing his call sign on the radio. The FAC had them in sight and requested to be briefed on his role in the operation. Mike asked him to recon the canal bank on the western shore for an inconspicuous insertion site that would enable them to circumnavigate the streams heading west to the Ba Thu area.

Mike looked up to see the gray Cessna L-19 dip its wings as it flew over the convoy of boats, then bank westward out toward the Cambodian border and Ba Thu. He kept his eyes on the gray speck as it executed a series of maneuvers, slowly turning in circles before heading back toward the canal and the procession of boats.

"Aaahh, Goose One-zero... Angel Eye-eight, over."

"One-zero... Go."

"Aaahhh… See a pretty good insert point about one click to your Sierra. It will give you access to a series of streams that lead back to the area you requested, over."

"Roger that, Angel Eye. Could you give me a heads up when we reach it, over."

"Will do, One-zero… You're going to have to travel west about two thousand meters before you locate the streams, over."

"Understand two thousand meters west, over."

"Roger that, One-zero. Be advised there're a lot of trails in the reeds… Probably some bad boys been moving through that area recently, over."

"Thanks for the heads up, Angel Eye. Give us a shout when we're in range of the insert site, over."

Mike looked out over the vast expanse to the west, looking for any prominent terrain feature to determine his position. He could only make an estimate based on the distance he thought they had traveled down the canal from the camp.

"Tally ho!" the voice on the radio exclaimed.

Mike stood up and waved to the men in the lead boat to have the driver pull into the embankment to his right. The boats behind him followed suit, and within minutes, the entire company had clambered ashore. He told Thiệu to tell them to move inland and establish a perimeter. When he was satisfied the insertion site was secure, he radioed back to the FAC. "Angel Eye… One-zero."

"Angel Eye, go."

"Could you give me a good fix on my ten-twenty using today's Zero Mike shack code, over?"

"Roger, One-zero… You ready to copy?… Over."

"That's affirmative, over."

"X-ray… Tango… Juliet… Mike… Papa… Quebec… Golf… India… Bravo, over."

"Roger, good copy, Angel Eye, and thanks for your help. Goose out."

Mike heard the double-click breaking squelch, indicating that the FAC had signed off the air. He quickly decoded the letters to numbers and plotted the coordinates on his field map. He smiled, satisfied with the choice the FAC had made to enable him to continue the mission.

He called Sergeant Watson to his side and showed him his plan of action. "Angel Eye said there're numerous trails of bent reeds in this area here," he explained. "I want to parallel this narrow stream here, moving northwest until we reach the junction of these two waterways near Bụng Báo Vội. Looks like a coupla' tree squares still left near there... I guess that's what those little black spots on the map represent."

"That's only about a thousand meters east of 'AO Keep Out,' Captain. We don't usually get that close," Watson advised him.

"From what I've seen so far, Sergeant, Charles is probably well aware of that," Mike replied. "We can change the rules, too. I guess at least they won't be expecting us." Then to his interpreter: "Thiệu, go find the *trung sĩ* and tell him we're ready to move out."

Thiệu stood up and scurried off. The young captain felt confident in his plan and was determined to see that the operation would continue to function utilizing sound military tactics. He checked his web gear, fighting knife securely taped to his harness, strobe light tightly packed in its sheath. The World War Two–vintage BAR belt he chose to wear housed the twenty magazines of 5.56mm ammo he carried in his six pouches. His ruck contained additional magazines, a Claymore mine, two white phosphorous grenades, four fragmentation grenades, and numerous PIRs, plastic packets of rice and dried fish to sustain him for the week. He had also packed two blocks of C-4 and a loop of det cord, wrapped in a thin nylon hammock rolled up within a small green towel. *Loaded for bear,* he told himself, confident he would be ready for anything they might encounter.

Thiệu hurried back over to the captain, an anxious expression on his face. "*Đại úy,*" he exclaimed, "*Trung sĩ* no here."

"What do you mean, 'no here'?"

"He *di di mau, Đại úy,*" he informed Mike, telling him that the *trung sĩ* had run away very quickly. "He go back to camp on boat."

Mike looked at Watson, shaking his head as he allowed the full meaning of Thiệu's statement to sink in.

Watson chuckled, clearly undaunted by the revelation at hand. "Now you know why we call the LLDB 'little, lazy, dirty bastards,'" he said. "They're fuckin' worthless."

Mike turned to Thiệu, his confused stare begging an explanation.

"He tell men you *điên,* you *beaucoup dinky dâu,*" Thiệu admitted.

"He thinks you're crazy, *Đại úy*," Watson confirmed.

"Fuck him and the sampan he rode in on. Let's get this show on the road before they all *di di*," Mike told the sergeant. "I want that point element at least a hundred meters out in front of the lead platoon."

With the operation finally underway, the dark, flat clouds lingering in the distance countered their move by unleashing a steady stream of soaking rain on the plains. Mike watched the curtain of showers slowly creep toward the formation, kicking up small spurts of water as the pebblelike droplets splashed heavily on the still waters below. What had been unlimited visibility swiftly diminished to a mere several hundred meters, and the foamy surge created by the swelling downpour eliminated any chance the men would have to detect any trip wires beneath the murky water in their path.

They moved westward for hours, toiling through the muddy marshes and islands of tall reeds. Mike watched some of the men ahead periodically break formation, chasing snakes and frogs, gathering various plants and berries and tossing them into large cooking pots that a couple of them carried on bamboo poles. He became amused at their techniques, how they grabbed the long snakes by their tails as they slithered away, then spun them over their heads like cowboys ready to lasso a calf, and finally snap their heads off by cracking them like a bull whip, very much like what he'd seen in some western movie.

"These guys ever get bit grabbing those snakes like that?" he asked Watson.

"Naw, they've got it down pat. Just remember, out here, eat anything that doesn't eat you first, *Đại úy*."

Word finally came back that the lead element had found the stream the captain was looking for. The formation stopped, and Mike headed to the front to verify the location on his map. Satisfied that it was the tributary he was looking for, he instructed them to cross it and follow it eastward, paralleling it by at least fifty meters, until it turned north and intersected the larger stream near the deserted colony known as Bụng Báo Vội. Based on their rate of travel, he estimated they would arrive at the junction by 1700 hours, allowing them time to set up a hasty ambush site on both rivulets just before dark.

The unrelenting rain saturated the men and their equipment throughout the afternoon, adding encumbering weight and requiring additional energy to be expended as they sloshed their way through the seemingly endless labyrinth of everglades. Mike regularly flipped open his compass, keeping a constant vigil on their direction of travel. The weight of his harness dug deep into his aching shoulders, while the constant rubbing of his magazines on his waist chafed his irritated skin through his flimsy wet tiger fatigues. The men's only relief was an occasional rise in the terrain, allowing them to at least take a knee for brief moments of reprieve from the constant drudgery they endured.

Mike finally realized why so many of the men wore shorts and tennis shoes rather than the issued tiger fatigues and jungle boots. He envied the fact that all they carried was their weapon and a harness holding their magazines and canteen. He considered himself fortunate that he at least had Cowboy humping his heavy ruck, and when Thiệu told him that Captain McNutt had always given the boy a big tip after each operation, he knew why the young lad was so eager to engage him.

"How much far we go, Đại úy?" Thiệu asked, squatting in the scant foot of water.

"Oh, I'd say about another two klicks," Mike replied. "We'll be there on schedule as long as we don't run into a pack of alligators on the way."

"What 'alle getta'?" the interpreter inquired, a puzzled look on his face.

"Never mind. It loses a lot in the translation," the captain said with a smile. Then: "Thiệu, why aren't many of the men carrying rucks?"

"*Beaucoup* heavy, Đại úy. They small. *Ti ti.*"

"Well, where are they carrying their chow?"

"They carry rice for eat."

"Yeah. Where?"

Thiệu patted his ammo pouches, smiling back at his captain. Mike took a quick glance around at the men squatting near him in the shallow water. The ones carrying rucksacks seemed to have a determined look on their faces, the others were chatting with one another, making small talk and smoking cigarettes, the butt stocks of their weapons stuck vertically in the mud.

"This isn't a fuckin' picnic, Thiệu. I don't know what they're used to out here, but their universe is about to change."

Mike stood up and went forward to where Sergeant Watson was chatting with some of the Kit Carsons. He noticed the nonchalant swagger they conveyed, the manner in which they held their weapons, along with the confident look on each one's face. He felt there was something distinctly different about them.

"Watson, we need to talk," Mike said. "Did you know that a lot of the men are carrying rice in their ammo pouches instead of magazines?"

"That doesn't surprise me, *Đại úy*. Most of these guys are deserters from the ARVN, and a lot of the others are wanted by the White Mice for God knows what. They're out here running away from something, and as long as they're out here with the Sidge, nobody will mess with them. Kinda' like the Foreign Legion."

"White Mice?"

"Saigon National Police, *Đại úy*. They're not here to fight. They're runners. If we get hit, they're the first to *di di*. That's why they travel so light. The pay is great, so it's just like a paid vacation to them."

"What else don't I know about this clusterfuck, Sergeant?"

"Just stay close to your radio, Captain," he advised. "If we get hit, we're really gonna need it. That's why you never see me far from mine."

Mike went back to the company commander, and with Thiệu's help, they sent all the men without rucksacks up to the front of the formation, right behind the point element of scouts. The intense concern on their faces verified the captain's suspicions. *If they don't get hit in the opening volley of fire, then at least they'd have a lot farther to run,* he felt, justifying his decision.

The pace quickened, and within two hours the operation had found its objective. With the sullen skies continuing to darken, the captain went forward to assess the situation. He confirmed his location on his map and then noticed a series of small tree squares visible about four hundred meters to the east. The black dots on the map further verified his assessment, and he decided to send a platoon of men to secure the first two for a RON position for the main body of the company. "Watson, who *are* the most reliable troops we have in the field with us?" he inquired.

"Gotta be the Kit Carsons," the sergeant quickly replied. "They're mostly local guys who were kidnapped by Charlie when they were boys and forced into service after the VC had raided their villages and slaughtered their families. They're highly motivated," he assured Mike. "I've seen them in action before."

"Great! I want you to hand-pick a squad of them and set up an ambush at the junction of these two streams," he said, pointing to the wide intersection of water. "Top told me the team has a protocol for this maneuver, so I'll leave it up to your ingenuity to set it up based on what has worked in the past."

"Claymores and det cord make for a lethal recipe of damn damn, *Đại úy.*"

"Your call," Mike replied. "Although I'd rather stay here and have some fun, I'm going with the main body over to those tree squares to get these guys out of the water. These damn socks are full of mud, and it's driving me crazy slidin' around in them anyway."

"You're wearing socks?" Watson chided. "Didn't you go to the COC course in Nha Trang, *Đại úy?*" He was referring to the combat orientation course taught on Hòn Tre Island.

"Naw, I kinda' missed that one on purpose," Mike confessed.

"Suppose you're wearin' some boxers too, aren't ya?"

Mike knew his sergeant, regardless of rank, was about to make an obvious statement directly related to his FNG status.

"That's a double whammy, *Đại úy.* Crotch rot and jungle foot. Now, that's a nasty combination," Watson observed, chuckling.

"*Touché,*" Mike said and sighed.

"Too bad we don't have any leeches down here. That shit attracts them like flies."

"Well, at least my boots will be broken in after we get back from this one," Mike replied, squeezing the mud with his toes. "Get your men together and get into nametag defilade. After you're concealed, we'll move off. If any bad guys are watching us, they'll follow *our* movement. We'll use this as a stay-behind, so give me a heads-up when you're in place. I want to limit the radio traffic, so just send 'Bingo' when you're settled in."

"Roger that... Our normal signal for bogies in the kill zone is three keys on the handset, so just keep your squelch on low."

"I'll set up two defcons to your northwest... Defcon number one here... And number two... here," Mike said, indicating the spots on the map. "If you need them, I'll have the coordinates designated with our fire base, so when you call for a fire mission, just refer to them as such."

"Sounds like a plan, Captain," the sergeant replied, marking the spots on his own map. "Just don't let them light any cooking fires. We're too close to the Fence. Burnin' C-four's OK, though. Just make sure it's all out by dark."

"Don't worry about that."

After the main body moved off to the northeast, toward the tree squares in the distance, Sergeant Watson surveyed the ambush site, conjuring up different scenarios, depending on which waterway the enemy might approach from. Before long, he decided on a course of action that would accommodate up to five sampans in the kill zone. He considered the fan radius of each mine, including back blast areas and interlocking fields of fire. His other concern was finding areas to conceal the men with some degree of cover and with enough elevation to be able to visualize the kill zone. After the Carsons had set all the blasting caps in place, the sergeant had them conceal the mines and det cord along the marshy banks. Just before dark, the ambush settled into place.

Bingo.

Having ensured that the tree squares were swept for booby traps and having established a fighting perimeter and listening posts, the captain sat down on the soggy, elevated ground, still saturated with foul marshy bog but somewhat sheltered by the overhanging trees. He quickly unlaced his boots, poured the muddy water out of them, and placed them over two short sticks he had stuck in the mud. He pulled his socks off, wrung them out, and hastily buried them in the soft ground beside him.

Somewhat relieved, he pulled out his field map and selected points on it where he wanted artillery concentrations impacting if they were hit during the night. After plotting the coordinates, he shacked up the codes and called back to the camp for them to hand-deliver the defcons and numbers for each to the field howitzer battery there.

Exhausted, he reached into his fatigue jacket to retrieve the pouch of rice that had been cooking all day. To his surprise, it had almost tripled in size, and he was grateful for the bountiful portion. He soon realized, however, that he had forgotten his spoon. Undaunted, he pulled his knife from its sheath, cut open the top, and began to eat the tasty concoction with his dirty fingers. When that didn't work anymore, he just held it up and, just like he had done with a box of Cracker Jacks when he was a kid, poured the contents directly into his hungry mouth. *Damn, this is good shit!* he concluded, amazed how the flavor of the peppers and fish accented the rice.

He made one last check of the perimeter. Confident that all the men had finished eating, he made his way back to his position and looked toward the ambush site. He propped up his rucksack, pulled the radio close, draped the handset over his shoulder, and—with his weapon in his lap, the steady hiss of the squelch in his ear—simply closed his eyes.

The sudden lull in the monotone hissing startled his senses. Mike awoke abruptly to the intermittent cadence of some station-breaking squelch in his handset. It continued: Three short keys of the mike jolted the captain up into a sitting position. He cleared his eyes and strained to focus on the dark horizon ahead. He gazed down to the luminous hands on his watch: 0310.

He had no sooner readapted his eyes to the total darkness when the first explosion lit up the horizon, followed in rapid succession by two more. A volley of bright red tracers streaked amid the darkness, crisscrossing repeatedly from several locations like dotted laser lines until they disappeared into the blackened void. A single line of green tracer rounds flew directly up into the shallow sky, weaving slowly until they suddenly disappeared in the darkened clouds. Then... total silence.

He thought he heard a low, moaning sound, but as he listened intently, he heard no more. The captain pulled on his web gear and buckled it tight, scanning the darkness using the off-center technique he had been taught for detecting movement in the night. He clipped the handset to his harness and strained to hear any more breaks in the squelch.

Fifteen or twenty minutes had passed, and he continued to kneel, anxiously scanning the vague horizon for any sign of activity. Finally, the hissing sound broke.

Bingo, the voice whispered.

Relieved, Mike felt the tension in his body subside. His alert eyes continued to scan the gloomy night, keenly aware that the brief firefight would have alerted any additional infiltrators in the area. The time passed slowly with the light, steady rain finally transitioning unto a fine, comfortable mist. He maintained his vigil until he sensed the welcome arrival of early-morning nautical twilight.

"Thiệu," he whispered. "Go tell the *đại tá* to have the men stand to."

Mike knew that if the enemy had crept up on them during the night, the most probable time they would attack would be just as dawn broke. He was making sure that his men would be ready.

The morning light slowly traversed over the marshy plains, creating a mirror effect on the freshly irrigated fields. Mike told Thiệu to tell the *đại tá* that he was going back to secure the ambush site and bring the rest of the men back to the tree square with him. "And get the rest of the Kit Carsons together, Thiệu. I want them to come with me." Together, they left the tree square and headed cautiously back to the ambush site. Mike radioed ahead to Sergeant Watson and informed him of their approach.

Arriving at the scene, Mike witnessed the true carnage of war for the first time. His men had stacked the bodies up in two of the sampans that were still afloat. Two more shattered hulls rested partially submerged in the middle of the fluid stream. The enemy lay lifeless, clad irreverently in ragged black shorts, AK-47 ammo vests strapped to their lean chests. They were barefoot, with their contorted bodies riddled with bullet and jagged fragmentation wounds. Several limbs lay severed or partially detached, and Mike wondered why there was very little blood covering the corpses.

As he gazed over the brutal manifestation of battle, Mike realized that the enemy had not just lost their lives. Each one of them had surrendered his own personal identity. Not a one of them had retained the benefits of humanity, but had just unwillingly assumed a new label from battle: *enemy KIA*. The young captain now knew why the term *body count* seemed so inertly impersonal. He took a last look and decided he could live with that.

"They never knew what hit 'em, Captain," Watson told him, his voice a little drawn and raspy. "Only one of 'em was even able to get a burst off. They were loaded down with rice and crates of B-forty rockets. Had the scouts stack 'em up over there," he said, pointing to a large stack of wooden boxes and gunny sacks of rice.

"Everybody OK?" the captain asked.

"Yeah. Could sure use some extended *poc* time, though," Watson replied. "When you come down from that adrenaline rush, kinda' wipes out your energy factor, big time."

The captain observed the dreary expression on Watson's face, coupled with an apparent uneasiness in his demeanor. He had taken notice of the sergeant's staunch work ethic and the manner the rest of the team regarded him in their leisure time. Mike considered himself lucky to have Sergeant Roy Watson on his team, in spite of the fact that he was the junior NCO at the ripe age of twenty-four. "We need to move out of the RON position ASAP, but I'll make sure we settle in midday, to let your men stand down a little longer."

Mike walked around the edge of the stream. Red clumps of coagulated blood clung submissively to the base of the tall, stationary reeds. He realized that the bodies must have bled out in the water during the night, leaving behind a gruesome testament to the fury of war. A hint of sweet chicory and cordite teased his nostrils, urging him to draw another breath of the unfamiliar scent. He walked slowly up the stream past the ambush site, retracing the final path the enemy had taken to their violent deaths. He noticed that the stream took a final turn before flowing into the juncture, prompting him to wander up a little more to determine how far it flowed to the west. The narrow waterway etched a long, straight line through the reeds, at least a thousand meters directly toward the Cambodian border. His curiosity satisfied, he turned to rejoin his men.

Then he caught a glimpse of something that drew his attention. Just around the crook in the stream, a red smudge of blood covered some reeds that lay broken on the opposite bank. He brought his weapon to the ready and carefully crossed the murky stream, mindfully creating as little noise as possible. Creeping up on the layer of bent reeds, he noticed a smeared trail of blood leading back away from the water's edge. He stepped cautiously up to the bank, stealthfully following the telltale track. Twenty meters inland, he observed two small bare feet, their callused soles caked in dried blood.

He pointed his weapon at the figure lying motionless face down in the reeds, silky black pajamas, tan, floppy-brimmed bush hat obscuring the face. Mike remained uncertain whether the person were dead or not. *Looks like a young boy,* he thought. *What the hell is he doing out here?*

Instinctively, he poked the lifeless figure with the barrel of his M16. It responded immediately, emitting a full, guttural moan, then a pronounced, painful, shrill-like whimpering. The figure suddenly drew his arms up to cover his hidden face. Mike hesitated, wondering if the figure might be baiting him, might be slyly coaxing him to roll him over and then explode a live grenade in his face.

Just as Mike was about to retreat to a safe distance, the figure slowly rolled over, bloody hands still covering his face in fear. The black pajama top flipped open, exposing a small female breast, astounding the foreboding American warrior standing over her. "Watson!!" Mike yelled. "Watson!!" The urgency in his voice was enough not only to summon his sergeant but also to set the young girl into a frenzy of wailing and tears.

He carefully reached down to pull her bloody hands from her face, exposing a pair of dark, ebony eyes filled with tears and mortal fear. He tried to calm her, pressing his open palm up and down, then placing one finger to his lips, beseeching her to quiet down. *Don't know if I'm ready for this*, he told himself. *She can't be more than fourteen years old.*

Watson and Thiệu scurried across the stream, alarmed by the tenor in the captain's voice.

"We've got a live one," he told them. "It's a young girl!"

Mike stared down at the trembling youngster, instinctively reaching down to pull her black silk top over her breast.

"She VC!" Thiệu yelled, stating the obvious.

"Somebody was protecting her or musta' pushed her out of the boat when the first Claymore went off," Watson reasoned.

"Thiệu, get her to calm down. Tell her we're not going to hurt her," the captain told him. "Ask her where's she's hurt."

The young girl continued to wail, covering her face with her blood-stained hands. Thiệu rattled off a series of questions, his tone and emphasis demanding quick answers. Her wailing subsided to low, deep, rasping sobs, pain and anguish apparent in her every bridled breath. The interpreter reached down and jostled her shoulder firmly, repeating his questions in a deeper, more menacing tone.

Suddenly she stopped. Her hands slowly drifted away from her face. Her breathing seemed to cease. She lay limp, her shiny, blood-smeared face expressionless, her head tilted calmly to the right. The captain pulled Thiệu away and then knelt down beside the lifeless maiden. He gently clasped her throat, looking for any sign of pulsation in her carotid arteries. "I've got a faint pulse," he reported, a concerned emphasis apparent in his tone. "She probably passed out because she's lost so much blood."

He drew open her bloody blouse, searching for any puncture or bullet wounds. He found the source of the blood on her hands: a series of cuts high on her right arm that appeared superficial. He determined that her arms weren't broken and that she didn't have any significant chest wounds. He turned his attention to her legs, finding a small tear in her pants high on the right side of her thigh. He ripped the fabric open, exposing a deep wound to her upper thigh.

"It's not pumping," he told Watson. "She's lucky. It missed the femoral artery. Otherwise, she would have already bled out."

He unsnapped his field dressing from his web gear and told Sergeant Watson to hold her leg up. Applying direct pressure to the wound, he securely wrapped the dressing around the gaping gash in her thigh. "She's not gonna make if we don't get her out of here ASAP," the captain declared.

"Captain, Dust Off's not gonna fly out to this area so close to the Fence for some wounded VC," Watson told him. "That would only compromise our position for sure."

"She's gonna die," Mike told him, a quiet calm in his statement. "She needs blood… *now.*"

The captain drew back on his haunches, noticing the group of Kit Carsons staring at him from the opposite bank. It seemed to him as though they were asking him, "What you do now, *Đại úy?*" That question was already churning feverishly in his mind. He quickly reassessed the situation, the courses of action, and their consequences. He unbuckled his web gear, took the can of albumin blood substitute off his harness, and told Thiệu to take his belt off and strap it around her arm. He swiftly searched for a vein, and when he found one, he inserted the needle into the crook in her arm. He handed the IV pouch to Thiệu and told him to hold it up.

Then he reached down into his trousers for his battle map, studying the various waterways leading back to the Kinh Gẫy.

"What'cha got on your mind, Captain?" Watson inquired.

"Well, if we off-load some of those bodies in one of those sampans, we could use it to ferry her back to the Kinh Gẫy, where they could rendezvous with one of our airboats or a PBR from the navy. We could get her back to camp in about an hour."

Sergeant Watson looked intently at his captain, and his eyes dimmed as he listened.

"This stream actually flows just another five hundred meters north," Mike continued. "Then it turns east and intersects with the Kinh Gẫy about seven hundred meters from where we inserted. I don't know how fast those motorized sampans travel, but it sure beats carrying her out in a poncho."

"Would you be going to all this trouble if *she* were a he?" the sergeant inquired.

Mike hesitated before answering. When he did, he echoed Watson's emphasis on the girl's gender. "I know *she's* the enemy, Sergeant, if that's what you're asking. But *she* also happens to be a POW, one who at the moment requires medical attention. I'm also sure *she* has useful intelligence regarding the enemy's recent activities, and it's my responsibility to ensure that I protect that valuable information and get it to the people who can make good use of it."

"*Đại úy! Đại úy!*" Thiệu yelled. "She open her eye!"

"Good," Mike replied. "Let me know when the pouch is empty."

Then he turned his attention to the task at hand. "Watson, get the Carsons to pick out one of the boats so we can get her headed in the right direction. Pick out two men to escort her back to the canal. Make sure at least one of them knows something about driving the boat as well," he told him. "I want those crates of B-forties loaded on them if there's room."

Then: "Thiệu, I want you to blindfold her so she can't see what happened to her friends. Tell her we are taking her to get some medical attention, and make sure she knows we're not the barbarians they've told her we are. We're not going to hurt her."

While Watson returned to the ambush site with the men to prepare a boat for the prisoner, Mike opened a morphine ampule and knelt down beside the dazed young girl. "Tell her I'm going to give her something for the pain, and she might feel a prick from the needle," he told Thiệu. He quickly inserted the injection into her thigh and then pinned the empty tube to her soggy collar. He looked briefly at her tormented face. Then he untied the red and blue scarf from around his neck, opened his canteen, doused the scarf with water, and gingerly wiped the cakes of drying blood from her forehead and face.

"I want her bound, Thiệu. But make sure her arms are in front, not back." Within minutes, they had her loaded onto the sampan. After making sure the escort knew where they were going, and the consequences of *anything* happening to her, Mike watched the sputtering sampan head north up the stream, heading to the main canal, hidden somewhere off in the distance, where it would rendezvous with either an airboat or a navy PBR.

After the captain had explained the situation to Sergeant Miller over the radio, the team sergeant assured Mike that the navy would be the fastest method to get the prisoner back to camp. After Miller contacted them on the in-camp landline, the navy folks readily complied. They were excited about the opportunity to see what a female VC actually looked like. *Bác sĩ* and a navy corpsman would set out in a PBR, bringing medical kits with them, to rendezvous with the sampan carrying the two Carsons and the female prisoner. They could properly tend to her wounds en route back to the camp.

The captain and his weapons sergeant returned with the remaining Carsons to the main body within an hour. Together, they spent the next six days arduously crisscrossing the desolate Plain of Reeds without making any contact with the elusive enemy. Mike could only wonder *who* might have told them where they were. And now where they were going.

* * *

CHAPTER THIRTY-TWO

THE WEARY LEAD SCOUTS CROSSED the narrow stream and stepped up through the tall reeds onto the end of the old, abandoned dirt airfield at the south end of the camp. The captain and Sergeant Watson followed close behind, unshaven, wet, and redolent with a variety of foul odors emanating from their weary bodies. They watched the surplus three-quarter-ton truck traveling rapidly down the runway toward them, a cloud of brown, dusty smoke trailing lazily behind.

"Welcome home, *Đại úy*," *Bác sĩ* Braxton said, sliding out of the driver's seat and taking the captain's ruck from Cowboy. He slung it up into the back while Watson lifted the two PRC-25 radios up onto the wooden seats in the rear. "Hear ya had a little excitement for a change," he told Watson.

"Nothin' to write home about," the weapons sergeant replied, stomping his boots on the hard clay to clear them of the last lingering remnants of reed water.

"What's the status of the girl?" the captain asked.

"Well, that created a little excitement around here, that's for sure," Braxton told them. "After I patched her up, we decided to keep her down at the navy compound for safekeeping. The LLDB wanted us to turn her over to them, but Top didn't trust 'em."

"Well, where is she?" Mike asked as he slung his wet web gear into the back.

"Top had her back-loaded to the C-Team in Biên Hòa on the mail chopper two days ago. When the LLDB found out, we about had an incident in the inner compound."

"What were they going to do with her?"

"Exactly..." Braxton replied, a smirk on his face.

"Where's Sergeant Miller now?" Mike inquired, stepping up into the passenger seat.

"He's in the TOC. He's on secure to the B-Team, trying to sort it all out. They relieved *Đại úy* Tran while you were in the field, and there seems to be a power play going on for who's going to replace him."

"So… how's the girl?" the captain asked once again.

"She lost a lot of blood. I'm surprised she made it. Whoever put that tight field dressing on her probably saved her life. I just sewed her up, transfused a few liters of blood, and pumped her full of antibiotics. She's good to go," *Bác sĩ* related. "Pretty tough little girl."

The squeaky truck bounced and swayed through the dried ruts in the hardened lane leading back to the team house. When they arrived, Mike told Braxton that he wanted to meet with Sergeant Miller as soon as he had time to shower and shave.

He relished soaking in the warm rainwater as it slowly poured from the elevated tank through the makeshift spout above him. His thoughts continued to reengage the image of that young girl, brutally injured, lying near death amid the soggy reeds. He nourished the compassion he felt for her, and as it lingered within him, he tried in earnest to determine the circumstances that led her down the dark stream that fateful night. Mike felt he needed to know *why* she was there. Was it her own choice or some form of dastardly coercion? He wondered if he would ever find out.

The dry jungle fatigues and boots soothed his mood as the captain walked carefully over the wooden artillery pallets that served as a crude sidewalk to the TOC. He opened the heavy reinforced door and promptly felt the comfy cool air initiate a series of chill goose bumps over his tepid skin.

Master Sergeant Miller sat talking to a stranger seated across from him at the table. "Captain Shannahan," he said, standing up as Mike approached the table. "Let me introduce you to Sergeant First Class Marshall. George and I served together when we were with the Two Corps MIKE Force up in Pleiku."

"Nice to meet you, Sergeant," Mike replied, shaking his hand.

"Sergeant Marshall is the best demo man in the Group," Miller continued. "I pulled some strings to get his happy ass down here to help us out."

"You're a tall drink of water. Where you from?" Mike inquired, noting that his toned, muscular physique was accented with a shiny new Rolex GMT on his wide wrist.

"Asheville, North Carolina," Marshall proudly reported. "Heard you spent some time with the Tenth in Tölz," he added, lighting up a dark, short cheroot with his shiny Zippo.

"Yeah. Tölz and Devens."

"Was Lieutenant Colonel DeLay there?" Marshall inquired, taking a deep hit on the cigar.

"Yeah, he was A-Company CO when I was there. Had a smokin' hot daughter who used to hang out at the club."

Marshall's expression changed. "His chopper went down just south of here in Four Corps a coupla' days ago," he said. "They were hovering over a spider hole on a berm near Seven Sisters when the viper popped his head up and got off a B-forty right into the crew compartment. Took 'em all out."

"He was a good guy," Mike told them, reluctantly recalling the casual times they had spoken together at the club.

Miller shook his head. "I heard the dumb-ass door gunner was trying to drop a mortar round down the friggin' spider hole," he said. "Fuckin' stupid-shit stuff."

"Speaking of stupid-shit stuff, Top," the captain interjected. "That wasted week of playin' hide n' seek out in the playpen is fuckin' ridiculous. They don't pass out Purple Hearts for crotch rot and snake bites."

"Don't count on it changing any time soon," Miller replied. "Not as long as the LLDB has anything to say about it, Captain."

"Ya don't have to slap this Irishman in the face with a wet mop for me to figure that one out, Top. We're going to have to find a way to change their mind-set or piss Charlie off enough for them to change their tactics as well. Regardless, our mission is clear," he concluded. "We just need to make the adjustments to make it happen."

His team sergeant fully agreed, and for the next several hours, the three of them explored methods and tactics that could generate the desired outcomes. They determined that the two most effective assets they had in camp were the Cambodes of the III Corps MIKE Force and the platoon of Vietnamese Kit Carson scouts. They collectively decided to develop their strategies using their assets' unique talents as the focus of their offensive operations.

The captain noted that the FAC who had assisted him in locating the insertion site had also been able to visually detect recent movement through the marshy terrain. It was apparent to him that if a body of troops, no matter how small or large, were moving through the area, there would be no way for them to conceal their tracks from aerial observation. He decided to request a daily visual reconnaissance chopper to take a member of the team and fly over the AO, looking for reed trails or any other suspicious activity.

"It'll take a company or larger-size unit at least two days to make it to the river," Miller pointed out. "We pick up their trail the first day out, and we can easily make them feel like Buddha just came down from the heavens to shit in their rice!"

They agreed that any sampan movement out of the Ba Thu area would be confined to the series of waterways leading east from the border sanctuary. Sergeant Miller plotted the streams originating from the area on the wall map, depicting the most expeditious route to intersect the Vàm Cỏ Đông River at various junctions. They then identified the most logical intersections that would yield the most productive outcomes if an ambush site were inserted at each.

"This isn't really brain surgery here, Top," the captain professed. "They've got to get from point A to point B, and their most expeditious method is to use the streams intersecting the AO." He indicated the points on the map. "We just have to be in the right place at the right time."

"We could also set up area ambushes by moving airboats in right before dark," Miller added, "and catching them in the open at daybreak."

"You're right, Top," the captain agreed. "But in my opinion, the key to the success of these operations is security. Right now, we're not fooling anyone. They know where we're going before we even start out."

"That's a scary thought, Đại úy," Miller agreed. "We're just gonna have to take the little bastards out of the loop."

"We could use the Sidge as a decoy. Let them do their thing like they always have. Same routes, same RON. Hell, let 'em even light fires," the captain joked.

"So, the word would get back to Sir Charles, and he'd just plot alternate routes around them," Miller concluded. "And in the meantime, we'd be waitin' for 'em to the north and south of the Sidge operation with the MIKE Force on one side and the Carsons on the other."

"Makes sense to me," the captain concurred. "Let's make it happen."

They agreed to set the operation in place once they knew exactly where the LLDB was planning the next excursion out into the playpen. They would not divulge any details of the alternate troop movements to anyone outside of the team, thereby ensuring that the enemy would be receiving only the information they wanted him to have from the moles within.

With a workable operational plan in place, the young captain turned his attention to the paltry state of repair the camp itself was in. He directed his engineers to work with the navy Seabees to cap the rotting sandbags off with a layer of cement and to devise an effective drainage system that would alleviate the standing water and congested gullies inside the camp perimeter.

He spent hours atop the camp's forty-foot observation tower, familiarizing himself with the camp defensive posture while noting the mundane daily life of the inhabitants below. Small individual groups of women and children ventured out regularly over the berms, gathering plants, frogs, and snakes within the marshy menagerie of defensive wires and trip flares. He witnessed the brutally arduous shantytown atmosphere, with lines of clothes and sheets hanging from various strands of wire crisscrossing between the hooches, mothers cowering around the seemingly infinite array of small cooking fires. Empty artillery shell casings lay scattered throughout the encampment, with rusting fifty-five-gallon drums burning trash and excrement in every compound.

He stood amused as half-naked women sat peacefully on the river's edge, calmly bathing in the river's murky waters while children frolicked in the nearby canal, which was heavily infested with nests of poisonous snakes. Others idly chatted while washing their clothes or cleaning their pots, completely oblivious to the occasional dead floater passing by on his long, soggy interment in the South China Sea. *This is a fuckin' hellhole,* Mike realized. *No wonder everyone is sick!*

He made his way down the steep tower ladder and adjusted the shoulder strap on his .45 as he headed toward the dispensary to speak with *Bác sĩ* Braxton. "We're going to have to do something about those rats," Mike told him when he got there. "I woke up last night with one of them gnawing on my toenails."

"Don't worry, *Đại úy*," Braxton claimed with a smile. "They won't eat much."

"Seriously… I was just up in the tower, and I saw a group of kids corner one near the north ammo bunker. The son of a bitch was the size of a possum!"

"They're pretty good at catching 'em. They've had a lot of practice," *Bác sĩ* said, wrapping gauze around a tearful young boy's leg.

"What happened to him?" the captain asked.

"Got caught up in the tanglefoot across the canal. He'll be all right. Didn't like the tetanus shot I gave him, though."

"Have these kids been inoculated against cholera?"

Braxton paused, a thoughtful expression looming, prefacing his answer. "Nope, I don't think so," he finally replied.

"Well, don't you think that might be a step in the right direction, given the circumstances?"

"There're over a hundred kids in this camp, *Đại úy*. That's a lot of vaccine."

"That could easily be a hundred dead kids, Doc. You want that on your conscience?" Mike inquired. "And what are we doing about getting these damn rats under control?"

"I'm glad you brought that up, Captain. Top and I were talkin', and you know how the VN are, so we figured if we put a ten-*piastre* bounty on 'em, we'd have the problem solved in no time."

"How much is a *piastre*?"

"About a penny."

"You think it will work?"

"It's worth a try. What'a we have to lose?"

The captain conferred with Sergeant Miller and put together a requisition for enough vaccine to inoculate the children in the camp, including any elderly or others who posed a risk of contracting the disease. *Bác sĩ* Braxton helped his young Cambodian nurse, Xian, post colorful *Wanted* posters throughout the camp, offering a reward for every rat turned over to the team.

Mike turned his attention to the most disturbing issue he had observed from the tower, and he sought the team sergeant's advice on how to rectify the problem. "I've noticed that there are a lot of the indig scrounging in the perimeter wires for plants and food," he began. "Why aren't they setting off the trip flares and booby traps we've got in place out there?"

"Good question. We need to do an inspection of the wire anyway, Cap'n. I'll have Sergeant Marshall inspect the trip flares and Claymores in the morning. He'd noticed the same thing. We may need to replace some of them. They've been out there for a while."

"Let the LLDB know that anyone from here on out who is caught in the wires will be considered hostile," Mike emphasized. "They want to fish, gather, or capture, they can do it down at the end of the runway, not in *my wire*."

Over the next long weeks, the improvements began to transform the camp's appearance to a more functional and stable environment. The bounty program seemed to be working as well. The rat population slowly diminished, along with the standing water and green algae that had been permeating the ditches along the camp's rutted lane. The B-Team sent a crew of medics down from Tây Ninh to help inoculate the children against cholera and diphtheria, and a centralized trash dump was set up to burn refuse at the south end of the camp.

Sergeant Marshall's inspection of the camp's perimeter disclosed that all of the Claymores had had their blasting caps removed, and the trip wires for the warning flares had all been cut. That revelation did not sit well with the team, and the captain let it be known to everyone that, henceforth, *anyone*—including LLDB personnel—caught out in the wires would be shot.

Mike gradually developed an affinity with the camp and the daily routine that he and his men endured. The true depth of his responsibility became abundantly apparent when the S4 sergeant from the B-Detachment arrived to have him sign for all the weapons and equipment issued for the camp, including all the small arms, crew-served weapons and mortars, ammunition, and miscellaneous equipment for more than a thousand men under his direct and indirect command. The list of inventory seemed staggering, and along with it came the intense realization that he was personally accountable for everything that happened to, or was a result of, the activities of Detachment A-326.

Mike eagerly carried that burden with him daily, awakening at dawn to be the first in the chilly shower, to be dressed and sipping his instant coffee at the team table before his men emerged from their rooms for the daily buffet of powdered eggs and Spam. His first task required him to check in with the commo shack for sitreps on operations in the field and messages from the B-Detachment in Tây Ninh City. He routinely filled his shirt pockets with gum and candy as he left the team house and headed out for his daily walks through the indig compounds to check on the human pulse of the congested neighborhoods.

The team regularly sent one member on a "scrounging" mission into Saigon, a brief in-country R&R where they could enjoy some down time from the rigors of camp life and operations, but with a laundry list of items the team needed for a project or job. As barter, they would take captured K-54 pistols, AK-47s, or other NVA possessions to trade with anxious rear-echelon types who for a cherished war souvenir would gladly surrender valuable government property: pallets of tin, Cokes, or beer; cases of steaks; or the precious fifths of Crown Royal to give to the chief navy cook in exchange for fresh eggs and bacon. Their prized achievement was the three-quarter-ton truck they acquired from an air force sergeant in exchange for a pistol belt with a pearl-handled K-54 taken off a dead NVA colonel.

The captain was discouraged to find that, unlike in the regular army, Special Forces teams were required to solicit their own food sources, a task severely complicated by the isolated remoteness of the average SF camp location. The indig in the camp strike force relied predominantly on the daily airlifts from the C-Detachment in Biên Hòa, with loads of native food supplies flown in on cargo nets suspended below the mammoth Chinook helicopters. Mike marveled at the sight of live cow and pig hooves dangling through the nets as the twin-engine helicopters hovered above the landing pad at the edge of the runway.

The team continued to take advantage of the vast array of surplus weapons they maintained, altering the old M2 carbines by sawing off the barrels and carving the butt stocks into pistol grips. With its twenty-round magazine, the World War Two weapon quickly became a favorite with the chopper pilots in the area, prompting some of them to fly in from as far away as Mộc Hòa in IV Corps to trade prime steaks and cases of chicken for the valued sidearm.

The captain soon adopted a protective, even paternal routine of climbing the tower just before dusk and surveying the perimeter and outlying approaches to the camp with his powerful field binoculars. He was firmly intent on detecting any enemy movement before darkness settled in. He watched the navy PBRs idling out of the canal to set up their night ambushes along the wide, winding river, a tactic designed to prevent the NVA from crossing the river on their way to Saigon. He sat concealed in his perch, maintaining his vigil for hours, listening intently or flicking on the new Starlight scope when he wanted to scan a suspicious movement in the canal or river. Occasionally, he would be treated to a distant firefight, with flares and tracers accenting the dark horizon, muffled impacts of artillery and rockets whispering audibly in the night.

A cautious peace settled nightly over the busy camp while devoted mothers tended to their children, and their men cleaned their weapons in the dim glare of the candle-lit hooches. The low, constant murmur of the sandbagged generators vibrated their dubious lullaby as they provided the necessary power to operate the numerous radios that served as the camp's lifeline to the world beyond the rusty wires. The black, impenetrable cloak of darkness provided the enemy with nocturnal anonymity, their coveted veil of invisibility, and along with it, their only true ally to assist them in creating an element of fear within the huddled masses anticipating their inevitable arrival.

Mike heard the baby cry, and he turned his attention to a pajama-clad mother who had stepped out of her hooch and onto the dark lane outside. As the sound intensified, he clicked on the Starlight and focused on the consoling mother cradling her child. She rocked the infant back and forth, desperately attempting to silence the shrill cries echoing throughout the camp. The child intensified his displeasure, prompting his mother to hold up the naked infant and place his limp penis in her mouth as she continued to cradle him back and forth. The response was immediate, restoring the tense calm as she fulfilled her maternal chore. *Never saw that one before,* Mike told himself. *Talk about resourceful.*

He looked at his watch: 2200 hours. He placed the scope back in its pouch, zipped it up, and headed slowly back down the steep ladder. *Commo watch,* he told himself as he prepared to spend the next two hours listening to the constant hiss of the radio, monitoring the camp's operation in the field as well as two more powerful radios linking them to the B-Team in Tây Ninh and the radio relay site atop Núi Bà Đen, the tall Black Virgin Mountain, clearly visible to their northwest.

Each team member endured two-hour shifts each night to monitor the banks of radios. The crucial yet tedious task could be tempered with the opportunity to communicate with sister camps located to their north and south, as well as the single-sideband radio traffic from ham operators around the world. Army Mohawk aircraft checked in occasionally as they silently orbited above, monitoring their high-tech sensors, which were designed to detect large troop movements along the Fence. An occasional firefight or ambush relieved the stale monotony, enabling the men to monitor the play-by-play action, an action filled with raw tension and vivid emotion apparent in the tone of the players as they called for artillery and air support.

The captain started a log, copying call signs and conferring with his men who the stations on the net were and the techniques used to communicate with them back channel so as not to violate military protocol. For weeks he had been trying to track down where Rich had been exiled to.

A couple of days before, during a conversation with Sergeant Marshall, Mike had mentioned an isolated mountaintop radio relay station somewhere in Laos. "You're not supposed to know anything about that, Captain," Marshall had informed him. "Call sign Leghorn. SOG uses it to bounce radio traffic from their RTs back to Covey and the FOBs in-country," he related. "Sits on top of a steep mountain with about a thousand-foot vertical drop."

"Leghorn," Mike had repeated, etching the call sign into his mind.

"If somebody asks you about it, it doesn't exist," the sergeant had warned.

Now Mike decided to take a chance. Toward the end of his commo shift, he put a call into the radio relay site atop Núi Bà Đen. "Matterhorn, Matterhorn… This is Red Bank Goose One-zero… Over."

"Red Bank… This is Matterhorn One-three, over."

"Matterhorn... Goose One-zero. Can you patch me through to Leghorn, over?"

"Goose... Matterhorn... Stand by."

Mike waited patiently, listening to the faint hissing sound from the radio monitoring the field operation. He scribbled on the pad in front of him, and growing anxious that his request would be denied, he adjusted the fans blowing on the bank of radios.

Finally a different voice replied: "Goose One-zero... Matterhorn One-zero, over."

"One-zero... Go."

"What is the nature of your traffic, over?"

Mike hesitated briefly. "Nontactical. Can you get them to push to an alternate frequency, over?"

Another long pause.

"Do you have a designator for Leghorn, Goose?"

Mike thought for a moment and then offered his best guess. "Ahhh, roger, Matterhorn. I need commo with Hammer Knocker One-zero, over."

"Say designator again..."

"Roger... Hammer Knocker One-zero, over."

"Roger...Stand by, Goose."

Mike waited patiently as his anxiety mingled with guarded anticipation. He noticed a pack of Lucky Strikes on the desk and searched for a match to light one up. He sat back in the worn swivel chair, blowing white plumes of stangnant smoke into the swirling fans. Minutes passed. Then, as he leaned over to put the cigarette out, the radio crackled to life.

"Goose One-zero... Goose One-zero... This is Matterhorn, over."

"Matterhorn... Goose... Go."

"Goose... Go to Fox Mike sixty-eight-dot-three on secure to receive your traffic, over."

"Ahh... Understand sixty-eight-dot-three Fox Mike secure, Matterhorn."

"Affirmative... Matterhorn One-zero, out."

Mike quickly turned the tuning dial on the secure PRC-50 to the designated frequency and waited.

"Red Bank Goose One-zero... This is Cyclops Nickel, over."

Mike grabbed the handset. "Cyclops Nickel... This is Goose One-zero, over."

"Ahhh... roger, Goose One-zero... Understand you have traffic for this station, over."

"Roger, Cyclops... Trying to establish commo with Hammer Knocker, over."

"Aaaahhh, you got him, Goosie, over."

Mike unleashed a broad smile, but he knew that someone of consequence might be monitoring his transmissions. He thought for a moment and then keyed his handset. "Cyclops... Goose. I need a sitrep regarding your status. Be advised that you can direct that traffic to Alpha three-four-eight minus the date that you departed CONUS. I say again: Send sitrep to Alpha three-four-eight minus the date you departed CONUS, over."

"Goose... Cyclops Nickel... Roger copy... Wilco, out."

Mike eased back in his chair, his broad smile still tweaking his cheeks. His gamble had paid off, and he felt confident that Rich would be sending him a letter within the week. He sat quietly in the confined quarters, reminiscing the carefree days he'd spent with his good friend, just hoping he would make it off that desolate mountain in Laos in one piece.

* * *

CHAPTER THIRTY-THREE

D ARKNESS SLIPPED BELOW THE VAST array of lush green mountain peaks, elevating a pink-rouge tint of morning twilight that steadily crept down the crowded treetops into the deep, shadowy gorges below.

Lieutenant Rich Mycoskie stepped out of his heavily bunkered lair, situated well above what he referred to as the "Kingdom of Sir Chuck and his dastardly Cohorts," who were confidently and leisurely dwelling in the extended valley floor below. Casually attired in the uniform of the day, he yawned and scratched his head as he buttoned the fly on his cut-off tiger fatigues. Slipping on his tatty flip-flops, he reached down and summoned Samson, his pet monkey, to scamper up his arm and take a perch on his furry broad shoulder. The lieutenant ran his fingers through his bushy, full beard while Samson sat contentedly, grooming his master's thick, matted hair, searching diligently for any critters that might have taken up residence while he slept. Rich found solace in the warmth of the macaque's smooth haunches, which eased the bite of the chilly morning air.

He gazed out over the panoramic view. Thin pockets of morning mist lingered between the lower mountain saddles, persisting a little longer only to evaporate in the inevitable heat that was rushing in from the south. To the north, he watched the low cumulus cloud banks floating aimlessly below him, gently careening off the elevated peaks as their chalky haze smothered the damp valley floors. He turned and looked up toward the TOC, where radio towers of all sizes and heights stood intertwined with a maze of support wires crisscrossing the summit in every direction. He started his climb up the sandbagged steps, winding his way through the series of fighting bunkers covered with layers of plastic and littered with empty C-ration boxes, tin cans, and trash.

As he passed the security element's hooch, he heard the Montagnard squad clanging pots as they prepared to boil some rainwater to make breakfast. "Hey! Keep it down in there!" he scolded them amiably. "Chuck is trying to get some shut-eye down there!" Rich felt lucky to have the Yards there with him, all seasoned fighters from the feared Hatchet Force in Kon Tum.

As he continued up the winding path between the huge boulders and the rocky peak, he noticed the twenty layers of sandbags over the TOC showing the first signs of rot and decay. Standing in the doorway to the command center and looking back down over the wide minefields and rolls of wire surrounding the perimeter, however, he decided a little wear and tear were the least of his worries.

"We've got an RT surrounded by an NVA company in the Bra, Lieutenant," Sergeant Jacob Sweeny told him as he entered the TOC. The sergeant was monitoring the traffic between the beleaguered team and Covey flying high overhead the intense action on the ground. The Bra was the major NVA base camp, known officially as Binh Trạm 37 and situated near a winding river at the intersection of Highway 110 and the Hồ Chí Minh Trail. Its terrain resembled a brassiere.

"What assets do they have available?" Rich inquired.

"Covey's got some fast movers headed in, but there's a coupla' A-ones on station and some gunships from Đắk Tô on the way."

The lieutenant sat down and picked up a headset. He lifted Samson off his shoulder and set him gingerly on the floor. He and Sweeny listened to the Special Forces sergeant, the Covey, in the backseat of the small plane talking to the one-zero on the ground and from his high perch directing the team to a landing zone where they could attempt a hot extraction.

"What was their mission?" Rich inquired, wondering why they would have directly inserted a team into such a hot area.

"POW snatch," Sweeny informed him, writing call signs down as they came over the net. "They lost track of a whole NVA division and need to find them."

Rich and Sweeny continued to monitor the traffic as Covey directed the team through a tall section of elephant grass, hoping they would be able to break through and head for a small clearing he had observed about four hundred meters to their south. They began firing their 40mm grenade launchers in a fan direction to their front, holding their fire with their rifles so the enemy would not be able to pinpoint them in the surrounding tall grass. The RT continued to fight, throwing hand grenades and leaving toe poppers and hasty Claymore mines set to explode in their wake and neutralize the pursuing NVA.

Covey fired a white phosphorus rocket, making highly visible the target for the A-1 Skyraiders to saturate the area with napalm and cannon fire. Rich and Sweeny listened as the Cobra gunships began their runs, firing salvos of seventeen-pound rockets and minigunfire into the tree lines and advancing enemy in the grass below.

"We're taking fire from three-sixty!" the Cobra pilot reported as he banked his chopper steeply up the mountainous slope.

"You're spewin' fuel," Covey advised, watching the trail of aviation gas swirl past the tail rotor on the heavily damaged gunship.

The fighting on the ground intensified as the Cobras broke off contact and nursed their wounded and now ineffective birds back in the direction of the Fence. Covey vectored the fast movers in. As they made their approach, he directed the team to make a run for it as soon as the first five-hundred-pounder hit.

Rich felt the tension in his body as he sat helplessly listening to men die. He'd been a reluctant party to numerous such encounters in the three long months since he'd begun suffering his lonely penance.

The team broke through the encirclement, and with their wounded comrades in tow, they finally made it to the clearing in the trees. Covey told them to be ready for the inbound slicks, or troop-carrying choppers, because he could see the NVA moving steadily toward them only two hundred meters away. He told the one-zero to pop smoke to enable the slicks to find them. The lead chopper spiraled down, flared abruptly to level off, and then began his high-speed run to the LZ. But just as the pilot flared to hover in the clearing, the NVA opened up from the opposite direction, springing the ambush they'd previously set in the obvious LZ.

As the team ran toward the open doors of the chopper, it violently tilted on its side. Bodies, blades, and ammunition exploded in the deadly barrage of gunfire and rockets. Totally exposed, the team lay helpless in the burning grass, with gunfire and explosions engulfing their quest for any hope of escape.

Rich looked at his sergeant, shaking his head. They had both witnessed similar escapades that had resulted in the loss of the men on the ground as well as those who risked their lives to save them.

"You know they're gonna have to send in a Bright Light team to retrieve the bodies," Sweeny said.

"They'd better bring a Hatchet Force and the Two Corp MIKE Force with 'em," the lieutenant declared. "I think it's about time to send an Arc Light in to show those fuckers we mean business as well." Rich was referring to an overwhelming aerial raid by B-52 Stratofortresses.

They listened quietly as Covey repeatedly tried to make contact with the one-zero on the ground. After about ten minutes, he finally relented. "Oscar Zulu… Oscar Zulu… Negative contact… Covey Two-six-seven out."

Rich took the headset off, stood up, and walked slowly over to the door. He put both hands on the threshold, staring out into the distant deep-green foliage while his heartbeat simmered to an even pace. "I know you're down there somewhere, big brother," he murmured. "And I'm not leaving till I find you," he promised.

He scanned the mountain ranges heading down toward Cambodia. He renewed his intent, whenever he could get back to Nha Trang, on questioning Major Aldridge about the exact location of his brother's operation. Whenever he could get back to Nha Trang, this time… under different circumstances.

I've got to get off this fuckin' mountain, he told himself, weary of listening to the men of his unit meet their demise. *If they're going down, I'm going down with them,* he concluded. *And not as a spectator in this nosebleed bleacher, just watchin' the fuckin' war go by.*

He turned and yelled back at Sergeant Sweeny. "When's the next resupply chopper due in?"

"Two days, Lieutenant."

"Good. Tell the FOB to put a straphanger on it to help you with the commo. I'm going back with it to Nha Trang. Heard my old team sergeant just took over as NCOIC of the Recondo School, and I think he can help me get a few extra credits to put on my résumé. I'll be back on the next chopper, so don't give my bunk away, and make *damn* sure the Yards don't barbecue Samson while I'm gone."

"Seriously?"

"Don't look so damn traumatized," he snidely remarked. "I do have my moments."

He lowered his arm, and as Samson vaulted up to his favorite perch, Rich left the bunker and headed back down to his hooch. He stood in front of the rusty wall locker, smiling assuredly while he inspected his reflection in the spotty mirror. He ceremoniously lifted the scissors up and began to crop away his crusty beard.

* * *

CHAPTER THIRTY-FOUR

T HE CAPTAIN AND SEVERAL OF his men sat leisurely around the team table eating lunch. The smooth, lamenting voice of George Jones filled the busy room with welcome vestiges of the lives they had left behind. Tin plates of sautéed hot dogs and beans meant that they would have to come up with another creative method to enhance their dwindling food supplies. Mike opened a package of grape Kool-Aid and poured it into his glass. As he watched it dissolve, he broke an iodine tablet in two and dropped the larger half into the dark mixture.

"The rats are back, Captain," *Bác sĩ* Braxton told him. "Thought we had it under control, but it's getting worse every week."

"I haven't seen any of the fuckers in about a month," Sergeant Daniels reported.

"Well, they just brought in about twenty of the creepy bastards this morning," *Bác sĩ* told them. "They weren't real big, but they were damn sure mean."

"Let me know if it gets any worse," the captain told him.

Mike got up from the table and walked over to the reel-to-reel tape deck and reversed the spools to listen to some more music. As he sat back down, he looked up to see Sergeant McDonald, the new junior commo man, walking down the hallway from the commo bunker. "Captain… Got a message from the C-Team and they want to know the results of the leech repellant tests that they sent us," he informed him.

"What leech repellant test?" Mike inquired. He looked around the table, but each man shrugged his shoulders, all professing their ignorance in the matter.

"Send them a message back and tell them, 'Negative results on the leech repellant test… One-zero sends,'" the captain told McDonald.

Master Sergeant Miller threw open the screen door to the team house. "Captain! Come take a look at this!" he demanded, an irritated tone in his voice.

Mike stood up, and with the other men close behind, he stepped down from the team house landing and looked in the direction the team sergeant was pointing. "What the fuck is that?" he asked, staring up at the small, blimplike balloon tethered to a dark line leading back down into the navy compound.

"Looks like the circus is in town, *Đại úy*," Top answered. "That thing's gotta be at least a hundred feet up," he estimated.

Mike walked over to the truck parked outside the team house, and as most of the men clambered aboard, he set off hastily in the direction of the navy compound. As he and his entourage entered the navy billet, he observed Lieutenant Bosworth conferring with a small group of civilian technicians. "You want to explain to me what that airborne aiming stake is doing flying over my camp?" Mike asked the lieutenant, interrupting their conference.

Bosworth smiled, a sheepish element garnishing his expression. "They just got it up," he explained. "We were just on our way over to the radio shack to give it a test."

"Give *what* a test?" the captain inquired.

A diminutive man in his fifties stood up from his chair and walked over to the gathering. "We're going to test the reception variances, based on the height and trajectory of the antenna in relation to the target sensors we've placed in the operational area," he informed them. "We may have to make some minor adjustments in the disposition of the receiving apparatus, so we wanted to conduct a dry run before we leave," he explained.

Mike stared at the technician, reacting more to his long curly hair and muttonchops than to what he had just conveyed to the confused group of men before him. "Say that in English," Mike told him.

Lieutenant Bosworth intervened. "We've placed some sensors out in the field, and we're going to test the reception values that we're able to pick up with the antenna on the blimp."

Master Sergeant Miller had heard enough. "So... You've *already* placed sensors out in my AO, and now you've strung a goddamn welcome sign up over the camp to pick them up?" he inquired.

"That's right," the technician confirmed, smiling, pushing his glasses up over his nose, seemingly anticipating approval.

"Let me make *myself* perfectly clear, Lieutenant," Miller interjected. "This geography here is known as a TAOR—*tactical area of responsibility*. It extends from the river all the way to the Cambodian border. Captain Shannahan and ODA-three-two-six own that piece of real estate. According to the highers at Mack-V, it's *our* responsibility, not the U.S. Navy's. Anything that comes into or goes out of the TAOR does so with *our* blessing and authority, *not yours*. Is that perfectly clear?" he asked Bosworth, eyes firmly focused for the response.

"I might remind you: You're standing on navy property right now," Bosworth replied.

"Wrong answer, Lieutenant," Sergeant Miller informed him, turning to the captain.

"Who's your commanding officer, Bosworth?" Mike inquired.

Bosworth just stared at him, reluctant to respond.

"Never mind," Mike told him. "I'll have *my* commander contact him directly. In the meantime, take that damn blimp down immediately, or I'll have my men shoot it down." He turned and walked out the door, his men close behind.

*   *   *

For the next six weeks, operations in the field intensified. The Mekong, as the commander of the Cambodian troops was fondly known, had finally returned from his lengthy rehabilitation in Vũng Tàu and reemerged with his able Cambodes as a potent adversary to anything that resembled a VC or NVA combatant. The tactic of subverting the CIDG field operations with alternate ambushes on their flanks proved an effective deterrent to the enemy's ability to move men and supplies through the Plain of Reeds. The Cambodes and the Carsons' kill ratio soared, an increase whose effect was a sudden intensification in enemy activity in their sister camp to the north. A-325, at Duc Huế, began to take a series of barrages of 82- and 120mm mortars, and in a twenty-minute interval during a single evening more than a hundred Russian 107mm Katyusha rockets rained down on that camp from the direction of Ba Thu. Mike regarded this as an effort to keep the camp pinned down and occupied while the bad guys moved their troops and supplies through the southern sector of the camp's AO.

Along with the successes of Mike's team in the field came an unexpected lull in enemy activity against it. The ambush sites quickly dried up, and the visual reconnaissance flights verified that the enemy had decided to take alternate routes to get their supplies to their brethren in-country.

Mike received the long-awaited letter from Rich, in which he learned that Major Aldridge had reassigned his friend to a unit operating out of Buôn Ma Thuột. He did some back-channel checking and discovered that that particular unit was, in fact, Command and Control South, a reconnaissance element of the secretive MACV SOG. He knew Rich would be running cross-border operations deep into Cambodia, performing a variety of top-secret missions. He envied his friend's assignment and yearned desperately to join him.

Instead, the captain continued to take his turn drudging through the endless swamps and tree squares in the field with the indig, slowly developing a deep, simmering resentment for the monotonous charade perpetrated by his LLDB counterparts. With their constant and highly justified doubt and suspicion about the motives of the Vietnamese Special Forces, the team exposed an elaborate system of premeditated corruption, carefully orchestrated and enforced with an element of fear directed at the camp strike force.

For example: Early one morning, the C-Team delivered several pallets of new uniforms and boots for the CIDG to wear to the field. Master Sergeant Miller directed each company to line up at the end of the airfield and pick out a uniform and pair of boots that fit. He found it curious that instead of putting the boots on and wearing them, they tied the boot strings together, threw them over their shoulders, and took them back to their compounds. Sensing something just wasn't right, Miller returned to the inner compound and scaled the tower for a better look at what might be occurring. He discovered that in each compound, the LLDB had set up a field desk, and as each man filed by, they either collected money from him or confiscated the man's boots and uniform. This blatant extortion proved to be a standard practice implemented by the Vietnamese cadre: reselling anything of value that the team had issued or given the indig, including the occasional pallets of Cokes flown in on special occasions.

The scope and extent of the exploitation far overwhelmed the captain's basic feelings of trust when his men discovered that the LLDB were routinely *ghosting* men through the pay line—that is, using imposters to collect pay for deserters and KIA. The cadre would also send the same men through several times, using a different name each time, and then force the Sidge to turn the money over to them. Sergeant Miller put a stop to that practice by having each man dip his finger in indelible ink after receiving his pay. The LLDB quickly countered by imposing a *security tax* on each man and his family, insisting it be paid directly to the LLDB.

Sergeant Miller attributed the cultural corruption to the arrogant French influence imposed on them during the numerous decades of colonial rule. The captain took it personally, however. He continued to mount the tower in his usual manner, but now he spent as much time watching what was going on inside the camp as he did monitoring the bayou beyond the wires. He eventually felt more like a warden than a noble guardian *patrón*.

One hot, lazy afternoon, just at the conclusion of *poc* time, he observed a young boy sliding a plywood cover off what looked like a buried Conex container hidden beside a sandbagged ammo bunker. The captain positioned his binoculars for a closer look and watched the teenager dip a large, green nylon net on a pole down into the shadowy hole and then pull out a dark mass of squirming creatures caught in the mesh. Mike focused the lens for a closer look and then swiftly straightened up in amazement. "Fuckin' rats!" he exclaimed.

He climbed down the ladder and headed straight for the dispensary. "*Bác sĩ!*" he yelled.

Braxton peered over from his hammock, a little confused from being awakened abruptly from his midday nap.

"You got any diesel in here?" the captain inquired, hastily looking around the empty beds.

"No sir," the *bác sĩ* replied, slipping out of the nylon netting.

"Well, I need your help. Get your shirt on, and come with me. You're not gonna believe this."

Braxton followed him out the door, buttoning his fatigue jacket as he watched the captain walk over to the airboat shed, pick up a five-gallon bucket of diesel fuel, and head toward the 327th compound. Confused by the intensity he saw in his team leader's gait, *Bác sĩ* hurried his pace to keep up.

Mike walked over to the edge of the ammo bunker and set the bucket down. He knelt down and brushed away the loosely strewn dirt, exposing the edge of a four-by-eight sheet of weathered plywood. "Get a load of this," he told Braxton as he lifted the lid.

"Jesus fuckin' Christ!" the *bác sĩ* exclaimed, peering down into the putrid mass of scrambling rats and excrement.

"They're fuckin' *breeding* them for the bounty!" the captain exclaimed.

Bác sĩ wasted no time, picking up the pail of diesel fuel and pouring it over the rebellious rodents below. The regiment of frenzied rats careened off the slick walls of the deep metal container, leapfrogging each other in pyramid fashion, desperately trying to escape the dense malodorous fumes. "This is a fuckin' epidemic just waiting to happen!" he said. "Back up, *Đại úy*. The friggin' vapors could explode."

Mike looked over at the ammo bunker and the blast barrier erected in front of it. Braxton noticed it as well and offered his assurances. "Don't worry, Captain. It'll take more than this to set *that* off."

Mike turned to see a small crowd of indig gathering outside their hooches. Their irritated expressions indicated that he hadn't made any new friends this day. He watched Braxton ignite the diesel fuel, sending a thick black plume of smoke tumbling up into the breathless air. The *bác sĩ* covered his nose and mouth with his shirt as the distinct odor of singed hair and burning flesh purged the fresh air in his lungs. The din of squeals was horrific. "Wonder what they'll come up with next?" Braxton asked the captain as they watched the critters fry.

A sharp vibration of automatic weapons fire echoed loudly from the inner compound. The captain and Sergeant Braxton knelt to the ground as the onlookers of the rodenticide scurried back inside their hooches. Mike unsnapped the loop on his .45 and drew it from his shoulder holster, looking over to *Bác sĩ*, who was running back toward the dispensary.

Loud shouts and a lone woman screaming led Mike around the guard shack and into the inner confines of the camp. He immediately saw the frantic woman lifting the young girl off the dusty ground, the child's arm bloodied and dangling by several threads of muscle as it flopped by her mother's side. He saw the arm lazily flop back and forth while she cradled her child, dropping to her knees and screaming in horror. He looked to his right and saw a man standing inside the doors of an open Conex container, desperately trying to insert another magazine into the M16 in his hands. As Mike leveled his .45 at the apparent shooter, the LLDB sergeant stepped from behind the open door and delivered three point-blank shots from his .38, knocking the man back into the container, blood spewing freely from the final head shot.

The captain quickly surveyed the scene, looking for any more hostiles he might encounter. Several members of the team converged on the site, armed and confused by what had just happened in the midday afternoon, just outside the team house.

Mike went over to the young girl and her wailing mother. As a small crowd began to gather, he turned and told Sergeant Watson to lock down the inner compound. *Bác sĩ* slid in next to the mother, opened his aid pouch, and pulled out a pair of hemostats. "Severed her humeral artery. Got to stop the bleeding," he told anyone who was listening. "Get my tourniquet out of the bag," he instructed Mike. "I've got to clamp off this bleeder," he said, tending to the limp child, still resting in her mother's arms.

Bác sĩ found the artery and clamped it shut. Then he took the tourniquet from the captain and tightened it around the young girl's arm. "Get these people out of here," he demanded, turning his attention now to the apparent bullet wound in her cheek. "I'm gonna' have to bag her, *Đại úy*. Here, hold this," he told him, handing the dangling arm to the captain.

Mike took a closer look at the child and realized that she was his favorite "China doll," the one who camped out with the other kids at the front door of the team house. She was always wearing two pink bows in her tiny pony tails, clapping her dainty hands together, smiling in glee whenever he walked out the door. Now he gazed at the nearly severed arm in his hand, the petite fingers extended lifelessly with the palm outstretched, just as he had seen it many times before, excitedly accepting the pieces of candy he enjoyed giving her. He drew her image to him, recalling all the times she would hug his leg after he'd given her a treat, how she was always thanking him *before* tasting the sweets.

"What needs to happen here, Doc?" he asked Braxton.

"Doesn't look like we can save her arm, but she definitely needs a vascular surgeon at the very least. They've got a good one at the Twelfth Evac in Củ Chi."

Mike turned to see which of his men were still there. "Sergeant McDonald," he ordered the new commo man, "get on the horn and get me a medevac in here from the Twenty-fifth, ASAP."

"They may not come if they know she's VN," *Bác sĩ* reminded him.

"Tell them we have a friendly-fire incident!" Mike shouted at McDonald, already on his way to the commo bunker. "That's all they need to know!"

The mother continued to sob as she stroked the blood-soaked hair of her limp daughter. Braxton stayed busy securing the IV he'd inserted and continuing to make sure her airway was clear.

"What the fuck happened here?" the captain asked Thiệu, who was jabbering away with several of the LLDB.

"He get *beaucoup* drunk last night," the interpreter began, pointing to the dead man in the container. "He make fight with everybody, so *Trung sĩ* Nguyễn put him in box and lock door. When *trung sĩ* open door, he start shooting at everybody. Hit little girl."

Mike turned and looked inside the sandbagged container. He looked at the stacks of M16s, M14s, and other weapons stored on wooden racks. "That's a fuckin' weapons bunker. What the fuck did he put him in there for?" he asked incredulously.

"He no think ammo there… Ammo in another bunker."

Mike turned and stared at Sergeant Nguyễn. "Stupid fuckin' bastard," he said to his face. "Your scrawny butt sucks canal water, shit-for-brains!"

"Medevac's on its way, Captain," McDonald reported.

"Let's get her over to the pad," *Bác sĩ* told them. He reached over and gently took the child from her mother's arms. "Tell her we're taking her to Củ Chi to see the doctors, Thiệu. Tell her she can come with us, but we need to get them over to the chopper pad for the medevac coming in."

Mike reached down and picked up Braxton's medical bag. As they hurried to the boat, the *bác sĩ* requested permission to accompany mother and daughter up to Củ Chi. "I've got to keep her airway clear, sir. It'll also give me a chance to scrounge up some supplies I need from the Twenty-fifth

Medical Battalion and some of the good stuff from the Twelfth Evac. I'll
be back in the morning," he assured the captain.

"Just get her there. Once that's done, do your thing."

"Thanks, Captain," Braxton said as he stepped down into the boat
with his precious cargo.

Mike helped the mother down into the boat and handed her the *bác
sĩ's* medical bag. He watched the chopper flaring rapidly over the river and
sliding quickly onto the landing pad, which was obscured in a cloud of red
smoke. The medic jumped out and helped Braxton put the young girl on
a stretcher, then lifted her up with the IV still attached to her other arm.
With all on board, the chopper quickly lifted off the pad before "Pierre"
had time to slide a round down his irritating tube. Mike watched his
sergeant arguing with the medevac's crew chief as they rotated left and
headed back to Củ Chi.

The captain turned to see *Trung sĩ* Nguyễn staring back at him from
the gate to the airboat shed. "You are one worthless motherfucker!" he
yelled, pointing directly at the Vietnamese sergeant. "*Mông của bạn xin
lỗi* sucks *kênh nước!*" he added, the only English being the word *sucks*.

* * *

CHAPTER THIRTY-FIVE

MIKE WATCHED THE CAMP BUNKERS whizzing by as the Huey sprinted along the still canal searching for altitude, the anxious door gunner laying suppressive fire from his M60 along the riverbank just in case the notorious "Pierre" was on the prowl. Firm G-forces pinned him to his seat as the pilot engaged the collective, elevating the bird in a steep, banking climb to relative safety.

Mike reached up and took the headset off the overhead clip, adjusting the soft earphones as the welcome voice of the DJ on the Armed Forces Network taunted the troops before announcing the next song. The chill air flowed freely through the crew compartment, and as he gazed out toward the Fence, the captain found himself squinting, desperately looking for any signs of Charlie in the distant haze. The chopper carved its way north above the caramel-tinted river and the lush, thick palms and other trees that lined its narrowing banks. As the chopper leveled off high above the wasteland, the captain keyed the mike to find out the flight time from the pilot. "How long to Tây Ninh?" he asked, looking up front, into the cockpit.

"Not long, Cap'n. About thirty mikes," the pilot responded, cutting through the lively Zeppelin tune. "Gotta drop some mail off for your guys on Núi Bà Đen on the way in."

"Roger that," Mike replied, looking forward to getting a close look at the mysterious radio relay site perched atop South Vietnam's only mountain.

He looked out the door on the right, recognizing the tree patterns of the rectangular rubber plantation that encompassed a majority of the infamous "War Zone Charlie." The height of their flight plan provided him with a panoramic view of the vast countryside, neatly proportioned with green rice fields and brown-tinted hamlets. An occasional dusty red road connected the villages while scattered pockets of dark-bermed bomb craters verified the only evidence of war in the seemingly idyllic farmlands below.

The opening refrain from one of his favorite songs beat through the headset, encouraging him to groove with the beat as he started tapping his toes. The energetic tempo soon melded with the heavy strokes of the beating blades as Duane Eddy hit the first chord on his guitar solo. Mike smiled broadly as he began to mimic the instrumental melody of "Ghost Riders in the Sky." He quickly slipped out of his webbed seat, sat down on the floor, and slid over to the open door. He dropped his legs out, letting his boots dangle in the rush of wind flowing just above the skids. He looked over to the door gunner, who was smiling in approval at the captain's impetuous antics, nodding his helmet in unison with the beat of the pounding drums.

Fresh adrenaline rushed through Mike's veins, and the thin, cool air filled his lungs with a spirited concoction of bravado as he slapped his hands on the edge of the door, keeping in tempo with the inspiring tune. *I am that ghost rider,* he told himself. *This is bitchin' boss!* he thought, feeling motivated enough to lead the charge on the whole NVA army if need be.

His spirits soared, high in the light blue sky, with nothing between him and mother earth except his youthful exuberance, cascading freely at three thousand feet and holding. *There's nothing like a rookie team leader at three thousand feet and thirty klicks from camp,* he assured himself, suppressing the compelling instinct to launch himself out into the beckoning breeze, soaring wickedly through the clouds as he had done so many times in Tölz. He eased his boots down on the skid, grabbed hold of the up-strut, and swung himself out, soulfully caressing the chill airstream blasting in his contorted face.

"I heard you guys were a bunch of crazy mothers!" the gunner broke in, shaking his head as the young captain challenged the hundred-knot wind.

Mike let the gale force blow him back against the open door, then eased himself back into the crew compartment and settled back in. He turned to see the gunner tapping his helmet with his finger. "Sorry... Musta' lost my head," the captain said. "I've been outa' town, and they don't let me outa' the cage too often anyway."

He realized it had been months since he had had the opportunity to just be himself, an individual with basic instincts and quirky larks, out from the constant scrutiny of subordinates and peers, finally oblivious to the heavy burdens he bore. His mindset ricocheted through the past four years, finally settling back in Kingsville with Jim hunting at his side. Duane strummed the final chords to his melody, gradually easing the young warrior back down into the reality he currently managed, some days better than others.

Now he focused on the tree-lined mountain in the distance beyond, which crept ever closer as the chopper drifted through the scant ripples of developing clouds. His mood sobered, quelled in part by the lament-filled, soulful ballad, with Marvin Gaye's smooth voice reminding him that "war is not the answer," a notion his conscience was just beginning to debate.

The door gunner pointed ahead, and Mike watched the chopper maneuver in the strong head winds, watched it jockey for position over the metal landing pad, which was surrounded by jagged boulders and sandbagged bunkers. He read the large sign posted with the Twenty-fifth Infantry Division's tropical-lightning patch, declaring that they were welcome, courtesy of the First Brigade Lancers of that division. As he surveyed the cloudy summit, he was reminded of a medieval fortress, accented by bunkers encased in huge rock formations, with anachronistic radio towers and antennas extending skyward like giant metallic porcupine quills impaling the granite terrain. A lanky redheaded soldier ran over to the chopper while the gunner released his seat belt and dragged the large canvas bag to the door. He pushed while the soldier pulled, and finally the heavy bag slipped out the door and onto the metal pad below.

"What's in there?" Mike asked. "Looks like a month's worth of movies."

"Don't need them, Captain," the gunner told him. "They've got TV up here," he said, pointing to the large, layered antenna pointing receptively toward Saigon.

"Must be nice," Mike replied, looking up at the pagoda-shaped building faintly visible on the summit.

The soldier struggled at dragging the large bag off the perforated pad, and the pilot revved up the turbines to lift off as the crosswinds swirled and the heavy downdrafts collided, creating a collective effort to keep the bird captive in the grips of the vengeful mountain. Mike heard that they had lost twenty-three men in a sapper attack back in May of the previous year, and the stories circulated that their souls still lurked among the cavernous and war-scarred boulders still harboring their blood. The fickle Black Virgin finally released her death grip on the struggling chopper as the pilot lifted her off to a forceful hover, then pressed the cyclic forward as the blue sky greeted their grateful return. The chopper turned to the side, slipping away from the mountain fortress, easing its nose down toward the distant runway, clearly visible in the built-up area below.

"That's the Cao Đài Monastery down there on the left, Captain," the pilot told him, directing his attention to the opulent structure with decorative towers and ornamental gold trim.

"What are they, Buddhists?"

"Don't know," he replied. "Just know Charlie doesn't mess with them."

"That's your B-Detachment compound there, next to the airfield," the copilot added.

Mike felt the blistering heat envelop the crew compartment as the chopper flew along the runway, then slipped to the left and settled down by a Cobra hunter-killer team parked next to the fuel dump. He stepped down from the Huey, pulled his beret out of his trouser pocket, and once it was in place, waved to the pilots, thanking them for the ride. He threw his web gear over his shoulder and carried his M16 by the handle as he walked toward the guard shack at the end of the runway.

"Where's the head shack?" he asked the Vietnamese guard.

The man didn't reply, but he pointed in a general direction down the dusty road inside the wire. Mike noticed the whitewashed cement bunker with the colorful invitation: *Welcome to B-32 Tay Ninh. Home of the Professionals.* He followed the narrow road and soon came upon a long wooden building with the headquarters' logo arched above the door.

"I'm Captain Shannahan from Three-two-six Trà Cú," he told the sergeant behind the cluttered metal desk. "I'm here for the commanders' meeting."

"That's been put on hold," the busy sergeant told him. "A-Three-two-two Katum got hit last night and is still receiving heavy rocket and mortar barrages from across the Fence. The ol' man's in the commo bunker now, directing the reaction forces. Looks like you're gonna have to cool your heels for a skosh, Captain."

"Got any hot showers anywhere?"

"Reed, show the captain where the billets and showers are," he told the clerk. Then to Mike: "Most of the team leaders are in the club on the other side of the volleyball pit. Hope you brought your wallet with you."

Mike followed the spec-four down the sidewalk through a neatly manicured grove of trees with a line of wooden cabins nestled in the scant shade beneath.

"Take any one that's empty," the clerk told him. "The showers and latrine are over there." He pointed to a large, open-sided structure, with a tin roof covering the stalls and sinks on the concrete slab.

Mike opened the screen door and walked over to the neatly made bed. He pressed his hand down on the thin mattress and smiled. *Clean sheets,* he told himself as he picked up the pillow and sniffed the casing. *Bet they couldn't find any river water to wash 'em in around here.*

He unbuckled his web gear and draped it over the back of the chair in front of the small desk. He wasted no time in getting out of his jungle fatigues. He grabbed the neatly folded towel on the desk and headed straight for the showers. He was elated to see two knobs on the shower wall, and he turned the left one on as far as it would go. Within seconds, steamy vapors enveloped the shower stall, washing away the months of grime and grit embedded in the young man's fingernails and toes. He stood there, transfixed by the soothing water softening his calluses, gently massaging his shoulders and back, turning his skin a rosy pale. He lingered until he felt a little guilty, disgusted with himself for not finding a bar of soap to finalize his transformation. He reached over and turned the hot water down, cooling his body as the water ran cold. He grabbed his towel and headed back to the hooch, feeling refreshed and clean but a little lightheaded from the experience. He turned on the small black fan and lay down naked on the clean white sheets. Within seconds, he drifted off to sleep as the flowing breeze teased his limp, damp body.

"Đại úy... Đại úy...," the soft voice uttered.

Mike stirred, confused about where he was and the strange voice interrupting his shallow sleep. He opened his eyes to see a young woman standing over him, her long, petite fingers gingerly touching his chest.

"Đại úy," she repeated. "*Thiếu tá* Wilson send me."

"Major Wilson?" he asked, clearing his throat.

She shook her head yes, smiling at him as he abruptly sat up to shield his nakedness. She handed him the damp towel, and as he covered himself, she put her hand on his shoulder and motioned for him to lie down.

"*Thiếu tá* Wilson say give you numba'-one lubbing," she told him, picking up a bottle of lotion out of the straw basket she had placed on the desk.

"Rubbing?"

"Lubbing… You know, massage," she said and giggled. "You funny, *Đại úy.*"

"What's your name?" Mike inquired.

"You call me Co," she replied.

"I know you're a *co*," he said, using the generic Vietnamese term for any unmarried young woman. "But what's your name?"

"My name Co. Everybody call me Co."

"You sure you no VC?"

Co giggled again, her breasts jiggling just beneath the black silk blouse as she rubbed the lotion into her hands.

"Me no BC, *Đại úy*. BC numba' tan," she assured him. "You *beaucoup* funny, *Đại úy*," she repeated. Then she motioned him to lie on his stomach. "You loll obah now."

Mike felt her silk pants straddle his legs as she started applying a warm, soothing lotion to his shoulders, gently rubbing her soft palms in a circular motion, plying and stimulating his tight muscles until the soreness dissipated and the pleasure emerged. She ever so slowly worked her way down his back, and just before she reached his taut buttocks, he drifted back off into a pleasurable, trancelike sleep.

He continued to stir in and out, too relaxed to totally regain any true semblance of valid consciousness, in total submission to the touch of her magic fingers and the trail of ecstasy they conveyed. He felt her manipulating his toes, using slow, deliberate caresses as she elongated the weary muscles in the bottom of his feet. He remained captivated, entranced, eagerly anticipating the escalating essence of her enchanting spell.

Co gently rolled him over, reversing the course of her manipulation, deeply kneading his thighs as she worked her way back up his limp torso. Suddenly she stopped.

Mike stirred, abruptly anxious that she might be finished. He peeked down to see her unbuttoning her blouse, then watched her twirl her long black hair up into a bun as she slid a long ivory pin through it to keep it in place. She calmly slid off her blouse, exposing an exquisite display of femininity. She slowly bent over and rested her full breasts on Mike's eager thighs. He felt her welcome dark nipples tease his alert senses as she slid them up and down his inner thighs, the full warmth of her body clearly evident when she pulled back, allowing her breasts to cascade freely over his elastic legs. She slowly worked her way up, removing the towel as she skillfully manipulated her breasts over Mike's emerging manhood.

Oh, God, he thought. *I wonder if she's going to...*

He felt her warm hand begin to stroke him, slowly beckoning his libido to respond. She didn't have to wait long. When she was satisfied that he was fully stimulated, she teasingly used the caressing heat of her tongue to establish her dominance over the moment.

Oh, please don't stop! his thoughts pleaded.

Co sensed his desires, slipping her warm mouth over him while her tantalizing fingers found their way to his chest, tweaking his nipples as she continued to amaze him with her skillful mouth.

"I'll give you about an hour and a half to stop that," he finally muttered, knowing full well that his demise was imminent.

He reached down and cupped her intriguing breasts in his large hands, and as soon as the soft, magnificent feeling filtered through to his brain, he exploded in contractions that left him totally limp and fully exhausted. She continued to exploit his senses, adeptly applying herself until she was sure that all the vitality left in his body was fully exorcised.

"You like?" Co asked, smiling sweetly as the captain's eyes held transfixed to her beautifully contoured breasts.

"Are you out of your fuckin' mind?" he replied, unable to find a more suitable response. "Where'd you learn how to do that?"

"You no like?" she replied, a frown drawing down on her pretty face.

"No... no... I like! I like!" he said, concerned that she had misunderstood him.

She smiled and stood up. And with Mike still admiring the perfectly structured creature, she put her blouse back on and picked up her basket.

"You *beaucoup* pretty, *Đại úy*. I come see you again," she told him. She smiled and walked out the door.

Mike dropped his head back down on the pillow, totally spent of any vigor left in his body. *I guess that's why steam jobs and blow baths are so popular with the guys,* he surmised. *I wonder if I was supposed to pay her for that.*

He lay sprawled on the narrow bunk, semiconscious in a self-induced coma, intermingling his dream patterns with the distant sounds of chopper blades and small fixed-winged aircraft as they circled the runway nearby. His mind again spurned the horrid images of the two young girls, the VC prisoner and the "China doll" indig, images that had perpetually tormented his emerging nightmares for months. Again he rejected the subconscious indignity those images conveyed.

He awoke refreshed, stirred from his sleep by the boisterous shouts of men laughing and yelling somewhere within the compound. He put on his fatigues and, after a quick stop at the latrine, walked briskly down the sidewalk toward the club. Several men sat leisurely at a wooden picnic table, drinking beer as they yelled at the other shirtless men, who were aggressively playing volleyball in the sandy pit. It became readily apparent that this was more than just a friendly match, as the tall, muscular black player slammed the ball over the net to the raucous jubilation of his teammates.

Mike walked over and sat down on the bench, shaking hands with the spectators as they issued a series of insults to various players engaged in their own repertoire of verbal fisticuffs against the other team.

"You play, Captain?" Mike was asked.

"I have," he replied. "But that was in college, and I think they had rules in that game."

"We got rules! Nothin' like good ol' *jungle rules* to keep you on your toes, *Đại úy*," the burly sergeant told him. "There's some cold beer in the club," he added, pointing to the wooden double doors under the patio.

"Thanks. I think I'll get one," he replied, getting up and walking over to the long, wood-sided building. He stepped inside and was immediately embraced by the flow of chilled air. The bar in front of him was occupied by several officers, laughing and enjoying the camaraderie that was apparent in their tone. He noticed that several of them wore faded, wrinkled fatigues while others stood beside them with starched uniforms and polished boots.

"Shannahan! Get your butt over here!" a voice yelled from down the bar, drowning out the country and western melody that competed with the banter in the background.

He walked down the tall bar and noticed a blond-haired major with a wide grin on his face. "How'd you like the wax job?" the B-Team XO inquired, still smiling broadly as Mike approached.

"Wax job?"

"Don't tell me you've never had a wax job," he said in mock disbelief.

"Can't say I have, Major Wilson," Mike replied to the XO, trying to make the connection.

"Well, if you've got any wax left in your 'ears' after Co took care of you, you're a better man than me," Wilson said, laughing and slapping some of the other men on the back.

Mike blushed, a little embarrassed by the intimate revelation exposed by Major Wilson to the entire bar. He looked for a familiar face, but the only thing he had in common with them was their faded jungle fatigues and the same subdued sword-and-lightning patch they wore on their shoulders. He knew that would be enough, so he confidently slid in next to them and ordered a beer from the pretty *co* behind the opulently crafted teak bar.

"We rear-echelon types like to take care of you A-Team pukes when you finally decide to slip outa' the bush and rejoin civilized society," the major told him.

"Well, we certainly appreciate the sentiment and hospitality," Mike replied, holding the ice-cold beer up to toast in what he considered a noble gesture.

"Colonel Patterson has rescheduled the briefings for sixteen hundred in the head shed," the major related. "You've got time for a coupla' more before we have to head over."

The XO introduced him to the team leaders from his sister camps to the north, all situated along the border in obscure places that the regular army chose not to go to—places like Katum, more commonly referred to as *Kaboom*, and Ben Het, or *Been Hit*. Each remote Special Forces outpost had its own harrowing history, and the fact that they even still existed was a testament to the tenacity and courage of the men who valiantly defended them. The conversations focused on obscure parables of humor they had encountered, each more deviant and ridiculous than the last. Regardless of the situation—mortar attacks, ambushes, enemy sapper probes—they found an element of humor to rely on, which Mike knew they applied instinctively to buffer against the constant stress they each had endured. He knew, because he employed the same technique himself.

"Hell, every time we got hit with rockets or mortars, that damn monkey would start screamin' his fuckin' head off, then scurry up to the top of the fuckin' flagpole and start jackin' off!" one officer told them, providing a degree of levity that was well received.

Tales of terror or anecdotes of bravery and personal salutations went unspoken, for each team leader had endured similar encounters and their mission was still on-going. They all knew there would be time for accolades when, and if, they returned to "the world."

Major Wilson had just delivered the punch line to another of his off-color jokes when the B-Team commander entered the conference room. As everyone stood at attention, Mike was taken aback by the age and command presence that Lieutenant Colonel Patterson conveyed. His flowing white hair provided him with a distinguished, sagelike quality that was accented by the deep contours in his determined face. Mike had heard of the lieutenant colonel's World War Two exploits with Darby's Rangers as well as the numerous awards and decorations he'd earned in the icy mountains of Korea. The young captain now knew why Patterson's men had tagged him with the lofty demonstrative title Pappy.

Patterson looked around the room, then went up to each man and shook his hand, putting his other arm around their shoulders and hugging them with a brief display of concern. When he reached Mike, he shook his hand, put his other hand on top of his shoulder, and looked him sternly in the eyes. "I like what you're doing down there, Shannahan," he told him. "Continue to *press on*."

"Thank you, sir."

After taking his seat at the head of the table, Patterson directed Major Larson, the S2, to give the men the latest intelligence briefing regarding enemy activity relative to their area of operations. Each team leader then provided a briefback, either confirming or updating the assessment of the activity in his area, prompting a fluid discussion that followed with estimates of enemy troop strength and the projected intentions that each unit identified. The A-Team commanders continued to discuss tactics and personnel issues, supplies and fortifications, all elements critical to daily SF camp operations.

When the routine elements of the briefings seemed to be drawing to a conclusion, Pappy Patterson stood and addressed his men. "I can tell you there's something big dwelling on the horizon, gentlemen," he began. "But that's about it. It will be critical for each of you to ensure exactly where the base camps and assembly areas are across the Fence from your AOs." His eyes glimmered with the unexpected revelation. "Within the next month or two, I expect we will provide Sir Charles with a new and long-awaited dynamic to this war, and I anticipate it will shift the paradigm significantly."

What the fuck is a paradigm? Mike wondered.

With that said, Pappy concluded the briefing and directed the men back to the patio by the club, where the distinct aroma of grilling steaks tantalized their salivating palates. Other members of the B-Detachment were already lounging about, easily discernible in their starched fatigues, feasting on the large buffet of food that originally had been prepared just for the guests of honor from the outlying camps. The young captain mingled with the crowd and soon was introduced to the portly S4, Captain Thomas Meek, whom he suddenly realized was a classmate of his from OCS. Meek told him that two other classmates were with Group, stationed on A-Teams in the highlands and near the DMZ. The two captains enjoyed reminiscing about their time at Fort Benning, and Tom gave Mike a solemn update on more of their classmates who had made the *Army Times.*

The two friends meandered their way over to the club, drawn by the beat of drums from the live band ordered for the evening. Tom introduced Mike to more of the rear-echelon types, people who would be in a position to help him secure scarce equipment and special weapons, along with other favors based on his new elevated status as a *personal* friend of the S4. Mike marveled at the weight Tom had put on over the years, but he knew that the supply officers existed in a totally different environment from the rest of them, their secretive stature and contacts trumping the normal army chain of command.

Before long, the men began grumbling, complaining about the consistently off-key renditions played by the Filipino USO troupe. They had just finished totally destroying one of Elvis's popular ballads, and the S4 had heard enough. Captain Meek purposefully strode across the empty dance floor directly to the power box feeding the PA system and electric guitars. "You're fuckin' hurtin' my goddamn ears!" he shouted, pulling the power cords out of the box. "Turn on the stereo!" he yelled to the bartender.

Happy with Captain Meek's decision, the men clapped, whistled, and laughed, quite amused by the distraught looks on the Filipino musicians' faces.

"Come with me," Tom told Mike. "And bring your beer with you."

Together, they walked out of the club and up the dark dirt road leading to the main entrance to the compound. Just beyond the wire barrier that had been placed across the road at the guard shack, a throng of young women shouted and waved at the approaching officers, pleading to be escorted into the confines to provide their personal services to the wealthy Americans. "Đại úy! Đại úy!" they shouted at the captains, smiling and posing in their short skirts and dresses in the process. "Đại úy! I be lubbing you too many!"

Mike turned to Tom, an inquisitive expression on his face. "What's with all this *rubbing-you* shit?" he asked.

"*Loving you*," Tom replied. "They want you to get them in the gate to make *bang-bang* with you," he said, snickering. "Take your pick. You get only one, and she has to be checked out of the compound by twenty-two hundred," he informed him. "No excuses."

Mike surveyed the gaggle of young, anxious damsels staring back at him in paltry anticipation. Most of them appeared to be in their late teens, with a couple of older women clearly versed on seductive skills apparently acquired over years of mastering the world's oldest profession. He sensed that they all were there out of sheer desperation to help feed their families.

"Who's that tall one in the middle?" Mike asked, taken by the long slit up her Chinese skirt, exposing a well-toned leg in the process.

"That's Hairy Box," Tom told him.

"Hairy Box?"

"Yeah. She has a few pubes down there, so the guys call her Hairy Box."

"So the rest of them don't?"

"Not really…" he confessed, a slight shrug in his shoulders.

Mike stood there for a moment, gazing into the eyes of the assortment of young women before him. He then turned and patted his friend on the back. "I don't think so," he told him. "Not my type. But thanks anyway. I've got to be on the pad at oh-seven hundred to hitch a ride back to camp."

Mike started back down the road toward the club, leaving the commotion and women to Tom and the crowd of men walking up the road toward the gate.

* * *

CHAPTER THIRTY-SIX

MIKE FELT THE PELLETS OF hot sweat cascade off his nose and into the heavy sandbag he held open for Sergeant Miller. The scorching afternoon sun tinted the team sergeant's glossy pale skin, which was sopping with filthy sweat as he filled yet another burlap sandbag for the dilapidated mortar pit. The whole team had been taking turns putting on the finishing touches in repairing the last elements of decay within the inner compound, and the two shirtless men struggled in the stifling mid-afternoon heat as they formed the final top layer of sandbags around the 81mm mortar pit.

The sudden series of muffled explosions sent them scurrying over to the perimeter wall, climbing up on top of the bunkers to determine the source of the unusual disturbance. They watched the black PBR that was rounding the river's bend in the distance lurch abruptly in the water as the rocket skipped off the rolling wave and slammed violently into the bow. The fore gunner's twin .50s erupted amid the thick black haze, spewing a line of red tracers into the embankment only twenty-five meters to their port side.

Sergeant Miller bolted off the bunker, ran over to the tower, and scampered up the ladder to man the sandbagged .50-caliber machine gun mounted in the parapet. He quickly unleashed a steady volley of lead directed at the shoreline of the river, where the boat's tracers were cutting through the dense foliage. He swept his fifty's smoking muzzle back and forth to saturate the ambush site with a deadly lead curtain. The camp's attack siren slowly escalated to a high pitch, demanding that the troops man their bunkers.

"They're running east!" Miller yelled down, reloading another link of lead into the smoldering breach. Mike knew where the enemy was going, since he had himself memorized from the tower the outlying terrain and avenues of approach and escape across the river. He ran over to the team house, grabbed a flak jacket and his web gear, and headed down to the airboat house, his new CAR-15 assault rifle in tow.

"Get your gear and a radio and come with me!" he yelled to Sergeant Daniels, who was just running out of the commo bunker. "Tell the Mekong I need a squad of Bodes to meet me at the boathouse!" he yelled to Sergeant Watson, who was leaning out of the door to the airboat house. "And tell McDonald to get me some gunships on station out of Củ Chi!"

Mike got to the boat ramp just as a pair of PBRs raced past and up the canal, in their haste swamping several assault boats in their moorings. They careened off the muddy embankment at the mouth of the narrow canal and then banked sharply to the left as they sped off to the bend in the river, where their stricken comrades were fighting desperately to stay afloat in the volley of gunfire and rockets.

"They're gonna try to make it to that old trail to Bao Trai," Mike told Daniels as he threw the flak jacket into the boat. "We just need to get across the river and set up a *hasty* along that trail," he said, using the term for makeshift ambush. "Then we'll give 'em a taste of their own medicine."

A large group of the Cambodian strikers ran down the ramp, snapping up their web gear and looking anxious to get into the fight. Mike directed them to three of the functional assault boats. Then he reached back, cranked up the outboard, and headed out of the canal and into the river. He sped directly across the swift-moving water, glancing over to see the two PBRs pivoting sharply in their wake as they laid down a steady stream of .50-caliber machine-gun fire and 40mm grenades to blanket the shore and the thick, clustered tree line beyond.

The captain steered the boat carefully up the shallow murky ditch paralleling the trail and beached the craft in the tall muddy reeds that blocked the enemy's path nearly three hundred meters past the river. He signaled for the men to follow him as he crept through the thick reeds along the edge of the path for another two hundred meters. Peering up and over the elevated trail, he watched for any movement along the low berms separating the abandoned rice fields to the west. He didn't have to wait long.

"Wait till they all get out of the paddy trail before you open up," he told Sergeant Daniels. "Tell the tail gunner to cut loose when the last one steps up on the berm."

He motioned for two of the Bodes to move farther up the concealed reed line to provide security and to cut down any one who made it through the kill zone. He peered back up over the bank, counting at least twelve figures clad in black shorts and sandals scurrying out of the low-lying tree line and onto the pathway between the open fields, running directly toward Mike and his men, carrying empty B-40 rocket launchers and AK-47s, awkwardly hunched over to conceal their retreat.

Sporadic gunfire still echoed from the bend in the river, and Mike could hear the distinct churning of chopper blades in the distance. But he focused on the lead enemy runner, who was smiling broadly as he carefully picked his steps on the dirt-swollen berm. The pathway seemed clearly familiar to the runner, and Mike convinced himself that this group was a local VC squad from the village of Bao Trai, just a kilometer up the trail toward Củ Chi.

The captain quietly slipped the selector switch to full automatic and laid two magazines on the grass in front of him. He took a deep breath as the enemy lead runner jumped up to the trail and then sprinted directly for them as they lay waiting, barely concealed in the tall reeds to the runner's right. Mike waited anxiously for the last man, the one carrying the rocket launcher, to span the rise when he heard the tail gunner open up with his M16.

An explosion of gunfire erupted, with bodies careening through the pebble-laced dirt, face first as they lost control of their movement, some blasted backward as their bodies were torn to shreds. Mike found himself taking short bursts, directing a series of shots into their chests, aiming for the heart as he watched the enemy crumble like detached puppets. The two Cambodes he sent forward raced back down the trail, firing with full automatic volleys into the dead and twitching near-dead strewn in the kill zone before them. With the enemy completely decimated, the Cambodes moved quickly through the blood-soaked bodies, casually anointing finishing rounds into any trembling movement they saw.

Mike stepped up out of the ditch and surveyed the aftermath of their vengeance, the enemy once more mystically transformed into the bland category he preferred: enemy KIA. He walked over to where Sergeant Daniels was standing and told him to have the gunships make a strafing and rocket run in the thick vegetation beyond the tree line and to check whether any more bad guys were in the grove spanning the shore line.

"Have a coupla' the Bodes search the bodies for any documents, and police up the weapons before they head back to camp," Mike told Daniels. "I'm sure someone from the village will be down here tonight to retrieve the bodies."

He motioned to the men who had boated over with him. He had them pick the boat up out of the muddy stream and carry it back to deeper water, where they boarded and made their way back across the river to the camp.

"Navy had two KIA and three wounded, Captain," Sergeant Miller told him as he stepped out of the boat, dragging the flak jacket he had forgotten to put on.

Mike shook his head, still amazed at the audacity of the enemy to mount an ambush so close to camp and in broad daylight. "Well, we made 'em pay for it this time, and that's all I've got to say about that."

He looked overhead, watching the Dust Off chopper slowing to a flare as it eased its way down to the runway next to the navy compound.

"Braxton went down there to see if he could help," Miller told him, a stern look on his perplexed face. "Next time something like that happens, Đại úy, you might consider having some of the men take point on any reaction force," he advised him, a slight rise in his brow.

"Point taken, Top, no pun intended. Next time I'll jump up and man the fifty, and you can get out there and crawl around with the snakes," he replied, smiling as he unslung his wet web gear. "I knew where they were headed, and I didn't have time to write up an ops order. If I would have hesitated, they would have made it up the trail and been long gone."

"We already lost one team leader leading the charge, and I don't plan on having to explain to Pappy how I let another one get his ass out in front."

"I think I'm getting that warm fuzzy feeling all over again, Top," Mike replied. "Seriously, I get it. Just don't hug me up. I feel the same way toward every man on the team."

Sergeant Miller stared at him, forcing home the gist of his message to the young captain. Then: "We need to get down there and pay our respects to those fine young men who died here today, Captain."

"I suggest we get our shirts on and get the rest of the team to join us, then," the captain replied, walking up the embankment and heading for the team house.

He unlaced his wet boots and threw his mud-soaked trousers to the floor. He put on a clean set of fatigues and dry boots and met the rest of the team, waiting for him outside. Together, they walked down the long, crusted lane to the navy compound, toward the Dust Off chopper idling at the end of the runway.

Two olive-drab body bags lay zipped up on the ground with a bevy of sailors and several officers gathered solemnly around them. The captain and his men paused and took off their berets as Lieutenant Bosworth concluded his remarks, standing stoically over the bodies of his fallen men. They watched reverently as three sailors hoisted the bags onto the chopper floor, followed by several men assisting the three wounded up into the crew compartment of the medical chopper.

As the Huey lifted off, Lieutenant Bosworth strode briskly over to the captain and his men. "Why don't you have any men on the other side of that goddamn river?" he demanded. "That's the third boat this month that's been hit right around the fuckin' bend, just a thousand meters from your front door!"

The captain took offense to Bosworth's remarks, but he made an effort to maintain détente as he responded to the gruff inquiry. "We came to convey our respects to your men, Lieutenant. But to answer your question: It's not our AO. You're going to have to take that up with the commanding general of the Twenty-fifth Division in Cù Chi."

"That's bullshit," Bosworth contended.

"No, sir, that's army regulations. They have this thing about units operating in somebody else's AO."

"I heard you caught them. So how's that even possible if you can't operate over there?"

"I wouldn't say we *caught* them. And that wasn't an operation. That was a reaction force movement in response to an attack on U.S. personnel. We can react. We just can't *operate* over there."

"That's a crock of shit!" the lieutenant maintained as he pushed past the captain and his men and headed for his air-conditioned building inside the wire.

"Well, I'd say that went *really* well, Captain," Miller concluded, putting his beret back on and walking over to several of the navy NCOs gathered in a group beside them.

Mike noticed the damaged PBR, tethered to a sister boat being eased alongside the makeshift dock near the fuel dump. He walked over, trying not to breathe the foul kerosene odors, and he gazed down into the open deck awash in empty shell casings and dark swirls of thick, red blood. Two gaping holes with black cordite smears trimmed the open blast sites just above the water line. *There's nowhere to hide in those things,* he told himself, surveying the shattered cockpit and bullet-ridden hull. *Their only protection is their flak jackets and helmets,* he concluded, admiring the true, unbridled courage those men displayed daily in taking to the water in those floating death traps. "Like shooting ducks on a pond," he lamented.

Mike walked alone back up toward the team house, his mind calculating the impact of the day's events on his soul. He was gratified that the body bags had been zipped before he got there. He didn't want to see the faces of men he might recognize. He would never be able to discount their humanity the way he could with Sir Charles. These sailors were, after all, an extension of him. They were his countrymen, his brothers.

As he ambled back up the lane, hands in his pockets, nurturing regret in his heart, he noticed the small group of children hesitate, then step back out of his way. He concluded that they sensed a degree of despair in his manner. They all were reluctant to engage him as they normally did. Some had their tiny hands to their mouths, a sad expression draped over their innocent faces.

Mike stepped up into the quiet team house and headed down the hall to his room. Just as he turned into his doorway, Sergeant McDonald yelled down the hallway. "Captain, just got an urgent message from the C-Team. They want the results of the leech repellant test, sir, and they say 'Negative' is not an acceptable answer."

Mike stuck his head out into the hallway and replied. "Then tell them to go fuck themselves!"

He thought for a moment and then stepped out into the dark hallway. "Strike that last one, McDonald. Just tell them that the leech repellant really worked great. And tell them to send us a shitload of fuckin' elephant repellent, 'cause we don't have any of those motherfuckers either!"

Fuckin' idiots, he reassured himself.

Alone in his room, Mike leaned back on his musty pillow, one boot resting on the metal bed frame at his foot, the other on the floor. Instinctively, his churning mind rewound the event cycle and allowed his senses to catch up with what had actually just transpired.

He stared up at the loose tin roofing and the tips of rusty nails that jutted past the wooden cross beams that held them in place—anything to distract himself from the inevitable reconciliation he dreaded to face once it was able to penetrate the barriers harboring his soul. *Who built this hellhole in the first place?* he wondered. *The only thing keeping it together is the fuckin' termites holding hands.*

He fought the images demanding discharge from his subconscious, the stark realities that would reshape his values, consequences and events that would change his life. *I just killed human beings today,* he finally admitted.

He felt relieved that he took no pleasure in it, but still he struggled with the concept and how his God would perceive him after breaking one of His Commandments. He rechecked his value system, seriously debating if he needed to justify his actions to himself or to his Maker. He scrutinized the various scenarios that had led up to the event and then finally selected one that enabled him to make peace with himself, confident that his actions were, indeed, *honorable.* "Guess this is what they mean by *gut check,*" he said aloud.

It was only then, when he finally had unleashed the veiled, shadowy concept of Guilt, a concept he wasn't equipped to deal with, nor with the scope of its associated consequences. He realized that as long as he continued to dehumanize his enemy, he could avoid dealing with that particular soul-eroding emotion, at least for the time being. "I just wish Denny were here to tell me to *just shut the fuck up.*"

He sat up on the squeaky bunk, the unpleasant scent of dried swamp water and gunpowder still clinging to his clammy skin. As he reached down to unlace his jungle boots, the tremor caught his eye. He placed both hands palms down in front of him, verifying the slight vibration in both hands. He turned them over to see if that would calm them down, only to discover that it made them shake with greater fervor. *So much for any chance of ever becoming a surgeon,* he told himself, not really concerned such a career lay anywhere in his future.

The escalating pitter-patter of heavy raindrops careening off the rusting tin announced the arrival of a violent torrential storm, sharply accented with dazzling lightning flashes and rumbling, howitzerlike crashes of thunder. Mike slowly turned and watched the intense rain transform the dust-caked compound into a fast-moving tsunami of loose debris and mud, the deep gullies overflowing as the dark, churning water rushed toward the storm drains funneling the filth into the rising canal.

The sudden rush of wind propelled the heavy sheets of rain up under the overhang and through the rotting eaves, saturating the captain's tiny room with a dampening spray of misty rainwater.

"Hope you brought your rubber booties with you, *Đại úy,*" Sergeant Watson said, poking his head around the doorway. "The 'Go to hell' monsoon's here, and you don't have to worry about seeing the sun for at least a week or so. Better get used to it. The team house is going to take a mud bath."

"Yeah, that's all we need around here. More fuckin' water," Mike replied. He took off his clothes and draped them on the end of his bunk, grabbing the small green towel hanging on the wall and wrapping it around his waist. He picked up his soap, slid on his shower tongs, and headed down the dark hallway toward the makeshift shower stall. He stood at the doorway for a brief moment. Then he stepped outside into the small covered patio and the entrance to the commo bunker.

As he stood there, the dense curtain of rain methodically obscured the diminishing limits of visibility. Bunkers had disappeared, along with the tall, vague image of the observation tower, just thirty meters in front of him. He suddenly felt isolated—but not entirely, not spiritually. Impulsively, he hung his towel on a loose nail and stepped out into the soaking deluge. He stared up into the dark, ominous heavens and squinted repeatedly as the large drops of cleansing water baptized his body, inflicting a constant series of penance in the process as the sting of the wind-driven rain kept cadence with his silent pleas of *mea culpa. My God, I am heartily sorry for having offended Thee...*

He stood with his arms outstretched, allowing the heavenly flow to anoint him completely, cleansing his body and soul with absolution, purging the element of doubt that had tarnished the faith in his true worth. He felt intimately assured that his Lord could see the true nature and motivation of his intent, that he relied on His infinite wisdom and His clear vision to direct his soul. Having endured his first baptism under fire, he embraced the renewal of his worth.

*   *   *

The incessant rains inundated the plains and continued for weeks, elevating the water table to the point where only the large tree squares and the highest man-made berms emerged above the vast lake that the monsoon had created. In spite of the relentless typhoon conditions pounding the camp, the conflicted, weary men continued to press on with their mission: to deny enemy infiltration from the Cambodian border to the Vàm Cỏ Đông River.

The rising water enabled Sir Charles to abandon his traditional routes and take advantage of the low visibility and lack of air reconnaissance resulting from the impenetrable cloud cover. The bad guys altered their tactics to navigate off the winding, narrow streams and take a more direct route to the river, cutting their exposure time in half.

But the rising water helped the good guys as well. With the airboats able to traverse across the plains at will, the captain and the team continued to conduct lightning strikes into areas that had been inaccessible prior to the monsoon season. They could now cover a large area of terrain in a short period of time, taking full advantage of the forty-mile-an-hour speed the airboats could maintain as they raced across the soggy plains at full throttle. With the visibility consistently at less than fifty yards, the strikers were able to run up on the enemy sampan convoys and run them over before a shot was fired, inflicting terror and termination in their wake.

The captain also continued to take his turn operating with the CIDG in the field, a task he performed despite his mounting contempt for his corrupt counterparts who had no interest in finding or defeating the enemy. The arduous jaunts into the waterlogged playpen began to take a toll on his mental and physical stature. The constant intake of contaminated water resulted in his developing a persistent case of diarrhea, coupled with the inevitable weight loss that came with his paltry diet. He toiled through the waist-deep marshes for days on end, learning how to harvest the scarce edible plants and vegetation, begrudgingly cultivating a newly tolerated interest in the culinary aspects of tabasco-infused, Asian reptilian cuisine.

Rather than trying to locate and engage the enemy, the main priority of the day was to find some elevated area where they could at least heat their meals and keep their heads out of the water when they set up their nightly perimeters.

In spite of the hardships the team endured, Mike knew that the operations still provided a value to the overall mission. As long as Charlie knew where the CIDG troops were, he would make every attempt to go around them. Right into the deadly clutches of the vengeful Cambodes and Carsons.

*   *   *

CHAPTER THIRTY-SEVEN

RICH GAZED INTO THE SMALL mirror and tidied up the oblique pattern of dark greasepaint that concealed the tint and contours of his distinct Caucasian features. He carefully tied the olive-green cotton cravat covering his dark, bushy hair, which gave him the appearance of a modern-day Apache warrior. He took one last look. Then he smiled and sat down on the small bunk in the cluttered room, meticulously slid the vintage canvas leggings over his boots and pants legs, and snugly cinched them up. He slung the AK-47 around his neck and picked up his ammo pouches and bulging rucksack before heading out the door to the waiting truck and the remainder of his team.

They had spent the preceding two weeks together running training missions out of an isolated A-Team near Bu Đóp, exercises designed to enable the men to integrate their mission skills and develop the necessary tactical awareness to survive as a team. They had meticulously rehearsed immediate-action drills, a lifesaving technique designed to let them break contact with the enemy and elude capture long enough to be extracted from the target area. The team had perfected their nonverbal communication signals and had worked on contingencies that could arise in the worst-case scenarios. As a well-honed clandestine unit, RT Knife was equipped to perform such unique tasks as area reconnaissance, wiretaps, and bomb damage assessments. They knew how to direct air strikes on troop and convoy concentrations on the Hồ Chí Minh Trail. Finally, they could do body snatches, a critical element in real-time intelligence. These training missions were crucial, not so much for the seasoned team but certainly for the newest member to assimilate into their ranks, Lieutenant Rich Mycoskie, code name Samson.

Lieutenant Mycoskie gazed down at the flat, rolling terrain below, sliding steadily beneath the skids of the camouflaged insertion chopper on its way to the LZ somewhere across the Fence. His team had departed the launch site at FOB Six near Quân Lợi just before dawn, headed for the "Salem House" sector of eastern Cambodia. Two army 195th AHC gunships had joined the insert package from their base in Bu Đốp, heavily laden with miniguns and rockets to provide cover for the RT during the treacherous insertion maneuver.

Rich looked over to his one-zero, a seasoned staff sergeant who had run top-secret reconnaissance missions with other teams in the northern as well as the central sectors along the Laotian and Cambodian borders. He recalled the eerie stories of the man's bravery and prowess under fire, and he felt confident that his first mission would be well orchestrated under Sergeant William "Bad Billy" Gibson's firm and battle-seasoned leadership. Rank served no purpose in their mission, and consistent with the Special Forces credo, the lieutenant fully embraced his role as the one-one on the six-man reconnaissance team. He remained eager to learn all he could from this savvy veteran, the insight and tricks of the trade that would enable him to confidently assume command of his own team sometime in the near future. Their mission today: Locate and map enemy marshaling areas and ammo storage dumps in the Dog's Face region of eastern Cambodia—that name, like Parrot's Beak, referring to the shape the border made there.

The lieutenant had completed the grueling SOG One-Zero School at Long Thành and had requested to be assigned to CCS, the top-secret recon company that operated in the cross-border areas of Cambodia under the auspices of a shadowy entity known only as MACV SOG, the Military Assistance Command, Vietnam—Studies and Observations Group. Rich had requested it because it was the same company that his brother Brad had operated with until that day in late September '66, when he was last seen charging the enemy, providing covering fire as his wounded team members lifted off the LZ in the last chopper out.

Gibson took the headset from the door gunner while Rich watched him conversing intently with the 195th pilot in front. "We're about ten out from the primary target area," the pilot was telling Gibson. "Once we drop your team off, we'll make at least two more dummy insertions to throw them off."

"Roger that."

"We'll be in orbit out of earshot, but it'll only take us about ten minutes to return to the LZ if you run into some real bad guys," the pilot assured Sergeant Gibson.

The sergeant turned and motioned Rich over to him. "We're ten minutes out from the primary LZ," he said, competing to be heard above the roar of the turbines. "I want you and two of the Cambodes out the port door, and I'll lead Cuong and Cau out the other with me. Once we get on the ground, head for the nearest tree line in front of the chopper, and stay put until I give the signal to move. Got it?"

"Roger that," Rich replied, snugging up the AK-47 ammo pouches strapped to his chest.

Without warning, the recently modified chopper sped down to treetop level, accelerating just above the green cauliflower-shaped treetops to their target ahead. Rich studied the uneven terrain, not used to the flat, prairielike features, which offered little cover and concealment for their stealthy movements. There were no mountainous ravines, no triple canopy, no thick forests to help them elude and hide from the enemy. The tall, grassy knolls surrounded sparse clumps of trees, with vast open areas dominating the landscape. *You gotta be shittin' me*, Rich whispered to himself.

He slid to the edge of the door, dangling his boots above the skids skirting the treetops just below them. His spirits soared as the adrenaline elevated his heart rate, keeping pace with the rapid retort of the racing rotor blades. He checked the magazine and safety on his AK. The tails of his cravat whipped in the firm breeze as he anxiously sat balanced on the edge of the door. "Finally! I'm finally here, after all these years, Brad," he proclaimed, drawing deep breaths, searching for any scent of his brother.

He turned and pointed to the two Cambodian team members perched anxiously behind him, both clad in captured NVA uniforms, complete ensembles with AK-47s and pith helmets. "You on me," he said, gesturing to the veteran warriors. Both Than and Do grinned slyly, more like starved predators, just waiting to kill something.

Rich gave them the thumbs-up sign and returned his attention to the golden, grassy plains and the short, sparse tree lines whizzing by. The bird abruptly flared, like a wild Canadian goose with its underbelly fully exposed, back-flapping desperately to cushion its landing.

Rich looked down, gauging the drop from the skid to the ground through the high-waving strands of thick, wheat-colored grass below. His adrenaline overtook his judgment, launching him out the door before his mind caught up with his eyes. The extra six feet he fell through the tall grass confounded his perception and confused his reflexes, resulting in an awkward impact, expelling absolutely all the air from his lungs. He desperately tried to recover as Than and Do looked down at him crumpled on his knees below them. They looked at each other, acknowledging that *they* should have taken the lead instead. *Won't try that one again,* Rich told himself as the pain from his deflated lungs sparred with the aching sting in his bruised knees.

The chopper rose up briefly, then sprinted across the grassy plain, parting the tall grass in its wake. It quickly vaulted up over the clumps of trees and disappeared in the distance. The team remained silent in the tree line next to the drop zone, listening intently as the choppers negotiated two additional dummy insertions. Then total silence.

Rich welcomed the lull in the action. He rubbed his aching knees, thankful there were no bones protruding where they weren't supposed to be. He listened for any movement around the LZ but heard nothing. Not even a bird acknowledged their arrival.

The team remained poised and attentive for several minutes until Gibson felt satisfied that the LZ had not been compromised. Only then did he order the men to the nearest clump of scrub trees to their west. "We're going to have to expand our intervals more than we're used to," he whispered. "Just don't lose sight of each other. It's not like operating up north, where we can rely on heavy cover."

Gibson sent the point man, Cau, west in a direction away from the rising sun. They moved slowly, and after only ten minutes, Cau returned to Gibson's side. "*Beaucoup* VC, *Trung sĩ,*" he told the sergeant, pointing in a northerly direction. Rich sensed a seriousness that he hadn't seen in Cau over the past two weeks. "We go now, *di di.*" he said, pointing back in the direction they had come from.

Sergeant Gibson wasn't totally convinced. He delayed any decision to return to the LZ. The open plains seemed vacant to him, with no sign of any activity in any direction. Not wanting to abort the mission, he continued to move.

Then suddenly, the one-zero stared down at the numerous fresh tracks in the dusty earth ahead of him. *"Beaucoup* VC!" Cau repeated, clearly agitated by Gibson's nonchalance.

Rich sensed movement in the distance. Suddenly, scores of NVA pith helmets emerged, bobbing above the waving clumps of grass, barely visible, even though they were heading directly for the team. He tapped Gibson on the shoulder and pointed toward them. The sergeant immediately set the team off in a southerly direction, instructing Rich and Cuong to prepare two-minute fuses on the Claymores they were leaving behind.

Within seconds, another sea of pith helmets blanketed the horizon, moving rapidly toward them from the south. "Lob some M-seventy-nine rounds downrange, and see if we can slow 'em down," Gibson ordered his trusty Cambodes.

As the first round slid through the small tube of the grenade launcher, Gibson radioed to the C&C chopper orbiting in the distance. The command-and-control element instructed them to return to the LZ and informed them that there were gunships inbound to cover their extraction. As the first round impacted in the distance, a spread volley of green tracers and sporadic rifle fire cracked over their heads. "Set the damn grass on fire!" Gibson yelled as he set the delayed-time fuse on another Claymore.

Rich pulled out a star-cluster flare and ignited it. Within seconds, the dry, highly combustible grassy plains were ablaze in thick white smoke, with racing flames searching for more tinder to burn. The other team members joined in the effort, firing their weapons and retreating in an orchestrated immediate-action drill to cover their hasty departure to the LZ. Claymores exploded behind them. The Cambodes paused only to send volley after volley of high-arching 40mm grenades toward the advancing enemy as the team sprinted through the tall grassy fields toward the pickup site.

They reached the LZ intact and quickly set up a perimeter. They set out more Claymores with contact-detonator wires, and they set another fire to cover their positions from the NVA, who were charging down on them from the north. As the active Claymores they had left behind detonated, pith helmets and body parts vaulted above the high grass and billowing white smoke in the distance.

Than raced out of the perimeter to the lone clump of trees to their north and placed two Claymores up against their trunks. As Than retreated back, Rich witnessed several AK rounds tear into his rucksack, ripping the fabric to shreds as he tumbled to the ground. Do didn't hesitate. He dropped his weapon and scampered out to retrieve his wounded friend, who was clawing slowly through the grass toward the perimeter.

Like a dreaded bird of prey, the first gunship announced its arrival, roaring in at treetop level and banking hard to the left and back into an upward spiral, with green tracers trailing close behind its menacing trek. Sergeant Gibson popped a green smoke canister and directed the gunships to hose down the advancing enemy from the south. A solid stream of rockets and miniguns halted that threat.

Gibson then directed the second gunship to administer the last rites to the larger enemy element, just emerging through the dense smoke to their north. Rich watched the solid stream of tracers tear through the wave of startled NVA, decimating their charge as the awesome force of the attack helicopters came to bear on their ranks. *That's what I call pee-bringers!* he thought to himself, amazed at the sheer volume of fire and explosions blanketing the battlefield.

Rich expended magazine after magazine, directing his fire at the enemy survivors, who continued their relentless determination to annihilate the small team that had so rudely entered their sacred domain. He watched a small group of NVA running to gain cover behind the small clump of trees to their north. In an instant, the two Claymores Than had placed there exploded in a fiery blast, evicting the prospective tenants with a bloody bath of steel and C-4.

The army slick raced in, abruptly settling in behind the desperate team. Sergeant Gibson frantically gestured for Lieutenant Mycoskie to help Do get Than to the open door as the door gunner blasted away at the advancing enemy to their south. The covering gunships continued to lay down a steady stream of suppressing fire, allowing the team just enough time to scamper aboard the chopper as it lifted off and nosed down to the east, crabbing left and right to avoid the steady stream of fire directed at their departure.

Rich peered back out the open door, amazed at the sheer number of enemy still swarming into the LZ, firing green tracers at them from the fading battlefield in their last desperate effort to exact some form of revenge for the devastation the team had left behind. Exhausted, he turned his attention to Than, who was grimacing in pain as Sergeant Gibson tore open his shirt to expose a through-and-through, gaping wound just below his collar bone. He quickly turned his head away, disgusted by the large amount of blood and torn flesh exposed so close to him.

"Give me your IV canister" Gibson told him, his hand outstretched and waiting. "His is all shot up."

Rich pulled it off his web gear, and without looking back over, he held it out for Gibson to retrieve. The sergeant noticed the grim expression on the lieutenant's face, and asked, "Are you hit, Lieutenant?"

"Negative," Rich replied. "Blood makes me queasy. Just one of those things."

Gibson grabbed the canister, and as he pried it open, he scolded the rookie member of the team. "Well, you better get used to it in a fuckin' hurry, sir. Get over here and find a vein while I get this compress on him."

Rich slid over to take the IV from Gibson. Than's warm blood saturated his pants as it seeped across the chopper floor. He clenched his teeth as he searched for a vein, oblivious to his comrade's life slipping away as he finally found his mark. Sergeant Gibson finished patching Than up and laid the wounded warrior's head in Do's lap as he took the headset from the hook on the strut. "I've got one hit pretty bad," he told the pilot. "Radio Bu Đóp and have them ready to receive an inbound."

Gibson slid back over to where the lieutenant was sitting, knees bent up as he stared out the door to the distant rice fields below.

"Does that shit happen all the time?" Rich asked Gibson, who was struggling to light a cigarette. The door gunner stood up and handed the sergeant a lit cigarette, smiling as he pumped his fist, still highly excited as his adrenaline tweaked his trembling nerves, bolstering the elements of euphoria still peaking in his young heart.

"Hell, Lieutenant, I've been shot outa' hotter LZs than that in my dreams," Gibson calmly told him. "Trouble is, we didn't accomplish our mission." He took a long drag off the short Lucky Strike. "Better wash that nasty ol' blood outa' your gear when you get back. And get some sleep. We'll be going back in tomorrow."

Rich leaned back up against the bulkhead, his mind processing the sergeant's last words. He looked over at the grinning door gunner and gestured for a cigarette. The young spec-four complied, tucking the lighter inside his flight jacket as he lit the cigarette.

"Thanks," Rich said. *Guess I'd better get used to a lot of things,* he concluded, leaning back against the bulkhead as the cigarette shook lazily in his hand. ********

CHAPTER THIRTY-EIGHT

T HE CAPTAIN SURVEYED THE LINE of eight blindfolded men squatting down in the mud path in front of him, trying to piece together the mysterious circumstances that had brought them together. He quickly concluded they were not NVA regulars, and their lack of firearms or any other type of combative implements led him to believe they weren't active VC either. He studied them closely: All were clad in black shorts and a variety of loose-fitting civilian shirts, and all were barefoot. The other striking element they had in common was that each of them was at least fifty years old.

Mike sat down on the elevated dirt berm on the edge of the tree square, laid his weapon across his lap, and called Thiệu over to him "Ask the one on the end what they were doing out here again," he ordered.

Thiệu walked over to the stone-faced elder and began to question him. Mike focused on the blood-soaked teeth of the trembling old man, his feeble cheek cut and swollen from the brutal pistol whipping delivered by the LLDB sergeant an hour earlier. The circumstances leading up to their capture confounded the captain, and he remained determined to sort it out.

"He say they come to find wood for fire," Thiệu reported.

"Ask him again about the water buffalo and what they were dragging behind them, and tell him not to say 'wood' again. Wood floats."

Thiệu complied. He continued to interrogate the reluctant peasant, whose pain was evident in his contorted gestures.

The captain had seen and heard enough. He told Thiệu to stand the prisoner up and bring him over. The interpreter reached down and grabbed the old man under his arm, easily lifting him up to his feet.

"Take off his blindfold, and untie his arms," Mike ordered.

Thiệu looked over to the captain, uncertain what to do.

"Take it off!" Mike repeated.

Thiệu stepped behind the bony elder, removed his blindfold, and untied his frail arms. The man stood, uneasily maintaining his balance as he looked tentatively around, confused by and anxious about his sudden emancipation. Thiệu walked him over to the captain and stood by to interpret. Mike looked the prisoner directly in the eyes as he questioned him, fixating on his dark pupils.

"Tell him to squat down, Thiệu," Mike began, "and tell him who I am." The interpreter complied, and the prisoner responded in Vietnamese.

"He say you too young to be *Đại úy*," Thiệu said as he crouched down in the mud.

The captain paused a moment. Then he got up and stood towering above the diminutive white-haired man stooped nervously below him. He raised his CAR-15 up across his chest and swiftly chambered a new round. The operating rod handle slammed home with a loud report, and the old man cowered as he dropped his head.

"And tell him he's too damn *old* to be out here in the middle of nowhere trying to bullshit somebody who bullshitted his way to where he is today, standing over *him* with a loaded weapon in his hands."

Thiệu relayed the message as the old man put his hands up to his face to wipe the small stream of blood oozing from the crook of his mouth. The captain drew his weapon down to his side and placed it up against the berm behind him. He reached back and took the plastic canteen off his pistol belt and squatted down in front of his captive. "Tell him to wash the blood out of his mouth and take a drink," he told Thiệu, holding the open canteen in front of the man's face.

Mike sat down in the wet mud in front of him and crossed his legs. He watched as the elder cautiously washed his mouth out and then handed the canteen back. Mike motioned for him to take a drink, refusing to accept the canteen until the man complied. The elder finally drew it to his drawn lips, eyes still transfixed on his captor, a suspicious tint in his gaze.

"Tell him that funky taste is just iodine," the captain told Thiệu. "It tastes like poison, but it won't actually kill him."

His thirst quenched, the prisoner slowly handed the canteen back. Mike took it, and without wiping off the spout, he casually took a long sip of water as well.

"Tell him I know he's not VC," Mike said, screwing the cap back on the canteen. "He looks like a farmer. Tell him my grandfather was a farmer, so I know what one looks like."

The captain took the man's hands, held them in front of him, and turned the palms up. He studied the numerous calluses and the hard, stringy nature of his firm forearms, concluding that his labor was of lifelong duration. "Ask him where his farm is," he ordered Thiệu.

"He no talk, Đại úy," the interpreter told him.

"Thiệu, you're the interpreter! Figure it out, or make up something, like you normally do. Just get my point across to him that I need some answers. Now!"

Thiệu relaxed his tone as he began to translate, sensing a different approach in the captain's interrogation, an approach he wasn't used to.

"He say he no farmer, Đại úy," Thiệu reported. "He say they cut wood in the mountains. No land for farm in mountain."

"So they're woodcutters? There're no mountains except Núi Bà Đen anywhere around here. Where are they cutting the wood?"

"He say they from up north, far to north," Thiệu explained, pointing in a northerly direction.

"So how did they all get down here?"

Thiệu returned to questioning the old man, drawing out more information than they had been able to in the preceding two hours at the hands of the LLDB.

"Soldiers come to their village six months ago and take all men to carry supplies to south. They say if they no help, they kill all wives and children."

"What supplies?"

Thiệu asked the old man, and the old man replied.

"He carry two artillery shell."

"To where?"

"He say Ba Thu."

"Where did he get the shells from?"

Following a long conversation Thiệu related the old man's story. "He live Sơn La. That North Vietnam next to Laos in mountains. Soldiers take them to Hà Đông, next to Hanoi, to pick up shells to take to south. Many men carry supplies on Hồ Chí Minh Trail. They walk four months on Trail until they come Ba Thu. NVA in Ba Thu tell them to get wood from tree square. Then they all go home."

Mike had been evaluating the old man's manner and gestures throughout his rendition of events leading up to his capture and sensed a lot of truth in the story, but something just didn't add up. "If they were out looking for tree squares to harvest, then where are all their woodcutting tools?" he asked, focusing again on the nature of the man's response.

"He say they drop saws and tools when they try run away," Thiệu told him.

The old man reached into his breast pocket and pulled out a folded, wet piece of paper. He handed it to the captain, gesturing for him to keep it. Mike carefully unfolded it, realizing it was some sort of North Vietnamese currency. The face of "Uncle Ho" appeared on the front of the five-*đồng* certificate, and as he turned it over, he smiled as he saw an image of a steam shovel loading a large dump truck, the words *NĂM ĐỒNG* centered below it.

"This looks like Monopoly play money, Thiệu. What is it?"

"That North Vietnam money, *Đại úy*. They pay him five *đồng* to carry shell."

"How much is that?"

"Don't know, *Đại úy*. That no worth nothing in Saigon. He say you keep. He pay you for water."

"I don't want his money. Tell him I just want the truth," he concluded, stuffing the enemy money back in the woodcutter's wet shirt.

The old man drew his hands together, clasping them as though he were gesturing in prayer, bobbing his head up and down in gratitude as he paid tribute to the young captain.

"Tell him to stop that, Thiệu. Tell him nobody's going to hurt him anymore. He has my word on that."

Mike stood up, wiped the wet globs of mud off his pants, and walked out to the water's edge. He studied the three mammoth water buffalo standing idly in thigh-deep water, oblivious to anything except the flies and gnats competing for morsels as they swarmed around the docile beasts' overworked haunches. He walked out and inspected the long ropes trailing behind them, noting the freshly cut ends of the ropes floating in the calm green water. He looked to the west and saw Sergeant Daniels approaching with a platoon of CIDG he'd sent to learn what the animals were towing when his team had spotted them in the distance.

"It's like looking for a needle in a haystack, Captain," Daniels told him. "The water's too deep and murky out there to find anything unless you step on it. They wouldn't tow sacks of rice through that shit. It just doesn't make sense."

Mike shook his head. "Thiệu was able to find out that they're a bunch of forced laborers from the north. The oldest one admitted that they came down the Trail hauling ammo for the NVA, but afterward they were told to go out and cut down some tree squares for wood, and that's when we spooked 'em."

"Then why'd they try to run?"

"Thiệu said they were scared."

"Makes sense. But it sure looked like they were dragging something behind those water buffalo," Daniels added. "Whata' we going to do with them?"

"I've got a good mind to just let the old farts go, but something tells me we haven't gotten the whole story yet."

Mike stared out into the distance, toward the invisible Fence, no more than five kilometers to their west. He carefully weighed the circumstances and the story the old woodcutter had related. Then he concluded that he didn't have *all* the facts. "We're heading back in," he told Daniels, "Get on the horn and tell Top to have the B-Team send a chopper to pick up the prisoners in the morning. Tell them we have three NVA water buffalo CIA as well, and ask them what they want us to do with them."

"The Bodes will probably want to butcher 'em," Daniels said. "I hear some of 'em are pretty good eating."

"I thought they considered 'em sacred."

"I think that's the Montagnards and the Indians, Đại úy."

With the early rays of sunlight guiding them, the 328th CIDG Company wearily made its way back through the final shallow stream and onto the south end of the dirt runway outside the navy perimeter. Master Sergeant Miller stood leaning against the three-quarter-ton truck, his arms folded, anticipating the details of the capture of eight NVA grandfathers.

Following a brief after-action report by the captain, Miller recommended that they keep the prisoners sequestered right there, so as not to agitate the Cambodes and to give the mammoth CH-47 Chinook helicopter being sent from the C-Team in Biên Hòa room to land and take on the livestock and prisoners.

"The B-Team was on the secure horn last night and wanted us to provide primary and alternate avenues of approach to Chuck's SR-Three headquarters in Ba Thu, Captain," Miller reported. "I sent Watson down the canal at oh-dark-thirty this morning with the Mekong and ten airboats to recon the area. They should be linking up with Angel Eye right about now. He's going to guide them through the tall grass to get a closer look at the terrain and map out some primary and alternate routes."

"They're gearin' up for something," Mike surmised. "Looks like we'll be gettin' our passports stamped PDQ."

"Sure hope so. It's been getting pretty stale and boring around here for a while."

"I'm going to take the truck up to the team house with Daniels to slap on a quick shower and shave. I'll be back down as soon as I get some dry fatigues and some PIRs for the old papa-sans. We didn't have enough to feed them, and I'm sure they're ready to chow down."

"Chopper's supposed to be inbound, Captain," Miller added, looking off into the eastern sky. "Leave me the radio. I'll try to establish commo and get an ETA."

Mike handed Top the PRC-77, threw his gear into the back of the truck, and with Sergeant Daniels seated next to him, headed back up the muddy runway to the team house. The full aroma of roasted Spam greeted them as they stepped up into the empty team room, and Mike quickly walked over to the table, took three fried strips of his favorite breakfast meat from the platter, and placed them on two slices of stiff, stale bread. He anointed them copiously with watery mustard from the plastic dispenser, doused them with several drops of hot sauce, and with three swift bites, made short work of the tasty treat. He wiped his face with his bare forearm, grabbed his web gear, and headed down the hallway to his room.

The distinct churning of the dual chopper blades caught his attention as he languished beneath the tepid water draining from the rain-filled barrels above. Realizing that the Chinook was already landing, he grabbed his small towel and hurried back to his room. As he drove toward the pad at the end of the runway, he watched the massive work chopper ease up in a torrent of swirling dust, straining loudly in the early morning heat to gain momentum as it slowly skirted the canal and off into the light-blue eastern sky.

"Just got word from the C-Team that they are really anxious to interrogate the old farts, sir," Miller told him. "Seems as though the spooks we've got running recon across the Fence have been coming up dry with any live intel, and to have eight old papa-sans fresh from the Trail and Ba Thu has got a lota' S2 types excited up in Biên Hòa."

"Well, they'll probably tell them everything they want to know, as long as they don't pistol-whip 'em."

Sergeant Miller turned his attention to the faint chatter coming across the net on the radio. He held the handset up to his ear and listened, a concerned frown apparent in his stare. His grim demeanor drew Mike's interest. The captain moved closer, quietly straining to hear what was being said.

"Break… Break… Angel Eye, this is Red Bank Goose One-three," Miller interrupted. "Say again last transmission, over." Sergeant Miller's eyes focused clearly on the captain, his tense jawbone emerging as his eyes tightened. He listened intently for several minutes, taunting the captain's curiosity to its peak. "Roger copy, Angel Eye… Understand Dust Off is not an option at this time. Are you going to stay on station?"

"What's up?" Mike finally asked.

"Roger, Angel Eye… Standing by this station. Goose One-three, out."

Miller laid the handset on the top of the radio and ran his hand through the sparse growth of hair, then massaged the back of his sunburnt neck before he broke the news to his captain. "Angel Eye was directing the boats through a thick patch of elephant grass when he spotted something in the water ahead of them. He radioed Watson to veer fifteen degrees to the west to check it out, and when the lead boat approached it, it detonated. Angel Eye said the boat just vaporized and that the crater was about the equivalent of a seven-fifty- or thousand-pounder."

"Who was in the lead boat?" Mike asked.

"Don't know for sure. Angel Eye lost all commo with the boats right after the explosion. Said the only thing he could see intact was the engine, which splashed down about two hundred meters from the blast site."

Mike's mind raced immediately back to the woodcutters and their oxen. "They were draggin' the air force's bombs outa' 'AO Keep Out' into *our* AO!" he exclaimed. "No wonder they were stripped down. Anything metallic would have set them off! Thank God Daniels couldn't find them."

"Fuckin' devious bastards," Miller defiantly conceded.

"Have McDonald get me a chopper outa' Củ Chi. We need to get down there fast. No telling how many more of those things are still in the area."

Sergeant Miller picked up the radio and was told the mail chopper was inbound. He instructed McDonald to request him land at the end of the runway instead of the pad across from the team house. Within minutes, the aging Huey settled down next to the anxious pair, and Mike immediately ran over to talk to the pilot, who agreed to take him down to the boats. Miller hastily grabbed the mail bag and threw it into the back of the truck.

The captain settled into the crew compartment, put the headset on, and realized that the pilot had been monitoring the whole incident on the team's frequency. "I'm a little concerned about setting one of those babies off myself," he told Mike. "You have any idea how many of them are out there?"

"Not a clue," the captain replied. "But I would assume that if there were more in that immediate area, the other boats would have set them off by now."

He sat anxiously, carefully listening to the pilots assigning vectors, the cool air managing to restrain the nervous sweat building in his temples. He stared out into the flat, glassy plains, scanning the shiny horizon for any sign of the airboats in the distance. The lively melody from AFN suddenly filled the headset, and just as quickly, the captain keyed his mike. "Do you mind?" he said to the pilot. "Not really in the mood for any Steppenwolf right about now."

"Roger that, sir," the warrant officer replied, flipping the switch off.

Within minutes, the Bird Dog appeared on the horizon. It was circling above the squadron on airboats, which itself was circling around the dark massive cavern in the reeds. As they approached, Mike watched the small figures at the crater, the idle boats drifting listlessly while their crews searched for their comrades in the murky, waist-deep water. The pilot hovered over the devastation below. All eyes were searching the shallow water for any signs of bombs that might be lurking in the shallow marshes beneath them.

"Captain, I'm not going to try and land anywhere near that crater," the pilot told him. "I've got my eyes on some elevated berms about two hundred fifty meters to the east. I think I can get a stable touchdown if I keep the power up, but I don't know how long I can maintain hover."

"Roger, I appreciate anything you can do to get me down there."

The chopper slowly descended above the junctions of some old rice paddies while scores of the Cambodes below pushed through the grass-laced water toward the apparent touchdown. Mike scanned the Cambodes, hoping to see Watson towering above them. His heart sank as the reality of the situation took firm hold of his senses. He felt his chest tighten as the dull pain asserted its dominance over his emotions. *He's gone,* he finally allowed himself to acknowledge.

A group of six men emerged from the staggered group, drudging slowly through the murky field of water, a lone, limp body perched lifelessly above their shoulders. They moved with a degree of firm reverence, three on either side, grim faces, evidence of their emerging grief. As they drew nearer, Mike realized who the men were carrying. "The Mekong," he muttered to himself.

Mike's eyes and hope continued to search for his sergeant, seemingly lost in this oddly tranquil sea of death, or scattered to oblivion in a deadly wave of metallic fragments and TNT. He stood on the strut of the chopper as it touched down, the spinning blades painting a circular array of foamy ripples in the still waters beyond. He watched the men struggle with their heavy load, slipping and stumbling in the marshy waste. Then, beyond them, two lone Cambodes followed, one waving his hand, eagerly beckoning to be seen. The captain noticed that each had their arms clasped around a foot, two pale white soles clearly visible as they drug the corpse through the water behind them.

Mike launched himself out into water, sloshing wildly through the hot, thigh-deep aquatic maze of reeds and grass. Then he realized that a swift, straightforward motion enabled him to move at a quicker pace. He strode powerfully though the water until he finally reached the men with Sergeant Watson in tow. "I'll take him!" he yelled, panting fervently.

He put his arms under the partially submerged body and with all his strength focused on getting him out of the filthy water. He lifted Watson up and turned to make his way back to the waiting chopper. As he struggled with the overwhelming weight, he wouldn't let himself look at the sergeant's face, which lay arched backward, drooping lifelessly, the back and other bones obviously broken. His boots dug deep into the mushy soil with every laborious step he took. *God, give me strength*, he prayed.

He felt the blood rushing to his temples, his heartbeat accelerating with every step, the eyes of every Cambode fixated on the pulsating arteries in his neck. He dared not stop to adjust his slippery burden. His task was at hand, and he remained determined to carry his soldier off his final battlefield with the dignity that Sergeant Watson had earned.

The door gunner unplugged his intercom, jumped down to the berm, and took off his helmet. He cringed seeing the anguish in the captain's face as he struggled toward the chopper. The copilot quickly unleashed his harness, stepped down to help, and grabbed Watson's shoulders while the door gunner struggled to hold on to his fractured legs. They finally lifted him up into the crew compartment and slid him in to lie next to his fallen comrade, the Mekong.

Mike lingered on the skid, too exhausted to take the final, long step up into the chopper. As he gathered his breath, he turned to the assembled strikers and lifted his arms up. "Where're the others?" he yelled, gesturing with outstretched palms. Several of the Cambodes interpreted his query and just shook their heads. Mike nodded, understanding that only scattered body parts remained of the other three Cambodian KIA.

The captain then circled his arm above his head and pointed north, toward the camp. Reluctantly, in unison, they slowly turned and waded back out toward their empty boats.

The young door gunner reached down and offered his hand, pulling the captain up and into the door. The cabin was drenched with bodily fluids and dirty swamp water. Mike sat down on the nylon seat and put the headset on. "Guess that's all of them," he hastily told the pilot. "Could you raise Goose One-three on the horn and tell him that we have one USSF and four Cambodes KIA. And tell him to have two body bags ready when we land."

"Roger that, sir."

As the chopper lifted off, Mike looked down at Watson for the first time. The sergeant's waxy blue eyes offered no inference of pain or fear, his expression appearing peaceful and benign. Mike reached down to close the man's eyes, but after several attempts, he realized the rigor of the body would not cooperate. He looked around to find something to cover him with. Finally he took off his wet fatigue jacket and gently wrapped it around Watson's head. The sergeant's large thighs lay completely filleted open, the deep lacerations extending from his knees to his waist, a puddle of vibrating pink water dancing freely in the massive wounds. The force of the blast had blown off his boots, and Mike noticed the vivid white band around the sergeant's finger where his gold wedding ring once had set. His thoughts rushed back to the picture hanging on the wall in Watson's room, the picture of the sergeant's twin little girls hugging his broad neck as they each kissed his cheeks.

Mike turned his head and stared out the door, his vision completely devoid of any focus, his mind swirling independently of any clear direction. *I can't fix this,* he told himself. *Maybe if I close my eyes, it will all go away. Better suck it up. They'll be watching me.*

He regained an element of composure and looked back down at the broken bodies lying catatonically at his feet. The tattered shards of remaining clothing wrestled with the wind as it swirled through the cabin, providing the dormant remains of the warriors with a fleeting inference of life. The door gunner's eyes remained transfixed on the corpses. He was mesmerized by the tremor of viscous fluids, eerily skipping in the deep void in Watson's thighs with the steady vibrations of the turbines.

Mike reached down and lifted up Watson's broken legs, tilting them both until the water rushed out onto the floor, briefly mingling with the wet soil and grime, then suddenly swirling up again as the wind thrust the spray directly into the captain's face. He turned his head, coughing and heaving, spitting out the vile concoction. He drew up his wet T-shirt to wipe the slimy grit from his face and eyes. "That sucked!" he yelled to the door gunner, spitting the lingering taste out of his mouth.

The door gunner motioned for him to put on the headset.

"Captain, be advised that your highers want us to take the remains up to Biên Hòa instead of Củ Chi as soon as you're done with him," the pilot told him.

"Roger that," Mike replied, wiping his eyelids with his fingertips. He turned to look out the front of the chopper, over the harnessed shoulders of the pilots. A crowd of men scurried along the lane, running to the runway to meet the inbound chopper.

As the pilot flared the bird, he slowly rotated the chopper with the tail rotor, positioning the door facing the waiting men below. Mike jumped out, took off his T-shirt, and used it to wipe his face and chest before throwing it into the back of the team truck. "They never knew what hit 'em," he told Miller. "Wasn't anything left of that boat except part of the damn engine barely sticking out of the water."

Several of the team cautiously removed Watson's body from the floor of the chopper, slithering it slowly into the green rubbery body bag lying fully unzipped on the ground. Sergeant Daniels removed the fatigue jacket from around the dead sergeant's head and handed it back to the captain.

They then removed the Mekong's body from the chopper and placed it into the second body bag, leaving it unzipped because he would be there only temporarily. Placing him there was an important gesture of respect, elevating him in the eyes of his Cambode troops. None of the other indig were afforded such an honor. The final destination for the Mekong would be a funeral pyre later that evening, however.

"The C-Team directed us to make sure that the pilots understand they are to proceed directly to Biên Hòa, Captain," Miller told him. "After they process Sergeant Watson's body, they'll assign an escort sergeant to bring him home."

"The pilot already told me they were taking charge. That's where they're headed. Good for them." Mike knelt down and took one last look at his sergeant, lying prone and peaceful on the ground.

He looked up to see Lieutenant Bosworth and several of his men standing in the background, arms folded and expressionless. He immediately sensed an uneasiness swelling in his heart, and he knew it was time to go. "Go ahead and take it from here, Top," he told his team sergeant.

Mike turned and walked over to the idling chopper, thanking the pilots and door gunner for their help. Instinctively, he put his wet fatigue shirt back on and started walking up the narrow lane to the team house. He passed the lines of Cambodes and their tearful women, some carrying large segments of wood for the funeral pyre that would be erected on the runway for the Mekong that evening. At a loss for any lofty sentiment he could provide to quell their pain, he avoided making eye contact with any of them.

He moved quickly down the hallway in the empty team house, into his room, and closed the door. He ripped off his damp fatigue jacket and threw it against the wall, dropping to his knees as his emotions commanded his full attention. With his hands on his thighs, he sat back on the heels of his wet boots, staring blindly at the rusting tin above him. He gently ran his hands through his hair and then reluctantly embraced the foreign scent of death. He slowly held his palms to his face, drawing in the unmistakable redolence of the man he had carried from the battlefield only an hour before.

Warm tears swelled in his eyes, and before he could counter the emotion, they fell fully down his unshaven face and into his trembling palms. Hesitantly, he finally relented to the overpowering compulsion to submit, allowing the tears to flow freely as his body exhaled the pent-up remorse and sorrow tearing at his soul. *I can handle it, Lord,* he vowed. *Just be patient with me.*

He wept silently, mourning what he felt was a senseless loss of a valiant man, realizing also that there was no one to offer condolences to, even if he knew what to say. Letters of sympathy to the family of the fallen were taboo in the Fifth Group, since so many of their operations were highly classified.

In a desperate effort to purge himself of the demons dwelling within, Mike took a deep, cleansing breath, opened the vault, then slammed it shut with his vulnerabilities concealed in the darkness within. He sat up on the bunk, pulled off his boots, and reached under his mattress for the new bar of Lava soap he'd been saving for a special occasion. His small towel in hand, he headed down the hallway to the shower.

* * *

CHAPTER THIRTY-NINE

IKE EASED BACK AGAINST THE damp bulkhead with his hands clasped behind his head, fully entranced by the majesty of the Milky Way as its million-star menagerie spread like heavenly pixie dust drenching the dark Asian sky. He searched for Orion, his lifelong guardian, but to his alarm, the sky wasn't cooperating that night. The Hunter was nowhere to be found. He couldn't find the Big Dipper or the North Star either. *Of course,* he said to himself, *we're too close to the Equator. Those stars would be beyond the northern horizon.* Resigning himself that different stars would keep him company that night, he tested himself to remember other nebulous formations from Greek mythology that his father had pointed out to him when he was a child in Japan. Where the Milky Way displayed right above his head he saw the constellation of Aquila, the Eagle, with its bright start Altair. Far to the north he found the Northern Cross, which he knew was also called the Swan, and in the southern stream of the Milky Way he recognized the Southern Cross, far more prominent here than it ever had been in either Japan or Texas. A little higher he identified the constellation of Sagittarius, the Archer, which he had learned contained the center of our vast galaxy.

Lord, I know You know where I am and why I'm here, he confessed. *And as I look up into Your infinite kingdom, I know my voice is faint and my courage weak. But with Your tolerant blessing, I will do my duty honorably.*

He paused briefly, looking down at the luminous face on his watch: 0400. Three tense hours had passed since he and four of his men had quietly directed their squadron of airboats into position just southwest of the decimated hamlet of Ap Vinh. Now, as he scanned the faint horizon, he barely needed to squint to see the outlines of the deadly watercraft, silently afloat, motionless in the starlit night. Each of the fifteen boats carried at least six heavily armed Cambodes, their ranks bolstered by the five Special Forces advisors strategically dispersed among them. Mike remained impressed by the noise discipline the men had displayed throughout the arduous, stealthy movement. He felt confident that at this time in the early morning, not even the snakes knew they were there.

His thoughts wandered heavenward once again, his mind curious if some young maiden somewhere in the world was looking up into the stars to greet his lonely stare. A sudden trio of shooting stars lifted his spirits, a sight he hadn't seen since that starry night camping out on the bluff overlooking Yokohama Harbor. His thoughts had not provoked the waning image of Barbara in months. No longer could he even see her face. Carefully, he decided to unlock the sacred vault and summon her one last time. *How majestic do my words need to be before you hear my voice?* he silently asked her.

He paused for several moments, then concluded: *That's what I thought.* He shook his head slowly, took a deep, purging breath, and allowed her to linger aimlessly, unescorted, as he closed the vault behind her. With an hour and a half left to go until daybreak, he clipped the handset of the radio on his shoulder strap, folded his arms over his chest, and allowed himself an hour of nervous, shallow sleep.

The faint hiss of the squelch broke sharply, stirring the captain to check his watch: 0515. He listened intently as the squelch broke four more times with double clicks from his men in the waiting boats. He gave the thumbs-up sign to his driver as he took his seat, anxious to fire up the large 180-hp Lycoming aircraft engine mounted securely on the stern. The bow machine gunner quietly took his position, linking the folded belts of .30 ammo on the floor below him. The two M79 grenadiers slid in on either side of him, securing their 40mm projectiles in open rucksacks behind them. The captain took his place on the fuel tank beside the driver, waiting for the initial volley of artillery to initiate the assault.

The first hint of daybreak peeked slowly beyond the eastern horizon, casting a surreal spectrum of vague shadows and grayscale tint over slick, stagnant marshes, just before the first glimmer of light extinguished the fading flicker of the lingering morning stars.

"Shot out," the radio crackled.

Mike looked back over his shoulder to the northeast, listening for any sound of the incoming artillery. Within a few seconds, the first salvo of 175mm artillery rounds rumbled past, high over their heads, impacting moments later with a bright orange flash, smothered immediately with voluminous clouds of dark gray, cordite-soaked debris. "Light 'em up!" the captain yelled into the handset, circling his arms high above his head as he stood on the square fuel tank beside the driver.

In unison, the powerful Lycoming aircraft engines erupted into life, spewing clouds of white smoke as the long propellers churned up the tranquil waters behind them. The captain pointed to the middle boat and pumped his fist up and down, prompting the driver to ease out in front of the formation. Sergeant Daniels stood up from his position beside the lead driver, smiled, and snap-saluted the captain. Mike quickly surveyed the formation, and with all boats poised and ready for the assault, he pulled his goggles down and pointed to Daniels's boat, then turned and gestured emphatically to the west.

He swiftly bent over and shouted his orders to his restless driver, slapping him repeatedly in the back. "Giddyup, motherfucker! *¡Dalligas!*"

In an instant, the V-shaped onslaught of war boats lifted their snub-nosed bows on plane, above the low-lying reeds and grass-filled waters, speeding at full throttle toward their objective in the distance.

The captain adjusted his flight goggles, deflecting the stinging spray of water from the lead airboat's rooster tail blurring his vision as they led the furious charge. In the near distance, billowing black and gray plumes of smoke continued to erupt on the horizon, deadly evidence of the battery of 175mm howitzers' clout impacting from Cù Chi, nearly twenty miles away. He gazed to his right and left, the squadron of fifteen heavily armed airboats racing to their objective just inside the Cambodian border. Sergeant Daniels stood up in the lead boat, pulled the long whip antenna down, and tied a small American flag to the tip. As it flapped rapidly in the breeze ahead of him, the captain smiled contentedly, finally riding into battle under his beloved Stars and Stripes.

As the outline of hooches and buildings emerged in the distance, the endless expanse of marshy waters gave way to a series of rice paddies, long checkerboard fields with the first sprouts of grain peeking above the shallow brown water. Mike held on tight, watching the lead boat vault the first dike, flying airborne as it splashed twice before launching over the next low berm separating the fields. At 250 meters from the hooch line, the lead machine gunner opened up, spraying his calling card in the form of hot, molten lead.

The lead boat driver launched the craft up and over the final berm and skidded to a stop on the dusty road bordering the edge of the Plain of Reeds. The trailing boats quickly followed suit, their bow-mounted .30-caliber machine guns raking fields of interlocking fire on the unprotected village ahead. The flight of orbiting gunships pounded with rocket fire the surrounding buildings that housed the enemy's regimental headquarters, creating a firestorm of burning structures and secondary explosions.

Mike fired continuously into the confused mass of enemy troops, who were running in all directions, some pausing as they fired blindly at the chorus of choppers and strange, devilish boats delivering a deadly curtain of lead in their direction. An occasional B-40 rocket flew hissing over his head, only to splash down well behind them in the paddies beyond. With their boat's machine-gun ammo depleted, the company of MIKE Force Cambodes launched the ground assault, bringing accurate fire on the retreating enemy pockets as they ran from the burning village of Ba Thu. The contorted bodies of NVA troops lay scattered in all directions, the cadre and regulars apparently completely surprised by the early-morning *Blitzkrieg*-like attack from across the *other* side of the Fence.

Several large truckloads of frantic enemy troops attempting to flee the battle zone sat stalled, blocked by smoldering bomb craters at the north end of the village, exposed victims of the unrelenting cascades of fire from the persistent spray of miniguns blaring down from the flight of Cobra gunships pinwheeling above them. Mike cringed when the lead truck suddenly burst into flames, launching dozens of fiery bodies into the hazy morning sky as it exploded in a fireball of death. His men maneuvered their squads as they methodically moved through the village, dispatching their death blows to those unfortunate enough not to have escaped their terminal span of influence. The inspired warriors pumped a withering volley of 40mm grenades into the line of wrecked and stalled trucks, isolated on the lone road leading away from the mounting carnage. Towering flames from the series of wooden barracks obscured the morning sky as the dense white smoke merged with the dark cordite vapors lingering above the battle zone. Within a matter of only twenty minutes, the battle-savvy Cambodes secured the demolished village, pausing only to set up a perimeter on what was left of its outskirts.

The captain radioed to the commander of the Twenty-fifth Infantry Division, who was in the black C&C chopper orbiting high above, informing him that the proposed LZ was secure and ready for Phase Two of the operation. Minutes later, a light observation helicopter swooped down, dropping off three forward air controllers and their radios, who were equipped to guide in the first battalion of the infantry troopers.

Mike looked up and watched the four eagle flights of choppers turn and descend in formation, with the lead chopper bearing down on the forward air controller standing at the far end of the dusty road. In unison, they flared, churning up the heavy matte of dense smoke, then skidded to a bumpy stop, unleashing the scores of sky troopers, who quickly scurried to the perimeter and took up their positions. As soon as the first sortie had lifted off, another flight of Tomahawk slicks eased into the pattern and delivered their cargo to the LZ as nervous door gunners raked the diminishing ranks of retreating enemy stragglers. Within a matter of minutes, an entire battalion of Twenty-fifth Infantry troopers were on the ground, poised and anxious to pursue the enemy.

The nonstop exodus of mechanized troop carriers and artillery pieces continued to flow from the Củ Chi base camp, hoisted in under the wide bellies of CH-47 Chinooks and mammoth Skycranes. Within a matter of hours, the fuming village of Ba Thu had burned itself out, its former inhabitants replaced with the massive firepower and clout of the U.S. Army's Twenty-fifth Infantry Division. The May 1970 incursion into eastern Cambodia had begun, spearheaded by the Cambodian strikers of the Third Mobile Strike Force.

The captain made his way among his men, inquiring about the wounded and making sure the rest of his team had endured the assault unscathed. His ears rang constantly with the common aftermath of battle, creating a mild headache while the lingering adrenaline served to temper its effect.

"We've got four wounded, *Đại úy*," Sergeant Daniels told him, yelling above the sounds of chopper blades and outgoing artillery fire from the mobile 105s. "The Twenty-fifth's got Dust Off inbound to take them up to Củ Chi to get patched up."

"Have *Bác sĩ* Braxton go with them. Our work's done here. As soon as the fuel bladders arrive, let's get gassed up and head back to camp," the captain told him. "Get Top on the horn, and have him get a pallet of beer hooked in from the C-Team for the Bodes."

"Roger that. Sergeant Marshall is working on resupplying our basic load with the armory guys from the Twenty-fifth."

Mike surveyed the horrific aftermath of the assault. Several squads of infantrymen reluctantly toiled in the morning heat, dragging decimated bodies into a pile at the edge of the village, stacking row after row of enemy weapons beside them. The sweet, confounding smell of death infused the air, coupled with the distinct tang of cordite, gunpowder, and burnt flesh. He watched the men performing their dire tasks, their fatigues worn and faded, most laboring with small green towels draped loosely around their sweaty necks. He noticed the variety of graffiti emblazoned on their helmets—peace symbols, vile nicknames, various playing cards, and messages depicting their fragile state of mind. He wondered how they got away with it. The army he had known seemingly had been transformed into a political statement, tolerated, even endorsed by the civil turmoil back home.

"That's your army at work, Captain," Sergeant Marshall commented, noticing the look on Mike's face.

Mike slid his warm CAR-15 behind his back, adjusting the sling as he turned and replied. "Yeah, but at least they *showed up*. Unlike some other chickenshit bastards I know." The image of Jim resurfaced in his mind.

He walked over and helped a young trooper pull a body through the dust, wondering whatever had happened to his old *best* friend.

* * *

The destruction of the enemy's sanctuaries across the Fence put a sudden stop to enemy infiltration into the team's area of responsibility. An unwelcome sabbatical of activity slowly gave way to doldrums of repetitive tasks, embraced fully with innovative new schemes of graft and other corruption orchestrated by the resident LLDB. Operations in the playpen were transformed into weekly excursions of plantlife harvesting and reptile population management, accented only occasionally by the indiscriminate explosion of an undetected mackerel-can booby trap.

The team took this respite in stride, undertaking team house remodeling projects that included a fully enclosed shower with a kerosene heater mounted in the rain barrel on the roof. They constructed a round card table with a felt surface for their nightly games of pinochle and bridge, and finally, they installed in the ground behind the team house a 155mm howitzer canister with a screen attached to keep them from having to mount the berm in order to relieve themselves. The installation of a new stereo system and the acquisition of foam pillows provided a welcome element of the comforts of home.

Mike sat at the team table enjoying his instant coffee and final strip of Spam when Sergeant McDonald ran down the hallway with an anxious look on his face. "Better get to the radio shack, sir," he told him. "We've got a problem down the canal with the insert."

Mike stepped into the commo bunker just as Sergeant Miller stood up from the long banks of radios. "The operation we just sent in down the canal got hit. Ambushed or something, Captain. Apparently three of the boats are destroyed, and there's *beaucoup* casualties."

"Where?"

"About six clicks down the Kinh Gẫy. Near the junction of the Ap Kinh. Marshall thinks it was a command-detonated ordnance. Swamped his boat as well."

"Our folks OK?"

"That's affirmative. But we need to get down there. There's still a bunch of little people in the water."

"Are they still in contact?"

"Negative," Miller told him. "Weird thing is, there wasn't any contact."

The captain and his team sergeant hurried over to the boat house, only to find there were no assault boats available to take them down the canal. Mike hurriedly pushed an airboat down the ramp, and within seconds, he and Sergeant Miller were speeding down the narrow canal toward the stricken operation.

Mike looked ahead at the frenzy of commotion in the water: shouting men on both sides of the banks dragging bodies out of the murky canal, divers bobbing up and down searching for more victims of the blast. The captain idled the heavy boat to the edge of the melee, shut the engine off, and yelled to Sergeant Marshall, who was standing on the muddy bank, bare-chested and bootless, his wet trousers rolled up to his knees. "What do we need to do?"

"There's still some more indig in the water, Captain!" Marshall yelled back.

Mike pulled off his boots, took off his shirt, and jumped into the dark water. He took a deep breath and submerged, searching the invisible water with his hands for anything in front of him. He finally felt a leg, grabbed hold of it, and brought it to the surface. Several other men in the water swam over to him and took the body while he submerged again, searching for any other victims weighted down on the bottom. He dove and searched repeatedly, only to come up empty in his hunt for more victims. Fully exhausted, he swam over to the edge and pulled himself up on the berm. "What the fuck happened?" he asked Sergeant Marshall, still panting from the exertion.

"All I know, Đại úy, is that we were motoring down the canal when this 'Go to fuckin' hell' explosion blew right up front with the lead boats. Bodies were splashin' down like depth charges right in front of me. Then the fuckin' blast wave swamped my boat, and when I finally got my gear off and surfaced, shit was strewn everywhere."

"You didn't see any bad guys?" Mike asked, a little confused about the circumstances.

"If there were any, Captain, they didn't stick around to sign the guest book."

"Doesn't make any fuckin' sense," Miller put in. "Whatever it was, it had to be command-detonated."

"Have some of your people recon both sides of the banks for any wires leading to the canal," Mike advised Sergeant Marshall.

The captain walked over to where the bodies lay in line on the muddy embankment, tattered rucksacks and shreds of clothing scattered about. He counted fourteen corpses, some badly mangled while the others must have just drowned, he assumed. "There's probably a lot of ammo and weapons at the bottom, Top," he said. "We're going to have to retrieve all that gear when the water clears."

He sat down on the bank, watching several of the CIDG making their last desperate efforts to retrieve more of their comrades. The dark, murky water tightly held its secrets, and Mike knew that they probably wouldn't be able to make a final body count until the sediment cleared. He considered the callous destruction, emotions bearing down directly on the loss of life lying at his feet. He didn't know any of the men lying there on the muddy sepulcher of death, and he didn't want to. Death had become an omen of his destiny, his essence, his fragile fortitude. He had already resigned himself to that noble outcome that his father had predicted for him: *Croiche onoraigh*, a fate he was equipped to endure. He had already relinquished his selfish grasp on life. His fate lay in his Lord's keeping.

He drew his palms up to his face, sniffing lightly, concerned if the scent of death still lingered on him, concerned if the utter integrity and sanctity of the contents of the vault had not been terminally violated. *What is it about pulling bodies out of the fuckin' water around here anyway?* he asked himself. *There's no glory or honor in getting zapped on a stupid boat ride. It's all just a fuckin' senseless waste of humanity,* he concluded.

He looked up the embankment at Sergeant Marshall walking toward him. "Found this about thirty meters back," the sergeant said, holding up a split pair of 16-gauge electrical wires. "Almost missed it. It was just lying on the edge of the berm, but it leads back into the water way back up the canal. We musta' drove right past the sneaky fuckers right before they blew it."

Mike inspected the frayed brown wires, noticing the heavy-gauge plastic coating on each end. "Pretty heavy-duty stuff," he noted. "Not like anything I've seen out here before."

"Hop on board, *Đại úy*," Sergeant Miller told him. "Let's find out where they triggered it."

The captain held on to the wire and stepped aboard the airboat, pulling on it until it became taut. As he tightened his grip, the bow of the boat turned and floated out into the center of the canal. He continued to reel the connection in, spooling the slippery wire in coils on the floor of the boat beside him. "They were serious about this shit, Top," he noted, as the boat continued back up the canal. "Look how much wire we've already pulled in."

"I'm not getting a good feeling about this, Captain," Miller told him. "We're already over a hundred meters from the blast site, and that wire isn't getting any closer to the shoreline."

Mike turned and stared at his team sergeant, noting the edge of concern as he tightened his jaw. Miller turned the key on and pushed the start button, igniting the 180-hp Lycoming. He turned the rudders hard left to the bank. "Toss all that wire over to the bank, Captain. We're wasting our time."

Mike complied, then walked back and sat down on the bench next to Miller. "Are you thinking what I'm thinking?" he asked, slipping his muddy feet into his dry boots.

Sergeant Miller eased the throttle forward, turning the boat back out into the middle of the canal. "There's only one other explanation. And there's gonna be hell to pay if I'm right."

He slammed the throttle forward, lifting the bow of the airboat until it reached its plane, racing back up the canal toward the camp. As the camp finally came into view, they observed a navy Seawolf chopper approaching from the east. They watched it crab over the canal, then flair abruptly, churning the choking layers of dust as it drifted down to the pad. The crew chief tossed off several blue denim duffel bags, followed by a half dozen men attired in Hawaiian shirts and Bermuda shorts.

"Probably just got back from R&R," Mike yelled over the blaring drone of the propeller blades.

Sergeant Miller eased back on the throttle, coasting the large boat toward the edge of the bank. He let the engine idle, slowly coaxing the boat along the shoreline up toward the PBR slips near the fuel dump. "Keep your eyes open for some wires or tubing coming out of the water, *Đại úy*," he said as he peered over the side.

Mike leaned over, parting the small reeds and river grass as he sorted through the vegetation growing up the canal bank. Several startled water snakes slithered away, prompting him to look carefully before he stuck his hands back into the forbidding waters. Slowly, the boat eased its way up to the PBR docks when, suddenly, the captain made his discovery. "Tally ho!" he yelled back, leaning over the edge of the boat, pulling several strands of wire up for Sergeant Miller to see.

"Those fuckin' bastards!" Top yelled back, turning the engine off and coming forward to inspect the find. He pulled on the wires, then jumped ashore, ripping up the leads from their shallow trench buried beneath the moist but dusty dirt. Mike took the bow mooring line and tied it off to the dock before jumping up to follow his team sergeant.

"You might want to sit this one out, Cap'n," Miller yelled back, the fire in his veins evident in the red texture enveloping his neck and face.

"Maintain, Sergeant," Mike yelled after him, just as several naval officers stepped out of the ops center building.

Sergeant Miller stopped abruptly, staring down the trio of officers as they made their way toward him. Mike stepped by his side as Miller held out his hand, several strands of wire dangling loosely in his large palm.

"We were just coming to find you," Lieutenant Bosworth told them. "When I found out what happened—"

"Just who the *fuck* do you think you are, Lieutenant?" Miller asked him, his tone belligerent and forceful.

"Now, just hold on there, Sergeant," Bosworth replied, a little taken aback by the way he had just been addressed.

The captain stepped forward, easing between his team sergeant and the navy lieutenant. "No, Bosworth. You hold on," he began. "This is one of those times that I really wish my leg was about a foot longer so I could get a little more traction and get a good head start on putting my boot up your sorry ass. Who the fuck is your mother? Didn't she ever teach you to have any respect for authority? You got a problem when somebody tells you *No?*"

Several of the men standing behind them in the Hawaiian garb stepped up and stood next to Bosworth, expanding their chests in a display of defiance.

"So, who are *these* clowns?" Miller inquired, sizing up the unshaven, long-haired group of men who had just gotten off the helicopter.

"These men are part of SEAL Team One," the lieutenant said. "My headquarters mustered them in to help in whatever way they can, following the accident down the canal."

"*Accident?*" Miller replied. "You call the murder of fourteen of my people an *accident?* You're just a *whole* lot more arrogant and stupid than I'd given you credit for, Lieutenant!"

Sergeant Miller took his long Randall fighting knife out of its scabbard and swiftly severed the strands of wire he held in his hand, tossing the remnants forcefully to the ground.

"You got any more stupid surprises in store for us out there in our AO?" the captain asked, noting the agitated demeanor of the group of men in front of him.

"SEALs?" Miller injected. "You guys look like something outa' the movie *M*A*S*H*. Just got one question: Which one of you is Hawkeye?"

The captain turned to Sergeant Miller, attempting to avert the obvious altercation that was imminent. "Top, take the boat back up to the airboat shed. I'll be up there in a couple. I'll take it from here."

"Negative, *Đại úy*. Not leaving you alone with these fools. They look pretty queer to me."

"You need to get your sergeant under control, Shannahan," Bosworth retorted.

"You, sir, have no obvious inclination as to the consequences of your actions. I strongly suggest you just return to your quarters, pack your gear, and prepare yourself for the captain's mast or general court-martial that will put an end to your sorry-ass career. You want to take it any further, that's entirely up to you," the captain forcefully offered. "I'm the one who has to ultimately account for their senseless deaths, by not adequately protecting them from idiots like you. And, by the way, that's Master Sergeant Miller to you."

"I had nothing to do with—"

"You had *everything* to do with what went down today. This isn't my first sumo match, Bosworth. We made it very clear to you: 'No unauthorized intervention into our AO.' Your arrogance and sheer stupidity amazes me. You, sir, are solely responsible for instigating the deaths of fourteen of my men. That is on you, sir. You own that one. So just tuck it way into your sea bag along with those pretty little geisha dolls!"

"My seaman acted without authority, on his own. He panicked when he heard screws—"

"Bullshit! We told you '*No* ordnance in our AO!' this whole clusterfuck is on you, Bosworth. One thing about the navy I learned from my father is that the buck stops with the commander. No weak-sister excuses. Your ass is already grass, and I'm just getting ready to fire up the damn lawnmower.

Guess you haven't had a lot of time to think about what you're gonna do after the navy. Do they have any retirement homes in New Hampshire?"

Bosworth stared at the captain, his mounting disdain evident in the scowl and tense posture he displayed.

"And so we *both* understand each other," Mike went on, giving the navy lieutenant explicit instructions. "Until further notice, the operational area under *my* command is *off limits* to *all* navy personnel and contractors. That means you will confine your activities from the fuel dump north up the canal to the Vàm Cỏ Đông."

The distinct humming of the Johnson outboards emerged eerily from the edge of the canal as Sergeant Marshall and several of the heavily laden assault boats moved slowly past the PBR docks toward the airboat shed. Each boat contained the tattered bodies of the dead indig, irreverently stacked one on top of the other.

Mike looked at the members of the SEAL team eyeing the procession of boats, tapped Miller on the shoulder, and told him to get the boat and drive him back up to the team house. They turned and started to walk back to the docks when the captain turned again and offered a parting gesture. "Oh, by the way… Nice shirts, fellas."

Later that day, the captain met with the new LLDB commander, who promptly demanded immediate reparations from the navy for the men killed in the friendly-fire incident. Mike also made it a point to confer in depth with Sergeant Marshall and his team sergeant before filing his incident report with the B-Team. The subsequent investigation revealed that seven other explosive devices had been planted in the AO, both in the canal as well as in main feeder streams that traversed throughout the plains: hydrophones attached to 250-pound bombs that detected propeller vibrations in the water. Lieutenant Bosworth was summarily relieved of his command, and that was the last the team heard from him or the incident from the navy.

The senseless deaths at the hands of the navy created tension between the Americans and the Vietnamese, a tension that was palpable and that lingered over all activities within the camp. Despite the captain's efforts to suppress the true source of the explosion, rumors and insinuations surfaced, supporting the contention that the incident had been premeditated, a racial vendetta by the navy, targeting only Vietnamese, since no Americans had been killed in the incident. The fact that the LLDB hoarded the majority of the substantial death benefits to the families came to light when Thiệu's cousin's family complained to him that they were insulted by the ten dollars they had received for the death of their father.

"We better hope the LLDB don't start booby-trappin' the canal themselves just to collect a little extra cash," Sergeant Marshall remarked one night. "The bounty Charlie has on our berets is high enough."

*　　*　　*

CHAPTER FORTY

"Take me, take me to your darkest room,/
Close every window and bolt every door./
The very first moment I heard your voice/
I'd be in darkness no more./

"Take me to your most barren desert,/
A thousand miles from the nearest sea./
The very moment I saw your smile/
It would be like heaven to me./...

"Take me to Siberia/
And the coldest weather of the wintertime,/
And it would be just like spring in California/
As long as I knew you were mine./...

"Take me... Take me..."

MIKE EMBRACED GEORGE JONES PROSELYTIZING him, as he pleaded for someone to please *take him*... anywhere but here. He sensed the dark image in his doorway and turned his tape player off. *Girl, I don't know who you are, but I'm with you, I assure you.*

Mike looked up to see Sergeant McDonald's face peering at him from the shadows at the edge of the entrance to his room. "Just got a message from the B-Team, sir," he said, a somber look on his face. "It's from the Old Man, sir. You're to pack your gear and be ready to depart by sixteen hundred hours today, Captain."

"Depart to where?" Mike asked, sitting up and putting the week-old copy of *Stars and Stripes* down on his bed.

"B-Team, sir. Message says you're being relieved. Your replacement will be on the chopper when it lands... Pappy sends."

Mike sat in silence. The word *relieved* bore several connotations, none that were clear to him. "That's it? Never mind, Mac... But thanks," he said, still sifting through the meaning of the message. "Guess I'd better get packing."

Thanks, George, he whispered, noting the strange coincidence.

He quietly folded up his extra sets of fatigues hanging on the wall, picked up his worn pair of swamp boots, and threw them in the bottom of his rucksack. He looked around the small room, then gathered his wallet, a small box of letters and official papers, his shaving kit, his .45, and fresh underwear. He stuffed it all in before flipping down the flap. Then he went over to the far wall, picked up the captured SKS Chinese assault rifle and the NVA pith helmet riddled with bullet holes, and tossed them on the bed. He regretted not keeping the NVA officer's K-54 pistol he gave to Sergeant Daniels for barter in Saigon just two days before.

Better hurry up and get the hell out of here before they change their minds, he thought.

He spent the rest of the afternoon talking to his men who were in camp, thanking them for the jobs they had performed under such challenging circumstances. He was careful not to say good-bye, because in Group, there was no apparent need to. Top reminded him that after he got to the B-Team, he needed to fill out efficiency ratings on all the men. Then the sergeant said he'd just received his orders back to Bragg to join the Sixth Group, headquartered there.

"This is from the team, *Đại úy,*" Sergeant Miller told him, handing him a green box with the word *Rolex* in the middle of it. "Your share of the team fund."

"Thanks, Top," Mike said, taking out the shiny silver GMT Master and admiring its quality. "Thought I was going to have to go all the way to Hong Kong to get one of these."

"But I've got to tell you, it's just not the same around here anymore, *Đại úy.* The whole fuckin' war's gone to hell in a handbag. Ever since they arrested the Group commander for that double-agent fiasco in Nha Trang Harbor last year, they've been tryin' to reel us back into the regular army."

"That happened right before I got in-country. Seemed like somebody in Mack-V really had it in for us, can't stand the thought that we're not in their chain of command," Mike told him, adjusting the dials on the watch. "Bunch of lightweights if you ask me."

"Got some friends down at Mack-V in Saigon who tell me they're gonna turn over all the border camps to the VN Ruff Puffs," Miller added, using the American nickname for the Vietnamese Regional Forces and Popular Forces, or RFPFs. "Shut down the Projects. All part of the goddamn 'Vietnamization program.'"

"Well, Top, I got less than six weeks left in-country," Mike remarked casually, locking the clasp on his new status symbol. "So I'm not going to get all hot and bothered by it."

"It'll be good to get back to Bragg, and I can't believe I'm saying that. But the truth is, the VN don't really give a shit if we're here or not, just as long as Uncle Sam's greenbacks keep flowin' in their direction."

"If we were really serious about winning this war, it would have been over years ago," Mike concluded.

"That woulda' put a hell of a lot of people outa' work back in 'the world,' don'cha know. The fuckin' politicians don't have the balls to just declare war on these Commie bastards and get it over with. Same fuckin' thing they did in Korea, and see where that got us? Truman should have let MacArthur take out the Chicoms when he had the chance."

"Fuckin' hypocrites," Mike agreed. "They send our guys across the Fence every day to scout the Trail and get their asses shot off. Then they disown the poor bastards and hang them out to dry when they get zapped or captured. Hell, their families don't even know what happened to them."

"That's what we do, Captain. And we do it better than any other swingin' dicks in-country. Problem is, why do we *have* to do it? Because the fuckin' politicians are afraid to admit they are waging a *secret* war in those neutral countries across the Fence."

"I hear you, Top. But if they'd just send our conventional troops across the Fence and shut down the Trail once and for all, Sir Charles would have to pack up his shit and go to the house."

"They're afraid they'd piss off the Russians and the Chinese. They'd rather see our boys take the brunt of it instead. *Scumbags!*"

Mike paused, shaking his head as he tried to sort it all out. "You realize we're starting to sound like all those folks back home, don'cha?" he reminded his sergeant.

"I know, *Đại úy*. But sometimes it just pisses the fuck out of me. I've never given a rat's ass about politics. I'm a professional solider. I serve at the pleasure of the President, and I take orders. Fuck a bunch of politics."

"I'm right there with you. I'm not career. Just a citizen soldier. I've tried to sort it all out, but I just ain't that smart myself. Sometimes I have to take a deep breath, but when I do that, I conjure up all those fuckin' images of those things I *thought* I left behind," Mike commented, staring down at the timepiece's vivid colors on the bezel.

"We're on an island, *Đại úy*. And the shoreline is diminishing. They hate us at home, and they resent us here. I joined Group in '63. It meant something then. Still does, but only to us. They don't know who we are. But then again, why should they? They haven't seen the majesty of the Alps under our boot tips, sittin' in the saddle at ten thousand feet. The tropical jungles of South America, the deserts of Africa, or the lush mountains of the Highlands. They haven't heard the strange words we speak to oppressed natives all around the world. *Coherently*, I might add. They're not enthused at all with the concept we hold dear: *De oppresso liber*. We don't come to *kill*, we come to *liberate*. Strange concept, isn't it? But they don't get it, or even appreciate it. It really sucks when the only people we can trust over here are the hated Cambodes and Yards."

"Ya know, since I've been here almost a year, I haven't had one VN come up to me and thank us for laying our lives on the line, trying to save them from the Commies. Not one. Except that poor ol' NVA woodcutter from the North who thanked me for givin' him some water and not stealing his life savings. It's all about the greenbacks, Top. The only thing I've heard lately is that they want to 'lub me too many.' Just want to know, Top: How many *is* that?"

"What?" Miller asked, a bit confused by the Captain's drift.

"Exactly. That's just what *I* said," Mike replied mysteriously. "Just wanted to make sure I'm not getting cheated, Top."

Late in the afternoon, the work chopper eased down on the pad across the canal, with the new team leader on board. Sergeant Marshall ferried Mike over one last time, and as he stepped up on the pad, he shook hands with his replacement, Captain Lewis, an old friend from the Tenth. With no time to exchange pleasantries, Mike just climbed up into the cabin and sat down. As the chopper lifted off, he took one last look at the place he'd been calling home for the past ten months. Then he gazed over to the far river bank. His old nemesis, "Pierre," hadn't been heard from for months, and Mike assumed the local VC river watcher was either dead or had simply retired from the war.

He sat in the middle seat and rolled his sleeves down as the cool air chilled the cabin. He harbored no interest in gazing out into the countryside. He knew what it looked like, and he no longer embraced what he saw. Before long, the chopper slid in behind a row of Cobra gunships parked at the end of the Tây Ninh airstrip. He casually gathered his gear and threw it in the waiting jeep, which took him inside the compound to the S1 building, near the latrines.

"Pappy's in his office, Captain Shannahan," the S1 sergeant told him. "I'll let him know you're here." Mike looked around the office, still a little nervous about being *relieved*.

He didn't have to wait long. Lieutenant Colonel Patterson promptly made his entrance and extended his welcoming hand to the young captain. "Welcome back to civilization, Shannahan," he began. "Glad you were able to get up here on such short notice. Step into my office with me. I know you're probably wondering what this is all about."

Mike followed the colonel into his small office and took a seat in the metal folding chair in front of his desk.

"We received alert orders on you this week, since you're scheduled to DEROS next month," Pappy said, referring to Mike's official "date of expected return from overseas." "They've got you slotted to take over a company in Training Group back at Bragg. Just wanted to get your thoughts on that before we ship you outa' here."

Mike sat back in the chair, grateful that there was no drama lingering in the air. "Well, sir, I've been giving the army a lot of thought lately, and the way that things are going, I don't see a bright future for me without a college degree. A lot of my dad's friends got rifted after the war," he related, alluding to the military practice of reverting newly minted officers back to their NCO rank if they hadn't completed their degree requirements within a year of being commissioned. "And that's probably going to happen after this one, too."

"I can't argue with that," the colonel agreed. "Well, I guess that means you won't be extending your commitment, so we'll leave it at that. But, in the meantime, it's been brought to my attention that you haven't taken your R&R yet, Captain, so I want you on the first chopper out of here to Saigon in the morning. Specialist Morgan will type up the orders for you as soon as you decide where you want to go."

Mike smiled, the thought of going on R&R had never crossed his mind. "Well, I appreciate that, sir. I think I just want to go somewhere where they have an overabundance of large-breasted, round-eyed women, Colonel," Mike admitted.

The colonel smiled, thought for a brief moment, then offered his advice. "How 'bout Hawaii or Australia, Captain?"

"Australia, sir. Never been there, and I've always wondered what a wallaby was, and I've never seen a platypus or a koala up close. But more importantly, I've had encounters with *Fräuleins*, *jo-sans*, and *co*'s, but I've never met a real-live Sheila."

"Done. We have our own hotel there on Coogee Beach. It's called the Oceanic. I'll have the company S1 send them a wire to let them know you're coming."

"Thank you, sir. I really appreciate that."

"But when you get back, you'll be spending a lot of time with me, son."

"Sir?"

"Captain Willington just rotated back to the States, and I'll be needing a new S1 here at the B-Detachment. I've been reading your after-action reports over the last ten months, and you seem to have a distinct command of the English language, Captain."

"Well, thank you, sir, but I must tell you my English grades in high school certainly don't attest to that," Mike confessed.

"Well, at least you know how to spell, and that's a start. Captain Meek put in a good word for you as well. He told me you graduated near the top of your class in OCS, and that says a lot to me about your organizational abilities. You'll be handling all my correspondence and team assignments.

And you'll be responsible for the awards and decorations we submit to Group. And, as an added responsibility, you'll be in charge of the club and the other sundry fund."

"Yes, sir."

"You'll take Captain Willington's hooch, and I trust you will find the accommodations a little more agreeable than what you've been used to. Anything else, Captain?"

"Well, sir, we were all a little curious about what is going on with the incursion across the Fence. We don't get a lot of free information flowing in our direction, and we just wanted to know what progress we're making shutting down the Trail."

"To be totally honest with you, Captain, Chuck *knew* we were coming. As a matter of fact, the force you ran into at Ba Thu was a rear element protecting the withdrawal of the COSVN headquarter elements and the two NVA line regiments headquartered there."

"They seem to know a *lot* about what we are planning to do before *we* do, sir."

"Let's just say, Shannahan, that anything that is decided on in Saigon ends up in Hanoi in just a matter of hours. We ended up with a lot of weapons and equipment they couldn't move, but their main forces withdrew past the twenty-five-click zone dictated by Nixon after the invasion. They knew exactly how far we would go."

"We have any of *our* people still over there?" Mike asked.

"No, not really. Just the SOG recon teams running their missions, trying to keep an eye on them as usual. Anything else?"

"No, sir," Mike sadly replied, standing up. "We were just hoping that the operation was going to finally make a difference." Then he saluted the colonel and promptly left the room.

He picked up his gear and had the clerk direct him to his new hooch. His next stop was the showers, but not before he found a new bar of soap and a clean, fresh towel.

* * *

Mike peered out the small window of the aging 707 as it raced down the runway, finally lifting off from the sprawling Tân Sơn Nhứt Air Base, situated on the outskirts of Saigon. For the next *forever* hours, the young officer struggled to get comfortable in his seat, completely bored and restless in his stifled, confined environment. Rowdy rear-echelon types seemed to far outnumber the men aboard with the faded, worn fatigues and the million-mile stares. He had heard that for every combat trooper in Vietnam, ten support troops were required to keep him fighting. The men on board seemed to validate that disturbing fact.

He stared for hours into the endless blankets of white, billowing clouds, lazily formatted in contrast to the distant, white-capped sea as the freedom bird slowly migrated south. His spirit continued to linger, suspended aimlessly at thirty-eight thousand feet, aloof and unable to encounter any sign of the enemy. As the hours wore on, the stale scent in the cabin provided evidence of the grungy sanitary habits of the men confined within. Persistent shadows of smoke traversed the ceiling while the stench of burnt cigarette butts permeated the recycled air flowing down the aisles.

When the sun finally nestled below the western horizon, he reluctantly drifted off into a deep, sound sleep. He was finally able to shed the lingering apprehension that prefaced the dark dreams he'd had back in the swampland, bleak visions that constantly endeavored to possess him. The soulful whimpers of the wounded young girls continued to mock him, constantly chastising him for the brutal distress the war had brought into their lives. The vision of pink water shimmering in Watson's thigh wounds mingled with the pungent scent of death the captain carried with him daily. He desperately longed for new adventures, fresh memories to dwell on, fond escapades that would captivate his senses and put an end to the wicked subconscious torment he endured.

Several hours later, he awoke to find the jet nestled up to a large refueling truck parked outside a small terminal with the name *Darwin* illuminated in the evening sky. He quickly submitted again to the heavy urge to sleep, fluffing the small pillow against the bulkhead as he returned to his peaceful dreamland.

The abrupt jolt of the massive tires impacting the runway startled him swiftly back to reality. The early morning sun sent bright beacons of daylight throughout the musty cabin as he shaded his eyes and peered out into the vast expanse of quaint homes and brick buildings just beyond the edge of the runway. *The real world,* he thought, a smile creasing across his face.

The sleek, silver airliner taxied to a remote terminal, and as the noise of the aircraft engines finally faded, Mike watched the small white truck with the steps mounted above it position itself up against the forward door. The men from the other side of the cabin suddenly rushed across the aisle, leaning over to get a closer look at the two lines of animated young ladies pushing up against the restraining ropes that led to the terminal.

"What the hell?" Mike commented, amazed at the enthusiasm the girls were displaying, how they were pushing one another aside for a better view of the cabin door. "We got a rock star or someone on board?" he asked the man seated next to him.

"Naw, those are the Charity Girls," he casually commented. "They told us about them back in Saigon. If they take a liking to you, they'll give you their number and a time to call 'em. They just want to take you home. Show you the sights, here in the land of Oz, then cook and take care of you for a week. Think it's a feel-good thing for 'em."

"What's the catch?" Mike asked.

"No catch. They just love American men over here. We're generous. We open doors, pull out their chairs, treat them with respect. They're not used to that."

"Works for me."

The large side door swung open, and in stepped a tall Australian man clad in khaki shorts, wearing a bush hat with the side brim folded neatly to one side. He took the microphone from the stewardess and greeted all on board. "G'day, mates! Welcome to sunny Sydney! We're glad you made the trip all the way here, this special land we call Down Under. I know you've seen the lines of Sheilas waiting to meet you, but unfortunately, you have to clear customs before you're allowed to mingle with the locals. There'll be plenty of time for that later," he informed them in his heavy Aussie accent. "You'll each be given a voucher for some new clothes in the men's shop set up inside the terminal. This is a small gift from the Country Women's Association and the grateful citizens of New South Wales to our American brothers."

Following the instructions from the resident army sergeant with regard to their deportment while in Sydney, the men filed off the aircraft, past the throngs of women passing out their cards and pictures to select men, then into the terminal where they dutifully cleared customs. Mike had collected several numbers, but he was determined to let his first trip to Australia be guided solely by fate.

He stopped abruptly as he entered the men's store, amazed by the quality of clothing and the number of friendly people assisting the men to select expensive-looking slacks, shirts, and sport coats to wear during their trip. After spending a little more than the voucher afforded him, he packed as much as possible into his overnight bag and carried his new sport coat over his shoulder out to where the taxis sat lined up in front of the terminal. "Oceanic Hotel in Coogee Beach," he told the driver.

"Oceanic it is," the friendly cabbie replied, cranking down the meter. Evidently fond of Yanks like the captain, he chatted all through the ride, asking what the States were like. After a short ride, he dropped his American fare off in front of the beachfront hotel, full of gratitude for the excessive tip as he pulled away.

Mike surveyed the quaint white stucco design of the Victorian structure, then hurried in to get his room. The hallways and parlor rooms stood decorated with emblems and crests of the Special Forces regiment, accented by several pictures of past Group commanders and men of distinction. The friendly matron at the small desk selected his room on the second floor, and soon he stood peering out the open French window at the beautiful turquoise-blue ocean and sandy beach just yards away from the hotel entrance. *Now I know why they call it the Land of Oz,* he thought, scanning the shoreline and jagged rock cliffs abutting the eastern end of the beach.

He quickly undressed, hanging his khakis over the valet in the corner. The marble-floored bathroom soothed the soles of his feet as he turned the water on in the tall glass shower stall. He stepped in, opened the wrapper on the small bar of soap, and quickly lathered up before standing beneath the cascading flow of warm water comforting his body. He luxuriated in such unaccustomed luxury.

After the leisurely shower, he decided he didn't want the day to go to waste. He hurriedly put on a new pair of lightweight slacks and the blue plaid shirt he had bought. *Shit! Forgot to get a belt,* he realized, pulling the black army belt out of his khakis. Downstairs, he walked over to the middle-aged lady smiling behind the desk. "Excuse me, ma'am. How do I get downtown?" he asked, sliding the strap to his new Pentax camera over his shoulder.

"Just step out on Arden Street, in front of the hotel," she told him. "There'll be plenty of taxis. Tell them you want to go to Kings Cross. It's about five kilometers into the city."

He hailed the first cab he saw, and he sat back and enjoyed the strange sights of the suburbs surrounding the wonderful Kingdom of Oz. He felt mildly displaced, like a distant cousin in a peculiar land. A tranquil sense of normalcy surrounded him as he watched the neatly preserved neighborhoods and the citizens of Oz calmly going about their business.

Within minutes, the cabbie pulled up across from a small park, with benches surrounding a prominent, circular fountain, which looked like a large, aquatic dandelion spraying smooth mists of water into an elevated pool. "That's nice," Mike told the driver. "What's it called?"

"That's the El Alamein Fountain, mate," the cabbie said. "Dedicated to our Aussie veterans who fought in North Africa during the war."

"Got to get a picture of that!" Mike stepped out and handed the cabbie a crisp, new ten-dollar bill.

He walked across the street and started taking pictures of everything of interest he could see. Several of the businesses had American-sounding names—Texas Tavern, Whiskey-a-Go-Go, The Pink Panther—all empty, with just a few people casually walking up and down the mostly vacant sidewalks. He looked at his watch and realized it was only ten-thirty in the morning. He slung his camera strap over his shoulder and began to walk. Every person he passed smiled and greeted him with the local greeting, *G'day*. Although still suspicious of their true intent, Mike finally realized that they were actually being *genuinely* nice to him.

He strolled through the upscale neighborhoods sequestered off the beaten trail, past Victorian homes with wrought-iron fences in a turn-of-the-century motif. He stopped to watch a gathering of jovial mature men rolling small balls across a green, manicured lawn, attired completely in white: shirts, bow ties, pants, and shoes. *Must be a country club or something*, he thought to himself as he gazed over at the low, shrub-lined compound. *Grown men, fondly engaged in simple pleasures.*

He wandered on for hours along the promenades, savoring the fresh ocean breeze, smiling so much his cheeks actually began to ache. Soon he found himself standing on the edge of a high, rocky cliff overlooking Sydney Harbor, with the vast Tasman Sea looming peacefully in the distance. *Had to go fight a war for God to show me such a majestic sight,* he told himself, contemplating the beauty.

He lingered for some time, consolidating in his mind his good fortune and the arduous path he had taken to finally arrive at this place. He gazed out over the vast ocean, paying his respects to his fallen comrades, friends, and mentors. He stood there, so full of life, embracing the peaceful harmony more than halfway around the world from home, destined to return to the dark side soon, his own destiny still at hand.

He abruptly took stock of his worth, measuring his intentions with all of those who opposed him, not only the antiwar protesters at home but even the VC and NVA enemy he had been warring against. He reluctantly afforded an element of substance to their motivation, although inconsistent with his yet still in some ways valid, he conceded, even though their ambitions and their values were so different from his. He stood paradoxically confused, drawing deep breaths of the redeeming ocean air, allowing himself a welcome respite to dwell on his own aspirations, his motivation, his core. He regretted the confusion that ensued, along with the final fact that no resolutions could be drawn. *Ya just* had *to go there, didn't ya?* he scolded himself. *But my only true regrets are those imposed upon me.*

The tinge in his heels drew his attention. He realized that his stiff new shoes had finally worn through the firm calluses on his feet. He hadn't seen a cab in over an hour, and as he made his way back to the center of town, he decided to just take his shoes off, to limit further damage to his aching feet. He recalled seeing a corner apothecary and decided to stop and buy some moleskin and tape to take the pressure off his new blisters.

His excursion cut short, he finally hailed a taxi and made his way back to Coogee Beach to tend to his self-inflicted wounds. When the cab dropped him off in front of the hotel, he stood briefly, smiling in admiration at the scores of carefree sunbathers frolicking in the sun-drenched sand near the tranquil shore.

He reluctantly stepped inside, but as he turned to go up the stairs to his room, the kindly white-haired lady stepped out from behind her desk. "Mr. Shannahan, I have a gift for you from the American Australian Association," she said, handing him a large fresh-fruit basket, with an assortment of delectable-looking produce. "I hope you enjoy it, sir. They just dropped it off."

He thanked her and took the basket. With his shoes in his other hand, he limped gingerly up the worn, wooden stairs to his room. Inside the basket's bright foil wrap, he found a letter inviting him to an evening reception downtown in honor of the officers on R&R from Vietnam. He gazed several times at the fancy script with his name on it, ultimately deciding it would be in bad taste not to attend.

Attentively, he positioned the implements of relief on the bedside table. Then he set about in earnest to surgically repair his aching heels. *If you've ever worn combat boots,* he reminded himself, *you'd better know how to fix a blister.*

With the thin layers of moleskin firmly in place, he stripped down to his boxers and opened the tall French windows. The mild ocean breeze greeted him with a beguiling scent, which drew him back to the overstuffed bed, where he casually lay, welcoming the fresh salt air, allowing it to cleanse and purge the last vile remnants of cordite and stagnant vapors that had enveloped him. His fragile mind purged vague images and instincts, permitting the sweet depths of sleep to soon overwhelm him.

Hours later, he awoke, confused, urged back to reality by the blare of car horns and boisterous voices flowing through his open window. He stirred momentarily, then rallied his consciousness abruptly, suddenly aware that he had a dire commitment at hand. He peered out the window and watched the last vestige of the sunbathers leaving the beach, the setting sun casting dark shadows as they walked toward their waiting cars.

He glanced at his heavy watch, dutifully realizing that the event was scheduled to begin in less than fifteen minutes. He grabbed his tailored light-gray trousers from the closet, put on the button-down white shirt he had acquired, and within minutes, he stood in front of the hotel, anxiously looking for a cab, his new blue sport coat slung casually over his shoulder. *Shoulda' bought some Old Spice at the airport,* he briefly lamented.

The cabbie held his hand out, confident that his fare had ample cash on hand, considering the stature of the venue he had delivered him to. "Should you be needing a ride home, Governor," he said to the young man struggling to put his coat on. "I've left my cab's number on the card."

Mike walked through the large arched doorway, enamored with opulent murals and Olde English furniture assembled throughout the foyer, nurturing his swollen heels as he stepped into the vast, rustic ballroom, where he was greeted by a vision he had never before encountered. Princesses, adorned in fashion, energized his pulse as he gave the matron at the door his name. While she checked the guest list, he surveyed the crowd, fully entranced by the evident quality of talent, an abundance of sheer, utter beauty displayed in his presence. *Damn!* he thought. *Never seen anything like this up close before.*

Delightful girls, women (or those who purported to be women), were attired delicately in high fashion, full skirts and streamlined cocktail dresses—in any event, he felt, attired solely to be admired. They stood gracefully, intently engaged in conversations with their elder generation and numerous other, younger men in attendance. It appeared to Mike to be the upper echelon of Sydney society, gathered in accordance with their gentility to welcome their war-weary, honored guests.

He hesitated, then dolefully meandered over to the busy bar. With his back to the mélange of social opportunities, he ordered a Glenlivet with a twist, suddenly reluctant to engage anyone who might challenge his motives or inquire about his intent. He promptly harnessed a degree of social intrigue, guarding against any devious effort to query the self-righteous value of his resolve. He brushed the tarnished image of Eve—that is, Mrs. Carlson—from his mind, sipping slowly from the ice-filled crystal tumbler while he searched for telltale wedding rings on the various ladies' fingers.

Then he saw her. Across the room, the innocent, sweet naïveté in her smile immediately set him at ease. His eyes slowly scanned the flow of her vivid red hair, her long, shoulder-length locks accented fully by their contrast with her smooth, alabaster skin. The flowery, full-skirted dress drew tightly around her thin waist, and as his eyes followed the long contour of her legs, he strained to glimpse into her eyes. She stood casually talking to an older couple, her lovely profile demanding further attention.

He took his nametag out of his trouser pocket and adjusted it squarely on his breast pocket: *Captain Michael Shannahan, U.S. Army.*

With his drink in hand, he slowly merged into the energized crowd, nodding and smiling as he made his way through the thick variety of conversations. Moving with a purpose, he was careful not to become engaged or distracted from his mission. He stopped short of walking up to her, standing several steps away with her back to him. He stood quietly, debating the manner in which he would make her acquaintance. The tall gentleman she was talking with finally looked over her shoulder, making firm eye contact with Mike. He smiled and looked away, sipping his drink as he casually surveyed the crowd. *Probably not a good idea,* he decided, unsure of what to say if he did approach her.

While he pondered decorum and social etiquette, the gentleman placed his hand on the young maiden's shoulder. With his other hand, he motioned Mike over to them. The young captain haltingly obliged, cautiously stepping up to a position next to the young lady. The gray-haired gentleman smiled cordially, looking down at Mike's nametag as he made the introductions.

"Captain Shannahan... Ernest Anniston, and this is my wife, Elaine, and our daughter, Rachel."

"Michael Shannahan. It's a pleasure to meet you," Mike replied, reaching over and shaking Mr. Anniston's hand. He turned to Mrs. Anniston and took her hand gently, telling her it was his honor to make her acquaintance. She smiled approvingly.

As Mike finally glanced toward the Anniston daughter, he encountered the sparkle in her eyes, a gaze that captivated him instantly "Pardon me for my impudence, but you have the most beautiful eyes I have ever seen," he told her in earnest, admiring the emerald-green glittering in her eyes while he caressed her fingertips.

Her cheeks flourished to a blush, her sudden smile inviting and receptive. "You must be exhausted," Rachel commented. "Father was just telling us that it's over a ten-hour flight from Saigon."

"It seemed like a lot longer than that," Mike said to the three of them. "We must have had a headwind or something."

"Well, we were just going to be seated for dinner, Captain," Mr. Anniston told him. "And it would be our pleasure to have you join us at our table as our guest."

"I would enjoy that very much, sir," Mike replied, suddenly realizing that he hadn't eaten anything all day. He followed his new acquaintances into the dining room, careful to hold Elaine's chair as she was seated. He quickly pulled Rachel's chair out as well, glancing over to the approving smile on Ernest's face.

"So… Where are you from in America?" Ernest inquired.

"Well, my father is a career naval aviator, so I've pretty much grown up all over the world. But to answer your question: I call Texas my home."

"Ahhh, Texas," he replied, smiling broadly at the revelation.

"They have a lot of different breeds of horses there, don't they?" Rachel asked, smiling sweetly as her eyes continued to sparkle in the candle-lit room.

"Well, I worked on several ranches during my summers in high school, and I lived alongside the King Ranch before I joined the service."

"Father raises thoroughbreds on our ranch just outside Denham Court," Rachel was quick to inform him. "I love to ride when I'm home on holiday from the university," she added.

"Rachel attends nursing school at Catholic University in Melbourne," Elaine related. "We're thrilled to have her home now, for the summer break."

Catholic… Now, that's convenient. Mike felt encouraged with this unexpected revelation.

"Well, you're probably familiar with Assault, the Triple Crown winner, then?" Mike asked Ernest.

"Indeed I am," the gentleman replied. "He won it in 1946, just after the big war. They called him the Club-footed Comet," he added.

"Yeah, that's right." Mike smiled as he recalled the first time he'd seen the champion. "They say he stepped on a surveyor's stake when he was a colt and drove it right through his hoof. He walked with a limp, but when he was at a full gallop, you couldn't even tell."

"How very interesting!" Elaine remarked.

"Did you ever get to see him?" Rachel asked.

"Used to drive out to the King Ranch after school some days and just hang out in his stall near the Big House. I fed him salt and sugar cubes," Mike told her. "He's still a beautiful stallion, even today. He really puts on a show chasing the mares out in the pasture." Both Rachel and Elaine blushed at this suggestive image.

The conversation flowed with relative ease, with Mike and Rachel exchanging flirtatious glances whenever the opportunity arose. After a couple of rounds of drinks, the waiter presented the menu for the evening, and Mike quickly selected the most expensive entrée he could find. Although he had no idea what a *Chateaubriand* was, for that price, he knew it had to be good. The waiter informed him that the dish was prepared for two, but he insisted that he was hungry enough to finish anything that they could fit on the plate.

With their orders taken, Ernest took his wife's hand and escorted her out onto the dance floor. The orchestra's melody was unfamiliar to Mike, but when he looked at Rachel, he knew it was time to dance. He stood and offered his hand, pulling her chair out as they walked over to the crowded dance floor. Her intimate fragrance immediately enveloped him. He took deep, full breaths and filled his lungs with her sweet ambiance. They danced slowly to several songs, chatting about trivial things young people find interesting, drawing closer to each other as the romantic music accented their chance encounter.

"You're trembling," Rachel remarked, drawing Mike's attention to the fact.

"Oh, that. I gotta tell you that it's entirely all *your* fault. You've got my adrenal glands talking back to me," he confessed to her. "I haven't been this close to such a beautiful woman since *forever.*" He had just been thinking how dancing with her had made him forget the persistent pain in his heels, but he hadn't been aware that his tremor was acting up again.

She giggled, tightening her grip on his quivering hand. He took a deep breath, pleading for the slight tremor to stop, unwilling to tell her the true source of the malady. As the song ended, he escorted her back to the table, realizing that the sheer excitement of touching her had unleashed the surging overflow of adrenaline that his body could no longer manage.

"We'll be leaving late tomorrow morning to spend the rest of the week at the ranch," Ernest told him. "I'm sure Rachel would be glad to have you ride with her out to Lake Burragorang for the afternoon," he added. "You could stay in the guest quarters for a couple of days and see a bit of the Outback while you're here."

Mike turned to Rachel and watched her lovely smile puff the rose tint in her cheeks. She quickly took his hand and squeezed it firmly. "Oh *yes*, Michael. Please say yes. We could have a swell time, and Mum packs the grandest picnic baskets."

He stared daringly into her eyes, anticipating an adventure that would fill the void in his wounded soul. "That sounds great! I haven't been on a horse for over three years, and I love to ride. I can't think of anywhere else I'd rather be."

"Good! Then it's done!" Ernest replied as the waiters positioned the entrées on the candle-lit table. "We'll talk about it over dinner."

The smell of elegant food smothered Mike's senses, compelling him to temper the surging instinct to reject his manners and just *devour* the sautéed filet of beef filling the large plate before him. He waited patiently until Elaine finally took her first bite of thinly sliced salmon before he picked up his steak knife and initiated his assault on the tenderloin, braised in a thick, savory mélange of brown sauce and anointed with a slew of roasted shallots and mushrooms. *Damn! This is some good shit!* he told himself, elated with his choice from the menu.

He forced himself to alternate his tastes between the steamed asparagus and puffy whipped potatoes, pausing briefly to butter the fluffy yeast dinner rolls filling the basket in front of him. He noticed Rachel continually glancing over at him, smiling with delight as he neatly carved the large, barely bite-size pieces of filet before he had even finished chewing the last portion.

"Is it good?" she asked and waited patiently for Mike to pause in his eating and reply.

He took the napkin from his lap and, after several veiled efforts, was finally able to respond. "Excellent! This is the first real meal I've had in almost a year."

Then he looked around the table, a little perplexed by the sudden sad expressions on their faces. "No... really... It's *very* good. There's not a lot of five-star restaurants back where I've just come from," he said, smiling and hoping to restore the casual tenor to the table.

Rachel placed her hand on his knee and smiled. "Good! I'm glad you're enjoying it."

In an effort to defuse any further attention to the utter bliss his palate was experiencing, Mike slowed the pace of his intake. He even made a conscious attempt to limit the number of dinner rolls he was consuming, despite the glorious scent of freshly baked yeast beckoning his attention.

They made plans to pick Mike up at his hotel the following morning, and for the next hour or so, they talked about everything except the war. He enjoyed dancing several numbers with Elaine and Rachel, pleased that his tremor had finally subsided, along with the nervous perspiration on his palms.

Rachel placed her warm hand on the back of his neck, softly teasing him as she slowly rubbed her cheek against his. The orchestra collaborated to fuse the couple together, the smooth melody of *Moonlight Sonata* providing the essential glue. As the sultry refrain finally brought their entwined motion to a pause, she kissed him softly on the cheek and whispered in his ear. "Thank you so much for being here tonight. I hope you know how special you make me feel."

He looked into her eyes and smiled. "Now I know how it feels to be resurrected. Being with you tonight has truly brought me back to life. You have *no* idea. And… I'm really looking forward to spending the next few days with you and your parents."

He sat comfortably at the table, enjoying Rachel's laughter in response to one of Ernest's entertaining fables. His palate summoned additional endorphins as he sat spooning the final scrumptious portion of the large bowl of chocolate mousse when, suddenly, it emerged.

Abruptly, a feeling of lightheaded nausea began to materialize, coupled with a nervous layer of warm sweat seeping out above his creasing brow. He took a deep breath, then lightly patted his forehead with the dinner napkin. He reached over and took a long sip of the ice water, hoping to quell the crescendo of symptoms swelling in his churning stomach. Something wasn't right, and as he sat back in the chair, he feared the worst. "Would you all excuse me, please?" he asked, standing up and patting his forehead again. "I'll be right back."

He turned and hurried toward the men's room, the flora in his intestines and stomach rapidly conspiring to reject the contents of his welcomed feast, a decision that he knew would be made entirely without his consent. As he burst through the door to the men's room, his best and final effort to restrain the onslaught of consequences failed him. He barely had his trousers loosened when the deluge erupted, soiling the top portion of his pants as he drew them down to his knees. *Jeezzus fuckin' Christ!* he lamented as the sharp pain enveloped his midsection, doubling him over as he sat perched awkwardly on the chill commode. He reached behind him, flushing the toilet repeatedly as the episode escalated. The lingering nauseous feeling persisted, urging him desperately to vomit, but he refused to comply, swallowing repeatedly to thwart the overwhelming impulse. *I've got to get the hell outa' here!* he told himself, utterly humiliated by his current condition.

With the initial volley finally subsiding, he made a command decision. He carefully slid his trousers off, pulled the belt out, and stood up. After cleaning himself up as best he could, he dipped the soiled part of his pants in the toilet and flushed again. After several attempts, he finally rinsed most of the dark stains away. He wrung the wet pants out, slid them back on, took his sport coat off, and tied the arms around his waist. Without hesitation, he left the men's room and made his way past the serving waiters and through the busy kitchen, finally finding the loading dock, where he scurried down the alley and out onto the busy street.

For the next five days, he lay sequestered in his room, unable to eat or even venture out down the stairs, before he was finally able to restore the fragile flora that enabled him to function.

So much for a bunch of koalas and wallabies, he decided on his way to the airport. *But, dear God, I already really miss that sweet, lovely Sheila!*

* * *

CHAPTER FORTY-ONE

"W HAT HAPPENED TO *YOU*, CAPTAIN?" the familiar voice asked him.

Mike looked up from his desk to see Sergeant First Class Lanza smiling at him from the doorway.

"Looks like somebody took a shot at you and missed. Then took a massive *shit* at you and hit!" Lanza joked, his white teeth beaming through his dark five-o'clock shadow.

"If I hear one more *shit* joke about what happened to me, I'm going to take the rest of the afternoon just dreamin' up *shit* for you to do that'll take your mind off it for good," Mike said. "You obviously have entirely too much free time on your hands as it is."

"Don't take it so personal, *Đại úy*. I crapped in my pants all the time out in the boonies."

"It's not the same thing, and you know it, Sergeant."

"Well, I've heard lotsa' guys sayin' they were *dying* to take a crap, but you kinda' took it to the extreme, don'cha know."

"Why aren't you in the club counting napkins, Lanza?" he curtly inquired.

"Thought you might want to ride shotgun over to Tây Ninh East with me, *Đại úy*. Everybody else is hunkered down for *poc* time, and it's time you met my supply contacts at the base camp anyway."

The captain looked at his watch and decided he was just about caught up with the morning reports and correspondence. "Why not? I'd like to see what they've got in the main PX over there anyway. Gotta get one of those fancy Omega watches for my mom before I DEROS."

Mike grabbed his web gear and M16 and followed Sergeant Lanza out to the B-Team's three-quarter-ton truck, parked outside the front door. He had met Sergeant Ken Lanza on his previous trips to the B-Team and was glad to have someone of his caliber running the club and all the details and headaches that entailed. Kenji, as his friends called him, was just completing his fourth tour in Vietnam. A highly respected recon man with MACV SOG, he had also spent tours with the MIKE Force and several A-Teams throughout the country. Mike found it somewhat ironic that such a vetted warrior had allowed them to relegate his talents to just running a club in an obscure B-Detachment.

The pair sped out of the compound and onto the dusty dirt road leading into the bustling provincial capital city of Tây Ninh. Mike kept a sharp eye on the locals lining the road, suspicious of everyone they passed on the way—men, women, and children. As they passed over the whitewashed arches on the small bridge leading into town, he gazed up the smooth, murky river, still amazed at this tranquil, picturesque setting, which was totally oblivious to the raging war only a gunshot away.

"So, what'dja get yourself into down there, *Đại úy*?" Lanza asked, a conciliatory tone in his voice.

Mike sighed, paused for a moment, then painfully related the events that had led to his demise. "Just got stupid and greedy all at the same time," he said. "We landed at daybreak, and I was hot to trot to see *everything* as soon as I could. I was so hyped up, I forgot to eat anything. You ever been to Sydney?"

"Naw. Spent my time in Bangkok and Hong Kong. Got this thing for oriental women, cheap Rolexes, and star sapphires," Lanza explained, holding out his hairy arm for the captain to admire the large sapphire ring and the thick-linked, gold Rolex.

"Well, I met this really gorgeous girl at a reception in Sydney. Her name is Rachel. I had dinner with her and her parents in the ballroom, and things were going great until I pigged out on the lavish chow they had for dinner. Just couldn't stop eating. It was *fuckin'* good shit. About three hours into the evening, my stomach started talking back to me, and it obviously didn't agree with *anything* I ate. Bad move on my part. Barely made it to the latrine before all hell broke loose."

"How much did you eat?"

"I ate the whole damn thing and then some."

"Didn't anybody ever tell you—?"

"No, they *fuckin'* didn't!" Mike replied, clearly agitated. "And who do I talk to about that?"

Lanza laughed, running his large hand through his sparse black hair as he glanced over at the captain with a wide grin on his face. "No wonder you got sick. You can't pig out on a rich man's diet right away after what we eat here in-country. You're not supposed to do that shit to your body, Đại úy. It could fuck you up big time."

"*Now* you tell me! Now I know."

"So, what happened?"

"I E&E'd out the back door. Had shit all over my pants. I couldn't go back in there like that. Barely made it back to the hotel before it started up all over again."

"What happened to Rachel?"

"Thank God her dad came by the hotel the next day. He knew something went wrong. He saw how bad off I was and called his friend the doctor to make a house call on my sorry ass. I was so dehydrated, the doc put an IV in and gave me some pain medication for the stomach cramps and headaches I was having. I couldn't even keep a glass of water down."

"What about the girl?"

"Never saw her again," Mike said in a forlorn tone as he stared out the window. "But she did let me know that there's life after the Nam. And I was really beginning to wonder about that."

Lanza looked over at the young captain, gauging the expression on his face. "This shit here don't mean *nothing*. You know that, Đại úy."

Following a long, somber silence, Mike quietly replied. "I do now."

They rode through the noisy, pungent town, vile odors collaborating with disgusting vapors, duly noted by the irritated occupants of the truck. Lanza skillfully weaved his way through the narrow streets, dodging animal-drawn carts and smoke-spewing motorbikes, past ranks of women attired in black silk pants, colorful blouses, and straw coolie hats, who were either going to or coming from the massive base camp ahead. They finally passed through the guarded entrance, under the wooden archway constructed high overhead. Convoys of clay-covered deuce-and-a-halfs vied for position along the narrow dirt road, hauling weary soldiers and tons of supplies in and out of the Twenty-fifth Infantry Division headquarters.

Mike watched with keen interest as armored personnel carriers ferried dust-caked troops to destinations unknown, the men perched atop the "metal coffins" to escape the unbearable heat generated inside. Gangs of troops casually walked alongside the road, most without weapons, boldly secure in the confines of the sprawling assembly area. He observed tattered C-123 cargo planes rumbling toward the oil-drenched runway, patiently waiting for their turn to resupply some remote unit with pallets of ammunition and food.

As they drove on, he felt a degree of resignation witnessing the slouch and disrespect many of the men displayed in the manner they dressed and accorded themselves, accented by the prevalent "Do Wah Diddy" gait in their stride. He conceded that they were mere rear-echelon types, but still, to him, it *all* had taken on a character of its own, an emerging cycle of redundant indifference of those things he regarded as innately American: *duty* and *honor*. A firm commitment to the values and aspirations that had molded the post–World War Two American principles had been reduced into mere vestiges of the once-sacred American way.

Just go through the motions. Same ol' crap. Same ol' "don't give a shit" results.

Mike felt that America's benevolence had been tranformed into the lowest common denominator: hoards of cash for the venturists. He now realized that in order to maintain *any* façade of nobility, in order to substantiate and justify the inept policies dictating their actions, men had to sacrifice their lives. He reasoned that the perpetual protests and antiwar rhetoric spewing daily from the press, and from the American populace generally, had finally infiltrated the minds and attitudes of many of the men they sent to war in their stead, the men he gazed at now.

"There's a covey of Dust Off comin' in, Captain," Lanza said, pulling off to the side of the road.

"Why are we stopping?" Mike inquired, looking through the dusty windshield at the four Red Cross choppers flaring just over the road in front of them.

"You'll see…"

Mike watched carefully as each bird tilted its tail boom downward in landing on the Forty-fifth Field Hospital pad, spewing out of the open doors swirling layers of vaporized body fluids.

"They got me good the last time that happened," Lanza said, putting the truck back in gear and onto the road again.

Mike stared at the rush of medics and nurses to the doors of each chopper, pulling the blood-soaked stretchers out and rushing them into the large canvas-covered building, limp arms and legs dangling lifelessly from the poncho-draped bodies, most already expired despite the haste.

I wonder what worthless piece of shit jungle you died for today, he thought. *And for what? My armor is tarnished. You died a senseless death. I wish I had been there to fight with you, to save you,* he lamented. *And I don't even know your names.*

"They were bringin' load after load of those poor bastards in from that fiasco last year at Hamburger Hill," Lanza said. "And I made the dumb mistake of drivin' under one of 'em and got fuckin' *swamped* with splatter."

"We're supposed to be fighting a *fuckin'* war, but we're not," Mike suddenly proclaimed. "We're mere pawns in somebody else's game, Lanza. Fighting with bullshit *Marquess of Queensberry rules.* Been doing the same bullshit things for years, but nobody wants to step up and get the job done. Just accept the status quo. So long as the fuckers back home get reelected, doesn't matter how many young boys over here have to die. Bet they packed up their shit and left, right after all those brave paratroopers gave their lives takin' that meaningless fuckin' hill, didn't they?"

"What set *you* off, *Đại úy*?" a stunned Lanza inquired.

"American body bags and bloody stretchers. I'm fuckin' allergic to 'em."

* * *

The next several weeks provided the veteran captain with a bittersweet opportunity to recover from the primitive life he had left behind in the swamplands. In anticipation of his eventual emancipation back to the real world, he allowed his hair and sideburns to grow. His pandering hooch maid, Trần, ensured that his boots were shined and his fatigues were properly starched. Fresh towels and sheets greeted him every day, along with a steady diet of fresh eggs and poultry. He slowly began to regain the weight he'd lost, and the late-afternoon volleyball games outside the club restored his stamina and what was left of his muscular body. He reluctantly came to accept his new role as just another rear-echelon type.

The tedious, boring days behind his desk afforded him time to read the colonel's correspondence from headquarters, grim accounts detailing the transformation of the A-Teams in the entire region bordering both Laos and Cambodia. Camp after camp was eventually slated to be deactivated and turned over to Vietnamese Rangers and Regional Forces, their Special Forces advisors sent back home or to Groups stationed in other regions of the world. The politics of Mike's nation had finally caught up with their most trusted and valiant warriors. They were all going home, at least most of them.

*   *   *

Eighty kilometers to the north of Tây Ninh, a Bright Light team in Lộc Ninh readied their equipment for a hasty departure. Inside the makeshift tactical operations center, the CCS commander and his special operations staff sorted through the scant intelligence and other details they had accumulated to formulate a plan to locate and recover the remnants of RT Piston. Staff Sergeant Gibson and his one-one, Lieutenant Mycoskie, sat quietly at the back of the crowded TOC, staring at the large situation map on the wall, while majors and captains scurried to coordinate with support units in securing air assets and fast movers to bolster the recovery mission.

Sergeant Gibson's eyes narrowed and his relaxed posture stiffened as he observed the Vietnamese colonel and his aide walk into the room. Gibson stood abruptly and made his way directly to the CCS commander, Lieutenant Colonel Clifford Barksdale. "Sir, my team and I won't be a part of any operation that includes any LLDB or any other straphangin' indig involved in the briefing," he said. "If you don't get them outa' here, you're just gonna have to find another team to go in, sir."

The colonel put his hand on Gibson's shoulder and walked him to the corner of the room. "What's this all about, Gibson?"

"Sir, we've been shot out of the last four LZs my team has been inserted into, Colonel. That's *wayyy* too many to just be a coincidence. We've been takin' hits like that up and down the Fence for the last six months. The whole fuckin' NVA army knows we're coming. And they know exactly where to set up to intercept our inserts. I've done the math, and some worthless fuckers are tippin' them off."

The savvy silver leaf looked over toward the Vietnamese colonel, smugly attired in his crisp, starched fatigues. He smiled cordially at his counterpart as he contemplated Gibson's remarks.

"What the hell's he doing here in the first place?" Gibson demanded. "Does he have a *need to know?*"

"I'll handle it, Sergeant," Barksdale said. "You just focus on the mission at hand. You're right, he *doesn't* have a need to know."

The colonel strode over to the launch commander and quietly issued his directive. Gibson stared as the tall major walked over to the LLDB colonel and, with a little prompting, escorted him out of the briefing area.

A few minutes later, Barksdale stepped up in front of the map and began the initial briefing. "Yesterday at dawn, RT Piston was inserted without incident just south of Highway Seven in the Phumi Sre area in the "Salem House" AO. Covey made the scheduled contact when they moved into their RON position last night, and that's the last we heard from them. All subsequent attempts to establish commo with the team have produced negative results."

He pointed to the map and circled the insertion and RON position RT Piston had established before losing contact.

"Any beepers?" someone asked.

"Negative," the colonel replied. "Their mission was to investigate a reported isolated POW camp located in the vicinity of X-ray Zulu one-zero-five-two-one-zero-three-four," he said, indicating that spot on the map. "The team was light, with two Special Forces and three Cambodes on the ground after insert. Enemy activity was reported to be sparse, their main force units operating farther north, in the eastern sector of the AO. Weather in the target area is currently cloudy and overcast, with intermittent rain showers limiting our ability to get a good look at anything on the ground."

The briefing continued in detail, with the Bright Light team requesting medical supplies and additional special weapons and ammunition. The seasoned recon men studied the map diligently, looking for the obvious insertion sites as well as those they felt offered an alternative that would limit the enemy's ability to ambush them when they landed. They studied the relief and elevation markers on the map, factors that would dictate the equipment they would carry to negotiate the local terrain. Rally points were identified and plotted, along with the growing list of air assets scheduled to be on station.

They all agreed on one thing: If RT Piston was down, somebody had put them down, and recent similar encounters across the Fence indicated that the enemy was just lying in wait, fully prepared for the next team to come looking for them. Gibson stared at the map, focusing on RT Piston's last RON position. "They know we're comin' for 'em," he whispered.

The leaders of the Bright Light team planned their operational movement once they would be on the ground. They considered every contingency and finally determined that they were as prepared as they could be for the urgent mission at hand. "We're goin' in heavy, with just ammo and water," Gibson told everyone. "Once we find 'em, you can count on our fightin' our way out."

The supply sergeant dropped a large cardboard box on top of the table and then turned to leave the room.

"What's that?" Lieutenant Mycoskie inquired, reaching over to open the top.

"Body bags," the sergeant informed them. "Everybody grab one. You're gonna need them." There were enough bags in the box for each member of the RT Piston team and, ominously, a coupla' extras as well. The somber mood in the room intensified.

As the time wore on, the men were finally called on to give their briefback to the commander. Satisfied with the overall scheme they had devised, Colonel Barksdale finally authorized the dangerous mission. "Get some sleep, gentlemen. You'll be inserting at daybreak."

Lieutenant Mycoskie walked over to the map. Methodically he memorized the terrain features and elevations in and around the target area. He found himself searching for an avenue of escape back to the border, and he plotted the azimuth and distance of travel.

"This is gonna be a tough one, LT," Sergeant Gibson told him, handing him a vial of dextroamphetamines. "Put these *green hornets* somewhere you won't lose them."

"You think they found it?" Rich calmly asked.

"What? The POW camp? Haven't found one *yet*," Gibson answered. "The ones we did find were all deserted by the time we got there."

"Kinda' figured that. They *always* know when we're coming." Rich slung a body bag over his shoulder and headed out the door. He walked slowly back to the Bright Light hooch, dim vestiges of his brother looming profoundly in every step he took.

Sergeant Gibson quickly caught up with his one-one and placed his arm firmly around his shoulder. "Pretty flat terrain, Lieutenant," he told him. "Good thing is, there's a lot of cover in those chanti groves, and the elevation peaks out at about two hundred feet. I'm going to scrounge up some Bata boots for us. If we get spooked early, this damn thing could turn into a track meet."

Rich nodded his head and kept walking toward the hooch. He remained confident that Sir Charles would be waiting for them, and he was looking forward to the inevitable encounter. Unlike the case with many of the other men, this war continued to fuel a fervent fire in his soul. In spite of the moral burden that accompanied his arduous journey deep into that dark, soulful valley between good and evil, he would extract his measure of vengeance.

He threw the dense body bag on his bed and then walked over and pulled the heavy wooden crate of 7.62mm ammo back to his bunk. Samson scampered out from beneath the bunk, bounded up on the bed, and quickly found his perch on his master's broad shoulder. Rich carefully laid his empty magazines out, and one by one, he wiped each individual round clean, caressing every metal jacket before pressing it carefully into the magazine. Samson diligently performed his monkey-love ritual as his master assembled thirty-five twenty-round magazines, twenty-five of which he packed into the pouches of his World War Two BAR web belt hanging on the dusty wall.

Dumping the contents of his rucksack on the bed, he meticulously began sorting through the items he had taken on the last mission. He picked out a long piece of beef jerky and handed it up to Samson. The pesky macaque snatched the delicacy out of his hand and bolted up to the rafters to savor the treat. Rich threw the extra rations and medical items to the floor, then focused intently on packing the body bag and remaining M67 grenades and Claymore mines along with the extra magazines and det cord. He methodically stuffed the side pockets with mini-grenades and M79 rounds and then laid the time fuse on the bed to measure ten- and thirty-second fuses for the small quarter-pound blocks of C-4 he'd earlier fabricated, each infused with tiny ball bearings and rusty steel tacks. He carefully selected only violet smoke grenades, and he crammed several of them in the top of his pack.

With his nylon rucksack filled to the brim with implements of death and destruction, he pulled his Randall fighting knife from its scabbard on his harness and began to hone the razor-sharp blade, spitting repeatedly on the whetstone as he hummed a lonesome Orbison tune to himself. His critical battle chores complete, he stepped in front of the mirror, once again disguising the elements of his true nature with an assortment of oily, dark green war paint. He laid his head cravat and leggings neatly on the table, picked up the large butt can, and stepped outside the hooch. Scooping up as much loamy red clay and dust as he could, he made several trips until his bunk was completely covered in filthy, amber dirt. He pulled up his collar and lay down, crossing his arms over his chest as he shimmied his shoulders to spread out the uneven layers beneath him. He calmly closed his eyes and waited for the signal to deploy.

"Sweet dreams, Chucky boy. See ya in the mornin'," he whispered as his furry sentry stood guard at the foot of his filthy bed.

* * *

CHAPTER FORTY-TWO

THE MID-AFTERNOON HEAT SCORCHED THE captain's neck as he stepped up on the hot tailgate of the battered, rusty truck. The salty, dried, sweat-stained fatigue jacket irritated his skin as he bent down and slid the last cases of Coke and beer over to Sergeant Lanza for him to stack them up on the tall hand trolley.

"Gonna have to get some other lame-ass flunky to do your dirty work by Friday," Mike joked, jumping down and hurrying over to open the door for the sergeant.

"Don't rub it in, *Đại úy*. You short-timers can get *really* obnoxious."

"I'm so short, I have to look up to look down!" Mike reminded Lanza.

As the captain pulled open the screen door, Master Sergeant Donovan swiftly burst through, knocking him against the storeroom wall in his haste. "I need this truck!" the normally mild-mannered Irishman boldly insisted. "We've got an inbound recon team that's all shot up, and the slick is in trouble as well!" He slung his large medical bag into the back, then vaulted up into the driver's seat. "Need some help loading up the stretchers. Jump in! They're about five klicks out!"

The captain scurried over, pushed his weapon aside, and stepped up into the passenger seat, while Lanza hopped up into the back as the senior B-Team medic put the truck in gear.

"Why they comin' here and not over to the Eighty-fifth at the base camp?" the captain asked, a little confused.

"They don't think they can make it," Donovan quickly explained. "They're spewing what's left of their fuel, and their hydraulics are all shot to hell. They were tryin' to make it back to the FOB in Quân Lợi but finally had to divert. The pilot bought it, and the Peter Pilot is shot up pretty bad too. Folks from the Eighty-fifth are headed this way. Been listening to the clusterfuck over at the commo shed all morning."

"How many?"

"Don't know. It's pretty chaotic. Everybody and his brother are on the fuckin' net."

Donovan pulled alongside the dispensary, and Mike jumped out to help Specialist Emory pass the stretchers to Lanza, who was standing in the back. The junior medic handed the captain another large medical bag and then hopped up into the back with Sergeant Lanza.

"Why don't they just send a Dust Off in from the Eighty-fifth?" Mike asked.

"They're all tied up with some mechanized operation north of Katum," Donovan replied.

Speeding through the gate and onto the airfield, they quickly spotted the smoking Huey crabbing desperately through the distant haze, the dazed pilot struggling to keep the craft level as the tail boom swung like a drunken maestro's wand, the overheated turbines coughing large billows of white and dark smoke as it swirled behind and above the struggling chopper blades. Two dark green Cobra gunships trailed to either side, like helpless mother hens guiding their wounded chicks to safety. Mike noticed the convoy of jeeps and an army ambulance truck moving down the runway toward the stricken craft, which was descending rapidly just several hundred feet from the end of the tepid metal airstrip. The calm, cloudy peak of Núi Bà Đen loomed in the distance, providing a serene, panoramic backdrop to the calamity unfolding below.

"Who's on the chopper?" Mike finally asked.

"Some of the wounded from the Bright Light team they inserted across the Fence this morning," Donovan told him. "They still have folks on the ground but can't get to 'em. Chuck already shot down two more extraction packages after this one barely made it out."

Mike turned to watch the Huey's front skids snare the top strands of the concertina wire spools guarding the perimeter. The chopper abruptly dropped and skidded along the dusty rows of tanglefoot and trip flares just short of the end of the runway. They all watched in amazement as flare after flare vaulted into the brightly lit sky, exploding in vivid red clusters high above the crippled chopper careening through the wires, dragging and snapping row after row of razor-sharp wire now resembling failing arresting cables on an aircraft carrier. Suddenly, the chopper slid to a violent halt, its unexpired momentum causing the tail rotor to pivot around, spinning the Huey's nose back in the opposite direction.

Donovan drove within fifteen feet of the smoldering chopper and slid to a stop in the dust as the anxious men rushed toward the open doors. Mike winced at the blood-spattered Plexiglas cockpit, the pilot slumped over while still tethered to his harness, a lone, blood-soaked aviator boot dangling through the remnants of the shattered lower bubble. Bullet holes riddled the entire fuselage. Tatters of insulation and loose wires dangled throughout the cabin.

"Get 'em outa' here!!!" the copilot screamed as he fell out of the cockpit onto the dusty clay below. "This thing's getting ready to blow!!!"

Lanza reached in and grabbed the first man by his web gear, hoisting him over his shoulder as he scurried back toward the truck. Specialist Emory had laid out the stretchers and helped the sergeant lay the man down as he scoured his body for obvious life-threating wounds. The junior medic unbuckled the soldier's web harness and ripped open his blood-caked shirt as Lanza rushed back over to the chopper to help unload the remaining wounded warriors.

The captain continued to mount the slippery cabin, dragging out the semiconscious bodies, carefully handing them off to the scores of men who were standing ready to evacuate the ticking time bomb, its ominous dark smoke still smoldering out of the idle turbines. He felt a man brush by him, jumping up on the up-strut and spraying a large CO_2 canister directly into the overheated exhaust ports, the man's Nomex flight suit and helmet revealing he was one of the Cobra crews who had landed alongside them. Within seconds, three more crew members with extinguishers hosed down the transmission and engine, lessening the tangible threat of an imminent explosion.

Another ambulance from the Eighty-fifth arrived, with several nurses and a doctor to manage the makeshift triage set up at the end of the runway. Perceiving that the dead and wounded had finally been extracted from the battered chopper, Mike turned to the door gunner, who was still clutching his M60. He gestured that it was OK now for the gunner to leave his post. The man sat motionless, though, stoically ambivalent to what had been transpiring before him. *Probably scared shitless,* Mike reasoned, reaching over and nudging him on the arm.

The gunner sat passively, his visor reflecting the captain's confused glare in its smudged, mirrorlike finish. Mike reached over and slid the knob up, revealing the face of the Kansas boy he'd flown to Trà Cú with on his first trip in. "You OK, troop?" he asked, staring into the edge of the blue eyes accenting the gunner's freckled face, the young man's jaw drawn tight, his teeth firmly clenched.

The gunner's intent stare avoided looking back at Mike. As the boy sat transfixed on something in the distance, the captain reached over and slid his visor back down. *Probably still in shock and just needs some time,* he told himself.

Mike took one last look. Then he noticed the small dark hole just above the visor knob. He quickly stepped back up into bloody cabin, released the gunner's safety harness, and pushed the boy forward. Soaked in blood, the remnants of what was left of the contents of the boy's cranium completely saturated the back of his flak jacket. "Fuck me!" the captain whispered. "Can't get any more 'scared' than that."

Mike pushed the gunner back upright and stepped down from the compartment, his boots rimmed with globs of dark, viscous blood. He took a deep breath, turned, and hurried back over to where Sergeant Donovan and his junior medic were attending to the wounded. "We need a body bag for the gunner," he told one of the team of base camp medics standing there.

Once the first ambulance had been filled with desperate and dying men, it quickly turned and sped off back down the long runway, leaving only two less severely wounded Bright Light members leaning back on their canvas stretchers. The tall one with the head bandage and full leg splint lay on his side, feverishly taking short drags from a cigarette and talking passively to Sergeant Lanza. Mike walked over and squatted down to join the conversation.

"This is Sergeant First Class Spivey, Captain," Lanza told him. "Leroy and I go way back. He was just fillin' me in on the gunfight at the 'Go to Hell Corral.'"

"Es'cuse me if I don't get up, Captain," Spivey said, flashing a mock grin while he took another drag off the cigarette. "Like I was say'n, they had butchered them all. We were in the middle of putting the parts back together in body bags when they decided to open up the gates to hell."

He took another long drag off the cigarette, his fingers emitting a slight tremor as he exhaled. He coarsely spit out a loose piece of tobacco before resuming his tale. "We all knew they were there. Just didn't know how many of 'em. They had strung the torsos and limbs up in trees. Like bait in a snare, fuckin' bastards. They stacked the heads on top of one another, each one staring in a different direction."

"Who all is left in the target area?" Lanza asked casually, blatantly immune to the enemy's brutality.

The medics stepped in, lifting up the stretcher as Spivey lay back, flicking the butt as he answered. "Snake Charmer and Samson from RT Knife... And a coupla' their indig, I think. The rest didn't make it out of the kill zone."

"Snake Charmer and Samson?" the captain inquired.

"Bad Billy Gibson and his one-one, Lieutenant Mycoskie," Spivey yelled back as the medics shuffled him away. Mike stared at Lanza, a desperate frown now reflecting genuine concern.

"Ran a lot of real spooky duty trails with Gibson," Lanza recalled. "He's a damn good recon man, Đại úy."

"Mycoskie was my housemate back in Devens," Mike replied. "We were buds in Tölz with the Tenth."

The men abruptly cowered from the dust swirling around them as the two Cobra gunships jumped into the thin air and headed down the runway to the fuel trucks and armory near the B-Team compound.

"Guess Donovan and Emory went with the wounded," Lanza told him over the loud clamor from the blades. "Looks like that's all the excitement for the day, Đại úy."

"Coulda' damn sure done without *any* of it," the captain replied.

They walked back over to the truck and slowly headed back down the runway to the compound, Mike's thoughts invested solely on Rich's grim situation. "I need to find out what the fuck's goin' down. Pull over, Sergeant. I want to talk to one of the Cobra crews."

Sergeant Lanza carefully eased the truck between the two gunships, and Mike jumped out and hurried over to where the two pilots were talking while their war birds were being armed and refueled. "What's the latest?" he inquired, noting the resigned expressions on each of their faces.

"Fast movers and a coupla' gun teams outa' Lộc Ninh are keeping the bad guys pinned down," the tall warrant officer explained as Lanza came up beside Mike. "It don't look good for the home team, gents. From the last traffic we heard from the ground, they're runnin' outa' ammo fast."

"FAC's got aircraft bumpin' in to each other, just waiting to get into the fight, Captain," the other pilot told him. "They got approval from CINCPAC to jump the Fence with some TAC air, and we'll be heading back just as soon as we get gassed up. We got plenty of skin in this game, too. Lost two crews this afternoon."

"Looks like Gunslinger's comin' in now," the first warrant officer said, pointing back toward the apron of the runway. "He piloted the lead slick that dropped your guys off this morning," he confided with a distinct Texas drawl. "Expect he'll be waitin' to get back in there and do what he can to get the rest of 'em out before dark."

The lone Huey crabbed rapidly down the edge of the runway, stalling to a controlled hover beyond the refueling area until the gunship crews mounted their craft and lifted off, fully rearmed and obviously anxious to get back into the fight across the Fence. The Huey pilot then eased the bird next to the long refueling truck, shutting down the turbines as he touched down. With Lanza following close behind, Mike ran over to the open doors and pulled down the headset to talk to the pilots. "What's the latest?" he inquired, as the copilot lifted the fuel line and helped the ground crew insert the nozzle for the hot refuel. "Understand you were primary on the extraction efforts."

"They're ass deep in butt wipe, but as long as the fast movers stay on station, they seem to be holding their own," one of the pilots told him. "The C&C ship won't let anyone in to pick 'em up. The damn leprechauns got the PZ surrounded. Just need to top my tanks off, 'cause I ain't leavin' there till we get those poor bastards outa' harm's way."

Mike looked in the back and saw the crew chief tying several wooden boxes of ammo to the working end of a long, braided rope. "Anything we can do?" he inquired, suddenly feeling desperate and anxious to contribute.

"If they won't let me go in, I'm going to at least try to drop 'em some ammo and water," the pilot replied. "Got any medical pouches or bags?"

"Wait one…" Mike scampered back over to the truck to retrieve the large medical bag Spec-Five Emory had given him. As the copilot strapped himself back in, the slow, spinning blades recoiled into a high-pitched blast of hot, turbulent wind, accelerating wickedly in the vapor-thin air. Mike hurried back over, slung the bag up into the cabin, and stepped back, his mind hastily churning with the cadence of the blades, challenging the very core of his basic instincts. The powerful scent of JP-4 fuel swiftly infected his soul with the bouquet of bravado he cherished, accelerating his heartbeat as he drew deep, rapid breaths, soulfully fermenting the vitality of his resolve.

The pilot glanced back at him, smirking confidently as he dropped his dark visor down, a coy grin emerged as he drew the microphone to his lips, his farewell obscene salute derisively rendered to the lone officer who was standing anxiously a few feet away from the chopper that was about to fly back into combat. "Fuck *you*, too!" Mike shouted back with offense.

Then: "Not without *my* happy ass, motherfucker!" Mike suddenly bolted for the open door, jumping up onto the skid as the chopper shuddered, rapidly ascending into the open sky. Grabbing the up-strut, he rotated his body up and into the cabin, looking down at Sergeant Lanza staring back up at him, the sergeant slowly shaking his head with his hands on his hips.

The startled door gunner and crew chief exchanged puzzled glances, each shrugging their shoulders as the captain stood up and took a seat on the nylon bench, the cool wind swiftly drying the latent sweat saturating his fatigue jacket. "Those are my guys out there!" Mike yelled. "My friends. You guys could probably use some help anyway."

"Probably not the best career move you made today, Captain," the crew chief assured him. He reached under the bench seat and dragged out a bulky flak jacket. "Put this on, sir. If we make a run at the target, you're gonna be glad you got something to protect your vitals."

Mike grabbed the body armor, then realized he had left his weapon back in the truck. He looked around the cabin and saw two M16s clamped to brackets on the bulkhead. Several bandoleers of magazines hung next to them, so he made a mental note just in case the need arose. The crew chief coiled the long, braided rappelling rope on top of the wooden cases of ammo and then plugged his intercom back in. Before long, he had finished talking to the pilots and motioned for the captain to put on the headset above him.

"That was a damn fool move you made, Captain," the chief warrant officer told him. "I just hope you know how to make yourself useful."

"Just tell me what you need me to do. I'm pretty trainable. I even learned how to stack the blocks at a very early age in kindergarten."

"Jackson told me you have some buddies on the ground. That last slick that went in? It was carrying some of my friends, too. To put it all into proper *perspective* for you, Captain: They didn't make it out. Welcome aboard the Pony Express, *hero*," that last word spoken with a bit of ironic derision.

Suddenly, the pilot switched the feed to the C&C net, and Mike listened firsthand to the violence and confusion erupting over the airwaves. It took him several minutes, but he soon determined who the key players were and their call signs. He listened intently as the pilot of the Covey aircraft, orbiting high above the target area, directed the ordnance from the jets and Spads. "Keep your heads down, Bravo Delta," the Covey rider told the team on the ground. "They're gonna be unloading three more sorties of five-hundred-pounders to your November."

"Tell 'em to put it danger close," the excited voice replied, sporadic gunfire crackling in the background. "Ammo's gettin'a little scarce down here, don'cha know."

Mike looked into the distance, eager to *see* the action that was unfolding in his headset. He scanned the jagged horizon, looking for any telltale signs of smoke or aircraft circling in the late afternoon sky. The rolling, flat terrain below evolved into an emerging thicket of small, wiry scrub trees and tall grass, elevating gradually as the chopper navigated west. He eased over to the edge of the door, sitting down with his boots dangling freely just above the skids. The waving fields of tan grass beneath the skids ushered memories of the King Ranch and the high coastal grass meadows that had helped conceal Jim and him from the persistent watch of the assiduous game wardens. *This damn sure ain't the Ranch,* he reminded himself. *And the prey we're after today didn't just trade in their antlers for pith helmets.*

As the rhythmically beating chopper blades escorted them deeper and deeper into the foreboding foothills of Cambodia, the "Ghost Rider" melody suddenly slipped back into Mike's fluid mind. He looked over at the young door gunner, who was adjusting the thick metal plate between his legs. "Gotta maintain the family jewels, sir. Never know when they're gonna come in handy," he yelled. "There's *evil* lurkin' out there in them damn hills."

"Roger that..."

* * *

CHAPTER FORTY-THREE

RICH PEERED OVER THE BLOODY pile of decimated enemy bodies he had stacked around him, watching the thin, white vapor trail emerge from the wingtips of the silver jet as it banked sharply in the distance, steadily vectoring in on the target for its low-level bombing run. Bright, intermittent lines of green tracers zigzagged into the dusky sky, searching for the elusive angle to intercept the deadly jet as it roared in just above the treetops. The F-100 held firm despite the fusillade, releasing four bombs as it arched gracefully back up into the high, shadowy clouds above him. The sudden series of hot shock waves thrust him backward, jostling several corpses on top of him in the process. He barely heard the screams of dying men in the bloody aftermath, as shards of hot metal, smoldering dirt, and rocky debris cascaded down around him. "Cocksuckerrrrrrrrrrrs!!!" he screamed in defiance at the hidden enemy.

He looked to his left to make sure his team leader was still with him. He observed two pith helmets bob and weave as NVA soldiers emerged from the opposite tree line, sprinting toward their position though the tall, waving grass. He quickly slid to his knees, bringing his AK to bear on the charging enemy. Squeezing off two quick bursts, he cut the men down with well-placed shots to the chest.

"Get your ass down, LT!!" Gibson ordered. "They decided to take down the south side of the clearing with this next pass!"

Lieutenant Mycoskie lifted up the bullet-ridden corpse beside him and pushed it back on top of the pile in front of him. Swarms of flies and insects mingled amid the bodies, feasting on the smorgasbord of mangled intestines and splattered feces. Just as he nestled in beside the gruesome pile, he felt the heat of the jet's afterburner singe his hair, shadowed abruptly by the deafening explosion of its lethal payload. Large segments

434 | MICHAEL O'SHEA

of shattered tree branches and body parts assaulted their small perimeter, followed closely by a thick layer of benign, confettilike leaves, floating and dancing aimlessly in the still air above. The shrill, morbid wailing from men screaming and crying inundated the battlefield, followed by brief volleys of indiscriminate gunfire searching for his small team, concealed in the emergent shadows of swaying grass at the edge of the long, narrow clearing.

Sixty meters to their rear, through the tall, leafy, silver-toned trees, loomed a sheer rocky cliff, falling vertically more than a hundred feet to the narrow, rock-strewn rapids flowing down from the north. The setting sun sent shimmers of silver light reflecting eerily through the translucent leaves, casting vague shadows in the sparse grass clumped neatly below them.

"They're gonna make one more pass and then try to rope in some water and ammo while the bastards've got their heads down," Gibson told him, the radio handset glued to his ear. "I told 'em to come in over the river and get back out the same way. They'd never make it comin' in over the clearing."

Rich crawled over to check on his wounded Cambode comrade, Do, and realized his friend had finally succumbed from the sucking chest wounds he had sustained during the last brutal assault. He pulled two full magazines from Do's ammo pouch, crawled back over, and leaned his back up against the maze of corpses shielding him. *You were a good recon man, Charlie Brown,* he thought to himself, his lips and mouth parched from exhaustion and heat.

"The fast mover is inbound from west to east, Gunslinger," Covey informed the slick crew orbiting in the distance, waiting patiently behind the nearby hilltop to make a hasty resupply run. "He'll be dropping two canisters of napalm and a coupla' nickel bags of briquettes for the afternoon barbecue. Should muster up enough smoke cover to drop your load."

"Roger that, Covey. Kinda' partial to late-afternoon barbecues myself."

"You're clear to make your drop at the east end of the clearing as soon as he rotates. About fifty meters west from the cliff. How copy?"

"Roger Two-three-six... Understand fifty mikes west of the river... Got the fast mover in sight at my twelve o'clock, over."

"Gunslinger... Covey Two-three-six ... He'll be exiting the target area to the northwest."

"Bravo Delta... You copy last?"

"Covey... Roger, copy," Gibson confirmed. "Bravo Delta standing by." The gutsy one-zero low-crawled over to Lieutenant Mycoskie, parting the warm layers of spent brass tangled in the matted grass confines of the tiny perimeter.

"Take these two forty-five slugs and stick 'em in your ears, LT. Take your bandana off, shove it tight in your mouth, and keep your yapper shut and your nose pinched. That napalm they're about to drop will suck all the oxygen outa' your system and collapse your lungs, don'cha know. They'll be comin' in low from over the river to drop some ammo," he told him, a comforting grin spreading across his blood-stained face. "So don't let it hit you in the ass."

"Anything else, Mom?" Rich fired back.

"Yeah. Looks like you forgot to wash behind your ears this morning."

Gibson turned and crawled back to his position, signaling to the rear gunner, Chu, who was guarding their flank, to prepare for the next sortie. With his palms spread wide, he waved his fingers, the team's silent indicator for napalm. Within seconds, the accelerating jet's roar caught up with the tumbling wave of foo gas, as the fiery shower of death blanketed the shaded northern edges of the long clearing. The violent shock wave of the two five-hundred-pound bombs spread across the battlefield as the skyward jet's afterburner kicked in, the raging fire and rampaging decibels impacting friend and foe alike.

Rich pulled the .45 slugs from his ears, elevating his head just high enough above his gory bunker to survey the aftermath of the napalm's devastating effect on the enemy, who were violently consumed as the gates of hell burst open to greet them. The welcome sound of inbound chopper blades drew his attention to the east as the smoke and fire wandered aimlessly north, prodded gently by the slight, fickle breeze drifting in from the south. He smiled, watching two obscure figures in Gunslinger's open door slide a cargo net filled with wooden boxes and rucksacks over the skids, rapidly lowering the welcome payload as the chopper cleared the tips of the trees behind him.

Unfortunately, the intruding bird immediately began to take fire from the south edge of the clearing, as green tracers found their mark in the slow-moving target that was hovering above their position. White trails of propellant from B-40 rockets crisscrossed in front of and behind the vulnerable craft, and bright red sparks tap-danced along the fuselage: Volumes of deadly enemy rifle fire were impacting the thin hull and spinning blades.

"Just drop it, and get the fuck outa' here!!" Gibson screamed into the handset. "Abort! Abort!!!... Abort!!!"

Rich watched the rope go slack. The payload plummeted the last twenty feet to the ground. There was a loud, cracking sound as the heavy wooden casings smashed into the clearing. He saw the chopper dip to the right, losing precious altitude as it banked sharply away from the barrage while it attempted to accelerate out of range of the curtain of lead still pummeling it.

"Covey... Get some guns on the south side of that damn clearing!!!" Gibson yelled above the gunfire. "Now!!"

His urgent request had yet to be answered when, suddenly, Gunslinger's tail rotor spun into the coiling path of a streaking B-40, the abrupt explosion searing off the stabilizing fins and propeller, blasting the remnants wildly out into the center of the clearing. The stricken bird immediately started a rapid rotation, like a carnival ride spinning violently out of control. Watching it corkscrewing toward the ground, Rich saw pieces of cargo and equipment flying out of the open doors, along with a helmeted figure spinning limply through the air toward the trees at the southern edge of the clearing. Just before the doomed aircraft hit the ground, his eyes transfixed on another figure immediately ejected feet first, arms flailing, desperately attempting to stabilize as he careened forcefully into the tall grass beside their perimeter.

The chopper's skids utterly collapsed with the vigorous force of the impact. Then it recoiled briefly back into the air and spun again, its long blades cutting through the tall grass like the Grim Reaper as it cartwheeled into the edge of the clearing and exploded, showering the jagged tree line with burning fuel and armaments as it broke apart, impacting like a thin cardboard box into the dense clump of trees.

"Covey, Covey... Bravo Delta. Be advised... We have an asset down at the southeast edge of the LZ, over."

"Roger, Bravo. Smoke visible. Any survivors? Over."

"Negative, Covey... The bird nested in the trees with Uncle Ho."

A long pause followed as Gibson and the lieutenant watched the chopper burn, listening to the ammo cooking off or the enemy dispatching any survivors in the aftermath. Secondary fires quickly erupted, providing a welcome smoke screen between the team and the burning wreckage.

"Bravo Delta... Be advised that Covey Master has suspended all extraction packages for your location. Execute your E&E plan at your discretion, over."

"Roger, Covey. Wilco," Gibson responded to Covey. "We're in deep shit now, LT," he told the lieutenant. "Our only way outa' here is over that cliff, and until now, we didn't have a way to take advantage of it. Looks like it's now or never, but we have to move fast. They'll be comin' for us in force as soon as it's dark."

Gibson inched in closer to his one-one and looked back to signal Chu to join them. "Where the fuck is he?" he asked Rich.

"Donno. He was there last time I looked."

As the blood-red sun settled below the distant treetops, Covey suddenly came back on the net with his final transmission. "Bravo Delta... Covey. Specter Three-niner will be on station your location in two-zero mikes. When he gets on station, activate your transponder, and he will hose down your perimeter based on your call, over."

"Covey... Bravo Delta... Stand by." Then to Rich: "LT, I need you to crawl out to the ammo and get as many bandoleers as you can carry. Secure that damn rope, tie it to your web gear, and drag it back. We can use it to rappel down the big-ass fuckin' cliff. It's the only chance we've got, sir."

Without hesitation, Rich slung his AK over his back and began scurrying like a hefty lizard through the chest-high grass toward the ammo, about fifteen meters away. He located the rope tied to the small cargo net, slashed the knot with his razor-sharp Randall, and tied the end to his web gear. Scores of loose bandoleers of ammo lay scattered among the shattered crates—5.56 and 7.62 AK rounds intermingled with the shards of wood. He quickly looped a dozen of the green cloth bandoleers of ammunition to the rope, turned, and dragged the heavy load back to the perimeter.

"Covey Two-three-six... Bravo Delta. Be advised we will attempt to execute our E&E plan as soon as Specter can convince Chuck to keep his fuckin' head down. Remaining in this location is not an option. We will attempt to proceed to rally point Victor Zulu. How copy, over."

"Ahhh, roger, Bravo. Be advised you have weather rolling in from the south... Hope you brought your umbrella with you. We're runnin' on fumes, so we're headed back to the ranch. I'll be back at daybreak... Good luck tonight, ol' buddy... And don't forget to say your prayers. Covey Two-three-six, out."

*   *   *

Nearby, the dazed but conscious captain slowly rolled over, his eyes focusing on the enemy soldier kneeling down beside him. Suddenly realizing that he was unarmed, Mike searched his mind for an immediate solution. The worn barrel of the AK was pointed directly at his head, and he wondered what he would feel when the soldier pulled the trigger.

"RT Knife," the grinning soldier whispered, pointing to himself. "RT Knife," he repeated, pointing in a direction behind him. He motioned for Mike to follow him as he slid on his belly through the matted grass trail. The captain didn't dwell on his sudden change of fate, and he quickly followed the NVA-clad soldier through the entangled grass, pausing momentarily to shed the bulky flak jacket that was fully encased with vile, sticky blood.

Gibson's attention immediately shifted to the veiled movement behind him. He leveled his weapon as he watched the tips of the tall grass sway ever so slightly in front of him. "Gib-san," the faint voice whispered, and Chu emerged from the shaded stalks of high grass and into the perimeter.

"Where the fuck you bin?" Gibson scolded. But then he drew his weapon back up as the vague image of a man crawled out of the shadows behind him.

"He fall out of helicopter, *Trung sĩ*," Chu told him.

Mike stared up at Sergeant Gibson, then quickly looked past him to see Rich gazing at him with a questioning stare. "Hamma knokka," Rich whispered, still not relying on the validity of the image smiling up at him.

Gibson looked at both men smiling at each other, and then he quickly brought the tense situation back into perspective. "Sorry we don't have time for a fuckin' love-in, but our asses are about to get knee deep in alligator shit. Chu, reel in that rope and coil it up. LT, get this man a weapon and some web gear. This place is about to get lit up like the fuckin' Fourth of July."

Then to the radio: "Specter Three-niner... Specter Three-niner... Bravo Delta. How copy, over." Gibson stuffed his empty ammo pouches with freshly filled magazines, holding the handset tightly to his ear with his shoulder. "Specter Three-niner... Specter Three-niner. Bravo Delta. How copy this station, over."

Mike scurried over to where his friend was kneeling and hurriedly taking the web gear off Do. Grabbing the butt stock of Do's AK-47 and pushing it over to Mike, the lieutenant asked, "You A-Team pukes ever figure out how to use one of these?"

"Fuck you, Rich," Mike replied, pulling the operating rod handle back after he inserted the magazine.

"There's some bandoleers of seven six-two over there," Rich whispered. "Better grab a couple, and make sure your magazines are full. Take this," he said, handing over Do's ruck. "It probably has some Claymores or grenades and shit in it." Then, after fully eyeing Mike: "Looks like you cut yourself shavin' with a rake this mornin'. That grass is really sharp. Kinda' like that look on you."

"Specter Three-niner... Three-niner... Bravo Delta, over," Gibson whispered, the occasional popping sounds still echoing near the burning wreckage illuminating the southern tree line as the gray shadows submissively acquiesced to the dark masters of night.

"Bravo Delta... This *is* Specter Three-niner... Understand you gents could use a cheap date this evening, over."

"Roger that, Three-niner... Watch your screen, Three-niner... I'm going to activate my mini-ponder..."

"Positive fix on your location, Bravo Delta. My sensors are lit up with a large band of Commie Indians havin' a powwow two-hundred-ninety degrees around your location."

"Nothin' like bein' surrounded, Specter... Ya oughta try it sometime... Kinda' like cowboys and Indians, don'cha know. We're gonna give the fuckers one last chance to surrender... Then we're gonna attack."

"Well you're in luck tonight, Bravo Delta. Brought the cavalry with me. Since it's our first date, Bravo, you should know I've got appetizers of the twenty- and forty-millimeter cannon variety, with a one-oh-five howitzer for the main course. If you're still up for something sweet, I'd recommend the minigun soufflé for dessert. How copy?"

"Specter, we're starvin' down here, so could we just get to the main course? We are going to be exiting our position due east to the river, just as soon as you deliver the entrée. We'd appreciate it if you could keep them savages pinned down until we E&E down the cliff and across the stream."

"Bravo Delta, we're picking up a large renegade raiding party headed your way from the west end of the clearing. My guys are locked and loaded. Advise you might want to keep your head down."

"Roger, Specter... Just show me the magic, sweetheart... Bravo Delta standing by."

The sudden cannonlike explosions in the dark sky startled the team as the C-130 gunship belched volley after volley of deadly 105mm howitzer rounds into the enemy ranks that were sneaking up through the tall grassy clearing. Streams of green tracers immediately streaked skyward, searching for the kiss of death raining down on them from the silky, dark heavens.

Gibson rallied the tense group and sent Chu on point to lead them to the cliff in the darkness, the bright flashes of exploding shells heightening their retreat through the eerie, flash-lit thicket of trees.

Chu stopped suddenly, nearly falling off the jagged edge as he fought for his balance. Mike reached forward and grabbed the nap of his harness, pulling him back as he fell on his butt. Sergeant Gibson rushed forward, snatching the rope off the top of Chu's rucksack. "Set up a perimeter!" he ordered, clearly agitated at the near catastrophe. "And get your snap links ready to hook up!" he yelled, searching in the dark for something to anchor the rope to.

He found a small tree about ten meters away, double-wrapped the end of the rope, and tied it off with two half-hitches. Then he threw the coiled working end out over the cliff. Motioning for the men to join him, he pointed to the LT to take the lead. Rich clipped his snap link onto the rope, grabbed the trailing end, and swiftly stepped off into the blank void. Sporadic green tracers cracked and zinged through the treetops behind them, heightening the tension as Rich banged his way down the steep wall. When the rope slacked, he motioned for the captain to follow suit, then ushered Chu down next. Gibson pulled a blasting cap out of his trousers and tied it just above his grip, pulling the thirty-second time fuse as he lowered himself rapidly down to the dark embankment below.

The constant reverberating explosions lit up the darkened plateau above them, silhouetting the edge of the obscure cliff. A second later, the blasting cap blew, sending the rope cascading down to the rocky shore, eliminating any avenue of pursuit for the enemy above. "Get us outa' here, Chu," Gibson hastily ordered, pointing north along the river's edge.

Chu cinched up his gear and moved cautiously into the shallow flowing water and up the far embankment, where he encountered a well-trodden woodcutter's path through the scattered formation of moss-laden boulders. They all knew that walking the trails violated every recon man's sacred creed, but at this point, their only objective was to expand the space between them and the persistent enemy, still lurking in the distance above.

The audible rush of water from the adjacent rapids masked the occasional noises their trek created as they shuffled rapidly in the dark along the rock-strewn pathway. They continued to hear the gunship howling profoundly in the distance, relentlessly pounding the enemy with deadly cannon and Vulcan 20mm fire. Sergeant Gibson took a degree of comfort in knowing that Specter's sensitive infrared sensors would detect any enemy movement out of the "Death Zone," and their lifesaving mini-ponder pinpointed their new position. After an hour of their arduously humping the winding riverbed, the sergeant reluctantly halted their retreat.

Cautiously, they moved off the slippery path, taking up defensive positions in the wet rocks nestled just below the dense vegetation line above the trail. Gibson turned on the radio and whispered into the handset. "Specter Three-niner... Specter Three-niner... Bravo Delta, over."

"Bravo Delta... Specter... Go"

"Specter... Bravo Delta. Were you able to detect any troop movement or scouting parties headed our way? Over."

"Ahhh, Bravo Delta... Good to hear from you. Been tryin' to raise you on the horn. Saw you moving, but then lost your signal. Thought you might have stopped off somewhere for a cocktail. That's a big negative, Bravo... We had those savages' full attention and expended our entire basic load on their little powwow. Be advised that we are Winchester and have departed the AO, over."

"Specter... Bravo... Thanks for bailin' us out, good buddy, over."

"Any time, Bravo… Just remember: When you *care* enough to expend the *very* best, just call Specter Three-niner. Good hunting and happy trails, Bravo Delta… Specter Three-niner out."

Mike leaned back against the chill, slimy rocks behind him, anxiously gazing up into the dark, sullen skies for any sign of his faithful confidant, Orion. He had had no time to reflect on the predicament he now found himself in, adrenaline and endorphins still masquerading as suppressors of fear and anxiety, enabling him to endure the surreal circumstances governing his pending fate. His mind flashed back to that grim instant that crew chief Jackson was hit, his hot blood splattering Mike's face as the sergeant fell on top of him, the heavy jolt of several more rounds impacting into Jackson's flak jacket as he lay atop him. The captain replayed the sensation as the chopper was hit, the deafening eruption of metal shearing away from the fuselage, the sheer force of rotation pinning him firmly under the seats. He felt the blood rushing back to his head again, as he recounted the death grip he had on the aluminum railing supporting the seats, the wild sensation of free fall as the angry, wounded bird finally spit him out feet first, his tense body skipping like a smooth, flat stone as he hopscotched through the flat, grassy plain. *Why me, Lord?* he silently inquired. *Why didn't You just take me, too?*

The sudden crash of lightning startled him, snuffing out the line of communication he had established with his Lord. He felt the cool, swift breeze as it rustled the trees and swirled the palms in the invisible grove above him, announcing the arrival of the imminent, welcome shower. The sheets of nippy rain danced heavily on the rocky formations, splattering his face while he squinted over toward Gibson for direction. He knew the loud mixture of wind and rain would surely muffle their movement.

Within seconds, he watched the team leader point Chu up the gentle hill and into the tangled vegetation above. Mike crouched low, moving cautiously through the slick rocks to follow him up. As he passed Gibson, the one-zero offered the captain some words of advice: "Don't lose sight of him," he whispered. "We'll be right behind you. We're headed due west, and if we do get spooked, the rally point will be the second prominent terrain feature to the south. Here, take a couple of these," he told him, handing him two green pills. "They'll help keep your head in the game. We'll be moving steadily till first light."

The persistent rain lingered well into the early-morning hours, affording the small team a chance to move continually through the tangled heavy bush and into several open groves of neatly manicured, low-lying, yet mysteriously swaybacked, chanti trees. They knew their movement through the tall, stalky grass and muddy groves would surely leave a robust trail that even a novice tracker could follow. Gibson remained keenly aware of that risky gamble and constantly looked for avenues of rocky or firm terrain to traverse the distance, zigzagging periodically, leaving only sparse evidence of their direction of travel.

The drenching rain stopped abruptly, casting an eerie silence that immediately slowed their pace. Mike tasted the distinct flavor of charred wood lingering in the heavy air, an indication that latent cooking fires were smoldering under cover nearby. Chu dropped to his knee, his outstretched palm signaling the men to take cover. Mike watched him creep forward, then gradually lie down and slither through the thick clumps of wet grass. Following several tense minutes, he finally returned, motioning the men to assemble. "Big trail no good," he quietly told them, a concerned look on his face.

"You know the drill, Chu," Gibson told him, pulling the coil of olive-green parachute line out of his ruck and handing it to him.

Chu grimaced but didn't hesitate. He took the neatly coiled suspension line and slowly headed back to the trail. The men followed cautiously behind his lead, taking cover near the path when he sat down and unlaced his waterlogged boots. They watched silently while he surveyed the adjacent tree line, apparently looking for an appropriate avenue to cross. Then he moved through the damp brush about fifteen meters to his right, looped the line through the lower branches of a small, bent tree, coiled it once, and after pausing for several more minutes, quickly walked the line across the now-soggy, high-speed trail. They sat silently for at least ten minutes, listening intently for any sound or movement around them.

Finally, Gibson rose and gave Chu a thumbs-up signal to secure the line. Chu quietly shimmied up the small tree, tied both ends of the line tautly above the lower branches, and used a small stick to wind the two strands into a firm, rigid cord.

"Watch the LT," Gibson instructed the captain as Rich stood up, snapped his link to the two twisted lines above, took several quick steps, and slid out over the smooth, muddy trail, reaching up and pulling himself over until he gingerly stepped down on the other side. Mike nodded at Gibson and repeated the process, making sure his boots avoided contact with the wet ground as he pulled himself over the wide, well-traveled trail. Quietly unsnapping his link, he moved to a defensive position behind two trees as he watched Sergeant Gibson execute the trail-breaching technique.

Another long, arduous hour slowly passed. The team finally emerged from the thick, scraggly underbrush and stared up at the dark image of two low-level mountaintops looming ominously in front of them. The first shadowy curtain of light struggled to blight the dark overcast sky in the distance as Gibson gathered the men and issued his directive. "The rally point is just beyond the reverse slope of that fuckin' mountain," he whispered. "We don't have time to go around the motha'fucker, and I'd rather be fighting 'em from above than below, so after *stand to*, Chu will take the point and we'll head for the saddle and just go between them," he told the exhausted men, pointing to the low ridge between the two mountain crests. "Stay crouched down, and make sure you don't get silhouetted movin' through the apex of that saddle."

The men hurriedly set up a defensive perimeter, placing Claymores and several layers of toe poppers in front of the likely avenues of enemy approach. Then they settled in to greet the illuminating daylight that would surely challenge their innate skills in negotiating the final leg to the rally point on the other side of the tall, rocky terrain. The captain sat back on his haunches, the chill, wet mud seeping through his damp fatigues, temporarily cooling the elevated body temperature that the long night march had generated.

The comfy drone of a lone aircraft's engine buzzed in the distance, somewhere beyond the gray clouds above. They listened intently, desperately trying to get a fix on its direction of travel. Soon, the invisible craft raced its engine several times, the signal for the team to turn on their radio. "Bravo Delta, Bravo Delta... This is Covey Three-two-six... Three-two-six, over."

"Covey... Bravo, over," Gibson whispered.

"Well, good morning, happy campers. Need a quick fix on your twenty, Bravo."

"Have you to my Sierra, bearing one-niner-zero, over," Gibson confirmed, staring at the needle on his compass.

"Roger, understand one-niner-zero. Computing reverse azimuth, and give me a heads-up when we're over you, Bravo Delta."

The small, L-19 turned right, above the low cloud cover, vectoring in on the team hidden somewhere beneath the thick blanket of haze below. As the men on the ground focused on the steady drone above, the first elements of daylight peeked pensively over the mountaintops, exposing the open, lush terrain in front of them.

"Tally ho," Sergeant Gibson whispered into the handset as the plane's engine buzzed past, hidden in the low cloud banks directly above them.

"Roger, Bravo Delta… Looks like you're about two clicks southeast of the primary rally point, brother. Should have eyes on you as soon as this soup burns off. Meantime, proceed bearing zero-eight degrees. Covey Master is putting together an extraction package that'll be on station when you get there, copy?"

"Roger, copy."

Gibson studied the terrain in front of them and quickly decided to skirt the open field inside the small tree line leading to the west slope of the low-profile mountain ahead. He instructed the men to gather in the Claymores but to leave a few toe poppers behind, in case the trackers had picked up their trail.

As Mike stuffed a Claymore back into his rucksack, Rich tapped him on the shoulder. "You tryin' to get us all killed?" he whispered, prying the top off the small grease tube. "Who the fuck dressed *you* this morning, fool?" he asked, smearing the loam-green war paint on his friend's pale face.

"What the fuck you doin' out here in the bush, Rich?" Mike whispered. "We're supposed to be on our way back to 'the world.'"

Rich finished toning down Mike's features and casually put the grease tube back into his cargo pocket. "Ain't going back. I extended," he confided. "Haven't finished what I came here to do."

Mike just gazed into his eyes and studied his friend's intimate stare, convincing himself that Rich was sincere and contentedly motivated. He reached over and patted him softly on the shoulder, then squeezed his arm firmly. "Press on, pal," he said, smiling slightly, in solidarity with his friend's intent.

"Rear gunner, LT," Gibson whispered, then turned and signaled Chu to lead the way. The men moved quietly through the small tree line bordering the wet, open field, expanding the security distance between each man as they moved closer to the final obstacle between them and the extraction zone.

Mike listened to the songbirds sharply chirping in the vaulted treetops as the sun finally melted away the gloomy skies lingering above. As the heavens cleared, he heard the familiar drone of Covey's lone engine circling high above. *Sure hope he doesn't attract any flies,* he thought to himself.

A short time later, the team reached the base of the small mountain, then turned east and began to weave through the rocky slope toward the dip in the terrain beyond. Their trek upward remained slow and tentatively deliberate. They were keenly aware that sudden movements would draw the attention of spotters or trackers who could be lurking in the area. Finally, Chu stopped beside a large boulder near the apex of the saddle, signaling the rest of the men to join him.

"We'll take a blow here while I get Covey on the horn," Gibson told them as they scanned the expanse back down the hillside and into the tree-lined meadow below.

Hundreds of nesting birds in the treetops took sudden flight, their cacophony followed closely by the distinct sound of a lone toe popper echoing in the grove. All eyes focused on the distant tree line as a solid mass of NVA troops emerged from the dull shadows and into the sunlit meadow below.

"Covey Three-two-six, this is Bravo Delta, over," Gibson proclaimed, an urgent tone in his transmission.

"Ahhh, Bravo... This is Covey, over."

"Be advised... We have company... Need that extraction package, ASAP, over."

"Roger, Bravo... We're coastin' off to your east... Didn't want to stir up the pot. You have a fix on the bad guys?"

"That's a *big* roger, Covey. They're just below us, comin' out of the tree line where we pinged you this morning. Need you to help slow 'em down, don'cha know, over."

"Bravo... Be there in about two mikes. What's your position? Over."

"Covey... We're sittin' in the saddle between hill two-eight-seven and two-six-eight. I'll give you my mirror when you get here, over."

"Roger copy, Bravo. Got two gunship teams about to be on station, and the fast movers are on their way."

Mike looked over at Rich, who was grinning broadly as he watched the steady stream of pith helmets emerge from the thick tree line below. "What the fuck are you smiling about?" he complained. "Those crazed bastards are trying to cut our guts out and make us eat 'em."

Rich turned to him with his classic sly, shit-eating grin on his face and replied, "I know. Kinda' gets the blood pumpin', doesn't it?"

"I knew I shoulda' stayed in fuckin' Tây Ninh, you *crazy bastard*."

"Saddle up. Get ready to move," Gibson ordered, turning back to the east as Covey approached their position. "We gotta get off this ridge line."

Sergeant Gibson aimed the small signal mirror skyward, tilting the angle several times before Covey came up on the net. "Bravo Delta, Covey. Got eyes on you and the bad guys below your position. I'm going to put some smoke out for the fast movers. They'll be vectoring in from the Whiskey, so get ready to move, over."

"Roger, Covey."

The small drab-green Bird Dog nosed down and fired two white phosphorus missiles directly into the horde of enemy troops scrambling for cover in the open meadow. Dense white smoke marked the target area for the two swept-wing F-4 Phantom jets streaking in above the trees from the west. The team watched from their elevated vantage point as the five-hundred-pound bombs hit their mark, delivering death and devastation to the exposed enemy below.

Suddenly, from the hillside on the other side of the saddle, two .51-caliber antiaircraft guns opened up on the small Bird Dog banking in the light clouds above them. Dark-green tracers homed in on their defenseless target, savagely ripping into its foil-thin fuselage as smoke and fire erupted from the sputtering engine. Mike watched in utter dismay as Covey braced into a gentle downward glide, dark, oil-fed smoke tailing behind the craft as the green tracers pursued its descent toward the sparse opening in the fields to the north.

"Where the fuck did *they* come from?" Rich shouted.

"Musta' been asleep," Gibson replied. "Let's move before they spot us." He pushed Chu out from behind the boulder and down the reverse slope of the mountain.

The team hurriedly navigated down the steep slopes, forsaking their stealth for distance once again. They could see the smoke billowing up from the downed Bird Dog in the distance, realizing that Sir Charles would be converging on the crash site from every direction.

"Break... Break... Any station," Gibson said into his handset, panting as he stumbled down the incline. "This is Bravo Delta, over."

"Bravo Delta, this is Death Dealer One-three, over."

"Death Dealer, this is Bravo Delta moving to rally point Victor Zulu. Be advised: Covey Three-two-six is down... Charlie has a couple of fifty-ones concealed about halfway up the southern slope of hill two-six-eight... Say again: Fifty-ones on the south slope hill two-six-eight. How copy, over."

"Roger, Bravo... I'll have my gun team take a rocket run at 'em, but we're going to have to come in from the north and sideswipe 'em, over."

"Roger," Gibson acknowledged, still out of breath as he tried to stay focused on his treacherous jaunt down the hill. "Any C&C assets with you? Over."

"That's affirmative, Bravo Delta. Be advised: Covey Master will be with the extraction package inbound behind us."

The distinct wind-churning melody of the Cobra gunships drew a welcome sigh from Mike as he struggled to keep pace with Chu's light-footed scamper down through the rocky terrain. He looked skyward in time to see the two gunships rotate to their left and head directly for them.

"Bravo Delta... Bravo Delta... Death Dealer One-three. Is that your people moving down between the twin peaks, over?"

Gibson heard the garbled traffic on his handset clipped to his harness. He slid to a halt and dropped to his knees, gasping for air. "Station calling Bravo Delta, say again, over."

"Roger, Bravo Delta... Death Dealer One-three... I'm about to engage a small group moving down the north side of the saddle... Is that your people? Over."

"Affirmative, One-three... Do not engage!" Gibson insisted. "I have you in sight to my twelve o'clock. Those fifty-ones are on the *other* side of the hill. To your Lima, over!"

"Roger copy, Bravo... Death Dealer team going hot."

Mike watched the shark-mouthed Cobras suddenly bank hard to the left, then suddenly arch vertically, seeming to stall before dropping their noses and diving, accelerating rapidly as their miniguns opened up on the hillside above them. A quick burst of green tracers danced around and past the attacking gunships while flashes of rockets screamed out of their pods, streaking downward, exploding with a vengeance into the battery of enemy .51 guns mounted on the hillside.

The team reached the bottom of the incline and then followed Chu at a dead run to the tree line near another open meadow to their right. Gibson halted the group and set up a perimeter while they struggled to catch their breath. Minigunfire and explosions echoed through the saddle as the gunship pilots pinwheeled above the advancing enemy below. The teams heavy breathing under the trees, their recovery from total exhaustion, soon subsided, leaving an eerie silence throughout the shaded groves. Gibson pulled out his map, orienting the location of the team and the distance and direction to the rally point. He quickly realized that Victor Zulu was already occupied, nestled beside the smoldering wreckage of their old friend, Covey.

"Death Dealer One-three.. One-three, over."

"You got 'em, go."

"There's a no-vacancy sign on the rally point, Death Dealer. When's that C&C chopper gonna be on station? Over."

"Break... Break... Bravo Delta... Bravo Delta. This is Covey Master. What is your current location? Over."

"Covey Master... Bravo. We are located in the south edge of the tree line just north of hill two-eight-seven, over."

"Bravo... Covey... Can you put smoke out? Over."

"Covey... That's a negative. We don't think they know where we are yet, over."

"Roger, Bravo. Wait one."

The team looked off into the horizon in the east, watching several Hueys orbiting high above in the cloud-strewn sky. They also saw the formation of

Cobra gunships departing the area, apparently having depleted their load of ordnance on the enemy beyond the hills. Abruptly, each man cocked his head slightly, listening intently to the ominous sound sharply reverberating in the distance. "They put the fuckin' dogs on us!" Gibson exclaimed. "It won't be long now! LT, you got any dog shit with you?"

Rich took off his rucksack and pulled out a glass jar wrapped in a green hand towel. "Mixed it up myself," he proudly proclaimed, holding up the pepper, CS powder, and cayenne mixture for all to see. He quickly unscrewed the top and sprinkled the caustic mixture throughout the perimeter.

"Bravo Delta. This is Covey Master, over."

"Covey Master, Bravo... Go."

"Bravo... Covey. Proceed to the wreckage, to your November, and attempt to retrieve the bodies. It looks like we can execute an ex-fil on the other side of that grove to the Echo of the impact site, over."

Gibson took a deep breath. Then he turned and conveyed Covey Master's instructions to the team. "Before they pick us up," he said quietly, "they want us to retrieve the bodies."

The men exchanged stares and glares, shaking their heads as they evaluated the consequences of that directive. "Chu, take us up inside the tree line as far as you can go," Gibson ordered. "We're gonna have to make a run for it, so conserve as much energy as you can. Anybody need a greenie?"

The captain quickly raised his hand, his energy and stamina severely challenged. Gibson reached over and handed him two of the pills, along with the verbal instructions. "Just chew 'em up. Ain't got nothin' to wash 'em down with, don'cha know."

"Bravo Delta... Covey Master... Did you copy last?"

"Roger that, Covey. Bravo en route, over."

Gibson motioned Chu forward. As the noise of the howling pack of dogs behind them intensified, they realized that every precious second counted. They moved swiftly though the sparse, grassy underbrush beneath the trees, catching fleeting glimpses of the still-smoldering wreckage of their old friend Covey's Bird Dog, crumpled ahead and to the right of them. Within minutes, Chu halted the column, pointing directly to the crash site.

Gibson moved up to the edge of the tree line and scanned the expanse in all directions. "We're gonna have to move fast," he told the team. He looked at Rich and asked, "You still have your body bag?"

Rich nodded in agreement, pulled off his ruck, dug down deep, and pulled it out.

"Good," the sergeant said. "I'll give mine to the captain, and I want you both to extract the bodies and zip 'em up. Chu will help the captain carry one, and I'll give the LT a hand with the other. Covey redesignated the PZ to just beyond that grove on the other side of the wreckage. As soon as we get 'em out, Hotel Alpha to that grove and set up a perimeter. Copy?"

The men confirmed his instructions. After one last look up and down the meadow, the one-zero signaled Chu to make a run for the crash site.

Once out in the open, Mike looked back down the grassy meadow toward the twin peaks in the distance. He could see tan-green helmets bobbing up and down over the tall grassland, with the main body of enemy troops entering the tree line that the team had just vacated. As they approached the fuming, tangled craft, the scent of fuel, smoke, and oil filled his lungs. A hint of burned flesh tingled his nostrils as he and Rich prepared to enter the mangled cockpit while Gibson and Chu set up a hasty perimeter. Rich ripped off the remnants of the door and looked in at the pilot, his contorted, singed body crushed by the simmering engine pinning him firmly up against his seat.

Mike looked in the back, where the sergeant lay lifeless, still strapped into his harness, his chest and arms perforated with bullet holes. "Quick, give me your knife," he told Rich, reaching back in and taking the headset off the Covey rider's head. He pulled off the man's blood-spattered beret and stuffed it into his side pants pocket. Then he took the knife from Rich and slashed the nylon harness. He reached under the Covey rider's arms and tried to drag him forward, straining profusely, the dead weight thwarting his every effort. "Give me a hand, Rich. He weighs a ton," Mike said, his energy spent and colluding with the amphetamines swirling in his system.

Rich pushed Mike aside and grabbed hold of the lifeless Green Beret, grunting and cursing as he finally pulled him free. Mike unzipped the body bag, and Rich slid him head first into the damp green sepulcher.

"We ain't gettin' the front-seater out," Rich yelled over to Gibson. "The damn engine's sitting right on top of him."

"Take your Pen double-E, and take a picture of him, then," Gibson ordered.

Gibson motioned for Chu to head toward the adjacent grove as Mike and Rich each grabbed one of the looped straps on either end of the body bag. The smooth grassy mat below them eased their effort as they broke into a trot, trailing a short distance behind Chu.

They had no sooner departed the crash site when the first mortar round impacted well behind them. They quickly surmised that Chuck had apparently sent a spotter up a tree, and they cringed with every impact as each subsequent round walked in closer to them. They heard shouts and frantic commands in the distance as they scurried for cover in the groves ahead of them. "Pick it up!!" Gibson yelled as green tracers cracked loudly over their heads.

Mike looked back and watched three figures clad in black shorts and headbands sprinting through the grass behind them, firing their AKs as they rapidly closed the distance. Gibson spun and dropped to his knee. His CAR-15 leveled at the determined marauders, he squeezed off several short bursts on full automatic, halting the frenzied enemy charge. *Renegade trackers,* Mike surmised by their native garb.

Gibson quickly pulled a Claymore out of his ruck, snapped the thirty-second fuse, and shoved it into the ground. As he stood to rejoin the group, he saw a wooden-handle grenade flying out of the tall grass toward him. He spun and was able to take several steps before the blast thrust him face first into the ground, shards of hot metal peppering his legs and neck. He quickly regained his balance, ignoring the bee-sting-like pain, and ran determinedly toward his men, who had just reached the shaded edge of the grove. Green tracers streaked above his head just as the sudden blast of the Claymore behind him silenced their source.

Chu tilted his pistol-gripped grenade launcher, aiming just over Gibson's head, and launched a pair of high-explosive rounds into the grass behind him. The one-one slid into the edge of the shade, scrambling around to lean up against a small tree as he gasped for air. All finally at the far edge of the meadow, the brutally fatigued team watched the scores of dull-green pith helmets intermingled with the lines of trees in the distant grove. "There must be a couple hundred of them bastards," Mike reported, checking his magazines as he unbuckled his pouches. "We musta' really pissed somebody off."

Gibson pulled the handset to his ear, wincing slightly as the pain disbursed evenly throughout his body. "Covey Master... Bravo Delta, over," he sputtered but then realized there was no hissing sound to be heard. He slid his ruck off his shoulders and noticed the line of bullet holes in the ragged fabric. "Fuck!" he cursed, pulling the shattered relic out of his ruck. "They trashed the goddamn radio!"

He slung the useless PRC-25 to the wet grass and pulled out his emergency URC-68 survival radio from his vest. "Covey Master, Covey Master... Bravo Delta, over."

"Bravo Delta, we've been tryin' to raise you. What's your status? Over."

"Covey Master, Bravo. We were just a little preoccupied, don'cha know. We need some ordnance on that tree line to our Whiskey, yesterday, over."

"Be advised we have Covey Two-seven-seven inbound, and he's vectoring the fast movers to your location as we speak, over."

"Tell them to light up the whole tree line to the Whiskey of the crash site. It's swarming with bad guys just itchin' for a fight. And I need them to fire up that grass with some napalm for good measure, don'cha know, over."

"Bravo... Covey Master... We'll pass it on, Bravo. Do you have Covey rider and the pilot with you? Over."

"Roger on the backseater, negative on the pilot, over."

Gibson turned to Chu and told him to move through the grove and recon the PZ on the other side.

"This is our last chance, gents," Gibson told the team. "Take any Claymores you have left, and rig some trip wires on 'em between the trees. I have a bad feeling about this one. We're gonna need a fuckin' miracle to get outa' this hellhole. Might as well get rid of any toe poppers and other good shit you got stashed in your rucks. They're not gonna do us any good later."

The treetops swayed as the first sortie of ordnance erupted in the far tree line, the visible shock wave rustling their damp uniforms as it reverberated through the small grove. The sudden roar of afterburners followed closely behind as the pair of F-100s arched skyward, the fusillade of green tracers chasing their sonic ascent. Through the dark smoke and fiery aftermath, scores of B-40 rockets arched high through the bright sky, hissing like vengeful snakes as they showered down around the huddled team, spitting red-hot fragments of metallic shards, shattered branches, and other debris. Gibson stumbled to his feet and waved for the other two to follow him through the grove to the other side.

The air suddenly filled with the streams of green tracers, indiscriminately manicuring the layers of branches and leaves, snapping off bark as the men frantically zigzagged through the dense grove of trees.

"Covey, Bravo!" Gibson yelled into the radio as Mike and Rich ran past him. "That didn't slow 'em down a bit!"

"Roger, Bravo. You've got a coupla' battalion-size units converging on your location from two directions. We need to get you out of there now!" Covey Master replied. "Covey Two-seven-seven's got some fast movers with napalm on final. I've got the extract bird lined up, but you're gonna have to pop smoke when you're in position, over."

Gibson put the radio back in its pouch. He struggled to keep up with the others as he felt his strength gradually dissipating with every labored step, the sheer essence of vitality slowly abandoning his body. He willed himself forward through the maze of trees, loud, cracking sounds peppering the air above him. His vision began to blur, and a light-headed sensation soon overwhelmed him. His strenuous trot simmered before long to a lazy walk, then into a drunken stagger as he moved from tree to tree, holding himself upright as he neared the edge of the grove.

Mike looked back to see Gibson slumping down against the tree, his face pale and his expression curious as he fell to his knees. *He's hit!* Mike thought as he ran to his side.

"Get me up," Gibson whispered as he threw his arm around Mike's shoulder. Rich looked back and rushed to help. They dragged the one-zero over to the edge of the clearing.

Emerging above the trees, the lone F-4 Phantom spiraled upward while two canisters of lethal napalm toasted the advancing enemy in the meadow below.

"Get on the horn, LT," Gibson ordered, his voice laboring as he handed Rich the radio. "Tell Covey Master to get the package in here now!"

"Where you hit?" Mike asked. Then he felt Gibson's sticky, saturated back as he laid the sergeant down in the wet grass.

"Get those choppers in here now!" the wounded team leader demanded, his eyes distant and confused.

"Covey, Covey... Bravo Delta!" Rich barked into the radio, gunfire and explosions creeping up on the isolated team.

"Roger, Bravo Delta... Extract bird waiting for your signal, over."

Rich looked down at his one-zero, a questioning look on his face. "What signal?" he inquired emphatically.

"Pop smoke, LT," Gibson stammered. "Pop the fuckin' smoke!"

Rich pulled the smoke canister off his web gear, pulled the pin, and heaved the sputtering can as far as he could into the grassy plain. "Smoke's out!" he yelled into the radio. "Identify, over."

"Ahhh, Bravo Delta... Hula Dancer One-five... I have violet smoke, over."

"Roger affirmative, Hula Dancer... Violet smoke, over."

"I'm inbound to your November, Bravo... So be ready to *dalligas*. I'm going out the way I come in, so let the tail boom rotate before you try to load up, copy?"

"Roger, Hula... Advise your door gunners we have an indig dressed in an NVA uniform... So don't light him up. He's one of us, over."

Mike looked up to see a pair of Cobra gunships zooming in at treetop level to their north. He watched the front-seater give him a brief thumbs-up as the choppers sped through the lingering smoke, orbiting high, having selected their targets. Within seconds, the sky lit up with a menagerie of red and green tracers as the gunships engaged their miniguns and rocket pods, exchanging a lethal duel of fire with the enemy below.

Mike watched the slick bearing down on them, tree branches and leaves fluttering wildly in the front skids from his treetop approach. The last remnants of smoke disappeared, obliterated into the gusting wind as the chopper flared, leveled off, and then spun with the tail boom rotating around in precise unison. Chu and the captain grabbed the loops on the body bag and dragged it through the waving grass to the open door awaiting them. As the crew chief reached down to pull it up, a B-40 rocket streaked inches behind them, careening off the curved cockpit as it sailed off into the meadow beyond. The door gunner suddenly opened up, spraying the tree line where the rocket had been fired from. His red tracers tore through the grassy edge, while several hidden muzzle flashes joined the fray. Mike could hear rounds impacting around him as he labored to push the body up into the compartment. He turned to see Rich struggling with Gibson, and ran back and grabbed him by the waist as the sergeant put his arm around his shoulder. Mike looked up at the pilot, who stared back at him, his dark visor shielding any emotion as his bird took hit after hit.

"Let's go!!" the crew chief yelled as Mike jumped up and pulled Gibson aboard.

Rich vaulted up on the skid while the chopper shuddered violently. As it abruptly lifted off, he grunted loudly, his arms flailing forward, his chest slamming hard to the floor. He began to slip backward, back out the door, when Mike reached down and grabbed his harness. Dark blood oozed freely down Rich's back as the captain pulled him back in. With both door gunners furiously blasting away, the chopper's tail rotor rose high in the air, sliding the men inside against one another as the pilot skimmed the tall grass, accelerating rapidly, dodging clumps of scrub brush and small trees as the tracers danced and tinged along the fuselage.

"Rich! Rich!" Mike yelled above the screaming turbines. "Don't you fuckin' die on me now, brother!!" He rolled his friend over and tore open his shirt. Two dime-size dark holes spewed frothing red blood outward each time he struggled to take a breath. Mike felt someone behind him pull him away. He turned to see a Special Forces medic in tiger fatigues kneeling beside him. "Looks like a sucking chest wound. I'll take it from here," he insisted.

Mike slid back next to Gibson, who was sitting on the floor, his passive, dazed look competing with reality. He looked back over at Rich, whose respiration was faltering, and saw the sporadic, trickles of blood drooling down both of his dark, unshaven cheeks. The captain drew his legs up to his chest, resting his chin on his knees as he watched the chase medic wipe his friend's skin dry and then tape clear plastic squares over the wounds. He sat stoically, totally exhausted, his brain waves ricocheting through the amphetamine-induced swirl in his abused mind.

After several tense minutes, Rich's breathing stabilized. As the medic administered a second vial of morphine, Mike slid back over to his friend and took his hand. "You still in there, Hamma knokka?" he asked, staring down into what he considered the true face of a warrior.

Without opening his eyes, Rich rolled his head over and licked his parched, bloody lips. "That's probably gonna leave a big-ass scab, ain't it?" he whispered. "I hate fuckin' smelly big-ass scabs."

Mike smiled. *What color is the sky on the planet you came from?* he silently wondered.

"Minor detail," Rich uttered. "Now leave me the fuck alone. I need some shut-eye," he said as he suddenly drifted off to savor the morphine high.

Mike let go of his limp hand and sat down on the thin nylon seat. He watched the medic insert the Ringers Lactate IV into Gibson's arm. Then the chase medic looked up and asked, "You hit anywhere?"

"What? No… I don't think so," Mike finally replied after struggling through the haze to decipher the question.

"Couldn't tell with all that blood on you."

"Is he gonna make it?" Mike asked, nodding toward Rich, lying on the floor.

"Don't rightly know, *Đại úy.* Some do, some don't, with that kind of wound. I've done all I can for him. His lungs collapsed. They'll have to drain and try to reinflate them once we get back to Lộc Ninh… If he can hold on that long."

Mike shook his head and leaned back in the seat, peering up into the center console of the cockpit. The tan-skirted hula dancer mounted above the instrument panel shimmed provocatively, in perfect unison with the rhythmic vibration of the blades. His thoughts drifted back to the last time he saw that same rendition, years ago, on the dashboard of a rusty green Fairlane. He focused closer on the figurine, which was accented by a prismlike glare from the weird light deflected from the shot-up windshield. Mike concentrated on the spiderweb cracks in the windshield behind the dancer, his bleary eyes now squinting as he scrutinized the colorful detail.

"Looks like you guys were in a world of shit back there," the medic remarked, adjusting the flow in Gibson's IV.

"Yeah," Mike softly replied, his eyes still deftly focusing on the swaying skirt. He hesitated briefly but then stepped forward. He leaned over and tapped the pilot on the side of his shoulder. The warrant officer looked back, then slid up his dark visor. Mike's bloodshot eyes enlarged in wonder as he stared into the smiling face of his old friend, Jim.

* * *

CHAPTER FORTY-FOUR

C APTAIN SHANNAHAN SAT ON THE edge of the worn nylon seat, merely gazing over at Sergeant Lanza and the B-Team executive officer, Major Wilson, both casually leaning up against the jeep as the chopper slowly lifted off the tarmac. He rendered the men a final snap salute while the work chopper lazily rotated up and to the east, initiating its pursuit for altitude in the stifling afternoon heat. He looked down between the skids at the mysterious Cao Đài Monastery sliding below. Then he turned his attention to the gruff ridges surrounding the battle-scarred peak of Núi Bà Đen.

Staring down at the dotted, green farmlands below, following the winding Vàm Cỏ Đông as it turned several shades of dinge while it gradually meandered its way south toward Trà Cú, he felt like he had been here forever. He quickly slid over to the other side of the crew compartment, leaned out, and looked back across the Fence for one last glimpse into the forbidding complexities of Cambodia. *At least I know what I'm gonna get over there,* he told himself. *Not going to miss a damn thing about this place. We didn't accomplish a goddamn thing the whole year I was here. What a total waste of humanity!*

He wondered how many young men had lost their lives in that year, and how many more had lost their minds. The bellicose trace of death lingered in his taste buds as he recalled the melancholic scene on the landing strip in Lộc Ninh two days earlier, watching his brother Rich's limp body being placed on the stretcher and whisked away while Staff Sergeant Gibson insisted on walking to the waiting ambulance. He pondered the scene in vivid detail how he had unzipped the body bag to place Covey rider's blood-stained beret back on his lifeless head, and how much reverent respect the recon men had displayed for Master Sergeant

Carlisle as they slowly zipped up the body bag, lifted him gently onto the stretcher, and carried him away.

And Jimbo—another brother who had actually saved their lives. The tears that rolled down Jim's cheeks as he bear-hugged his old friend, calling him a "fuckin' Chinaman" while he related the circumstances of their unlikely reunion. Finding out that everyone in Kingsville had thought Mike was dead—a mistaken name on the casualty list of the 1968 Tet Offensive—and how that fallacy had motivated Jim to renounce his fears and broker a deal with the feds, a deal skillfully orchestrated with the help of his uncle, the banker in Alice. It had all been a challenge for Mike to process. His mind now swirled as he put the pieces together, sorting out his feelings and struggling to place them all into a manageable perspective.

There but for the grace of God go I, continued to echo in his frail consciousness as he struggled with the fact that he and Chu had survived the harrowing retreat virtually unscathed. Feelings of deep resentment, remorse, and pride conflicted, subjecting him to this paradoxical state of mind.

In Lộc Ninh, he had been astonished to learn from the men in Rich's unit that the RT's casualty rate was rapidly approaching 100 percent—whether killed, wounded, or MIA. He realized that the unsung heroes of SOG, men like Rich and Gibson, were well aware of the statistics, yet they strapped on their gear every day and set out into the badlands of Laos and Cambodia to do their duty, despite the odds against their ever returning. He was resigned to the fact that there would be no valor awards for their heroic exploits, no accolades for their gallant accomplishments, not even an acknowledgment of their citizenship if they were killed or captured. As they lay entangled in the wet underbrush of the rotting jungles, surrounded by regiments of bloodthirsty insurgents, their only reward lay in their own personal knowledge that they had fought the good fight, for their country, for their families, for their brothers in arms. And that, he concluded, would be good enough for him.

As the Huey banked right, following the wide Saigon River, Mike's mind focused on actually going home. He understood the reception he was likely to receive, and he prepared his magazine of tolerance, with tracer rounds of indifference, locked and loaded. He prepared himself for the onslaught of jeers and utter disrespect he knew was imminent.

With his ears still ringing from the crescendo of combat, Mike leaned back in his seat while the Freedom Bird raced down the seemingly endless Tân Sơn Nhứt runway. The anxious silence erupted into unbridled cheers and shouts of joy as the plane shuddered, the landing gear locking safely inboard. Mike sat passively, however, uninspired by this festive event, which marked the end of a long, treacherous journey for the men on board. He did welcome the solidarity he shared with them, and he did know that each one of them had his own unique story to tell. At that moment, though, he did not want to talk to anyone.

The Freedom Bird took its time shepherding the weary men home, with intermittent stops in Tokyo and Anchorage, a long and mentally draining trip, in no way a recompense for the new veterans' many sacrifices. The heavy tires finally rolled to a stop outside the dark, mostly deserted terminal at Travis Air Force Base. As Mike peered out into the dimly lit night, he noted that there were no celebrations, no cheers, no waiting families. And oddly enough, the men felt just the looming despair of having to engage another adversary: their ungrateful countrymen, who were nestled peacefully asleep in the warm sanctity of their beds.

The headlights from a convoy of army buses pulled alongside the metal stairway and then callously shuttled their sleepy cargo directly some thirty miles west to Oakland Army Depot. As the captain stepped off the bus, he gazed down at his shiny Rolex: 0300 hours, Pacific Daylight Savings Time.

The men endured the extended predawn physical, numerous tests to verify and document that they would not become wards of the Veterans Administration. Then they were brashly ushered along to cope with an administrative out-processing fiasco before they were tersely administered the final *coup de grâce*: Apathetic civilian clerks deftly cut up their military ID cards and threw them in the trash. The thankless, uncontested divorce was final.

Mike put his khakis back on and laced up his jump boots. He found his overseas bag in a green pile of baggage against the far wall, picked it up, and headed to the front door. Outside, where he stood in a long, single line for a taxi to take him across the gigantic Bay Bridge to the airport in San Francisco, the chill morning air brought goose bumps down his arms as he stared up at the tall, bare flagpole in front of the depot. When he finally arrived at the nearly empty airport, the spry, blond ticket agent informed him that the next flight to Dallas wouldn't leave until ten. He paid cash for his ticket and found a small coffee shop to pass the time. Mike lingered impatiently until nine-fifteen, when sheer boredom finally motivated him to head down to the gate.

Mike strolled casually down the long corridors with his small overnight bag in tow, people staring and snickering rudely as he passed by. He eventually reached his assigned gate, walked into the crowded departure lounge, and found a vacant spot at the far end of the concourse. He had no sooner taken his seat when people began to stand and move to other areas of the departure lounge. Before long, he sat sequestered, with empty seats spanning the entire area around him, mute people just standing and staring at him with condescending, menacing looks on their faces. Staring straight ahead, he ignored them all, his beret deflecting the incoming arrows of ignorance and hate, his hands spread wide on his thighs.

Before long, out of the corner of his unfocused eyes, he noticed a petite, demure lady slowly making her way toward him, her halting gait barely aided by the rubber-tipped cane she relied on. Before he knew it, she deliberately took the seat beside him. Her wrinkled, crooked fingers quivered as she methodically lifted her purse off her frail arm and set it down beside her. Then she propped her walking cane up on the adjacent arm rest. He felt her chastising eyes carefully scanning the room for several minutes. Then, suddenly, he sensed her trembling hand anointing his, squeezing it firmly as he turned slightly toward her. His eyes followed the thin line of tears drifting gradually through the uneven rouge paste accenting her furrowed cheeks while she gingerly patted her hand up and down on his leg. She sat silently, just holding on to his hand, daring anyone to intervene, virtually diminishing any selfish notions he might have vehemently conjured up, such as defiance, anger, or self-pity. Her gesture neutralized any such unproductive attitude he might have harbored. It liberated his sore, troubled heart and set it at ease, bestowing upon him the absolute finest tribute he could ever have imagined.

*　*　*

CHAPTER FORTY-FIVE

Twelve Years Later

T HE BUSY SECRETARY TURNED AWAY from her typing and picked up the phone buzzing audibly on her desk. "Procter and Gamble," she answered in a pleasant tone.

The gentleman in the adjoining office sat comfortably in his tall leather chair, peering out the nineteenth-floor window, gazing down at the idle boats moored securely in the Inner Harbor, leisurely admiring the new, modern structures transforming the landscape in dreary downtown Baltimore.

"Mr. Shannahan, your brother is on line one," the voice on the intercom reported.

"Thank you, Melissa," he replied, pushing the button on the speaker phone, wondering which brother was calling him. "This is Mike," he said.

"Yo! Well, *hello* there! It's Dan. Say… Andrea and I are coming up to Cambridge to see the folks this weekend, and we thought we'd swing by Columbia on the way and stop in and see you."

"That sounds great! Ya know, it's been a while since I've seen that gorgeous wife of yours. I've got to go to New York tomorrow for a corporate meeting, but I'll be back late Friday afternoon."

"Well, we thought we might take a side trip into DC for the dedication of the Wall on Saturday, and we wanted to take you down there with us... ... Mike... Mike... You there?"

"Don't take me back to somewhere you *know* I don't want to go, Daniel," Mike said quietly. "I'm not ready for that," he confessed in a mildly chastising tone.

"I know, but we thought—"

"Who's *we?*"

"Well, *all* of us. We thought it would be good for you to—"

"To *what?*" he sharply interrupted. "To read some more names on a wall that I would rather not know about? I canceled my subscription to the *Army Times* years ago, pal. Some things, the *less* you know, the better off you are."

"I didn't mean to upset you. We just wanted to be with you when they *finally* dedicated the Wall.... ... Mike?"

"I'm not going."

"We thought we could go out for dinner afterwards.... ... Mike?"

"Look, Dan, I appreciate what you're trying to do, but it's not working. I've made my peace with that war and the men I left behind, and I lost the combination to the vault where it resides *years* ago. There could be some names on that Wall that, well... *therapeutically*... I'd rather not see. Get it? They're still alive in my mind, so if I see their names on the Wall... ..."

"Mike?... *Michael?*"

"Tell the folks hi, and give Mom a kiss for me. I've got to go." He quickly disconnected the call, stood up, and pulled his vest down as he straightened his Italian silk tie. Walking over to the valet across the room, he took his tailored jacket off the stand and put it on. He leaned down and picked up his dark leather briefcase and headed smartly out the door.

"I'm taking the rest of the afternoon off, Melissa," he announced to his secretary. "Just pass any important messages to the service, and I'll check with them tonight. I've got some things to do before I leave for New York in the morning."

"Yes sir, but Mr. LaBarbera called from Cincinnati while you were on the other line, and he wanted to know if you'd made dinner reservations for tomorrow night."

"Could you call his secretary back and tell him I've got it handled. He hates surprises," he reminded her, flashing a coy grin as he left his office.

"Certainly."

Mike walked briskly past the smiling receptionist in the lobby and over to the bank of elevators. As the doors slid closed, his expression grimly changed as his mind drifted back "across the pond," toward the shady images he'd left in Never-never-land. He glanced down at his hands. The perpetual tremor still prevailed.

* * *

The doorbell chimed in the vaulted foyer, and Mike laid down the small orbit sander he was using to profile the maple coffee table he'd been meticulously constructing in the basement. He walked up the split-level stairs to see his brothers Dan and Tom standing vigilantly on the landing. He paused briefly, then reached over and opened the tall, glass-paneled door. "Let me guess," he told them, stepping over and giving each one of them a brotherly hug. "You were just in the neighborhood and thought you'd stop by for a beer."

"Something like that," Tom replied.

"Get your coat. The dedication starts in an hour and a half," Dan instructed. "Louise and Andrea are waiting in the van."

"Nothing like putting me on the spot and making me look bad in front of your ladies, is there?" Mike replied, trying in earnest to mimic one of the Commander's classic glares of displeasure.

"We're not taking no for an answer," Tom added, opening up the hall closet and rummaging through his older brother's collection of coats.

"I'm covered in sawdust," Mike complained, shaking his T-shirt for them to see.

Tom pulled out an old army field jacket with the Special Forces patch on the left arm. "Here, put this on," he ordered, handing him the faded jacket.

"I'm not wearing that," Mike insisted.

"Why not?" Dan inquired. "We just went by the Mall on the way up here, and all the guys are wearing their Vietnam jungle fatigues and stuff. Musta' been about ten thousand of them."

"*How* many?"

"The whole area is packed with Vietnam vets. We couldn't get anywhere near the place," Dan informed him. "That's why we need to get in gear. Otherwise, we'll never find a place to park."

Their older brother stood silently, grimly contemplating the circumstances, reluctantly acknowledging that the event was, indeed, not just about *him*. "Just let me change my shirt, then," he pleaded, hurrying up the adjacent stairs to his bedroom.

Tom vaulted up the short stairway to the living room, walked over to the fireplace, and took Mike's worn beret off the mantle. He tucked the relic into his coat and then quickly skipped back down the stairs to the foyer.

The thirty-five-minute ride from Columbia to the Beltway afforded Mike ample time to get caught up on all the extracurricular activities of all of his siblings' sons and daughters. He was stunned to learn that Seamus, his youngest brother, was marrying a German girl he'd met in Heidelberg when he'd been stationed there, flying gunships for an infantry unit.

Mike directed them through the side streets of Bethesda, his familiar back route toward downtown Washington he'd mastered during his many trips to National Airport. He knew just where to park, having frequented the upscale pubs and restaurants around Twenty-second and M Streets. They walked together along the wide boulevards, across Constitution Avenue, and toward the Reflecting Pool, where throngs of people were congregating *en masse*.

Mike felt varying degrees of self-consciousness while they skirted and dodged the festive throngs of strangers. He hadn't worn any part of his old uniform since he'd left Fort Devens for Vietnam. He'd forgotten how warm the old fatigue jacket had kept him, and as he reached his hand into the pocket, he pulled out a thirteen-year-old pack of gum. "Anybody want a piece of pocket litter?" he inquired. "It's vintage stuff... '69, I think."

He smiled as he opened the wrapper. The ladies cringed as he stuck the gum into his mouth and began to chew. "Ahhh... The bouquet... *Magnifique!*" he proclaimed, drawing sneers and smiles from the group.

"You're crazy, Mike," Louise told him. "That's probably going to make you sick."

"Girl, you don't *know* crazy. If we run into some of *my* guys today, I'll show you *crazy*, up close and personal."

They soon merged with the slow-moving crowds gathering in front of the deep depression in the ground to their right. A crisply attired multiservice honor guard stood above the apex of the memorial, the speaker's platform congested with top-coated dignitaries situated directly behind. Bands of restless men roamed the grassy knoll, selectively attired in remnants of uniforms from all the services, but most were army and marine infantrymen, long-haired and unshaven, with leather vests displaying mottos and slogans, their bush hats styled and adorned with varying degrees of rank as well as obscure pins and symbols. Hundreds of civilians pushed forward toward the Wall in front of them, held back only by a hastily constructed yellow picket fence, which was overladen and adorned with hundreds of bouquets of colorful flowers.

"If you guys think I'm wading into *that* mob, you'd better take another long hit off that dope you're smoking," Mike told them, staring down at the thousands of people standing shoulder to shoulder below.

"We don't have to, Mike," Tom told him. "We can see everything from right here. Here," he said, handing Mike his beret. "Put this on."

His big brother stared at him, then took it, stretching out the liner before he attempted to put it on. "It doesn't fit. Got too much hair, I guess."

"It looks fine," Dan told him. "But then again, you always did have the big head."

They stood on the periphery of the dedication, under the tall trees between the memorial site and the Reflecting Pool behind them. They listened, despite the chill air and damp ground, tolerating several long-winded politicians and chaplains, fund raisers and obvious proponents of the project. Mike continued to scan the crowd from their vantage point, hoping to see another Green Beret amid the black and red varieties so many of the men were wearing.

The formalities finally concluded with the retirement of the colors, and immediately, families and tearful loved ones rushed to the Wall, searching in earnest for the inscribed name of their fallen hero.

"Y'all go ahead," Mike said, backing up against the tall tree behind him. "I'll wait for you here."

"We'll be back just as soon as we walk the Wall," Tom told him, not wanting to risk a squabble. "Can't really see the names that well from here."

Mike watched them move into the slow-moving crowd, swiftly assimilating into the procession of pilgrims assembled to pay homage to the 58,195 names on the shiny granite Wall. He observed the array of former men-in-arms hugging one another, the constant phrase "Welcome home, brother" echoing in the nippy air beneath the tall trees. He objected to the atoning connotation it bore, hoping someone wouldn't test his deference to it by unwittingly using it on him. *We knew what to expect when we got back, even before we ever left to go over there,* he figured. *So what's the big deal? We didn't need a stinking parade or patronizing confirmation,* he told himself. *An element of respect would have been just fine.*

He felt a damp chill; the frigid, wet, rippled bark sapped his warmth as he leaned against the sturdy tree. He put his hands back into the field jacket's warm pockets, stood erect, and intensified his quest for a familiar face. He searched earnestly for the men in the funny green hat, longingly for the focused gaze of the warrior of extreme intent. He shared that look. It was only the unenlightened who failed to appreciate the extent of the Green Berets' commitment, their sacrifice.

The horde of long-haired men at the Wall drew his thoughts back to his post-service college days in Kingsville, back to his attempted resurrection into civilian society, when he, too, had cultivated a Fu Manchu to complement his long, wavy hair and sideburns. That convenient disguise had served him well—but only for a while. His time in the U.S. Armed Services inevitably cut off a number of brief romantic encounters; each time the lady was appalled when she found out that he was *one of them.*

But for the most part, the benign attitude of the students attending his south Texas university enabled him to assimilate rather well. He joined a fraternity, and he never looked back. He allowed his harrowing memories to ricochet at will until they finally found the elusive center of gravity within the sacred vault.

After sincere deliberation, he realized that he harbored absolutely no ill will toward the generation of protesters. Regardless of their passionate opposition toward the war, it had been their right to have their voices heard. After all, he finally concluded, that's exactly what he had fought for. He only regretted that they showed no similar respect for what he had done.

But he could never come to terms with the fact that one particular American antiwar activist had actually traveled to Hanoi and had made it a point to defile and mock the sacrifices of her nation's youth, the very ones who had spent their allowances to elevate and embrace her when she had enticed them in her role as Barbarella. No, he could never forgive the collaborator, the traitor, Hanoi Jane. *I only wish I live long enough to piss on Fonda's grave.*

Despite that, he cherished the unique honor of having had the opportunity to serve his country, to ride into battle under the Stars and Stripes, to associate with men of honor and distinction. No token parade would ever be able to provide him with the personal satisfaction that could possibly equate to the life lessons and honor his experiences had afforded him. His decision to fight for his country required no validation. It stood in the face of selfish dissension and endured the deafening silence of the complicit lambs. However, in the end, he acknowledged, it all came with an enduring price.

Mike wondered if the other men had struggled with their emotions to the same extent that he had, had suffered from the same persistent feelings of guilt and remorse, had sometimes detonated the same precipitous emotional outburst triggered by another's innocent display of perceived disrespect. Like him, most veterans of that war walked alone through the gathering, a guarded anticipation lurking on their faces. Apparently, they were searching for a lost comrade, a friend, a buddy. But most of all, they were just hoping to restore the bruised, tarnished virtues lost somewhere within themselves.

He felt genuine gratitude that the constant nightmares had finally faded after years of sleepless torment. He had finally acknowledged that his own wary reluctance to allow anyone to nestle comfortably within the confines of his guarded heart actually continued to perpetuate his lonely existence. He accepted the aching pain he had been suffering over these years as a form of penance he was required to pay, a retribution for whatever transgressions he may have unwittingly committed during the war. Yet, he wondered again, why he just didn't trust *anyone*.

He felt the large hand on his shoulder. "You here by your lonesome, Captain?" the gruff voice inquired.

Mike turned to see a face he didn't recognize, but the beret the man was wearing, accented with the Fifth Group flash, meant he was indeed in the company of a friend. "Mike Shannahan," he said eagerly, briskly extending his hand.

"Jake Jancinko," the Special Forces sergeant replied. "Didn't see you here last night. You just get here?"

"Yeah, I'm here with a couple of my brothers and their wives. What happened last night?" he was curious to know.

"Well, the SF Association orchestrated our own dedication ceremony," Jancinko said. "Matter-a' fact, most of the guys are still back celebrating at the hotel. We didn't want to get caught up in all this hoopla. We like to do our *own* thing. You know how we roll."

"Yeah, I remember. Hadn't heard of the SF Association. And what hotel?"

"It's the Association outa' Bragg. You know, former SF guys. There're local chapters all over the place. Where you from?"

"Well, I live just up the road in Maryland."

"There's a big chapter right here in DC, and they're the folks who are sponsoring the suite up at the Hilton. We established an FOB up there, and that's where everyone's hanging out."

"Really?"

"Yeah. About seventy-five to eighty guys up there. They sent me down to see if there were any stragglers like yourself hangin' out here today. I'm headed back up there now. Come on, I'll give you a ride."

"Well, I told my brothers I'd wait for them here," Mike said. "What's the suite number? I'll just get them to take me up there."

"Sixteen-thirty-eight. The bar's stocked and there's plenty of decent chow. See you when you get there," Jancinko said as he walked away. "And if you see any other SF types, pass the word."

"Roger, that." *Haven't said that in years,* he reminded himself, recalling the common ancient phase of memories past.

His brothers and their wives finally emerged from the waning crowd, the women visibly shaken by the experience. "There's a lot of pain going on down there," Daniel told him. "I think the girls are ready to go."

"We're all just thankful your name's not on that Wall," Tom remarked, holding tightly onto Louise's arm.

Mike told them of his encounter with the Special Forces sergeant and asked them to drop him off at the Hilton on Connecticut Avenue. They all expressed immediate relief that he finally would have the opportunity to reconnect with men of his unit after all those years, vastly altering the mood of the somber occasion. They soon pulled up in front of the busy hotel and let him out, his beret clutched tightly in his hand. He hastily bid his good-byes, tucked his beret in his belt, and swiftly strolled through the lobby to the elevators, restless anticipation soaring when he pushed the button for the sixteenth floor.

Loud chatter and laughter greeted him as he stepped off the elevator, and as he walked briskly down the hallway, he was greeted by a corridor full of men attired in dark green blazers and berets. Others stood attired in class-A green dress uniforms, highlighted with rows of medals and ribbons, all accented with the distinctive CIB and silver jump wings. *Looks like a bunch of frat rats*, he mused to himself, even though he knew better.

The faces looked elusively familiar, adorned with a few additional wrinkles, supported by bodies that had clearly benefited from a leisurely existence. Mike wandered into the social melee, nodding casually while desperately looking for a particular face.

"Shannahan!" a vaguely familiar man proclaimed loudly, staring at the nametag on Mike's field jacket. "I knew a Lieutenant Shannahan back in Tölz in the 60s. He used to run with my team leader, Lieutenant Stevenson!"

"Hollis Stevenson?" Mike inquired of the visibly drunken man, who was wavering with his beret cocked to one side.

"You got it!" the man confirmed. "Hell of a guy! The fuckin' women loved his happy ass."

"You heard from him lately?" Mike inquired, eager to hear any news about his old friend.

"Last I heard, he got out right after he lost his team across the Fence," he slurred. "He went back over to Tölz and opened a bar called *Der Stumpf,* or something like that."

"Is he still there?" Mike anxiously inquired.

"Don't know what they did with the body," the man informed him with a slim degree of nonchalance. "He went an' got his ass killed in a wreck on the Autobahn comin' back from Munich with a bunch of French broads in his Jag."

The grim news left Mike no other option than to just shake his head. *Knew this probably wasn't such a good idea,* he lamented.

He slid slowly through the gauntlet of animated men reminiscing in the hallway into the spacious double suite filled with smoke and banter. As he scanned the robust gathering of jovial men, his anticipation slowly dwindled to apprehension, with the stark realization that none of *his* men or old friends were here. He wandered slowly around the room, nodding to veterans wearing the variety of Group flashes on their berets, the Trojan Horse crest from the Tenth on some lapels, the slanted red and yellow on the black Fifth Group flash. Troopers from the First Group in Okinawa huddled in the far corner, their distinct yellow flash adorning their worn berets.

It had been over a decade since he had been in the company of men of this caliber, yet the impromptu reunion left him dealing with a hollow, ostensibly melancholy feeling about the affair. He found himself speculating about Rich's fate, just as he had done for all those years. Also about Allen, Jacques, Val, and all the others from his teams—Miller, Marshall, and *Bác sĩ* Braxton. Real men, patriots, warriors all. He now regretted not having heard anything about his SF brothers after he had set foot on the chopper in Tây Ninh, contentedly immersed in the emotional cocoon he had spun for himself those many years ago.

Making one last tour of the adjoining suites, gazing in amusement at the overflowing porcelain bathtubs of ice and beer in the bathrooms, Mike walked out into the crowded hallway and sadly made his way back to the elevators. The muffled shrieks of Janis Joplin flowed lazily from beneath the threshold of a guestroom as he passed by, adding a kind of flavor to old memories of times past. He reluctantly pressed the silver elevator button and stepped back, wondering how much the cab fare to Columbia was going to be. He stood patiently, caressing the fond image of Hollis back in Bad Tölz, that brash young warrior and his gaudy diamond pinky ring. The elevator door slid open.

Just as he took his first step in, he heard a distinctive laugh erupt from the room across the hall. The hair stood erect on his neck, his eyes widened abruptly. He put his hand out and stopped the heavy door, forcefully pushing it back open as he stepped back out into the landing. "O my God!" he exclaimed aloud, as the two distinctive resonances—Joplin's raspy voice and that familiar laugh—merged poignantly together.

The boisterous laugh echoed again, surging above the melody from behind the closed door, prompting Mike to rush over and bang forcefully on it. He banged again, and as the door suddenly swung open, the startled man in the room stared inquisitively at the intruder, then abruptly and jubilantly proclaimed, "Hamma knokka!!!!"

The brothers embraced, Rich's full tumbler of ice and scotch pouring lazily down Mike's back, saturating the musty field jacket, the astonished men in the crowded room merely smiling in solidarity and delight, while Janis soulfully pleaded yet again for *someone* to take another little piece of her heart.

*   *   *

GLOSSARY OF TERMS

1049	*See* **form 1049**.
A-1 Skyraider	The large single-engine prop plane used for close ground support. It was also known as Spads or Dusty.
A-4 Skyhawk	The navy single-seat attack jet aircraft, primarily used in missions over North Vietnam.
A-Team	The basic twelve-man team of the U.S. Special Forces.
AFN	Armed Forces Network, the radio and TV station transmitting out of Saigon.
AHC	Assault Helicopter Company.
AIT	Advanced Individual Training, also referred to as Advanced Infantry Training, a specialty training following Basic Training.
Airborne	Soldiers who are uniquely qualified as paratroopers.
AK-47	The Soviet-made Kalashnikov automatic rifle carried by the NVA and Viet Cong. It had an explosive, popping sound.
AO	Area of operations, a defined geographical area assigned to a unit.
APC	Armored personnel carrier, a track vehicle typically provided with a .50-caliber machine gun, which transported army troops or supplies.

Arc Light An overwhelming bombing raid by B-52 Stratofortresses along the Cambodian-Vietnamese border, an operation that shook earth for ten miles away from the target area.

ARVN Army of the Republic of Vietnam, Saigon's regular army.

AWOL Absent without official leave; leaving a position or post without official permission.

azimuth A compass bearing from the north.

B-40 A rocket-propelled grenade launcher, held on the shoulder.

B-Team The field headquarters for six A-Teams.

backseater The Covey, or Special Forces member riding backseat above an RT in a forward air controller's spotter aircraft.

bác sĩ Vietnamese for *doctor*. The term was also used to refer to U.S. medical personnel.

bandoleer A belt of machine-gun ammunition.

BAR Browning automatic rifle, a magazine-fed automatic .30-caliber rifle.

base camp A large resupply base for field units, usually at the brigade or division level.

battalion A military unit consisting of a headquarters and two or more batteries, companies, or similar units.

battery An artillery unit provided with six 105mm or 155mm howitzers or two 8-inch or 175mm self-propelled howitzers. It is equivalent to a company.

BDA Bomb damage assessment.

beaucoup French (and Vietnamese) for *much* or *many*.

berm A raised area around a defensive perimeter.

bird Any aircraft, but typically referring to a helicopter.

Bird Dog A forward air controller, or Covey, usually a small, maneuverable, single-engine prop plane, such as a Cessna L-19 observation plane.

blouse	To tuck trouser legs neatly into boots.
Bode	Cambodian.
body bag	A green plastic zippered bag used to transport bodies from the field.
body count	The number of enemy killed, wounded, or captured during an operation, a term used by higher-ups and politicians as a means of measuring the progress of the war.
boom-boom	Sexual relations.
BOQ	Bachelor officer quarters, living quarters for unmarried officers.
bought it	Or "bought the farm." If someone did this, he is KIA.
breaking squelch	To press the transmit bar on a radio to disrupt the natural static of another radio set that is to the same frequency.
Bright Light	A SOG team sent in to save or retrieve an RT in trouble.
briquette	A 500-pound bomb.
C-4	A plastic explosive that burns like sterno when ignited.
C-119	A military transport aircraft designed to drop cargo and troops by parachute. Also called "Flying Boxcar."
C-130	The large Hercules propeller-driven air force plane that can carry people and cargo.
C-rations	Combat rations, canned meals for use in the field. Each typically consisted of some kind of basic course, fruit, powdered cocoa, some type of dessert, chewing gum, and cigarettes.
C-Team	Company headquarters for three B-Teams.
call Ralph	To vomit.
CAR-15	A carbine rifle, a short-barreled version of the M16.

carbine A lightweight, short-barreled automatic or semiautomatic rifle.

Carson *See* **Kit Carson.**

C&C Command and control used by unit or reconnaissance commanders, usually orbiting a battle zone in a helicopter.

CCC SOG Command and Control Central.

CCN SOG Command and Control North.

CCS SOG Command and Control South.

CH-47 The Boeing Chinook twin-engine, heavy-lift helicopter used for troop movement, artillery placement, and battlefield resupply.

Charlie Viet Cong fighters.

chase medic A Special Forces medic sent to assist in treating casualties in extraction operations.

check six A directive to look directly behind (at six-o'clock).

Chiêu Hồi The "Open Arms" amnesty program for repatriating Viet Cong and NVA soldiers and cadres who had stopped fighting and had returned to South Vietnamese government authority.

Chinook *See* **CH-47.**

Chippewa The distinctive mountain boots worn by the Tenth Special Forces Group for mountain activities, including skiing.

chopper Helicopter.

Chuck The enemy, NVA regular troops.

CIA Captured in action.

CIB Combat Infantry Badge, awarded to soldiers who had been fired on in combat. The badge is worn on dress and fatigue uniforms.

CIDG Civilian Irregular Defense Group, American-financed mercenary troops that were led by members of Special Forces A-Teams. Pronounced "Sidge."

CINCPAC	Commander in chief of all U.S. forces in the Pacific region.
Claymore	An antipersonnel mine that, once detonated, propels small steel cubes in a fan-shaped pattern up to a distance of 100 meters.
clusterfuck	Any attempted operation that was disorganized or that ended badly.
co	Vietnamese for *unmarried woman*.
Cobra	The AH-1G attack helicopter, armed with rockets and machine guns. Also known as a gunship.
COC	Combat orientation course, held on Hòn Tre Island in Nha Trang Harbor.
commo	Communications.
company	A military unit typically consisting of two or more platoons along with a headquarters.
concertina	Coiled barbed wire.
Conex	The corrugated metal packing crate, approximately six feet in length, used to transport goods, often seen now on cargo ships.
contact	Firing at or being fired at by the enemy.
CONUS	Continental United States.
COSVN	Central Office of South Vietnam, the Communist headquarters for political action and military operations in South Vietnam.
COT	Commander of troops, the term for designating the officer in charge of troop movement.
Covey	The Special Forces member riding backseat above an RT in a forward air controller's spotter aircraft. This person was also known as Covey rider, or backseater.
CW	Continuous-wave radio signals. Slang for Morse code.
đại tá	Vietnamese for *colonel*. As an address or before a name, it is capitalized: *Đại tá*.

đại úy	Vietnamese for *captain*. Pronounced "die wee." As an address or before a name, it is capitalized: *Đại úy.*
¡Dalligas!	South Texas Spanish for "Let's clear out!"
defcon	Defensive concentration of preplanned artillery coordinates.
DEROS	"Date of expected return from overseas," the date a soldier is to rotate back to the States, the day he has been waiting for.
det cord	Detonation cord, a clear plastic tubing, resembling a clothesline, filled with explosives.
deuce-and-a-half	The M35 2½-ton army truck.
di di	Vietnamese for "Hurry up!" or "Let's get out of here!"
dinky dâu	Vietnamese for *crazy*, not to be confused with the American word **dink**.
dink	American slang for *Vietnamese enemy*, or for any Asian.
DMZ	The Demilitarized Zone, the no-man's land between North Vietnam and South Vietnam.
dogface	Infantry soldier.
dog lab	Specialized training for SF medics, utilizing dogs and typical combat injuries.
drogue chute	A parachute designed to slow its cargo load released from an aircraft, or a pilot chute to deploy a larger chute.
Dust Off	Medical evacuation of wounded soldiers by helicopter.
DX	To discard, dispose of, or kill.
DZ	Drop zone.
DZSO	Drop zone safety officer.
E&E	Evasion and escape.
Echo	East.

elephant grass	Tall, razor-edged tropical plant indigenous to Vietnam.
ETA	Estimated time of arrival.
ETS	End of term of service.
F-4	The Phantom jet fighter-bomber, the workhorse of the tactical air support fleet, with a thousand-mile range, a speed up to 1,400 miles per hour, and a payload of up to 16,000 pounds.
FAC	Forward air controller, the person who coordinates air strikes, usually sitting in a Bird Dog single-engine spotter plane.
fast mover	Jet aircraft.
fatigues	Standard green combat uniform.
Fence	The border of Vietnam with either Cambodia or Laos.
Flying Boxcar	*See* **C-119.**
FNG	Fucking new guy.
FOB	Forward operating base.
foo gas	Napalm, supplied and deployed in 55-gallon drums.
form 1049	The form used to request a transfer to another unit.
Freedom Bird	The contract commercial jet airliner that flew soldiers out of Vietnam.
front-seater	The pilot in an FAC (Covey) plane.
GCA hut	The checkered ground-control-approach hut, usually beside the runway.
gig line	The line formed by the shirt, the belt buckle, and the fly of one's pants.
gook	Derogatory term for Asian.
Green Berets	U.S. Special Forces.
greens	The army class-A uniform.
Group	An entire battalion of Special Forces companies—for example, Fifth Group or Tenth Group.
grunt	Infantryman.

gunship	Armed helicopter.
HALO	High-altitude–low-opening parachute jump.
Hamma knokka	I have no idea what it means.
Hatchet Force	A company-size unit of indig warriors who were used as a reaction force.
head shack	Headquarters building.
Hercules	*See* **C-130**.
hooch	A hut, simple dwelling, or any other living quarters or barracks, either military or civilian.
horn	Radio microphone.
Hotel Alpha	Haul ass. In other words, "Let's get out of here!" Same as *di di*.
howitzer	A short cannon used to fire high-trajectory shells at medium velocity.
Huey	The Bell UH-1 helicopter.
hump	To hike or march while carrying a rucksack; to do any difficult rask.
in-country	Vietnam.
Indian country	Out in the field, or in enemy territory.
indig	Indigenous troops (or civilians), regardless of ethnicity.
insert	To deploy into a tactical area by helicopter.
intel	Information on the enemy, gathered by human, electronic, or other means.
IV	Intravenous, a fluid solution injected directly into the veins.
JATO	Jet-assisted takeoff.
Jody	The person back home who took your girl when you were away.
JP-4	Jet fuel.

jumpmaster	The expert paratrooper in an Airborne unit who trains and teaches the military techniques for jumping from an airplane. He is responsible for training soldiers who enter the army's Airborne School to become paratroopers.
KIA	Killed in action.
Kinh Gẫy	The canal near Mike's camp, running through the Plain of Reeds, straight as an arrow for many miles from the Vàm Cỏ Đông River. It is like an expressway.
Kit Carson	A VC or NVA soldier who surrendered under the *Chiêu Hồi* program.
ki úy	Vietnamese for *second lieutenant*.
KKK	The *Khmer Kampuchea Krom*, Cambodian nationalists fighting against the Viet Cong and NVA. (There are no references in this book to the Ku Klux Klan.)
klick	Kilometer, approximately 0.62 mile (approximately $5/_8$ mile).
leg	Anyone who is not a paratrooper.
Lima	Left.
little people	Montagnards, or indigenous people generally.
LLDB	Lực Lượng Đặc Biệt, the Vietnamese Special Forces.
loadmaster	The aircrew member on a military transport aircraft who calculates and plans cargo and passenger placement to maintain permissible center-of-gravity limits throughout the flight. He is also responsible for determining the load order of the aircraft so that more tactically important material, such as ammunition, is off-loaded first.
low quarters	Military footwear.
LT	Lieutenant.

LZ Landing zone, a helicopter pickup or drop-off spot in the field, a cleared area large enough to accommodate the landing of one or more helicopters.

M14 The standard-issue 7.62mm semiautomatic/ automatic rifle, the last "battle rifle" issued in quantity to U.S. military personnel.

M16 The standard-issue 5.56mm semiautomatic/ automatic rifle made by Colt's Manufacturing Company. It was the mainstay of U.S. ground forces.

M60 A light, belt-fed 7.62mm machine gun.

M79 An individually operated, single-shot 40mm grenade launcher.

M80 A large firecracker used in training to simulate an explosion.

MACV Military Assistance Command, Vietnam, the main American military command unit responsible for all U.S. military activities in Vietnam. Pronounced "Mack-V."

Mae West A parachute malfunction that contorts the shape of the canopy into the outward appearance of a gigantic brassiere. Also called "blown periphery."

mama-san Any older Vietnamese woman.

medevac Medical evacuation. *See* **Dust Off.**

MIA Missing in action.

MIKE Force Mobile Strike Force Command, the fierce strikers, an indigenous component trained and commanded by the Special Forces, that reinforced or supported SF units or camps under attack. Each TAOR had a MIKE Force.

minigun An electronically controlled, extremely rapidly firing machine gun, typically mounted on aircraft for use against surface targets.

Montagnards	Dark-skinned, short native mountain people, the original inhabitants of Vietnam. Referred to as Yards for short. Also referred to as little people.
mortar	A muzzle-loading cannon with a short tube in relation to its caliber, which fires high-trajectory ammunition.
MP	Military police.
Mr. Charles	The Viet Cong or North Vietnamese enemy.
MRI	"Meal, ration, individual," field rations.
Nam	Vietnam.
nametag defilade	A condition of keeping one's head down, out of enemy fire.
napalm	A jellied petroleum anti-personnel weapon that burns fiercely.
NCO	Noncommissioned officer, an enlisted sergeant, E-5 and above.
net	Radio frequency setting.
November	North.
number one	The best, or highest, possible.
number ten	The worst, or lowest, possible.
Nungs	The Nùng people, an ethnic minority in Vietnam, many of whom fought alongside the NVA.
NVA	North Vietnamese Army.
O club	Officers' club.
O&I	Operations and Intelligence.
OCS	Officer Candidate School.
ODA	Operational Detachments—Alpha.
one-one	Assistant team leader. As an address or before a name, it is capitalized: One-one.
one-two	Radio operator. As an address or before a name, it is capitalized: One-two.
one-zero	Team leader. As an address or before a name, it is capitalized: One-zero.

ORT	Operational Readiness Test.
papa-san	Any older Vietnamese man.
paratrooper	A soldier, usually functioning as part of an Airborne force, who is trained to parachute into an operation.
Parrot's Beak	The portion of Cambodia north of the Mekong River and southeast of Phnom Penh.
party of the second part	The Viet Cong or North Vietnamese enemy.
PBR	"Patrol boat, river," a heavily armed fiberglass navy river patrol boat, used for patrolling and safeguarding the major waterways in South Vietnam.
PDQ	Pretty damn quick.
perimeter	Outer limits of a military position. Whatever is outside of the perimeter belongs to the enemy.
permanent party	A soldier permanently based at a post along with his family.
Peter Pilot	A copilot.
PF	South Vietnamese Popular Forces, similar to the National Guard in the U.S.
PIR	"Packet, indigenous ration," field rations.
playpen	The area CIDG troops preferred to deploy in, where they were assured that combat with an enemy force was unlikely.
PLF	Parachute landing fall.
poc **time**	Traditional midday, after-lunch nap.
point	The forward man or element on a combat patrol.
pop smoke	To release a smoke grenade to mark one's position.
POW	Prisoner of war.
PRC-25	Portable Radio Communications, Model 25, a back-packed FM receiver-transmitter used to communicate over a short distance.

PRC-77	A larger, very heavy long-range receiver-transmitter used in the field. It had a cryptographic scrambling/descrambling unit attached.
Projects	Top-secret operations run by Special Forces during the war.
PSP pad	The pierced-steel plank pad, also known as Marston mat, consisting of interlocking steel strips, which was used extensively during the Vietnam War as a temporary, portable runway for aircraft.
pucker factor	Adrenaline response.
PX	Post exchange.
PZ	Pickup zone.
Q	**BOQ** (bachelor officer quarters).
R&R	Rest and recreation (or recuperation), a three-to-seven-day vacation from the war.
rally point	The predetermined point to rendezvous following a skirmish.
Rangers	Elite infantry and commandos specially trained for reconnaissance or combat.
recon	Reconnaissance, going out into the jungle to observe, in order to identify enemy activity (or for some other specific operation).
Recondo School	The training school in-country for recon patrol, for going deep into the jungle to observe enemy activity without initiating contact.
regiment	A military unit typically consisting of several battalions.
RF	Military units, similar to a militia, organized within each district in South Vietnam to engage in offensive operations against local Viet Cong forces. RF units were better paid and equipped than PF units and could be assigned duties anywhere within the home district.

riser	One of four vertical wide nylon straps that attach to the cape wells of a paratrooper's harness. The other riser ends are attached to the numerous suspension lines sewn into the outer rim of the main canopy. The paratrooper holds on to the risers, using them to steer the canopy. By pulling down on a selected pair of risers, the paratrooper can either run with the wind or turn into the wind, thereby slowing the lateral drift.
RON	Remain-overnight position.
ROTC	Reserve Officers' Training Corps, the program offered in many high schools and colleges, geared to prepare students to become military officers.
RT	MACV SOG reconnaissance team.
ruck	The backpack issued to infantry in Vietnam.
Ruff Puffs	Vietnamese Regional Forces and Popular Forces (RFPFs)
S1	Personnel and administration officer.
S2	Intelligence officer.
S3	Operations officer.
S4	Supply officer.
saddle up	To put on a pack and ready oneself for marching.
sampan	A peasant's boat.
sapper	A Viet Cong or NVA commando, armed with explosives, who was trained to penetrate defense perimeters and destroy fighting positions, fuel or ammo dumps, and command and communication centers with demolition charges, usually prior to a ground assault by infantry.
SEALs	Highly trained navy special-operation force for conducting small-unit maritime military operations that originate from, and return to, a river, ocean, swamp, delta, or coastline.
SF	Special Forces.

SFOB	Special Forces operations base.
SFOC	Special Forces officers course.
shack up	To encode.
shavetail	Second lieutenant.
Sidge	*See* **CIDG.**
Sierra	South.
Sir Charles	The Viet Cong or North Vietnamese enemy.
sitrep	Situation report, a radio or telephone transmission usually to a unit's tactical operations center to provide information on that unit's current status.
slick	A lightly armed UH-1 (Huey) helicopter used for transporting troops in tactical air assault operations.
SOG	Studies and Operations Group, a designation to conceal cross-border operations.
Spad	*See* **A-1 Skyraider.**
spider hole	A camouflaged, one-man fighting position frequently used by the VC or NVA.
SR III	Subregion III, a North Vietnamese military region in South Vietnam, whose headquarters was in Cambodia.
stand down	A period of rest after completion of a mission or operation in the field.
stand to	To take up positions for action.
Starlight scope	A handheld telescope that used ambient light to see images at night.
stick	An Airborne troop on either the inboard or the outboard side of the aircraft.
strack	Extremely "gung ho," straight and squared away. A strack soldier acts strictly "by the book."
straphanger	Someone who participates in a unit's operation even though he does not belong in that unit.
striker	*See* **MIKE Force.**

tail gunner	Rear security, or the last man in a patrol.
tally ho	Target in sight.
tanglefoot	Single-strand barbed wire strung in a meshwork pattern at about ankle height, constituting a barrier difficult to cross by foot. It is usually placed around permanent defensive positions.
TAOR	Tactical area of responsibility, effectively within the boundaries of an AO.
thiếu tá	Vietnamese for *major*. As an address or before a name, it is capitalized: *Thiếu tá.*
Three	The radio call signal for the operations officer.
tiger fatigues	The military jungle-warfare uniform with a camouflage pattern resembling a tiger's stripes.
Tigerland	The army training camp at Fort Polk, Louisiana, whose focus is readying troops for combat in a jungle environment.
TOC	Tactical operations center, usually housed in a fortified bunker.
TO&E	Table of organization and equipment.
toe popper	A small antipersonnel mine or booby trap, whose explosion could blow off one's foot.
Top	A form of address to a first sergeant or master sergeant, the top NCO.
tracer	A round of ammunition chemically treated to glow or give off smoke so that its flight can be followed.
Trail	The Hồ Chí Minh Trail, mostly in Laos but somewhat in Cambodia, used to supply manpower and material from North Vietnam to the Viet Cong.
trung sĩ	Vietnamese for *sergeant*.
un-ass	To immediately leave an undesirable area very quickly.
unblouse	To free trouser legs that had been tucked into boots.

VC	Viet Cong.
VN	Vietnamese.
web gear	Canvas belt and shoulder straps for packing ammunition and other equipment.
Whiskey	West.
White Mice	The white-uniformed South Vietnamese city police.
white phosphorus	A sunstance that in contact with skin continues to burn all the way through the body. Water will not extinguish it. It can be fired from artillery, mortars, or rockets.
Willy Pete	*See* **white phosphorus.**
Winchester	Out of ammo.
world	"The world" was wherever was away from the war in Vietnam.
XO	Executive officer, the second in command of a military unit.
Yards	*See* **Montagnards.**

* * *

ACKNOWLEDGMENTS

M Y FATHER, COMMANDER JOHN AUGUSTUS O'Shea, Jr., initially inspired me to undertake this endeavor prior to his untimely death in 1990. While a Ph.D. at George Mason University in Virginia, he had just started writing his memoirs when he was suddenly taken from us. In amazement, I read facts about his childhood growing up on the streets of Brooklyn, New York, and about his state of mind as a young man facing the same challenges that I had confronted. Regrettably, there were too many chapters of his life left unwritten. I wanted *my* son to know who *his* father was and what it took to be able to bring him into the world.

I would like to thank my family for their love and understanding over the years, and I regret that the big brother they had known never came home after the war; he had been replaced by a more sober, more seasoned, but somewhat tarnished man. John-Michael, you are the most precious entity in my life. Special thanks to my brother Daniel, whose magnificent artistic talents are displayed vividly on the front cover of the book. Thanks, too, to my best friend, Dr. Danny Wayne Nicholls, Colonel, USAF (Ret.), and his fabulous wife, Marlo, who help navigate the ship. And of course, I thank my good friend Barbara Odom, whose persistent prodding to dust off the old manuscript finally motivated me to revisit the dormant pages. Longing to know if my words would help her understand what had happened to her brother's soul before he finally came home from the war, she constantly encouraged me to finalize the work.

To all the brave and honorable men of the Special Forces regiment, I salute you and am grateful that you have permitted me to walk among your ranks. In particular, I am grateful to the late Major George William

Petrie, Jr., who continued to inspire me until his recent final insert into the regiment's heavenly LZ. George, you *are* John Wayne, brother.

And finally, to my good, old, best friend, Jim Geary, who is happily retired and spends most of his time fishing in Galveston Bay, just outside of Houston, Texas. And no, Jim, I'm not going back across that fence with you for old times' sake! I've had more than enough excursions across Fences in my day. I've learned that the only thing across the fence is the other side—depending on which way you're going.

*   *   *

ABOUT THE AUTHOR

GRANDSON OF AN IRISH IMMIGRANT who landed at Ellis Island in 1904 before fighting in France as a Doughboy with the New York Rainbow Division in World War One. Son of a career naval aviator who saw action in World War Two, finally retiring after thirty-five years of service following Korea and Vietnam.

Michael O'Shea grew up on naval airbases in Cuba, Hawaii, and Japan, where he climbed to the summit of Mount Fujiyama at the age of twelve. That same year, he was the captain of the first Japanese-American Little League team to compete in the Little League World Series. A highly competitive swimmer and diver, he was a member of the All-Navy junior Olympic swim team. His insatiable curiosity as a child once led him at the age of ten to stow away on a Japanese fishing vessel in Yokohama Harbor, only to be discovered while the vessel was setting nets miles offshore in the Pacific Ocean.

He left college and enlisted in the army as a paratrooper in 1966. He earned his jump wings later that year and was selected to attend infantry OCS at Fort Benning, Georgia. Commissioned a second lieutenant in 1967, he graduated from the John F. Kennedy Center for Special Warfare at Fort Bragg, North Carolina, and was assigned to the Tenth Special Forces Group in Bad Tölz, Germany. He served as an A-Team executive officer, detachment commander, as well as the

S3 officer for B-Company, Tenth SFGA while stationed at Fort Devens, Massachusetts. He volunteered for duty in Vietnam in 1969, where he served as the CO of an A-Detachment on the Cambodian border. He was later informed that, at the age of twenty-one, he was the youngest captain to command a Special Forces A-Team in Vietnam.

He left the service following his tour in Vietnam and returned to his Alma Mater, earning his business degree from Texas A&I University in Kingsville, Texas. Following a ten-year career with the Surgical Products Division of Procter and Gamble, he partnered in a medical device company in Dallas. He currently specializes in total joint replacement for hips and knees, servicing and working with orthopedic surgeons in Arlington, Texas.

He is active in the Special Forces Association and enjoys his profession, offshore sailing, woodworking, and gourmet cooking while spending time with his son and close friends.

"TILL CALLED AGAIN"

I've lift my glass and drank my share
Of the wine that's known as pride
And walked among some gallant men,
And matched them stride for stride.

I've crammed my mind with devious ways
To defeat the enemy's goal
And kept inside for loyalty's sake,
The tales that can't be told.

The need is gone for my service now,
I'll hang up my "Green Beret"
And sip no more of the wine of pride,
Till called again someday.

Author unknown…

Printed in the United States
By Bookmasters